Brokered Justice

Brokered Justice

Race, Politics, and Mississippi Prisons, 1798–1992

William Banks Taylor

Ohio State University Press
Columbus

Library of Congress Cataloging-in-Publication Data

Taylor, William Banks, 1944–
Brokered justice : race, politics, and Mississippi prisons, 1798–1992 / William Banks Taylor.
p. cm.
Includes bibliographical references and index.
ISBN 0–8142–0621–2 (cloth). — ISBN 0–8142–0622–0 (paper)
1. Corrections—Mississippi—History. 2. Correctional institutions—Mississippi—History. 3. Prisons—Mississippi—History. I. Title.
HV9475.M7T39 1993
365'.9762—dc20 93–32001
CIP

Text designed by John Delaine.
Type set in ITC Galliard.
Printed by Cushing-Malloy, Inc., Ann Arbor, MI.

The paper in this book meets the guidelines for permanence and durability of the Committee on Production Guidelines for Book Longevity of the Council on Library Resources.

9 8 7 6 5 4 3 2 1

Contents

Acknowledgments

This book was undertaken at the request of John Watkins, Mississippi commissioner of corrections during the last years of the administration of Governor Cliff Finch (1976-80). It began as a state-supported project involving a considerable number of academicians and public administrators, but research monies advanced by the Mississippi Department of Corrections (MDOC) were terminated in 1980, and most of the projected contributors fell by the wayside in the years that followed.

In the end, only three persons other than the principal author made direct contributions. Dr. Warrick R. Edwards, now instructor of history at Tallahassee Community College, deserves credit for the bulk of the second chapter. Dr. Edwards also made substantial contributions to the third chapter, as did Ms. Ruby E. Cooley, a former graduate student at the University of Southern Mississippi (USM) now employed by the state of Georgia. Ms. Cooley contributed to the fourth chapter as well, and Professor Ronald G. Marquardt, chairman of the Department of Political Science at USM, researched and wrote a large part of the eighth chapter.

Several former and current employees of the penal system devoted time and effort to the project. Mr. Leonard Vincent, now senior legal counsel at the Mississippi State Penitentiary at Parchman, penned a very good legal treatise that proved helpful in the early stages of research. Former assistant commissioner Dr. Joe Cooke furnished official statistics and valuable analyses during the 1980s and early 1990s. Mr. Donald Cabana, formerly warden at Parchman and acting commissioner of corrections, and Professor Tyler H. Fletcher of USM, the last chairman of the state's old penitentiary board of commissioners, advanced invaluable comment on penitentiary politics. Mr. Lonnie Herring, training officer at Parchman, and Mr. Ken Jones, MDOC director of public relations, provided reproductions of photographs. A number of other employees of the penal system, who understood the nature of the beast and prudently requested anonymity, contributed rare documents and many useful leads, including whispered instructions that sent the principal author stamping through the wilds of the Yazoo Delta searching for old-timers with tales to tell.

Several colleagues read the manuscript and offered helpful comment. Especially useful were the suggestions of Dr. Charles A. Marx, formerly chief assistant to the Mississippi attorney general and Mississippi commissioner of revenue. Others, most notably Professor William K. Scarborough of the USM Department of History, clarified matters of fact and prevented errors of judgment.

When MDOC funds dried up in 1980, USM graciously allocated a small research grant and continued to provide financial assistance until the project was completed. Without the support of President Aubrey Keith Lucas and his administration, the manuscript never would have gone to press.

Special thanks also go to the staff of the Mississippi Department of Archives and History and that of the William David McCain Graduate Library at USM. Valuable indeed was the assistance of Mr. Henry Simmons of the McCain Graduate Library, who displayed remarkable expertise, patience, and good humor in leading the principal author through the nooks and crannies of his beloved Mississippi Collection.

Finally, several former state legislators contributed a great deal to the project. Mr. Con Maloney, formerly chairman of the senate corrections committee, boldly supported the project at its inception despite nagging reservations about the legal and political ramifications of "skeltons in the closet." Feeling that the exposure of skeletons might well prove useful to the public interest, the late senator Bill Harpole lent a hand in the latter stages of the study, and several others, agreeing with Senator Harpole but frankly admitting that they were among the skeletons, assisted on condition of anonymity.

In no case does this work seek to suggest solutions to the problems of modernity. Yet today, as the state's elected officials grapple with this troubled sphere of public policy, perhaps they might find some little wisdom in a book that attempts to chronicle and explain the successes and failures of the past.

Introduction

Buried in the closed stacks of the British Library is an anonymous pamphlet of early nineteenth-century vintage entitled, quite simply, *What to do with our Convicts?* That was a leading question among the first generations of Britons who contemplated the erosion of feudal life, the appearance of a "criminal class" within the new cities, and the apparent failure of common law institutions. But neither the Georgian pamphleteer nor any of his Victorian successors solved the riddle; and today, nearly two centuries later, policymakers in Britain's colonial progeny, the United States, ponder the same question with a much greater sense of urgency. What to do with our convicts?

The essential problem, yesterday and today, is one of oversupply: there are simply too many convicts, and their maintenance weighs heavily on the public purse. Then, too, few people can agree on what the state should seek to accomplish through legal punishment, and a resulting confusion of goals and means gives considerations of political economy the ascendancy in policy decisions. For well over two centuries, the fiscal tail has progressively wagged the legal dog, and at last we have arrived at a very unhappy juncture. By all appearances, American penal policy is bankrupt, more harmful than helpful, with no relief in sight.

The contemporary policy dilemma is at least partly attributable to an imperfect understanding of the factors that have led us into the bog. Indeed, few aspects of the American past are more under-researched than penal history. There is also much reason to be suspicious of what we think we know. Sensationalists and a wide array of authors with axes to grind figure quite prominently in the historiography of legal punishment, as do those who subscribe to the old Whig view of history—the notion that the past is a chronicle of progress to an enlightened present. We read a great deal, for instance, about "pioneers in penal reform"—men and women who have been instrumental in carrying policy from one point to a presumed better one, always nearer our own time. The underlying thesis is shaky at best, puerile at worst. Historical changes are just that, changes, and it seems safe to say that we have made a number of wrong turns along the way to modernity.

Intellectual narrowness thickens the fog. The formulation and administration of penal law is first and foremost a study in politics. Yet virtually everyone has assigned the subject to the realm of social history. Incredible as it seems, we know much more about the sociology of prison life and its attendant horrors than we know about the political factors that have manufactured convicts and dictated the horrors.

Overgeneralization has taken its toll as well. Most of those who have tackled American penal history have produced synthetic national or regional accounts. The problem is that such scholarship tells us very little about the essence of the subject—the history of legal punishment within the separate states. Every state has a distinctive penal history owing to peculiar economic, social, political, and legal phenomena, the influence of powerful individuals, and the long reign of state sovereignty over the formulation and administration of penal law.

In recent years a number of scholars have attempted to dispel the haze. Among the resulting publications have been histories of legal punishment within the states of Illinois, Louisiana, Texas, and Virginia. By and large, the authors have neither ground axes, embraced the Whig view of history, nor fallen prey to the bogey of national or regional homogenization. Instead, they have sought to let inductive facts speak for themselves, and one is hardly surprised to find that their work has uncovered evidence that challenges many interpretations of the past.

This book seeks to accomplish the same ends. It focuses on the state of Mississippi. The story commences in 1798, when territorial status was achieved. It concludes in 1992, amid the continuing chaos of federal intervention into a sphere of public administration that was reserved to the separate states until only recent years.

The breadth of the study has forced me and my co-authors to define our mission succinctly and to pursue it doggedly, often to the exclusion of interesting materials and perspectives. The reader can glean much information about the lives of convicts and their keepers, and on occasion the narrative sheds light on the fascinating culture of Mississippi. This book is not a sociological study, however, and it does not qualify as social history. Rather, it falls within the realm of political history, traditionally defined. The primary goal has been to write a dispassionate account of the factors that have molded a state's penal law, of the plight of policymakers functioning within a difficult scheme of governance, and of the tactics employed by those who have presided over a penal system.

Whenever pertinent, international, national, and regional influences have been noted and analyzed. The chief value of a study assessing the penal history of an American state, however, does not lie in synthesis relating the story to external developments. So in no case have my co-authors and I knowingly muddled the specific for the sake of the general. To do so would have been to mislead the reader by attempting to force square pegs into round holes.

Still, there are aspects of Mississippi's experience that should interest students of law, politics, public administration, and sociology everywhere. The first involves the most fundamental variable in the criminal policy equation—the character of public law.

Excluding only recent years, and those somewhat reluctantly, Mississippi politics has revolved around an elaborate campaign designed to control a large African American underclass. The campaign was waged via republican political process and legitimatized by public law. The police powers of the state were committed to its fulfillment. The nation's first elected judiciary presided, and the state's apparatus of legal force—the punitive powers delegated to the executive branch of government—functioned as the campaign's last line of defense.

Prior to 1865 the monetary value of African Americans screened them from the mainstream of criminal process, if not from the rigorous provisions of a slave code administered by local magistrates. But the difficulties inherent in a dual, racially motivated body of public law weighed heavily on the local administration of legal punishment, bore strongly on the decision to establish the first state penitentiary, and influenced its brief history.

After Appomattox the pathetic economic and social plight of black Mississippians and the policies pursued by both Republican and Democratic politicians rendered penology an exercise in the private exploitation of "criminal Negroes." Competing notions about who should exploit the labor of black convicts, and the best means of exploiting it, were a major theme in Mississippi politics during the twenty-five years that followed the conclusion of the War Between the States.

Shifting political alignments and the resulting state constitution of 1890 at last banned the direct exploitation of convicts by private parties and delivered to the public sector exclusive control of the state's felons. Thereafter, for well over three-quarters of a century, penology in Mississippi reflected the institutionalized racism imposed by the heavy hand of Jim Crow.

Racial inequity was the principal agenda of the body politic, the core of the state's constitutional and statutory law; and the preservation of white rule demanded separate arrangements for the respective races in all state institutions. The penitentiary was essentially an institution for black felons, and most public officials found it absurd to ground penal policy on a medical model, on alien notions of social justice, or on anything else that conflicted with the entire superstructure of public law. More rational were policies of social control, and the state pursued them.

The vehicle was the sprawling state penitentiary at Parchman. There, in remote Sunflower County, Mississippi established a huge cotton plantation, organized and administered it on long-standing principles of slave management, and sought to turn profits. Parchman's financial productivity sagged with the cotton market in the early 1950s, and political inertia ended profits altogether later in the decade, but the plantation's antebellum foundations did not crack until the mid-1970s. The history of legal punishment in Mississippi turns on an axis of racial inequity, and there is no escaping it.

On the other hand, the public record of no American state contains greater revelations of the iniquities of criminal policy, or more evidence of a desire to root them out. Mississippi's penal history, therefore, is a paradox, a chronicle of conflicting impulses.

The paradox is partly explained by the tactics of political warfare. Surely no branch of public administration has been exploited for private gain more notoriously, or employed as a political rapier more frequently, than penal administration. The first charge of the historian is to learn that lofty political rhetoric and accompanying "reforms" have not always equated with lofty motives. Mississippi's penal history provides graphic illustration.

Paradox also arises from the theory of the inferiority of black persons and the related paternalism of the ruling white majority. From the days of slavery, the black man was regarded as genetically handicapped, as a social inferior created by God to toil in the vineyards of a superior Caucasian race. The advantages of the white man's favored position, however, were thought by many white Mississippians to impose social obligations. That curious mind-set, so similar to the condescending paternalism exhibited by European aristocrats in their dealings with serfs, is easily discernible in the master-slave relationships of antebellum times. It is a recurring theme portrayed by William Faulkner, Eudora Welty, and the many others to whom Mississippi owes its rich literary heritage. A version of Tennyson's "white man's burden" permeates Mississippi history, and it explains many apparent inconsistencies in the state's penal history.

Other inconsistencies are bound up in a related conflict that has existed elsewhere in the American republic. Mississippi has had no monopoly on legal inequity. Nor have Mississippians been alone among Americans in their attempts to reconcile the effects of legal inequity with the libertarian foundations of American jurisprudence and the callings of the Christian faith. In many ways, the state's penal history is a case study of a nationwide confrontation, one pitting the pragmatic legal commands and threats emanating from a republican political process against a nobler moral and jurisprudential heritage.

The story also focuses attention on difficulties imposed on the administration of justice by political structures and processes common among all the states. Throughout Mississippi history, the independent state lawmaking power, responding to the will of the republican electorate, has progressively expanded the purview of public law, all the while complementing its legal commands with popular, get-tough-on-crime penal sanctions. Meanwhile, nothing in the political formula has required legislators to appropriate monies on a scale commensurate with the supply of convicts manufactured by the state's independent judicial power. Furthermore, the legislature's ability to provide for convicts has been compromised at times when economic recession, always a strong variable in the criminological equation, has spawned an increased supply of convicts.

The result has been unfortunate. For whenever the legislature has failed to supply the monies demanded by the purview of public law and the fruits of criminal process, the state's independent executive power, presiding over the administration of legal punishment, has been left holding the bag.

The gap between legal cause and effect produced by the practical operation of the separation-of-powers doctrine has occasioned much squabbling among political actors, of course, and attempts to redress its manifestations largely account for every scheme of penal organization attempted in Mississippi. The state's successes and failures address a number of questions of contemporary interest. Is institutional centralization or decentralization conforming to the federated structure of state government a more plausible principle of organization? How much control should the executive branch of government have over a state penal system? To what extent should the executive power be checked by the legislative power? Is a popularly elected board of penitentiary trustees the answer? Is active intervention by the federal judiciary feasible?

The state's various schemes of convict management have been similarly inspired, and they, too, focus attention on many issues. Is a trained "professional in corrections" or a surly power broker drawn from the state's political apparatus a more efficient superintendent in this troublesome sphere of public administration? How much control, if any, should penal administrators have over the duration of sentences? Are probation, parole, and other mediums that mitigate the severity of penal sanctions important correctional tools, as advertised? Or are they merely the tools of legal hypocrisy—utterly pragmatic expedients designed to counter the effects of an unsystematic concept of political organization and legal administration? What is the net effect of such programs on penal administration?

Mississippi's attempts to render its penal system self-sustaining or remunerative also have been inspired by the gap between legal cause and effect. Since antebellum times, when cheap, expeditious corporal punishments confounded the conviction of all too many culpable defendants, the state's principal alternative has been legal incarceration and state-administered convict labor. A number of schemes have been employed. Some have succeeded, more or less, for a time. All of them have failed in the end, and the historical record inevitably leads one to reflect on issues being debated today.

Is there a fundamental conflict between a revenue-generating penal system employing cheap, captive labor and a republican political process serving a market economy? Is the public sector capable of managing such a large-scale business ethically and profitably? In the event of remunerative operations, what can prevent the legislative power from undermining the business with raids on its capital base? At all events, can the moral dictates of penal jurisprudence be realized within a system of legal punishment that functions on principles of political economy?

Another expedient pursued by the state has been the privatization of convict labor. Privatization was employed to evade the cost of an avalanche of newly enfranchised African American convicts in the immediate aftermath of the War Between the States. From the standpoint of political economics, the scheme worked brilliantly, disposing of an overabundance of convicts and generating considerable revenue for the state. Yet the "invisible hand" of the market economy also fashioned an incredible degree of human abuse and public corruption. Perhaps Mississippi's experience with the privatization of convict labor, herein described very vividly, might give contemporary advocates of private sector "corrections" reason to pause and reflect.

At times when convict labor has failed to generate sufficient capital, when the state's courts of criminal jurisdiction have continued to manufacture too many convicts, and when the legislature has refused to come to the rescue, Mississippi's chief executives have been forced to follow one of two courses of action. They have either employed the clemency powers of their office to reduce the size of the state convict population to a level commensurate with available financial resources, thereby overturning the fruits of legislative and judicial process, or they have abdicated responsibility, rationing an insufficient legislative appropriation among the convicts. The former tactic has often exposed chief executives to the criticism of hypocritical legislators and to the wrath of the electorate. The latter, leaving the convicts wanting, has been more politically expedient.

Until recent years, nothing checked the resulting plight of convicts other than "reforms" born of partisan politics, the sporadic interest of journalists and humanitarians, and a vague, sometimes tactical, quest to be as "progressive" as other states. In 1972, however, U.S. district judge William Keady abandoned a long-standing "hands-off" doctrine pursued by the federal judiciary and extended to Mississippi's convicts most of the constitutional safeguards afforded other citizens in the landmark case of *Gates v. Collier*. Among those safeguards were legal access and a subjectively defined standard of living, most notably a specified amount of costly space for each incarcerated convict.

In operational terms, Keady, a veteran Mississippi politician, sought to force greater responsibility on the state legislature, to bridge the long-standing gap between legal cause and effect arising from the practical operation of the separation-of-powers doctrine. But the demands of the federal bench have bred conflicts that go to the very heart of the state's political structures and processes, and for some twenty years Mississippi has struggled with the legacy of federal intervention.

A number of perplexing questions have arisen. How can the fiscally strapped legislative power reconcile a standoff between the demands of a victimized, retributive electorate and those of a federal judge who, seeking to protect convicts, has carried the cost of legal punishment beyond the confines of political reality within the state? Two hallowed principles of American government are at odds, it seems: the unrestricted power of the people and the indefeasible rights of the citizen.

How can the executive branch of government navigate between a state judiciary generating an unprecedented supply of convicts, a federal judiciary effectively demanding money bills for the enhancement of convict life, and a state legislature generally unwilling, perhaps unable, to deliver them? Here, one discerns the age-old problem bred by the separation-of-powers doctrine but now compounded by the federated structure of American government. The intervention of the federal judiciary has trapped the state's governors and those within the executive branch of government who administer the penal sanctions of the state. Quite simply, the executive can no longer redress legislative truculence by leaving convicts wanting, and the alternative of clemency is no more politically expedient today than it was in the past.

With the back door thereby blocked, and the legislators at the front door either unwilling or unable to cough up the required cash, will not criminal process inevitably backwash? Must not an oversupply of convicts compromise judicial independence, erode prosecutorial integrity, and undermine law enforcement? Must not the fiscally strapped legislature turn to legal hypocrisy more and more, reducing the criminal policy of the state to a pathetic crusade seeking to evade the costly sanctions of public law? Will not the widening gap between the de jure and de facto faces of legal punishment increasingly impact negatively on the criminological equation? If so, at what point does the retreat from legal punishment undermine the very foundations of government?

Other questions relate to the day-to-day operation of penal institutions. How can those who preside over the state's felons function in the face of judicial edicts that presume iniquities by staff and seek to achieve a balance of power between the keepers and the kept? What impact has that legal adjustment had on state penal administration? Have the traditional tenets of penal jurisprudence been realized? Are convicts better off? The saga of Mississippi's attempts to grapple with the "justice model" of criminal corrections in an era of dearth and mounting convictions contributes to the growing body of literature inspired by federal intervention into state penal administration.

Mississippi's penal history is not a happy story. Yet it turns on economic, social, and political phenomena that are more or less common among all the states of the Union. It raises issues that challenge the most cherished ideals of the American people, and it leads the troubled reader back to the original question—what to do with our convicts?

1

Trial and Error in Antebellum Mississippi

In 1795 the United States acquired from Spain a huge expanse of territory extending along the 31st parallel north from the Mississippi River to the state of Georgia, and thereafter, following the courses of several rivers, southeast to the Atlantic Ocean. The western portion of the lands acquired became the Mississippi Territory, and in late 1798 an American governor, Winthrop Sargent, arrived at the river port of Natchez and began to plot the establishment of law and order. He was soon joined by three Federalist appointees to the territorial bench, and together the four men formulated Mississippi's initial code of crimes and punishments.

The Territorial Code

Governor Sargent and his collaborators were not learned jurists. They were, moreover, natives of eastern states who knew little of the frontier, and a notion that the citizenry was ill prepared for the responsibilities of civil government bore strongly on their deliberations. Loathe to legislate with an eye to local conditions, they perused codes operating elsewhere, found little instruction, and at last turned to the legal abstractions associated with what later generations labeled the Classical School of criminal jurisprudence.[1]

Classical dogma was rooted in the published works of the Italian lawyer Cesare Beccaria and in the later revisions of the English philosopher Jeremy Bentham. It rejected traditional retributivist doctrine, maintaining instead that the only rational purpose of a penal sanction was the deterrence of crime. Within the classical agenda, nothing was emphasized more than certainty of punishment, and to that end most corporal penalties were repudiated on the ground that a perception of undue severity might impact negatively on criminal process. Instead, financial penalties, striking at the motives of offenders, were thought proper for crimes against property, and a revolutionary scheme calling for time-sentences in penal institutions was recommended for most other public wrongs.[2]

These currents in legal philosophy influenced Mississippi's first lawgivers very profoundly, for the code they fashioned was a monument to deterrence theory, a complex body of multiple punishments anchored on two Benthamite principles—compensation and disablement. Compensation was of two types, vindictive and lucrative. Vindictive compensation was an essential component of Bentham's doctrine of general deterrence, threatening would-be offenders with an arithmetic scale of financial penalties calculated to exceed the amount of damage inherent in various culpable acts. Lucrative compensation, on the other hand, wedded criminal and civil liabilities via pecuniary restitution to the victims of crime. Sargent's code mandated both.

The code reflected Benthamite reasoning on legal disablement as well. Bentham had recognized four forms of disabling punishment: banishment, death, maiming, and imprisonment. Banishment was impracticable in Mississippi, and both capital punishment and maiming corporal penalties threatened to compromise two related qualities of punishment that Bentham had deemed essential—remissibility and popularity. Sargent and his colleagues eschewed maiming corporal penalties altogether and displayed extraordinary squeamishness on the subject of capital punishment. At a time when the penal law of England sanctioned capital punishment for well over two hundred offenses, that of the Mississippi Territory called for the sentence of death in only two instances.

The elimination of banishment and maiming corporal penalties and the virtual elimination of capital punishment left imprisonment as the only plausible means of legal disablement. Here, though, theory was pitted against practicability, for the Mississippi Territory had nothing resembling a proper place of confinement. Little wonder, then, that one of the government's first statutory enactments advanced guidelines for the construction and maintenance of jails. The statute required every county to erect and maintain a jail. It mandated strict classification by gender, age, and legal status. It provided for periodic inspections by justices of the peace. And it commanded justices to take "such legal measures, as may best tend to secure the Prisoners from escape, sickness and infection, and to have the Gaols cleansed from filth and vermin."

While the central thrust of the code accorded with classical doctrine, it also made allowances for the hard facts of frontier life. Most of the statutes making crimes punishable by imprisonment or fine included provisions empowering trial judges to impose alternative penalties—flagellation, imprisonment in the stocks or the pillory. Here was a safety net that contemplated the Territory's dearth of suitable places of confinement, the unequal distribution of property among those subject to financial sanctions, and the unsettling presence of Indians, outlaws, and troublesome transients. Hence, if space in a jail was unavailable, if the financial resources of a convict were meager, or if a criminal was considered notorious, judges had recourse to a number of the punishments of old. And if a convict proved incapable of paying a fine, sheriffs were authorized to lease him or her to a private contractor.[3]

Mississippi's initial code of crimes and punishments was logically calculated, but it placed a heavy burden on the executive branch of government. In the face of a rapidly growing population, suitable places of confinement had to be established and maintained; and until such resources were made available to trial judges, sentencing would have a distinct social bias—fines for the rich, forced labor or flagellation for the poor. Sargent tackled the problem immediately. His efforts to establish a territorial prison failed, however, and within five years his Jeffersonian successor, W. C. C. Claiborne, was bemoaning the resulting difficulties.[4]

The Early Woes of Legal Punishment

In 1798 only forty-five hundred persons resided within the Mississippi Territory. During the next decade the population of the Territory's two original counties, Adams and Pickering, increased by some thirty-five hundred freemen and six thousand slaves. By 1803 Natchez, the largest municipality, had a population of fourteen hundred, and by 1811 a tier of five new counties lying north and south of

Adams County and extending eastward to the present Alabama state line had been created. Immigration increased still more after the War of 1812. By 1820 Mississippi had a population of 42,176 freemen and 33,272 slaves, and the subsequent opening of the Indian lands brought hordes of settlers into the northeastern and central portions of the state.[5]

Population growth paralleled a considerable expansion of the purview of public law. Many of the new statutory requirements and constraints were born of the demands of domestic slavery. Others were necessitated by the independent spirit of rough, hard-drinking backwoodsmen and riotous boatmen from the emerging midwestern states who terrorized the ports of Mississippi's western river counties. Still others were attributable to notions of public virtue emanating from a pushy, politically active Protestant religious establishment. The result was a dramatic increase in criminal litigation that progressively swamped the legal resources of government.

Deficiencies in law enforcement inspired much extralegal activity. The courts of criminal jurisdiction were plagued by oppressive caseloads. Nothing, however, troubled public officials more than their inability to punish criminals in accordance with the provisions of law.[6]

Financial sanctions and the legal provisions that subjected persons incapable of paying fines to either corporal punishment or forced labor offended the democratic ethic of the citizenry. The penal alternative of imprisonment offered the bench little respite; the Territory had nothing but an old Spanish jail in Natchez when Sargent left Mississippi in 1801, and it could not accommodate those persons who were subject to legal incarceration. In the absence of even a primitive scheme of classification, criminals, vagrants, insolvent debtors, persons awaiting trial, and runaway slaves were confined together under beastly circumstances, and escapes were so frequent that the sheriff of Adams County was forced to adopt measures "repugnant to the feelings of humanity" in attempting to maintain security. On at least one occasion, overcrowding and the heartrending condition of inmates led Governor Claiborne to remit the sentences of convicted felons.[7]

The absence of proper places of confinement inspired Claiborne and his successors, like Sargent before them, to advocate the construction of a central prison capable of relieving pressures on local government. Legislators balked at the prospect of a large financial commitment, however, and such a unitary concept also ran afoul of the notion of local sovereignty that characterized the early years of Mississippi's political development.[8]

Failing there, chief executives placed great emphasis on the construction of additional local facilities, and jails were established in the Territory's major population centers of Natchez, Washington, Port Gibson, and Woodville quite early in the century. But planning considered neither the demands of a rapidly growing population nor the criminological implications of an expanding body of public law. Overcrowding worsened, producing a number of embarrassing incidents, and a hostile press displayed little sympathy.[9]

The problems associated with the jails of Mississippi's larger municipalities hardly inspired authorities in rural areas to comply with the provision of the law that required counties "to mark and lay out the bounds and rules of their respective prisons." Fiscal considerations discouraged jail construction in municipalities and counties with weak tax bases, while the relatively demanding statutory guidelines for the construction and maintenance of jails and the financial and legal liability attached to their operation also delayed compliance with the law.

The territorial code held counties responsible for the proper maintenance of jails; if a prisoner escaped due to the physical inadequacy of the structure in which he or she was confined, the county stood accountable for the amount of money for which the escapee had been committed. Sheriffs also had reason to be leery of legal incarceration. If an escape was attributable to negligence by the sheriff, that official stood "Chargeable to the Plaintiff, Creditor, or other Person at whose Debt, He or She was committed; or to whose use any forfeiture was adjudged, against such Prisoner."[10]

Subsequent statutory revisions imposed more exacting requirements on local officials. Dating from 1822 the law required retiring sheriffs to provide their successors with a certified list of the names of all prisoners confined in their jails along with an account of the reason each prisoner was confined. Later, the legislature imposed financial sanctions to cover cases in which prisoners escaped or died in consequence of negligence, inattention, or inhumanity on the part of county officials.[11]

Apparently jail standards were not enforced rigidly during the early years of the nineteenth century. In 1822, however, circuit judges were required by statute to conduct or oversee an inspection of jails at least once a year, to assure that a report on the state of the jails was filed with the court, and to fine jailers up to fifty dollars for each count of neglect. The transfer of such powers from local and more sympathetic justices of the peace to circuit judges was accompanied by legislation that terminated the sheriffs' one incentive for maintaining jails. During the early years of the century, sheriffs were allowed to sell food, intoxicating beverages, and other commodities to their prisoners, but in 1822 such profitable concessions were banned by statute. Thereafter jails were both financial and legal liabilities to local officials. Few counties and municipalities maintained them, and authorities in one rural area, lacking an adequate jail, actually chained a prisoner to a tree.[12]

Retreats from the Penal Law

With meager financial resources and the requirements of law discouraging jail construction despite increasing demand, public officials adopted every conceivable tactic capable of screening existing lockups from overcrowding. As early as May 1800 a statute empowered justices to release prisoners who had been committed to jail through civil process if they were capable of posting financial surety.[13] Mississippi thus experienced the first of many compromises of its penal law.

The government retreated further as pressures mounted. In July 1804 Governor Claiborne issued an ordinance demanding immediate trials, banning unspecified terms of imprisonment, and forbidding legal incarceration altogether unless a judge first conducted "a careful enquiry into the circumstances of the case." That ordinance was complemented by the granting of executive clemency whenever fiscal considerations or overcrowded jails rendered the government incapable of executing the punishments mandated by the courts. Claiborne once admitted that "a view to political economy" often had "an influence in pardoning offenders, whose claims for mercy were very doubtful."[14]

Succeeding governors pardoned criminals for the same reason, and in 1822 the legislature lent chief executives a hand by allowing all prisoners except those committed for felonies "to walk . . . out of prison, for the preservance of health" provided they were capable of "giving good security to keep within the . . . rules and bounds" established by a county court. But if propertied persons were to be allowed an avenue out of the jails, then surely something had to be done for the propertyless. The legislature therefore forbade the imprisonment of those who could not pay fines once it became clear that they had no estate. Persons awaiting trial were no less expensive to maintain than convicts, so the legislature stipulated that bail would be granted to all persons except those charged with capital offenses in cases where the proof was evident or the presumption of guilt great.[15]

Other revisions of the law removed vagrants and debtors from the jails. In 1818 the new state legislature authorized the establishment of county workhouses and work farms for vagrants, and soon local governments were profiting from the labor of a class that formerly had been a financial liability. Dating from 1822 the law provided debtors with several loopholes that screened them from legal incarceration. Several more appeared in 1839; and a year later—amid much high-sounding rhetoric about the God-given "rights of man"—the legislature abolished imprisonment for debt, thereby removing a heavy burden from the shoulders of county and municipal authorities.[16]

Such compromises promised to reduce the inmate population substantially, but a problem bred by the institution of domestic slavery thwarted every legislative effort. Mississippi's slave population grew prodigiously after about 1820, occasioning a corresponding increase in the number of runaways, and slave patrols delivered to jailers an unmanageable number of slaves whose owners were unknown. Quite early in the nineteenth century, sheriffs were authorized to recoup their expenses by selling runaways at public auction after advertising their whereabouts for six months. But even that compromise failed to solve the problems bred by a growing class of human chattel, so in 1824 the legislature empowered municipal authorities to exploit the labor of runaways within the limits of incorporated towns. Five years later county authorities were given a similar plum when the legislature authorized the employment of runaway slaves on highways and bridges immediately outside corporate limits.[17]

These legal provisions provided local governments with a cheap labor force, but they also created a demand for the confinement of runaways that reduced both the ability and the willingness of local officials to accommodate persons committed through criminal process. Jails came to be regarded as little more than sleeping quarters for runaway slaves. The sheriff of Wilkinson County once based a plea for a new jail on the argument that the existing facility was "unfit to receive negroes as a Public jail."[18]

The influx of runaway slaves led to steady degeneration within the few existing jails. On January 29, 1829, the Natchez *Southern Galaxy* protested that the inmates of the state's jails formed "a school of experimental villainy, in which each is taught new lessons by the other, and from which issues a band of wretches, infinitely better fitted to accomplish their nefarious designs upon society, than before they entered the walls of the prison." Under the circumstances, incarceration came to be regarded as an unrealistic penal option. "When the courts have the alternative," noted an eminent attorney in 1830, "they rarely order imprisonment, owing to its expense to the state."[19]

Increasing Severity and Decreasing Certainty

The inability of local jails to meet the demands of criminal process forced the legislature to do something; and the politicians, altogether ignoring the legal currents of the age, opted for more cost-efficient corporal punishments. By 1824, when George Poindexter's digest of the existing laws of Mississippi was printed, the penal code was bloody and retributive, presenting a striking contrast with the spirit and the letter of the original territorial code. Poindexter's digest mandated death by hanging for murder, arson, rape, robbery, burglary, forgery, counterfeiting, second offense manslaughter, second offense horse stealing, stealing or selling a free person, stealing a slave, bearing false witness that threatened life, and accessory before the fact to most of those crimes.[20]

Secondary forms of punishment were also much more severe, especially with regard to criminality by slaves. During the early years of the century, criminal process had been spared extensive involvement with the servile proletariat by statutes that practically defined criminal acts by slaves as private wrongs, or torts, and assigned such litigation to local magistrates.[21] The awesome growth of the slave population bred alarm among freemen, however, and by 1824 slaves were well within the purview of the criminal law.

Since only runaway slaves, and not those who violated the provisions of the criminal code, could be employed on public works projects, it was not cost-effective to imprison slaves adjudicated guilty of criminal acts. Because slaves could not own property, it was impossible to fine them. Consequently, a larger number of offenses by slaves were made punishable by bloodcurdling corporal penalties.[22]

The increasing severity of legal punishment assured conflict between the penal law and the people it ostensibly served. Corporal punishment often left telltale scars that reduced the monetary value of slaves, and slave owners stopped at nothing in attempting to shield their property from criminal process. The desire to protect a considerable financial investment was all the more evident in cases where crimes by slaves were punishable by death. A proposal to reimburse owners the full value of slaves put to death through criminal process was narrowly defeated at the Constitutional Convention of 1817, and that decision pitted the criminal law against the economic interests of a large and powerful segment of the population.[23]

Severe punishments also rendered the conviction of free defendants more difficult. Owing to the expense of imprisonment, the abysmal condition of the jails, and the merciless nature of penal alternatives, trial judges often confounded prosecutors by attaching what many considered unrealistic importance to the rules of criminal procedure and the quality of evidence necessary for conviction. Then, too, jurors were frequently intimidated by the severity of penal sanctions and reluctant to convict obviously guilty defendants, especially those charged with serious crimes.[24]

Executive clemency freed many convicts who failed to profit from the benevolence of the bench or the reluctance of jurors. During the late twenties District Attorney Robert K. Walker prosecuted a case of forgery to conviction and a sentence of death, only to create a stir in the legal community by recommending a gubernatorial pardon on the ground that the punishment was disproportionate to the offense. Dating from about 1827, chief executives were exposed to similar pressure from influential citizens, and clemency was granted more frequently. Governor Hiram Runnels received more than sixty petitions for clemency during the early thirties, all charging that the enforcement of existing statutes was too stringent and that punishments were too severe.[25]

The "Crime Wave" of the Thirties

Public awareness of the gulf between the letter of the criminal law and the operation of criminal process heightened during the early 1830s as a number of factors combined to produce an unprecedented level of anxiety, violence, and criminality in Mississippi. Many of the problems were attributable to a sudden acceleration in population growth, especially in municipalities. Jackson, the new state capital, seemed to rise from the banks of the Pearl River overnight, and after 1832, when the construction of public buildings brought in many unruly laborers, disorderly conduct was rife. Natchez, Vicksburg, and the other river towns did not grow as rapidly, but a considerable increase of commerce on the Mississippi River attracted "villains of every description, outlaws from other States, [and] refugees from justice" to the seedy ghettoes near the docks.[26]

The emergence during the thirties of the state's fabled cotton economy bred anxiety and violence as well. With "King Cotton" came a huge increase in the slave population that, according to one informed observer, occasioned "a sense of insecurity" among freemen that rendered them "continually subject to groundless and fanciful alarms and apprehensions." Uneasiness mounted with the beginning of systematic attacks on slavery by abolitionists, and it gave way to paranoia after 1831, when the gory details of Nat Turner's slave rebellion in Virginia became generally known.[27]

Economic development also brought the many problems that seem to plague emerging market economies everywhere. With the value of realty appreciating substantially, entrepreneurs successfully dispossessed Indians of their landed property and then turned on one another in vicious legal and political warfare. The development of capital also bred wild financial speculation and a ruinous struggle for control of the banking resources of the state. Going hand in hand with these disturbing influences was dire socioeconomic cleavage between the humble farmers of the eastern portion of the state and the great planter-capitalists of the western river counties. That rift, which found expression in the dogma of Jacksonian Democracy and Whiggery, fomented an uncommonly vicious political duel. General Sam Dale remembered that almost every Mississippian "wore pistols and bowie-knife, and a row once a day was the rule, not the exception." Legislators came to the statehouse armed for combat, and on one occasion nearly the whole population of Jackson gathered at the public square in battle array.[28]

To these problems were added the effects of an increase in alcohol consumption and a corresponding degeneration of public morality. According to the politician Henry S. Foote, there was "nothing more noticeable in the social status of Mississippi" during the thirties "than the immense quantities of intoxicating drinks" consumed by all classes. The result was an "astounding" increase in violence. Foote was certain that a majority of the state's serious criminal offenses "were to be traced to the direct influence of intoxicating drinks," and he found the indiscretions of drunken trial judges appalling. Another observer noted that declining morality in public officials had an adverse effect on the entire population. Mississippi politics, wrote yet another, was little more than "a series of selfish plots and counterplots for the benefit of . . . inferior men!"[29]

The anxiety, violence, and crime of the thirties gave rise to a spirit of reform that grew in intensity as the decade progressed. Many reformers held that the state's statutory law needed a thorough overhaul. The code had grown prodigiously. Declaratory statutes, remedial statutes, enlarging statutes, and restraining statutes all too often had been enacted in a vacuum, nobody had coordinated the resulting expansion of public law, and the corpus juris was therefore ill-classified, contradictory in nature and object, and extremely ambiguous.

The Jacksonian Democrats, who swept to power in the elections of 1831 and a year later enacted a new and radically democratic state constitution, found the code inconsistent with the most hallowed principles of popular government. Democratic spokesmen criticized the law as "a sealed book to the great mass of the community" and argued that it was "unjust to punish those who cannot readily ascertain what is prohibited." The confused condition of the law was also regarded as a threat to the efficiency of popularly elected officials because "but few, even of the judges and other public officers," could understand it. In 1832, therefore, the legislature commissioned the attorney P. Rutilius R. Pray to "amend the phraseology of the existing statutes and to prune, correct and arrange, alter and amend" its provisions. Pray's primary mission was to render the law "capable of being understood by all who read."[30]

However, Mississippi's essential problem arose less from the forms of the law than from its substance and administration; quite simply, the state's legal resources were incapable of coping with an ever-increasing supply of litigants and convicts. While influenced by the extraordinary economic, social, and political currents of the 1830s, that phenomenon was rooted in the law-generating propensities of republican governance. The substantive commands of public law were heavy, they were supported by unrealistic penal threats, and the dilemma promised to worsen, notwithstanding the efforts of lawyer Pray. Numerous Mississippians, while protesting the inefficiency of criminal process, clamored for more legal requirements and constraints, in effect arguing for an expansion of the penal code.

Many reformers felt that the excessive consumption of alcohol was the root of all evil, and in 1830 the Mississippi Temperance Society was founded. Others, who regarded gambling as the work of Satan, established antigambling leagues. Still others, offended by the widespread practice of dueling, formed a statewide antidueling league, and many citizens wanted to disarm the gun-toting members of the community. More numerous, especially among the classes who owned few or no slaves, were outraged citizens who blamed everything on wealthy planters and demanded more constraints on their Negroes.[31]

Often encouraged or led by the Protestant clergy, such groups lobbied state and local officials for statutes and ordinances reflecting their respective notions of public virtue. If unsuccessful, they damned the insensitivity, immorality, or corruption of the politicians and, feeding on mutual indignation, sometimes turned to extralegal activities. If successful, the resulting expansion of the purview of public law compounded the difficulties of criminal process, highlighting its inefficiency and frequently leading indignant mobs to take the law into their own hands. It was a serious, if temporary, dilemma; and between 1832 and 1835, as vigilante activity mounted steadily throughout Mississippi, politicians considered reforms in the several components of criminal process and at last concluded that a centralized penal institution might prop the sinking ship of state.[32]

The Case for a State Penitentiary

A number of considerations recommended a fundamental change in the means of legal punishment. Paramount among them was the political economy of penology under county administration. In 1822 the counties' fiscal embarrassments had led the legislature to retreat from the statutory requirement for all counties to build and maintain jails, and to allow those counties without suitable places of confinement to lodge prisoners in the jails of adjacent counties. Thereafter, counties with comparatively secure jails had contracted to house the prisoners of their less fortunate neighbors, and poorer counties had thereby relinquished a degree of sovereignty.[33]

One must suspect that the profitability of labor by runaway slaves also diminished the enthusiasm of local governments to involve themselves with the fruits of criminal process. While convicts were expensive and troublesome to maintain, runaways performed valuable public works and, not incidentally, offered public officials and other well-fixed members of the community a very handy tool for personal aggrandizement. It was better, from all points of view, to foist the convict problem on state government.

Earlier victories by local government made state politicians willing to take on the load. In 1822 the legislature had agreed to reimburse all expenses incurred by counties in providing food, drink, fire, and bedding to prisoners confined in their jails, and in 1829 the state had assumed responsibility for the medical expenses of indigent prisoners. Mounting state involvement had bred increased support for the construction of a state prison. Governor Gerard C. Brandon told the legislature in 1827 that such a facility would spare the state much of the "enormous burden" of supporting prisoners in local jails. Two years later the editor of the Natchez *Southern Galaxy* observed that the matter was one "of mere practicability," and afterward a growing number of state politicians agreed.[34]

Political and fiscal realities within Mississippi seemed to mesh nicely with a penal philosophy that was emerging in other parts of the country. By the mid-thirties the penal systems of Pennsylvania and New York were regarded as blueprints for enlightened penology throughout the United States and Europe. Pennsylvania's eastern penitentiary, Cherry Hill, had begun receiving prisoners in 1829. A successor to the famous, Quaker-inspired Walnut Street Jail in Philadelphia, the institution based its operations on principles borrowed from monastic Christianity, cloistering its inmates in separate cells. There the lonely convicts ate, slept, worked at a craft, and received religious instruction from visiting clergymen, their only contact with the outside world. The prison reflected an influential philosophy of punishment, and the bulk of professional opinion agreed with the assessment of the Englishman William Crawford, who observed that the Pennsylvania system was "powerfully instrumental not only in deterring but also in reclaiming the offender."[35]

Crawford was less enraptured with New York's Auburn system, but it had its supporters, and those who bothered to think about such things generally regarded the system as the only enlightened alternative to what was going on in Pennsylvania. Auburn Penitentiary was the progeny of New York's celebrated Newgate prison, where the eminent penologist Thomas Eddy had plied his trade, and the institution had quite literally opened for business in 1821. It was a compromised version of separate cellular confinement with both architecture and discipline designed to achieve maximum cost-efficiency. Tiny cells and inexpensive block architecture stood in marked contrast to Cherry Hill, as did workshops where inmates labored together in forced silence during daylight hours. Such a scheme facilitated large-scale prison industry, potential profits for the state, and, according to the system's advocates, the reformation of criminals.[36]

News of the achievements of penologists at Cherry Hill and Auburn had occasioned much excitement. Indeed, a crusade for penal reform was underway across the nation, and by the early thirties the states of the lower South were embracing Yankee penal philosophy. Kentucky, Georgia, and Tennessee had been the first to establish penitentiaries, and more recently Alabama and Louisiana had followed suit.[37] By 1836 Mississippi's retributive penal code stood as an anomaly among the more developed Southern states, and some observers contended that progress was leaving Mississippi behind.

Legislators could not escape the fact that the principles underlying the penitentiary concept were operating quite successfully in other spheres of social control within the state. Important precedents had been the establishment of county poorhouses and work farms in 1818 and the statutes that allowed local governments to exploit the labor of runaway slaves. The system of "poor relief" had proved very successful, actually producing profits through forced labor and the sale of commodities on the open market, and the gangs of manacled runaways, noted one observer, were "merely moving penitentiaries, appropriating that amount of labor, which at the north is expended within four walls, to the broader limits of the city."[38]

All this opened the door to penal reform. There were those who had doubts: a state penitentiary was an expensive proposition, and there was something fundamentally unsound about a proposal that preserved local sovereignty over criminal process yet divested local government of responsibility for its offspring. But the depredations of vigilantes had reached galling dimensions by 1835, the republican electorate was screaming for relief, and it was, after all, an election year.

The hopeful candidates jumped on the bandwagon. A state penitentiary was not necessarily a good idea, but it seemed to be the only idea.

Penal Reform

A bill calling for the establishment of a state penitentiary was enacted with little difficulty on February 26, 1836. The statute specified that the prison would be located within two miles of Jackson, made capable of housing at least two hundred convicts, and otherwise designed on the basis of "the best and most approved plans" adopted in other states. In April the state's commissioners of public buildings selected the eight-acre plot in central Jackson on which the present state capitol stands, and state architect William Nichols, armed with a generous $75,000 appropriation, began to draft plans.[39]

Nichols's blueprint conformed to the "simple but excellent and much admired" design of New York's Auburn Penitentiary. It called for a three story structure consisting of a round center and two wings containing several offices, workshops, a kitchen, a dining room, an infirmary, and a place of worship. The prison would have three hundred cells, each seven feet long, seven feet high, and three and one-half feet wide. According to Nichols, such an architectural plan would allow the state to combine "salutary discipline and profitable labor, with moral instruction."[40]

Construction, which began in April 1837, was slowed by the devastating effects of the national banking crisis of that year, but a subsequent $30,000 appropriation allowed the contractors to resume operations. Then legislative squabbling about the provisions of the new penal code and the respective virtues of the Auburn and Pennsylvania systems cast doubts on everything. Even so, in 1839 the Democratic majority at last pushed through a revised penal code that reduced to three the number of capital crimes, banned public punishments, and substituted imprisonment at hard labor for most of the financial and corporal penalties that had been mandated for felony convictions by the old code.[41]

Meanwhile, construction on the penitentiary continued in the face of severe economic dislocation. By April 15, 1840, twenty-five cells were ready to receive convicts, and an impatient governor proclaimed the official opening of the institution. Great fanfare ensued as the legislature declared the prison's "beauty, strength, durability, health, and convenience" a wonder of the age, equaling the praiseworthy attributes of any penal institution in the nation. Curious citizens and public officials looked on as Superintendent Charles M. Hart and his staff admitted the first twenty-eight convicts.[42]

The Philosophy of Punishment

Mississippi's new scheme of legal punishment was a maze of widely divergent ideals. Everything began with the distinction, first made by Bentham and the British school of legal Utilitarianism, between apparent punishment and real punishment. By abandoning corporal penalties and embracing time sentences in a penal institution, the state sought to make its penal sanctions more apparently lenient. Such sanctions, the theory went, would be more popular among trial juries, thereby enhancing certainty of punishment.[43]

The Utilitarian ideal also found expression in the location and design of the penitentiary. The attempt to render penal sanctions more lenient in the perception of the public led to the abandonment of publicly administered corporal punishments. That concession, which terminated the long reign of the public executioner, threatened to compromise the ancient notion that the example of punishment deterred crime among the general population. Bentham had addressed this omission by emphasizing that prisons with ominous appearances should be erected in the center of cities. Mississippi acted accordingly. The chairman of the senate committee on public buildings, noting the high, dark, and imposing walls of the prison looming in the center of the state's capital city, contended that the institution would "create in every citizen fear, respect and esteem" for the commands of law.[44]

As for real punishment, the state relied on fixed terms of imprisonment exposing convicts to "much deprivation and strict obedience to severe but just requirements." In the "American Penitentiary Code," a legislative committee noted,

> the requisites of punishment blended with benevolence are to place the criminal instantly and effectually out of reach of the influences of criminal association—to make the living world a blank to his vision—to make temptation voiceless—to show that the pleasures of vice were the seductive lures which have immured him for years in cells, that reverberate only to his sighs. . . .[45]

But imprisonment, by cloistering felons, threatened to expose them even more to the influences of criminal association. So Mississippi's legislators mandated separate cellular confinement and, following the example of New York, prohibited communication among convicts whenever labor brought them together.[46]

At this point the state's new scheme departed from the tenets of traditional penal philosophy and entered the world of social philosophy. The "*ne plus ultra* of the science of penal infliction," a legislative committee observed, was to remove the causes of criminality before releasing a felon back into society. Causation was not assigned to aberrations in the social fabric or to rational conduct on the part of the criminal. Instead, the assumptions were that society was blameless and that crime was "the bitter fruit of long continued lapses from a course of virtue and respectability." The primary mission of the penitentiary, then, was to bolster the "moral sense" of criminals through "a course of training calculated to restore its vitality."[47]

Training had four components. The first was the promotion of healthfulness among convicts. The cells were equipped with small windows, and air ducts were installed at each end of the cellblock. Woodburning stoves would provide warmth in winter, a physician would be on duty at all times, and food would be wholesome. Clothing and bedding would be comfortable, but not too comfortable; the legislature was aware of Bentham's doctrine of "less eligibility," which cautioned that the deterring effect of legal incarceration would be compromised if living conditions within the prison were superior to those of the lowest social class within the free community. Hence the law mandated that clothing and bedding would be made of "coarse materials" and that food, while wholesome, would be "inferior" in quality.[48]

Secondly, "benevolent" treatment by a "humane" staff would promote the "cardinal virtues" of fortitude, justice, prudence, and temperance in inmates. The principal keeper of the penitentiary was a superintendent or agent. He and his family were required to live within the walls of the prison, and his "constant attendance" was necessary unless he was performing official business elsewhere. The superintendent's administrative staff included a deputy keeper, two assistant keepers, and a clerk. Security was entrusted to a sergeant who commanded a fifteen-man security force.

To assure benevolence, the operations of the internal staff were to be supervised by a three-member board of inspectors. The inspectors were to visit the prison every two months to inquire into any alleged misconduct by the staff and to hold judicial proceedings "in the same manner . . . as in cases of arbitration." Appointed biennially by the governor with the advice and consent of the senate, the inspectors were also required to submit an annual report to the legislature containing assessments of the penitentiary both by themselves and by every principal member of the staff.[49]

The third component of training was religious instruction to inculcate the social ideals of Christian doctrine. A full-time chaplain would preside and would teach the convicts to read and write. Religious literature would be distributed among the convicts.[50] The penitentiary, it was hoped, would manufacture literate men and women possessed of the spirit of Christian love.

Finally, training would instill "habits of strict and regular industry." This component of penitentiary discipline was rooted in Calvinist dogma, which hailed the presence of a work ethic in socially adjusted citizens, and it was supported by those who called for hard labor and productive labor. Legal retributivists were consoled by the thought of forced convict labor, the harder the better, so the legislature took care to employ the term "hard labor" in the statute. The prospect of a captive labor force contributing to the public weal appealed to those who spoke of productive labor. This latter group propounded the popular argument that those who transgressed the laws of the state had no just claim for public support. The ideal of convict labor, therefore, united otherwise discordant factions and constituted the nexus of the state's new penal philosophy.

Although the design of the prison accorded with that of the Auburn system, a fiscally conservative legislature renounced the industrial sweatshops of New York in favor of the trade-oriented labor associated with the Pennsylvania system. Clearly, however, remunerative convict labor was the fondest hope of the politicians. The law stipulated that convicts would be "kept constantly employed . . . during the daytime, except when incapable of laboring." The superintendent would "use every proper means to furnish . . . prisoners with employment, the most beneficial to the public, and the best suited to their various capacities." He would enter into contracts "with such persons and upon such terms, as may be deemed . . . most beneficial to this state." He would supervise convict labor and sell all manufactured articles for the benefit of the public.[51]

Here, then, were the philosophical underpinnings of the state penitentiary. Optimists theorized that the scheme would enable the state to operate a cheap, even profitable, penal institution capable of making right "loved for its own sake, and wrong loathed and despised for its inherent deformity, rather than for the danger which attends its perpetration."[52]

An Unhappy Beginning

A considerable portion of the public had soured on the penitentiary even before the first convicts were admitted. The effects of the banking crisis, which extended well into the forties, caused many citizens to reevaluate the decision to invest such a large amount of public money in an institution for criminals. Others, straining to survive the recession within the confines of law, resented an institution that gobbled up their taxes for the purpose of providing felons with all the essentials of life. Furthermore, the "crime wave" of the 1830s had petered out by 1840; now there was ground to argue that the penitentiary bill had been enacted needlessly. Three months before the grand opening of the penitentiary, the governor observed that the appropriation of funds to construct the prison was regarded by many citizens as a "premium paid for vice."[53]

Fights over patronage and ill-advised revisions of the legislation that had established the penitentiary confirmed the critics. The original penitentiary act divided authority between the superintendent and the inspectors in a simple system of checks and balances. Those arrangements came under fire early in the 1840 legislative session, and in February, before the penitentiary admitted its first inmates, legislation stripped the inspectors and the superintendent of the power to appoint and dismiss members of the staff. The revised statute, which empowered the legislature to hire and fire all employees, crippled the inspectors, hamstrung the superintendent, and allowed the politicians to meddle in the affairs of the penitentiary. The meddling, of course, inspired still more legislation, and soon the prison's administrators were confounded by a statute mandating an exacting and most confusing system of bookkeeping.[54]

Problems were compounded by Section 6 of the original penitentiary act, which mandated that the convicts would complete the construction of the prison. That was a tall order, for when the first inmates were committed, 125 cells were uninhabitable, the walls were uncompleted, and more than 1.5 million bricks had yet to be manufactured and laid. The subsequent use of convict labor in constructing the prison satisfied the retributive urges of the community and the perceived fiscal interests of the state, but it compromised the principle of separate cellular confinement around which the theory of the penitentiary ostensibly revolved. The first twenty-eight inmates were lodged in twenty-five cells. Those committed later were assigned cellmates, and the work of the convicts often carried them far outside the walls of the prison.[55]

Such compromises did not make the maintenance of discipline easy for the staff, and the vagueness of the provisions of the law relating to disciplinary procedures virtually guaranteed iniquities. Injury to a convict was punishable in the same manner as injury to a free citizen. But "injury" was not given a precise definition by the legislature. The whipping of female convicts was expressly forbidden by statute, so the law implied that male prisoners could be disciplined by the lash. Solitary confinement on a diet of bread and water was also authorized by statute, but the law said nothing concerning the terms upon which it could be imposed. Furthermore, while the superintendent was required to summon the coroner of Hinds County in all cases of death "from any cause other than ordinary sickness," the term "ordinary sickness" went undefined, the coroner was not given jurisdiction over the penitentiary, and inquests were held only if they were requested by a principal officer of the prison.[56]

Less than a year after the opening of the penitentiary a legislative committee released an unsettling report. Severe corporal punishments were being inflicted. One inmate had been kept in solitary confinement on a diet of bread and water for almost a year, another had committed suicide, and still others had died under suspicious circumstances. Superintendent Hart possessed a foul temper and had exploited public property for private gain. Public confidence in "benevolent" operations at the penitentiary was hardly enhanced when Hart was allowed to retain his job. But an embarrassed legislature soon reassured the citizenry by banning corporal punishment, requiring an oath of all employees not to abuse convicts, and mandating monthly visits by the inspectors.[57]

While fostering human abuse, the decision to employ convicts in the construction of the prison also prevented the institution from generating revenue, thereby thwarting the popular notion that a profitable enterprise would emerge overnight. A great deal of criticism erupted after November 1841, when financial records disclosed a substantial deficit, and declining public regard led to declining public support. On February 14, 1842, the legislature abolished the office of deputy keeper, restricted the penitentiary to one assistant keeper, and reduced the salaries of all remaining staff members.[58]

Further disappointing financial returns led the politicians to continue their retreat from first principles. The use of convict labor in the construction of the prison precluded education in letters and reduced religious training to weekly services conducted in a "light and airy chapel" formed by an open space in the cellblock. The chaplain came to be regarded as an expensive luxury, and in 1844, when the legislators lowered the salaries of the superintendent, the remaining assistant keeper, and the clerk still further, they abolished the office of chaplain. Thereafter, preachers from the Jackson area provided spotty, gratuitous religious instruction.[59]

Criminological failures fed the fire. The notion that the location and grim architecture of the penitentiary would deter crime became suspect as early as September 1841, when one of the offices at the prison was burglarized. Later, when three of the first inmates released from the penitentiary promptly landed in jail, a journalist protested that convicts departed the prison as "the rank enemies of society, and almost immediately, and with singular recklessness, return to their old habits of villainy." Even one of the penitentiary's principal staff members acknowledged failure. Criminals, observed an imprudent physician, regarded the prison as "an asylum where their wants and sufferings may be ministered to." According to the report of a legislative committee, a substantial number of citizens believed the prison was nothing more than "an expensive State Seminary for the accomplishment and graduation of eminent roguery."[60]

The staff of the penitentiary tried to muddle through. In the summer of 1843 the superintendent sought to generate revenue by employing gangs of convicts at "rambling outdoors labor." That was yet another compromise of penal discipline, but it brought in a little money. Later in the year, after a number of new commitments increased the size of the labor force, several shops within the prison began operations. The convicts worked as blacksmiths, carpenters, wheelwrights, tailors, cooks, and cobblers with a degree of success. Jacksonians happily paid the modest prices charged for such services, and the penitentiary recorded a small profit during the fiscal year that ended November 1843.[61]

Such apparent progress enabled penal authorities to fend off the attacks of their more determined critics. In late 1843 a legislative committee toured the prison and later released a report praising the "neat, well-furnished, well-ventilated workshops, where busy industry works out its moral effects upon minds and bodies distempered by crime." By December 1844 fifty cells on the lower tier and thirty-six on the second tier were "complete and in good order" and fourteen more were nearing completion. Sheds for the storage of manufactured articles had been constructed, and trade-oriented labor was well established. The revenue-generating enterprises of the prison employed forty-six convict-artisans. In November 1845 the prison reported a net profit of well over $5,000.[62]

The Unfortunate Political Economy of Success

Ironically, the financial success of the prison, and the release of even "reformed" convict-artisans into the community, offended the public no less than insolvency and recidivism. The popular fear, which of course was exploited and promoted by aspiring politicians, was that vocational training threatened to secure released convicts "a place at the fireside of every member of the community." One candidate went so far as to equate the release of convict-artisans with the demise of Southern womanhood. A released convict with a trade acquired in the penitentiary, he warned, could pose as a respectable citizen and "marry some innocent and unsuspecting woman, who, when it is too late, will discover, that she has married a cold hearted villain, and that she has been receiving the embraces and caresses of a man polluted by crime and degraded by imprisonment."[63]

Nor did the business community like the penitentiary. The state was spending tax revenues to teach convicts a trade. If successful, the state released a convict-artisan into a marketplace where free artisans understandably resented a competitor whose training had been financed by their taxes. Free artisans were no less pleased when the state dumped cheap, convict-produced consumer goods into the marketplace; in effect, their taxes were being employed to depress prices. It was a dilemma that was beginning to develop across the nation; and between 1842 and 1845, as the penitentiary expanded its operations and sold greater amounts of produce on the open market, increasing numbers of free artisans voiced protest.[64]

The disenchantment of artisans, merging with the suspicions of the general public, set the republican political process in motion. As early as 1842 T. L. Sumrall, an eminent state senator, published a circular letter calling for a change of prison labor. Former governor A. G. McNutt printed similar sentiments in the summer of 1843. By late 1843 tradesmen throughout the state were mobilizing for political combat, and in December the legislature's joint standing committee on the penitentiary, noting the receipt of numerous petitions, observed that every "acknowledged . . . axiom in political economy" recommended a slow conversion of prison labor to textile manufacturing.[65]

The 1844 legislature, attempting to placate the artisans, allocated $1,500 for a wool-carding machine and an iron foundry. Those concessions did not satisfy the penitentiary's critics, however, and during the election year of 1845 hopeful political candidates succumbed before the muscle flexing of the state's small but remarkably influential artisan class. On March 5, 1846, the new legislature enacted a bill "to change the labor of convicts in the State Penitentiary." Quickly signed into law by a sympathetic governor, the statute directed the superintendent to procure an engine and fixtures, and to use convict labor to erect an industrial plant capable of employing eighty hands in the manufacture of textiles. The machinery was to be "kept constantly at work and in operation"; the proceeds of the mill were to reimburse the state.[66] Mississippi would follow the example of New York.

The Industrial Prison

The decision to manufacture textiles at the state penitentiary solved a dire political problem. The termination of trade-oriented convict labor disarmed the state's artisans, and, because there was only one other mill within the state, the advent of textile manufacturing excited no great hostility among the electorate. Like all political compromises, however, that of 1846 came at a cost. It exposed the state to all the pitfalls of public sector business administration.

The dilemma posed by the demands of political geography is the most glaring example. Purely economic reasoning would have placed the prison on the Mississippi River in the first place, but the Democratic majority in the legislature had frowned on a proposal to build the institution in Whiggish Vicksburg. Now, with the coming of heavy industry, the insular location of the capital city guaranteed inaccessibility to out-of-state markets. Nor could the Jackson metropolitan area easily supply the demand for wood to propel the furnace in the new mill, and the distant proximity of the Pearl River assured difficulty in procuring water for a thirsty steam engine.[67]

Problems were compounded by the purchase of an undersized engine and by the legislature's delay in authorizing the employment of a skilled engineer. Although the original plan called for a twenty-five horsepower engine, an insufficient legislative appropriation resulted in the installation of a twenty horsepower engine. It wheezed and coughed amid chronic woes for some five years before mercifully dying. More mechanical difficulties ensued in the following years, disrupting operations sometimes for several months at a time.[68]

Other problems developed due to the politicians' reluctance to appropriate funds for new equipment until disaster proved it essential. The most notable example was the legislature's inexplicable failure to equip the prison with a fire engine despite repeated warnings by the staff. On November 1, 1857, a fire broke out in the mill and completely destroyed the building and its contents. Eighteen days later, while the embers were yet smoldering, a chagrined legislature appropriated funds for the purchase of a fire engine and a hose.[69]

More serious were the effects of the legislators' contradictory view of inmate labor. Everybody in the statehouse expected the penitentiary to make money. That was difficult, though, because they also demanded non-revenue-producing public works projects of the convicts. The construction of the new textile mill required the inmates to manufacture and install some 250,000 bricks, but while that project was underway a large detachment of convicts was building a brick wall around the state capitol. Then, while the mill was still under construction, the convicts were required to manufacture bricks for the state lunatic asylum. That task demanded the manufacture of more than one million bricks, and thirty-five convicts were employed in a brickyard nearly two miles from the prison during 1848.

Legislators also demanded that inmates maintain the prison's physical plant, despite shoddy work by the convicts. During 1847 the front wall and the buildings connected to it began to deteriorate rapidly, and by early 1848 the superintendent's house was uninhabitable.

The building of a "valuable and substantial brick residence" for the superintendent monopolized the labor of a large number of convicts during 1848, and in 1851 the inmates made substantial repairs on the front wall and the buildings connected to it. By 1855 the superintendent's house was about to collapse, the front wall was giving way, the roof on the connected main building was cracking, and the offices below were being flooded every time it rained. Later, authorities discovered that prisoners lodged in the cells on the upper tier were escaping because of faulty construction.[70]

The legislature also opposed business practices that could have increased the penitentiary's sales. Mississippi planters, who constituted the prison's primary clientele, were dependent on credit prior to harvest time, but legislators insisted on cash transactions. So sales were diminished, and the superintendent was forced to engage in the burdensome practice of barter with many of his customers. Even barter was difficult, though, because the penitentiary was not equipped with a store at which business with the public could be conducted. Buyers, staff members, and convicts stumbled over each other at the front gate while someone went to fetch the superintendent. Meanwhile, the legislature was curiously tardy in authorizing the appointment of agents to sell the prison's produce outside the Jackson area.[71]

Business was also affected adversely by the public's perception of the penitentiary. A number of buyers displayed sympathy for the grieving artisans by boycotting the penitentiary during 1847. The resulting drop in revenues crippled the transition to textile manufacturing and produced angry remonstrances by the public. Four years later, when the price of raw cotton dropped suddenly, another storm of protest erupted because the penitentiary continued to sell its manufactured goods at prices consistent with the former price of raw materials. Protest was no less adamant whenever mechanical difficulties slowed operations in the mill, and sales always plummeted whenever there were rumors of sickness within the penitentiary. Somehow a sick convict was feared more than a sick freeman.[72]

The many problems of the textile mill undermined the operations of the entire prison. Harassed superintendents reported deficits through fiscal year 1848, and a strong legislative offensive to lease the penitentiary and all its inmates to private business interests failed in a sparse house late in the 1848 session.[73] Subsequently, the commissions and omissions of the legislature, the bungling of the staff, and the outrageous demands of the public thwarted productivity and generated incessant criticism.

But an indefinite continuation of deficits was almost an impossibility. The account of the penitentiary was assessed nothing for the construction of the expensive physical plant. Legislative appropriations provided interest-free capital for maintenance and permanent improvements. The prison was assessed no taxes. Labor was paid no wages. There was, moreover, a substantial market for coarse cotton and woolen goods in Mississippi and little competition from the private sector.

Hence the business affairs of the penitentiary improved steadily during the 1850s. Modest profits were reported in both 1849 and 1850 as the traumatic conversion to heavy industry continued. During 1851 workable machinery was at last procured, a full-time engineer for the troubled mill was hired, and a store for the sale of prison-made products was opened at the front gate. In 1852 the legislature finally authorized the superintendent to "appoint . . . agents in this and other states, for the sale of manufactured articles."[74]

Reported profits mounted, and by 1855 the transition to heavy industry was complete. Of the eighty-two convicts in the prison in December, sixty-eight were working in the mill, and sales for the past fiscal year totaled $32,372.89. Such numbers pleased the politicians. In 1856 the legislature approved a relatively simple system of accounting and gave the superintendent greatly increased control over his staff. In November 1857, when fire gutted the factory, there was little opposition to a speedy appropriation of $40,000 to rebuild it. When the superintendent purchased new machinery without prior authorization in 1858, an ungrumbling legislature appropriated $30,000 to pay for it. And in December of the same year, after the superintendent had recommended the construction of new cells, legislators responded with a liberal appropriation of $5,000.[75]

The new factory, which was completed by the convicts in late 1858, was described by the governor as "an excellent piece of work." A visiting journalist went further in his assessment, contending that "no factory in the Southern States . . . can compete with it in size, durability, and the perfect system observed in all its parts." Complementing the new factory was the addition of fifty-four new cells over the third tier of the prison; that project enabled penal authorities to increase the size of their labor force to 207 separately housed convicts.

An artesian well was added in late 1859. By July 1860 it was providing the steam engine with fourteen thousand gallons of water daily.[76]

These improvements led to the emergence of one of the greatest industrial prisons in the nation. In 1860 the textile mill recorded some $80,000 in gross sales. The next year manufacturing was increased and diversified to meet the demands of the Confederate war effort. Convicts not employed in the mill remodeled rifles, mounted cannon, and produced other materiel of war; for 1862 the prison recorded $143,964.47 in gross sales. After December 1862 the superintendent was authorized to employ free labor in the manufacture of military ordnance, and in the single month of April 1863 the prison's sales reached $81,574.84. When federal troops entered Jackson a month later, they found "really a great manufactory."[77]

Convict Life

By all accounts, the transition to prison industry brought an improvement in the standard of convict life. Inmates were well fed and well clothed. Great pains were taken to keep the prison clean. Despite inadequate medical facilities, the penitentiary recorded a relatively good health record. Unlike many other antebellum prisons, Mississippi's was never seriously criticized as a breeding ground for insanity. Few iniquities and nothing resembling a scandal were reported. Inspectors and superintendents penned glowing reports of internal discipline. Journalists who visited the penitentiary noted that the staff was efficient, even loving, and that convicts were humanely treated.[78]

Through it all, however, few Mississippians took the earlier talk of convict reformation seriously. In 1846 the philanthropist Dorothea Dix visited the penitentiary and donated a "valuable little library." But few of the convicts could read, the absence of a chaplain assured that nobody taught them, and the demands of labor allowed little time for such things. In 1848 the inspectors submitted a revealing report. The unpaid clergymen who dropped by from time to time were getting the job done; to their efforts the staff attributed a "general disposition to subordination and good order" among the convicts.[79]

Similar motives led to a brief revival of interest in convict reformation two years later. A legislative committee, contemplating the pending release of a large number of felons, warned that "very soon . . . these delinquents . . . will be turned loose upon the world perhaps again to prey upon society." That unpleasant prospect inspired the restoration of the office of chaplain, regular religious services, and a spirited campaign to teach convicts to read and write. But during the next year all the enthusiasm waned, and soon the office of chaplain was abolished once more. It was restored in 1858, on the eve of the release of another large group of convicts, and a man of the cloth remained on the staff of the prison until Yankee guns made it all futile.[80]

By the standards of later generations of behaviorists, the most enlightened program of the antebellum era was implemented during 1858 and 1859, when Governor William McWillie employed the clemency powers of his office to effect the early release of convicts whose conduct suggested social improvement. He did it for all the wrong reasons, of course. The state's trial courts were generating too many convicts, the penitentiary could not accommodate them, the jails were full, and local politicians were complaining. Then, too, McWillie regarded the entire penitentiary concept as "a morbid philanthropy which taxes honest industry for the benefit of felons." So he overturned the legislative and judicial processes by releasing convicts prematurely. Retributivists responded with a spirited but unsuccessful attempt to strip the chief executive of his clemency powers through a constitutional amendment.[81]

Too Little, Too Late

Mississippi's antebellum penitentiary failed to realize the heady goals held out at the time of its creation. Certainly it was not a profitable venture. The clerks' annual financial statements are incomplete and confusing, but available records depict red ink, and much of it, through 1848. From then until the outbreak of the war, modest operational profits were reported, but the official accounts are rendered dubious by a degree of fiscal juggling. The gaudy receipts reported during the war are also misleading; an inflationary economy and the sagging value of Confederate currency assured that disbursements mounted in almost direct proportion to receipts. On balance, even the most optimistic account of operational profits fails to approach the almost $240,000 appropriated by the legislature for the construction and maintenance of the physical plant alone.[82]

There is also ample reason to question whether the penitentiary had a constructive impact on the administration of legal punishment. The scope of the institution's operations was very narrow. The monetary value of slaves excluded them in all cases, the social values of the time excluded women in most cases, and the penal code excluded all convicted criminal offenders except felons. The prison accommodated less than fifty convicts through 1843. Between 1844 and 1855 the inmate population never exceeded one hundred. In 1858 the effect of overlapping sentences, combined with a substantial increase in the number of felony convictions, carried the population to 144; the same factors explain the presence of 207 convicts two years later. But the legislature never got around to authorizing the construction of the originally planned second 150-cell wing of the prison, and the penitentiary processed only 808 commitments between April 1840 and November 1860.[83]

The meager number of convicts dictated that the administration of legal punishment remained in the hands of county authorities in the overwhelming majority of cases. Unfortunately for the inmates of county jails, the incarceration of felons in the penitentiary allowed counties to imprison and exploit the labor of larger numbers of runaway slaves. Jails degenerated greatly after 1840. Even wealthier counties were slow to make improvements, while others maintained pathetic shacks designed for runaways or nothing at all. In 1855 the superintendent of the penitentiary complained that the abysmal condition of jails often allowed felons to escape before a member of his staff could arrive and convey them to Jackson.[84] By establishing a penitentiary, the legislature inadvertently opened the door to retrogression among the state's jails.

There is also reason to question whether the prison improved the administration of justice even within its narrow jurisdictional limits. From first to last the operations of the institution were affected adversely by contradictions inherent in the philosophy that launched it. Ever present was conflict between those whose first priority was financial profit and those who felt that the prison existed primarily to deter crime or reform criminals. In this debate financial reasoning emerged so frequently as the first priority in policy decisions that one frustrated politician found it necessary to remind his colleagues that "our object should not be to make profit by the convicts, but to reform them."[85]

Perhaps the nature of the convicts diminished enthusiasm for the ideal of reformation. A large percentage of them were guilty of manslaughter, a crime that by legal definition involved either gross recklessness or negligence, not malice, and therefore undermined the justification for moral training. Much the same was true of the prison's hefty population of Negro-stealers; while no reliable records exist, surely many of them were abolitionists who, on moral grounds, fed the underground railroad that transported slaves to freedom in the Northern states.

The public record, in fact, suggests that political factors figured very prominently in the sentencing practices of judges. During the 1850s, when the sectional controversy was generating unprecedented heat, a disproportionately large percentage of commitments were natives of northeastern states that did not contribute substantial numbers of settlers to Mississippi, notably New York and Pennsylvania. Moreover, the penitentiary reports confirm that the bench viewed a sentence to the penitentiary as an effective means of ridding society of undesirable transients. In 1841 only two of twenty-seven inmates had been born in the state, in 1848 only six of ninety-seven, in 1851 only nine of eighty-five, and in 1855 only thirteen of ninety-six.[86]

Whatever the cause or causes, there is no reason to conclude that "The Walls"—as Jacksonians dubbed the ugly prison—reformed or deterred anybody. Certainly that was the opinion of most Mississippians. In March 1850 the legislature authorized county authorities to execute condemned criminals outside the confines of jails whenever they could establish cause, thereby renouncing a major component of the philosophy that had launched the penitentiary. In January 1854 Governor Henry S. Foote revived the language of the 1830s with a plea for a "thorough *Reformation*" of criminal jurisprudence. The revised penal code, Foote contended, had failed to increase the certainty of legal punishment, and the administration of justice remained "so crude and imperfect, that the conviction of the most atrocious culprits is found to be well nigh impossible." In 1957 a sweeping revision of the penal code restored corporal punishment in a number of instances.[87]

Mississippi's antebellum penitentiary was a victim of unrealistic expectations. Regarded as a panacea by the prevailing wisdom of the 1830s, it was erected to solve a broad range of legal, social, and financial problems. But it was incapable of reconciling the many contradictions in the ill-formed logic that gave it birth. It provided the state with a means of removing a limited number of felons from society. That pleased local governments, to be sure, but there is no reason to think that the penitentiary accomplished much else. Indeed, it may well have done more harm than good.

2

The Privatization of Convict Labor

with W. R. Edwards

The operations of Mississippi's penitentiary ended abruptly in the spring of 1863 when federal troops penetrated the central portion of the state. Governor John J. Pettus transferred twenty-five of the most dangerous inmates to Alabama's penitentiary, pardoned forty others, and distributed the remainder among county jails. Confederate forces evacuated Jackson shortly thereafter, and elements of General William Tecumseh Sherman's army entered the city. The invaders dismantled the prison's mill and shops, and set fire to a number of buildings within the walls. Two months later, when Sherman's "scorched earth" policy reduced Jackson to rubble, those structures still standing within the penitentiary were put to the torch.[1]

For the balance of the war, the shell of the prison stood abandoned, and the convicts remained scattered among the several county jails to which they had been remanded. Their upkeep was a point of bitter dispute between state and local authorities. Attempts made during the February 1865 session of the legislature to secure reimbursement for the affected counties were soundly defeated, thereby placing a heavy financial burden upon the respective local governments. The last days of the Confederacy and the months immediately following its fall were chaotic. Where civil government existed, criminal convictions mounted sharply, exacerbating an already near intolerable situation. When the first postwar legislature convened in October 1865, one of the most pressing problems facing politicians was the rehabilitation of the penal system.[2]

The task was of monumental proportions. Nothing posed more difficulty than the dramatically altered size and composition of the convict population. Prior to the war, Mississippi's penal law had left the resolution of crimes by slaves at the county level, thus screening the state penal system from involvement with roughly half the population. But after the war, emancipated blacks were no longer shielded from the sanctions of the penal code, and the abysmal social and economic plight of these new freemen assured much criminality among them. The woeful condition of the surviving white citizenry, especially the state's large class of yeoman farmers, was little better. Virtually overnight, the courts of criminal jurisdiction began to manufacture a dramatically increased number of convicts.[3]

State government was incapable of relieving pressures. Although the Yankee host had spared the walls of the penitentiary, the factory and the buildings within were a shambles, the cellblock was uncovered, and roughly half the cells were in need of costly structural repairs. Meanwhile, the state's indebtedness amounted to some $5 million, the treasury was exhausted, and there was no prospect of immediate tax revenues. From the first, Mississippi's postbellum criminal policy hovered between the poles of justice and fiscal utility.

The First Stage

A proposal to lease the penitentiary and its inmates to private business interests attracted much support in the 1865 legislature, and proponents of the measure maintained that leased convicts could be "managed and treated as humanely as heretofore." A majority of the politicians rejected that argument, however, instead endorsing an optimistic plan to restore the industrial prison of antebellum days. Operating with a meager $25,000 appropriation, contractors began renovations in early 1866, and in March a number of convicts were transferred from county jails to the penitentiary.[4]

Optimism waned during 1866 as the legal implications of Negro emancipation became more evident. The first group of sixty-five convicts to enter the penitentiary was 76 percent black, and within a matter of weeks, as the number of convictions mounted and as sheriffs sought to clear their jails, the penitentiary was filled to capacity. By summer the situation was acute: one hundred and thirty prisoners were housed in fewer than one hundred cells, and county jails were inundated with convicts awaiting transfer to Jackson. The editor of the Jackson *Clarion and Standard* found the situation farcical. Judges, he noted critically, were sentencing as if the penitentiary had "unlimited capacity," so "either the laws should be repealed or the Penitentiary abolished."[5]

In October 1866, when the state architect estimated that an additional $65,000 would be required to complete essential repairs at the prison, Governor Benjamin G. Humphreys called a special session of the legislature. Leasing the penitentiary to private business interests was the only available option, he told the assembled politicians, and the Oxford-based firm of J. W. Young had tendered a "quite attractive" offer. Opposition collapsed almost immediately; within days the legislature hammered out a scheme that authorized the leasing of the penitentiary and its convicts to private parties.[6]

The privatization of legal punishment in Mississippi was born of perceived necessity. It was, moreover, adopted reluctantly as a temporary expedient, and the resulting statute imposed every conceivable check on lessees. The leasing law of 1866 authorized the chief executive, with the advice and consent of the senate, to appoint four commissioners. The commissioners, in turn, were empowered to lease the penitentiary to one or more private parties at no expense to the state for an indefinite period.

Under no circumstances were convicts to be removed from the prison grounds. Lessees were to control the labor of prisoners only during specified working hours. They could not punish convicts or make them work at tasks "deleterious to their health" or threatening to their safety. Responsibility for the physical and spiritual well-being of the convicts also fell on lessees. They would provide the inmates with proper food and clothing, with "suitable medical attendance in case of sickness," and with religious literature and instruction. A state-employed superintendent would serve as watchdog, and the governor would act as "umpire" if disputes developed.[7]

The provisions of the statute sounded safe enough, but the legislators, however well-meaning, betrayed an ignorance of the principles of political economy worthy of their antebellum predecessors. In January 1867 the commissioners concluded an agreement with J. W. Young. Under its provisions Young's firm posted bond of $100,000 and assumed control of the penitentiary and its convicts for a period of fourteen years. The lessee promptly initiated the manufacture and sale of various consumer goods. Within a month, the mechanics and artisans of Jackson and several nearby communities held a meeting in the state capitol and protested a policy that came into "direct conflict with the mechanical industry" of the law-abiding citizenry.[8]

The legislature reacted to the public clamor almost immediately, and an amended leasing statute of February 1867 established a vital precedent. Over the warnings of a large minority, the politicians mandated that the produce of the prison could not compete with that of the private sector and stipulated, by way of compensation, that lessees could employ all but eighty convicts outside the walls of the penitentiary. Again, supposed safeguards were established: convicts would have to volunteer for labor outside the walls, the superintendent would establish regulations for such work, the governor would have to approve the regulations, and, finally, the duration of leases would not exceed three years.[9]

The revised statute was a monument to political rationalization, and it set the stage for further compromises. Displeased with the altered contract, Young and his associates soon forfeited bond and stripped the penitentiary of "everything necessary and required for the health and ordinary comfort of the convicts," thereby returning the state to its original dilemma. Receiving no subsequent bids for the penitentiary, Governor Humphreys attempted to muddle through with insufficient funds. At last, when confronted with a simple choice between starving the inmates or granting a general pardon, the governor turned to federal military authorities. Late in the year a squad of soldiers seized the penitentiary and placed it under federal control.[10]

An Assist from Uncle Sam

Federal authorities were no more successful than state authorities. By March 31, 1868, 263 inmates were living under horrid conditions in the prison's 131 habitable cells. Still more convicts were in county jails awaiting transfer to Jackson; their plight was worse than that of the inmates of the penitentiary.

Unable to obtain funds from the Republican administration in Washington, the military superintendent of the penitentiary sought to generate revenues on his own and, like Young before him, promptly ran afoul of the private sector. On May 20, when he advertised in the capital press that convict goods and services could be obtained at "20 percent less than charged elsewhere," local tradesmen resurrected the Jackson Mechanics Association and set out to counter what they regarded as a threat to their livelihood. Confronted by powerful opposition and presiding over nearly three hundred starving convicts, the military superintendent virtually begged Governor Humphreys for financial assistance. The governor could not resist such a plea, and in what was criticized as an act of "doubtful legality," he authorized the issuance of a small number of state warrants capable of providing bare subsistence until another means of financing the penitentiary could be found.[11]

Another means was not found, and in July 1868, following the refusal of the electorate to ratify a new constitution, all state officials were removed from office and replaced by federal military authorities. The suspension of the checks and balances of civil government came at a crucial juncture in the affairs of the state penal system, and a pragmatic military policy decision was forthcoming. In November, when the emergency funds raised by Governor Humphreys were exhausted, General Alvan C. Gillem, the federal military commander, concluded an extraordinary leasing agreement with wealthy planter-merchant Edmund Richardson.[12]

The terms of Richardson's contract, known popularly as the "military lease," relieved the state of primary responsibility for maintaining its convicts. However, in return for feeding, clothing, and safeguarding the prisoners in his charge, Richardson received from the state an annual fee of $18,000 and the right to retain every penny derived from convict labor. He was also permitted to work convicts at the site or sites of his choice, either in or out of state, and at whatever tasks he desired. The expense of transporting prisoners to and from the penitentiary and from one field camp to another was also borne by the state, a provision that would cost the public an additional $12,000 per annum while eliminating a major component of the lessee's overhead costs. In only one clause did Richardson fail to score: consistent with the terms of the amended leasing law of February 1867, the contract was restricted to three years.[13]

On December 1, 1868, the lessee assumed control of the penitentiary and its inmates. Early in the following year his agents transported, at state expense, the majority of the convicts to three plantations in the Mississippi Delta and set them to "making cotton." Later Richardson proposed and secured a series of state bonds which committed him to repair the state's shattered levee system. Thereafter he withdrew his convicts from the fields during slack periods and employed them in gangs on the levees. When sickness or infirmity reduced the effectiveness of convict field hands, Richardson's agents returned them, again at state expense, to the penitentiary in Jackson. There they manufactured various consumer goods, all of which were sold in direct competition with a private sector that was powerless under the reign of martial law.[14]

The military lease brought Richardson incalculable riches. He emerged as "by far the largest planter of cotton in the world," and as the state's first postwar millionaire. Others, of course, came to covet his prize.[15] A means of restoring the principal features of labor under domestic slavery, but without the crucial variable of risk necessitated by the ownership of human chattel, had been identified for a labor-starved community.

The Failed Alcorn Offensive

The seductive appeal of Richardson's contract was demonstrated during 1870 when, in the process of restoring civil government, the incoming Republican governor, James Lusk Alcorn, sought to recall the state to "the moral considerations entering into the reformation of convicts and the punishment of crime."[16] The moderate Alcorn was popular among the Republican rank and file. His attempt to terminate leasing, to return all convicts to the penitentiary, and to place them under the constant supervision of state officials had special appeal among black politicians, who constituted approximately one-third of the legislature and sympathized with the plight of the overwhelmingly black convict population. Outside the statehouse, Alcorn's campaign was supported by the Mechanics and Citizens Joint Stock Association, whose members were infuriated by the competition of Richardson's convicts. But the governor's offensive ended in smoke.

Neither the entreaties of the chief executive nor the lobbying of the tradesmen secured the support of legislative leaders. A bill calling for a new leasing agreement and providing greater protection for convicts never emerged from committee. An official investigation into the condition of leased convicts—the central thrust of Alcorn's attack—was frustrated when the legislative committee blamed all shortcomings on the former lessee and actually praised Richardson's management.[17]

Quite clearly, Alcorn's efforts were thwarted by the impending expiration of Richardson's coveted lease.

By the spring of 1871 the approaching availability of the convict concession had aroused feverish excitement in the capital. Politicians squabbled about the proper ends of justice and the most propitious means of exploiting convict labor for the public weal. Amid it all, interested parties "button-holed legislators in an attempt to secure the lucrative prison concession." Conspicuous among the suitors was Richardson, who reportedly distributed some $20,000 among key politicians.[18]

It was a wise investment, for soon a remarkable piece of legislation was being touted by Republican leaders. The "Richardson penitentiary bill" extended its namesake's control of the penitentiary and its inmates for fifteen years. It also appropriated $120,000 for physical improvements at the prison, stipulated immediate payment of the entire sum to Richardson, and delivered the lessee $1,500 per month for the maintenance of convicts. In turn, Richardson was required to purchase whatever machinery he chose to utilize in the penitentiary's shops and to surrender it to the state upon the expiration of the lease.

The reaction to such a blatant display of public venality was explosive, widespread and, initially at least, beyond the confines of partisan politics. Outraged artisans and merchants met repeatedly at the capitol "to investigate, expose, and protest" the offending legislation.[19] The senate, however, passed the measure almost immediately, and thereafter attention focused on the lower house, where a number of impressive counterproposals were debated at length.

When the Jackson-based firm of William S. Stanton and Company offered one thousand acres and one-third of the capital necessary to erect a new industrial prison, the editor of the *Clarion* decided that the state should conclude the best contract available. "Let the Legislature keep the question open," he urged, "so that the bidding [might] go on. . . . Do we hear two thousand acres and one half the cost of the buildings? Going! Going!" And as the bidding continued with an offer from J. M. Wesson and Company promising a bonus to the state, the editor continued his crusade. "Not much 'bonus' about that proposition," he scoffed. "Who next?"[20]

The final bid for the penitentiary, submitted by former Confederate brigadier Peter B. Starke, came during the last week of April. In addition to a sizeable performance bond, Starke offered the state a bonus of $75,000 as well as $120,000 for renovations and the purchase of machinery. It was to no avail. On the final day of the session, the Republican majority in the house delivered the penitentiary to Richardson. By what means "the adventurers were induced to vote for the . . . proposition," commented a local editor, "each reader will determine for himself."[21]

The passage of the bill placed Governor Alcorn in a difficult position. He had his eyes on a vacant seat in the United States Senate, an appointment which required the support of Republicans in the legislature. Alcorn therefore hedged, stating that although the leasing bill was a "corrupt and extravagant scheme," he would not veto a measure that would be "passed over his head." As the expiration of the original Richardson lease drew nigh, the governor refused to sign the new agreement, instead authorizing a brief extension of the existing one. Having thereby avoided a direct confrontation with legislative leaders, Alcorn abruptly resigned his office and accepted a seat in the United States Senate. In December 1871, when Lieutenant-Governor Ridgley C. Powers assumed the governorship, the penal system was on the verge of reverting to state control. The state had neither the facilities nor the funds to accommodate its convicts, and the Richardson interests had every reason to be confident.[22]

The Penitentiary Act of 1872

Governor Powers was unwilling to relinquish the state penal system to Richardson without a fight, and his opening address to the 1872 legislature damned the principle of leasing convicts and outlined a plan for the construction of a larger penitentiary in or near Jackson. Later in the session he vetoed the "Richardson penitentiary bill" and threw his support behind legislation calling for a new prison.[23]

The governor was not a skilled politician, and he was confronted by a formidable, if most unlikely, alliance of Conservatives, Democrats, and white Radicals who sought the perpetuation of the convict lease system. Among them, the most prominent were former Confederate general Robert J. Lowery of Rankin County and carpetbagger O. C. French of Adams County, the Radical Republican floor leader in the lower house of the state legislature. Every attempt was made to thwart Powers's campaign for a new penitentiary. The governor, however, was supported by the Republican speaker of the house, John Lynch, who commanded the allegiance of a large legislative following anchored on bloc-voting black politicians, and the administration's bill cleared the legislature by a narrow margin in March 1872.[24]

The act mandated a system of congregate industrial labor and separate cellular confinement on the same terms, and largely in the same words, as the penitentiary act of 1839. The single new element pertained to the methods by which the state was to achieve such an ambitious goal. For that task the antebellum board of inspectors was resurrected. Appointed by the governor and confirmed by the senate for staggered terms of office, its three members were authorized to spend up to $10,000 for the purchase of a site of not less than five hundred acres near a railroad and "convenient . . . to all sections of the state." Upon acquiring the land, the inspectors were to enlist the assistance of the state architect in drafting plans for a new prison large enough "to confine, safely keep, and properly work, at suitable manufacturing and industrial operations, at least four hundred convicts."

Utilizing inmate labor, the inspectors were to begin construction as soon as practicable and to complete the prison no later than April 1, 1876. Meanwhile a series of leases not exceeding three years in duration would be permitted. The superintendent was to hire all guards and to maintain total responsibility for the welfare of leased convicts. Convicts were not to work on plantations or in factories, but instead on public works projects. The inspectors were to assure that leases relieved the state of all expenses for the maintenance of convicts.[25]

The penitentiary act of 1872 had one glaring flaw: it left the advocates of the new prison entirely at the mercy of lessees. That fact was demonstrated in the spring, before the enactment of the statute, when the expiration of Richardson's extended lease thrust on the state a swollen convict population whose condition had "deteriorated sharply." Richardson, the party responsible for the worsening condition of the convicts, was eager to lend a hand, as was Nathan Bedford Forrest, the former Confederate cavalry commander and founder of the Ku Klux Klan. Presented with no other options, a reluctant governor allowed Richardson to retain custody of the prison and the bulk of the convicts on a temporary basis and provided for the remainder through a short-term lease with Forrest. When the penitentiary bill at last cleared the legislature, most of the state's convicts—malnourished, emaciated, many of them seriously ill—were scattered about on Richardson's Delta plantations and in the construction camps of Forrest's Selma, Marion, and Memphis railroad.[26]

The new board of inspectors set out to rectify the situation with vigor. They immediately advertised for sealed proposals from "parties desiring to employ convict labor outside of the prison walls" and eventually concluded a three-year agreement with W. P. Dunnavant and W. M. Forrest, the son of Nathan Bedford Forrest, who were doing business as Dunnavant and Company. Then the inspectors announced their interest in obtaining land on which a new prison could be built. A number of proposals were forthcoming, and late in the year the board selected a five-hundred-acre tract some four and one-half miles north of Jackson offered by one Bourbon Shotwell. In December the inspectors adopted a blueprint drafted by the state architect, hired a general contractor, recalled fifty convicts from Dunnavant and Company, and asked the governor to "urge upon the Legislature . . . the very great importance" of beginning construction immediately.[27]

The Rout of the Republican Reformers

Governor Powers opened the 1873 legislative session with lofty praise for the board's labors and a strong endorsement of the plan for the construction of a new prison. That project was placed in grave jeopardy in January 1873 when Dunnavant and Company suddenly forfeited its lease. The governor and the inspectors agreed almost immediately to purchase the lessee's interest in the penitentiary and then concluded a second contract delivering Dunnavant one hundred convicts "fit for outdoor labor" on public works projects within the state for up to one year. In turn, Dunnavant and Company assumed full responsibility for guarding and maintaining the convicts and agreed to pay the state twelve dollars monthly for each of them.[28]

The new lease relieved the state of the expense of providing for roughly one-third of its convicts but left it responsible for the entire cost of maintaining over two hundred prisoners and the old penitentiary. The prospect of self-sufficiency, much less of revenue-producing operations, no longer existed. Since the administration had based its case for a new prison on such a prospect, support in the legislature began to erode.

It eroded still more in the course of a bitter dispute among Republican leaders regarding the inspectors' selection of the Shotwell tract. Charges of graft, worsened by allegations that leased convicts were being abused, strained relations between the governor and the Republican rank and file. The administration was embarrassed further when Robert Lowery's house judiciary committee investigated the allegations and predictably issued a stinging indictment. During the second week of April, a Republican-stacked joint legislative committee released a report that exonerated Powers and the inspectors of wrongdoing. Yet the committee found the estimated cost of a new penitentiary, a staggering sum of $1.5 million, prohibitive.[29]

The report of the committee dealt the campaign for a new prison an almost fatal blow, and soon Powers was overwhelmed by the deteriorating condition of the convicts. Chronic overcrowding and the spread of infectious diseases within the penitentiary had troubled the governor and the inspectors throughout the spring. Now the situation reached crisis proportions, leaving no alternative to clearing the prison through new leasing arrangements. On May 26 the inspectors signed a contract with W. M. Francis delivering the labor of "a hundred or more" convicts for a period of six to eight months. Then Edmund Richardson, always at the right place at the right time, concluded his third leasing agreement with the state, this one involving some thirty convicts. Again, in early June, when prison physician T. J. Mitchell expressed alarm over the probable spread of epidemic diseases within the cellblock, Richardson obtained an additional thirty convicts for ninety days at no cost to himself.

By the onset of winter Mississippi was in the early stages of a severe economic recession, the penal system was insolvent, the number of commitments was increasing dramatically, and convicts within the prison were suffering greatly. Unable to mitigate the situation due to events beyond his control, Governor Powers in effect abandoned his campaign for penal reform. During the last days of his term he reluctantly endorsed the signing of two more leases and left solution of the problem to his successor, Radical Republican Adelbert Ames.[30]

Executive-Legislative Collusion

In many ways Governor Ames personified the partisan self-interest and political opportunism that had subverted Republican idealism by early 1874. His successful gubernatorial campaign had committed him to "a rigid economy and a strict accountability" in public finance. Now, as fiscal reform and retrenchment became the rallying cry of the new administration, Ames and his cronies largely neglected the state's manifold social problems and sought to broaden their political base.[31]

A major issue affecting the internal politics of the state Republican party was the future of the penal system, and here a political dichotomy appeared very quickly. In one camp were those politicians who felt that the state could not continue to lease its convicts. A majority of that group were black legislators who could not be ignored by Ames and his inner circle; blacks now occupied over half the seats in the lower house of the legislature. Opposing them was a shadowy confederacy bound together by the allure of private gain. Ames and O. C. French gave this alliance a strong political base.

French, who with Robert Lowery had led opposition to Governor Powers's crusade for a new penitentiary, was a venal, audacious, but very able character. Formerly he had been an officer in the United States Army and Freedman's Bureau agent at Natchez. He had somehow survived an indictment for embezzlement of Bureau funds, had been elected to the legislature as representative for Adams County in 1870, and had then involved himself in a succession of unsavory schemes to defraud the state. Now chairman of the house committee on railroads, French was closely identified with various railroad interests. Those interests were the largest employers of unskilled labor in the state, and French was thus in a position to reap enormous profits through the distribution of convict labor.[32]

The Ames-French group initially trod softly, taking care not to tip its hand. Ames prudently failed to mention the penal system in his inaugural message of January 1874. French followed the same course in the house. A legislative push to restore the penitentiary encountered very little opposition, and on April 6, 1874, a black senator, Robert Gleed, pushed through an appropriation of $70,000.[33]

Meanwhile, Ames and French were operating behind closed doors, quietly laying the foundation for an incredible chapter in public venality. In early 1874 the governor replaced two of the three Powers appointees to the board of inspectors with members of his own political faction. The new board dismissed Powers's superintendent, C. W. Loomis, and replaced him with Charles Cleyland, formerly sergeant of the guard. Cleyland promptly distinguished himself by killing a convict, and word leaked out. Under the circumstances, the homicide was a political indiscretion, so the inspectors returned Cleyland to his former subordinate position and replaced him with a crony of Ames and French, carpetbagger William Noonan.[34]

On March 2, the day after Noonan's appointment, the recently restructured board of inspectors negotiated the first of four new leasing agreements, all of which benefited French and his principal business partner, Charles S. Jobes. Under the terms of the contract, one H. Powers, of whom little is known, and Jobes, reputedly French's nephew, assumed full responsibility for the maintenance and security of an unspecified number of convicts for a monthly fee of $5.50 per head. The agreement went into effect on March 22, 1874, and the lessee immediately transported his convicts to railroad construction camps in the central and northern parts of the state. The inspectors concluded a second series of leasing agreements with Jobes later in the year, in this instance delivering an unspecified number of prisoners at a monthly fee of fifty cents per man.[35]

By the end of 1874 state criminal policy was headed in two altogether different directions. Renovations at the penitentiary were advanced. The old shoe shop had been enlarged to accommodate seventy-five craftsmen, the renovation of the cotton mill was almost complete, and the convicts had manufactured over a million bricks since the first of the year. Now the leasing interests heard unsettling talk about a new cellblock and new machinery; there was even a revival of interest in the construction of a new prison.[36]

French struck quickly. In early February 1875 he conferred with Edmund Richardson, offered to sublease to him a number of convicts, and secured a promise from Richardson of a large cash bonus upon delivery. Richardson, of course, had no interest in employing the convicts exclusively on public works projects, as stipulated by the penitentiary act of 1872, so explicit in the agreement was a pledge by French to amend the law.

Later in the month, despite the bitter opposition of black politicians led by Senator Charles Caldwell of Clinton, French pushed through a carefully worded bill that extended the practice of leasing until January 1, 1880, and removed all restrictions on the employment of convicts leased to private individuals. Then, in the face of vehement opposition by black legislators, Governor Ames at last abandoned neutrality and signed the "French Act" into law on February 26, 1875.[37]

The next day the board of inspectors, making no attempt to solicit competitive bids, concluded yet another leasing agreement with the firm of French and Jobes, this one delivering 250 convicts at no cost. Because the new statute imposed no restrictions on convict labor, the state gave the lessee tacit permission to sublease at will. Such an arrangement quite satisfied Edmund Richardson, and some two days after the enactment of the new legislation he concluded his prearranged agreement with French and Jobes. The contract brought Richardson one hundred able-bodied convicts for a period of almost five years. In turn, he paid French and Jobes a cash bonus of $7,500 and posted their requisite bond with the state. With no effective opposition, French and Jobes in late May concluded their fourth and final lease for an additional two hundred convicts, of which half were immediately subleased to Richardson on the same terms as the earlier agreement.[38]

This complex maneuvering required trade-offs in the legislature. County officials were especially interested. Their own constituents, like those of state officials, hungered for a source of cheap, reliable labor, and county tax revenues were as diminished as those of the state. Also, blacks were committing more misdemeanors than felonies, few had money to pay their fines, and the long-neglected county jails remained overcrowded and expensive. The demands of justice were thus married to those of economy; and in the spring of 1875, as French, Jobes and Richardson were teaching Mississippians a valuable lesson in the political economy of criminal justice, elements in the legislature struck to legalize leasing at the county level. They were opposed stoutly by black leaders, who commanded enough strength to force compromise, but in the end the leasing and subleasing of convicts was legalized in forty-five of the state's seventy-three counties.[39]

The Collapse of the Last Barriers

The foundation laid by the legislative enactments of 1875 was a firm one, and the resurgent Democrats and Conservatives, who carried all before them in the elections of that year, were quick to build on it. From the opening day of the legislative session of 1876, a coalition of Democrats and Conservatives set about purging state government of the more objectionable vestiges of Radical Republicanism, beginning, of course, with the Republican incumbents. On March 23 Lieutenant-Governor A. K. Davis, accused of accepting a bribe in exchange for his influence in securing a pardon, was convicted and removed from office. Then Governor Ames himself, under indictment for alleged fraudulent acts involving the manipulation of convict leases, voluntarily resigned his office and left the state. On the same day, March 29, 1876, Democrat John M. Stone, a consistent advocate of the convict lease system, was inaugurated governor of Mississippi.[40]

Meanwhile, legislative leaders, aided by a substantial diminution of Negro strength in the house of representatives, embraced Ames's earlier tactics to take control of the state penal system. In mid-February the superintendent and the inspectors were sent packing by statute, and two weeks later the new Conservative-Democrat coalition in the legislature elected more suitable replacements.[41]

On April 15, 1876, a bill drafted expressly "to provide for leasing out the Penitentiary and the convict labor of the State" carried both chambers of the legislature and was signed into law. The statute dispossessed the Republican lessees and their sublessees of an "alleged and pretended contract" and outlined terms by which an orderly transfer of the convict concession could be effected. Otherwise the penitentiary act of 1876 mandated a public solicitation of bids and authorized a new four-year lease while entrenching and expanding the convict lease system to its maximum limits. It removed every barrier to the leasing of convicts and it extended the practice to every county and municipality in the state. It sanctioned subleasing by omission, and it also established a number of procedures that screened iniquities from public scrutiny.

Convicts under sentence of ten or more years were to labor either within the walls of the prison or near enough to the prison to be confined at night. The announced intent of that provision was to discourage the escape of the most dangerous felons. Its effect, however, was to screen the Caucasian prisoners, who almost invariably were convicted of heinous crimes, from the field camps of lessees. Thereafter a double standard existed: all white convicts except a handful employed as strawbosses in field camps remained snug and secure within the walls of the penitentiary while their black peers were dispatched far and wide. The double standard surely considered the sensibilities of the white electorate. The racial segregation of convicts, which was demanded even by those who contracted for convict labor, was effected. Black convicts were put to "niggers' work," and leasing was thereby rendered consistent with a social system of long vintage.[42]

The statute stipulated that convict labor could be used in "any private labor or employment" anywhere, anytime. Convicts working in road camps would be confined in stout stockades at night. Except for a vague injunction against "inhumane or unkind treatment" unsupported by sanctions, the law included no provision relating to the discipline, security, or general welfare of leased convicts. That omission was rendered devastating by another; convicts in field camps could not communicate with anyone except their relatives, and then only in the presence of their keepers.

If every level of government within Mississippi was to profit by the lease system, more convicts were needed. Counties and municipalities were provided for by a provision of the act that rendered certain classes of felonies, previously punishable by less than one year in the state penitentiary, subject to confinement in local jails. Convicts sentenced to the jails could be employed at hard labor; those unable to pay fines could be hired out to private contractors until they worked off their debts.[43]

A reduction in the number of felonies threatened to reduce the state convict population, so the Redeemers subsequently enacted legislation that redefined the crime of grand larceny as the theft of any property valued in excess of ten dollars or of any livestock whatever. This so-called "Pig law" produced the desired result. By the end of 1877, the state penal system alone claimed more than one thousand convicts, an almost exclusively black labor force worth considerably more than one million dollars as slaves on the eve of secession. Enactment of the Pig law, observes historian Vernon L. Wharton, "made of the convict lease a big business enterprise."[44]

On June 6, 1876, the board of inspectors assigned the highly coveted state convict concession to Jones S. Hamilton and John L. Hebron, doing business as the firm of Hamilton and Hebron. The contract delivered the entire convict population of the state to the lessees for four years and obligated them to shoulder the expense of convict maintenance. No further financial obligation was incurred by the lessees unless the convict population exceeded 140; every convict over that number would commit the lessee to an annual installment calculated at $1.10 per month.[45]

The board quickly renounced the state's contract with French and Jobes, and the Republican lessees filed a bill in the chancery court of Hinds County that sought to block the implementation of the state's new convict lease. They obtained an injunction, but it was struck down on October 1, 1876, and a flurry of suits and countersuits ensued. At last resigned to the inevitable, French and Jobes came to terms, agreeing to a compromise that permitted them to retain the convicts already under their control until January 1, 1877. A second agreement was then concluded with the sublessee, Richardson, by which he was allowed to retain 150 convicts until January 1, 1878.[46]

In early 1877 Hamilton and Hebron received the bulk of the state's convicts from French and Jobes. As the new lessees organized and distributed their captive laborers, they struck further deals with the legislature. In return for a pledge by Hamilton and Hebron to spend up to $25,000 in repairing the deteriorating buildings at the penitentiary, the politicians extended the lease until January 1, 1881, and agreed to credit the lessees' account for all expenditures over $25,000, provided the claims did not exceed the amount the lessees owed the state in a given year. Later, the delighted lessees agreed informally to purchase and install machinery valued at some $75,000 in the old mill at the penitentiary. On January 1, 1878, the fabulously wealthy Edmund Richardson relinquished his subleased convicts to the agents of Hamilton and Hebron, who shortly thereafter distributed them among their own sublessees.[47]

Squabbles over the Convict Spoils

Exploiting the convict-generating Pig law, and riding the crest of an improving economy, Hamilton and Hebron turned immense profits during 1878 and 1879. All the while they courted prominent personages in the theater of state politics and sought to bolster their position through the distribution of hundreds of convicts among prominent sublessees. Like Richardson, French, and Jobes before them, however, the lessees found the politics of the convict concession increasingly problematic, and by 1880 the pending expiration of their contract had mobilized a powerful body of opposition in the legislature.

The broadening scope of conflict was fed by the railroad-building mania of the time. Prior to 1880 railroad construction had been monopolized by a relative handful of determined entrepreneurs, and certainly those few had received their share of the convict spoils. But by 1880 internal improvements generally, and railroad construction in particular, were emerging as key issues in Mississippi politics, drawing wide support and exciting interest among a substantially larger number of prospective investors. Hence the demand for convict labor mounted, and the jealousy and indignation of those denied access to the huge state convict population rose in almost direct proportion. Now there was a great deal of high-sounding talk about "public works projects" accompanied by criticism of a contract that delivered the state's convicts to a single lessee.[48]

In his opening address to the 1880 legislature, Governor Stone observed that there were "various and conflicting opinions" on the disposition of the state's convicts and, stressing the importance of public works projects, suggested a further division of the spoils among the various railroad interests.[49] Hamilton and his associates were, of course, none too eager to share the convict concession, and soon the legislators were at daggers drawn. As always, a number of politicians voiced opposition to the principle of leasing without effect; the emerging lines of political combat pitted the allies of Hamilton and Hebron against those who wanted their convicts.

Debate centered on legislation introduced by the excluded railroad interests of north Mississippi. The measure called for the creation of a board of public works "to better provide for and aid the various industrial interests and enterprises" of the state. The proposed board would be empowered to "control and direct" all convict labor "in the construction of railroads, the building of bridges, the improvement of public lands and navigable streams and . . . the improvement of sanitary conditions." Promising to change not the system, but instead the distribution of rewards within the existing system, the bill was immediately endorsed by the senate committee on penitentiary and prisons and applauded by the senate at large.[50]

The proposed amendment of the law provoked unprecedented political polarization, and for the first time the contending parties carried their battle from the antechambers of the capitol to the pages of the tabloid press. There the competitors gave graphic illustration to their respective personal motives while debate in the legislature revealed the sordidness of convict leasing as never before. At last the contending parties closed ranks in an attempt to protect what continued infighting alone could destroy.[51]

The penitentiary act of 1880 mandated the creation of a board of public works and the leasing of convicts "without loss to the State." The statute authorized the governor, with the advice and consent of the senate, to appoint a board composed of one member from each of the state's six congressional districts. Upon expiration of the Hamilton-Hebron lease, the board was to solicit sealed bids for the lease of the penitentiary and its convicts for a period of six years. The new contract was to be awarded to "the highest and best bidder." In addition to posting a performance bond of $100,000, the lessee was to erect, within two years, a factory at the penitentiary capable of manufacturing jute bagging, wagons, carts, and wheelbarrows. The cost of new machinery was to be credited to the account of the lessee; upon expiration of the lease, the factory and its machinery would become the property of the state.

Further provisions sought to placate as many interest groups as possible. While the lessee was to control the entire state convict population, the board was empowered to enter into leasing agreements with other private parties and to transfer the resulting monies to the primary lessee. Convicts under sentence for more than ten years—still the bulk of the white prisoners—were to remain in the penitentiary. Those under sentence for ten years or less were to be "put upon public works" if possible; if not, they were to be hired out to planters and other private parties. The board would supervise all convicts working outside the penitentiary. Under no circumstances were prisoners confined in the penitentiary to be employed in the manufacture of articles produced by free artisans. Nor were they to engage in "mechanical pursuits" beyond the walls except "upon the construction of works of internal improvement."[52]

When the new board of public works received twelve bids for the convict concession, the editor of the *Kosciusko Central Star* observed that "not one has been made yet but which is fathered by parties who are known to have in view schemes which will further their own personal interests." The most enthusiastic supporters of the new board of public works, he added, were "those who contemplate the building of railroads at the expense of the State and so manipulate the schemes as to own them as soon as built."[53]

Playing the Humanitarian Card

The editor's conclusions required only modest powers of perception, but nobody seemed overly concerned until the board made its decision. The firm of Hamilton, Allen, and Company, of which the incumbent lessee Jones S. Hamilton was the principal partner, bid $39,240 per year. The members of the board of public works, leaving no tracks behind them, accepted the bid, thereby extending Hamilton's lease for six years.[54] The contract may or may not have gone to "the highest and best bidder." At all events, the unsuccessful suitors, now dissatisfied with the new legal provision that allowed the board to sublease convicts to other railroad interests, cried foul.

Reinforced by men who favored total state control of the penal system, those parties played their last remaining card, almost immediately launching humanitarian attacks on the convict lease system. Ethelbert Barksdale led the charge. For years the editor had been a consistent apologist for leasing. Now, on July 27, 1880, his powerful Jackson *Weekly Clarion* reversed itself, admonishing the board of public works to consider the "probable treatment" of prisoners. The new contract, Barksdale warned, gave the lessee and his agents "almost absolute power over the unfortunate convict." There were "a thousand ways" that convicts could be "punished or even abused with no infraction of the law"; some effort should be made to protect such helpless souls.

The newfound concern of the *Clarion* was a development of major significance. Hamilton's renewed monopoly of the state's swollen convict population had alienated a strong minority in the legislature. Now the state's premier newspaper addressed the most odious feature of state penal policy. The convict lease system was indefensible on such terms. It violated every established maxim of penal jurisprudence, and already a mountain of evidence, duly recorded on the public record, confirmed that convicts, delivered to private parties who had no stake in their welfare, had died in droves.[55]

Impassioned pleas by governors, superintendents, and legislators had sought to awaken the conscience of a Christian community to the iniquities of the convict lease system, and in 1880 the celebrated penal reformer Enoch Wines had announced to the nation that penology in Mississippi had "retrograded and not advanced."[56] Yet through it all neither the press nor any political faction within the state had attacked systematically on humanitarian grounds. The *Clarion's* shift in stance marked a turning point in the history of Mississippi's criminal policy, a redrawing of the lines of political combat. Thereafter the opponents of convict leasing, however mixed their motives, would anchor their attack on humanitarian arguments.

By January 1882 the "humanitarian" opposition, capitalizing on always abundant reports of abuse in the convict camps, had succeeded in arousing a degree of public indignation against the Hamilton lease. Barksdale fanned the fire with a series of editorials, and Governor Stone expressed concern over "complaints of cruel treatment" in his opening address to the legislature. There followed a number of motions for inquiry. Several bills sought to restrict leasing and to mitigate its horrors. Among them was an unsettling measure, introduced by one of the few remaining blacks in the legislature, that advocated more humane treatment for the large number of children who had entered the penal system since enactment of the Pig law.[57]

Legislative leaders parried these thrusts in predictable fashion. A joint committee looked into the allegations of abuse, acknowledged that there were instances of "inhumanity" in the camps, but concluded that such instances were uncommon. New legislation charged county grand juries to conduct monthly inspections of the camps, to interrogate prisoners apart from their keepers, and to return indictments against persons suspected of mistreating convicts. However, the statute assigned only misdemeanor status to the mistreatment of convicts, mandated very mild sanctions, and assigned adjudication to the county courts—to precisely that level of government where lessees were most apt to command maximum political influence.[58]

Humanitarian protest erupted anew in late 1883 when the new superintendent of the state penal system, T. J. McQuiston, submitted an extraordinary biennial penitentiary report. McQuiston's political connections and motives are unclear, but his report constituted a stinging indictment of the Hamilton lease. The superintendent asserted that convicts in the railroad camps suffered greater hardship, a higher rate of illness, and "greater fatality" than any others in the state. During 1882 and 1883 at least 218 state convicts—roughly one in six during 1882 and one in ten the following year—had died. The mortality rate of black convicts, the vast majority of whom had been assigned to the camps of sublessees, greatly exceeded that of white convicts, virtually all of whom had remained in the penitentiary. In 1882, 126 of 735 blacks and only 2 of 83 whites had perished.

While mortality statistics for leased county prisoners did not exist, McQuiston's report stated boldly that county prisoners were being "kept over their time," denied adequate clothing, and subjected to severe physical abuse. The county system was not properly guarded; nobody, it seemed, "was required by law to look after [such] matters."[59]

The Alliance of the Railroad Interests

Released shortly before the opening of the 1884 legislative session, the penitentiary report strengthened the opponents of the Hamilton lease. One apparently disinterested politician, noting the mortality statistics of the state penal system, observed "an epidemic death rate without the epidemic." The incumbent governor, Robert Lowery, who himself had been instrumental in establishing and expanding the convict lease system in Mississippi, spoke at length of the "outrages with impunity" that characterized the state's criminal policy and called for remedial legislation. But then the governor contradicted himself, noting that "checks and safeguards are multiplied in vain where there is not a public sentiment to coerce officers in the performance of the duties with which they are charged." "You may," he observed, "pile statute upon statute, and double the penalties, and after all for enforcement of the law you must rely upon this public sentiment."[60]

Although such a sense of public responsibility had been dormant in Mississippi, it was by no means moribund. Indeed, shortly after Lowery's address, the cold statistics embodied in the penitentiary report were illustrated by a scandal of major proportions. It occurred in late January when a group of eighteen black convicts drawn from a Delta plantation and bound for the prison in Jackson arrived by boat at Vicksburg. Clad in rags, their fingers and toes frozen, and their bodies bearing "the marks of severe goading," the manacled convicts presented so "shocking a spectacle" that local authorities refused them passage through the city. Their overseers protested, negotiations ensued, and at last the prisoners were placed aboard covered wagons and, thus shielded from public scrutiny, transported to the railroad depot. The spectacle, however, was observed by a local journalist, whose newspaper printed a full account. Within days the story had spread throughout the state. Years later, one legislator recalled that the incident raised "the voice of outraged humanity . . . for the first time in indignant protest against the savage barbarism and fiendish cruelty" of the convict lease system.[61]

Governor Lowery responded with a public denunciation of "chain-gang brutality" and called for a full investigation of the incident. Amid motions seeking to abolish or to mitigate the harshness of the lease system, the house appointed a three-man investigative committee chaired by Representative Jeff Wilson of Pontotoc County. In mid-February the committee presented a "detailed and documented" report to the house-at-large. It was an ugly story, one replete with accounts of "brutal punishments, bad and insufficient food . . . filthy and crowded quarters which allowed full exposure to inclement weather, heartless neglect of the sick," and an appalling loss of life.

Following the publication of portions of the report by a number of state newspapers, a substantial number of formerly indifferent politicians voiced support for reform. Measures addressing the most glaring iniquities of the county lease system were proposed and enacted in rapid succession. Suddenly Hamilton's monopoly of the state convict concession, now under fire from both humanitarians and competing railroad interests, seemed very insecure.[62]

The leasing interests evidently went to considerable lengths to suppress the report of the Wilson committee. Shortly after the document had been presented to the house, it was inexplicably removed from the public record, never to be seen again. The same fate befell other damaging public documents. Representative A. J. Baker of Lafayette County moved for and apparently obtained a roster of convicts who had died during 1882 and 1883, an account of the details surrounding their deaths, and the names of their respective employers. That information also disappeared from the official record.[63]

The curious disappearance of the telling documents was apparently the result of back room compromise. Hamilton and his business associates came to terms with other railroad interests and remained remarkably tranquil in February, when the legislature enacted yet another remedial statute. The measure outlawed the subleasing of state convicts, strengthened the police powers of the superintendent and inspectors, and transferred the convict concession from Hamilton, Allen, and Company to a related firm, the Gulf and Ship Island Railroad Company.

The statute represented the transfer as a concession to public opinion and theorized that a concentration of the convicts would simplify supervision, discourage abuses, and promote "an enterprise in which the whole state was interested." That enterprise, a collaborative effort by Jones S. Hamilton and a number of Mississippi's other railroad tycoons to construct a line running the entire length of the state from Tennessee to the Gulf of Mexico, earned the stockholders sweet terms. The transfer of the contract was to be made "upon such terms as may be agreed upon" by the parties involved prior to March 1886. Because the state would be "greatly compensated" by the completion of the rail line, the new lessee would be permitted to pay the state with first mortgage bonds at their current market value. The railroad company would employ every able-bodied convict in the construction of its line until the project was completed and thereafter, until January 1, 1891, on other works of internal improvement.[64]

When the 1884 legislature adjourned, control of the state penal system was vested by statute in the hands of Mississippi's wealthiest and most powerful railroad interests. Those interests had come to terms so as to protect a mutually beneficial business enterprise. Their position was protected by legislation that distributed the convict spoils to local governments, placated free laborers, and appeased humanitarians. Their remunerative operations were screened from public protest by a tactical appeal to "public works" and by a racial double standard that, with but few exceptions, allocated only black prisoners to the horrid road camps. Seldom in American history has a branch of public administration been more baldly exploited for private gain.

3

The Transition to Penal Farming

with R. E. Cooley and W. R. Edwards

The penitentiary act of 1884 strengthened the convict lease system by forging an alliance between a number of the state's most influential men. All of them had close political ties with the monied Bourbon oligarchy of the Mississippi Delta that had controlled the legislature and the nominating conventions of the state Democratic party since 1875, and earlier concessions to local government assured that the principle of leasing enjoyed much grass roots support throughout the state.

Long experience confirmed, however, that the concentration of the state convict concession in the hands of a small number of private parties brought with it political liabilities, and recent events had displayed the vulnerability of the system to humanitarian attacks. Yet the contract of the Gulf and Ship Island Railroad Company disposed of all pretence: it directly linked state penal policy with the interests of the closed circle that ruled Mississippi. After 1884 the convict lease system was an inviting target for the politically disaffected; it was no more secure than continuing Bourbon control of the state's political process.

The Emergence of Partisan Opposition

In the spring of 1884, almost before the ink had dried on the new penitentiary act, the newspapers of the state reported the murder of a subleased convict on one of Edmund Richardson's plantations and the subsequent death of the responsible white overseer at the hands of a mob of local blacks. The double homicide excited considerable public concern. Then word broke that Governor Lowery, citing a legal technicality in the penitentiary act of 1884, had blocked the transfer of the state convict lease from Hamilton, Allen, and Company to the Gulf and Ship Island Railroad Company.[1]

All the reported iniquities and the curious retention of the lease by the firm that perpetrated them were exploited by the leaders of a vigorous insurgency within the ranks of the state's dominant Democratic party. The political schism pitted the Bourbon oligarchy against the depressed farmers who constituted a solid but until now inactive majority of the white electorate. Engendered by severe economic hardship and by the failure of party leaders to redress the plight of small farmers, the insurgency united "dirt farmers" behind reformers who sought to seize control of Democratic party machinery.

For years the farmers had grumbled ineffectually about the inequity of a policy that assigned cheap, competing convict labor to wealthy planters and land-grabbing railroad syndicates. Now, Agrarian leaders, influenced by the effectiveness of recent humanitarian complaints about leasing, came to see the system as a "sore spot" on the record of Redeemer rule, as an avenue for a successful attack on the moral authority of the Bourbons. The convict lease system, concludes historian Scott Curtis, was a "political stick" with which "to beat the Bourbons." Agrarian leaders, perceiving the effectiveness of the weapon at hand, put it in play. The farmers registered to vote in droves and returned a strong Agrarian minority to the statehouse in the elections of 1885. The so-called "Revolt of the Rednecks" had begun.[2]

Superintendent McQuiston provided the rebels with ample fodder. His biennial report, submitted in late 1885, disclosed that fully 21 percent of the state's convicts had died and that another 16 percent had escaped during the past two years. Furthermore, although the state had reimbursed the lessee $55,000 for renovations at the penitentiary, the physical plant was a wreck. Insult was added to injury when Governor Lowery opened the 1886 legislative session with fulsome praise of the lessee, explained the omission in the 1884 statute that had forced him to leave the lease in the hands of Hamilton and his associates, and then remarked, almost as an afterthought, that the account of the lessee was in arrears.[3]

Pandemonium broke out in the statehouse. A senate committee, investigating the finances of the penal system, quickly confirmed that falsified claims were behind many of the renovations at the penitentiary. Then other legislative committees made damaging disclosures.

The penitentiary's inmates, most of whom were under sentence for heinous crimes, were being permitted to roam the streets of Jackson without supervision. And despite the recent enactment of statutory provisions seeking to end the mistreatment of state convicts, many of those remaining in the hands of thirty subcontractors continued to be subject to the harshest abuse.[4]

Governor Lowery, whose signature had authorized all the pretended renovations at the penitentiary, successfully made his superintendent the scapegoat; the defenseless McQuiston was summarily removed from office and replaced by David Johnson, a former state legislator. Hamilton was less defenseless. He was a powerful man, the quintessence of Bourbonism itself, and there was little evidence of criminal collusion by his firm. But if the governor had been misled, and if Hamilton was beyond the reach of the law, something had to be done to redress the continuing iniquities of state criminal policy. An anonymous correspondent to the Jackson *Clarion*, quoting at length from the missing report of the Wilson committee, damned "blood money" earned at the cost of "the lives of helpless manacled human beings" and called on the legislature "to remove the cursed blotted page" from the state's history.[5]

Legislative leaders closeted with Jones S. Hamilton, now a principal stockholder in the Gulf and Ship Island Railroad Company, and afterward concluded that a simple transfer of the convict lease to that firm might disarm critics. So on March 17, 1886, the retreating leasing interests pushed through remedial legislation.[6]

The penitentiary act of 1886 allowed the Gulf and Ship Island Railroad Company thirty days to settle with Hamilton, Allen, and Company and to conclude a contract with the state. Otherwise the incumbent lessee would retain possession of the lease only until January 1, 1887, at which time the state would conclude a contract delivering the penitentiary and all its convicts to the Gulf and Ship Island Railroad Company until February 1, 1892.

The statute also mandated that the railroad company would assume full responsibility for all the expenses of the penal system, including the salaries of the state-funded superintendent and physician, and pay into the state treasury an annual installment of $20,000 in 6 percent first mortgage bonds. At all times the new lessee would employ at least half the state's convicts on the rail line running the length of Mississippi; the remaining half might be subleased to other railroad companies, to levee commissioners, to contractors involved in other public works projects, and, as a "last resort," to planters. The state railroad commission was designated as the penitentiary's board of control, thereby supplanting the old board of public works.

These terms, which constituted a more favorable lease than the one offered two years earlier, were counterbalanced by several legal provisions that displayed the growing strength of the opposition. No longer could the lessee reduce payments to the treasury by making repairs and renovations at the penitentiary. Convicts could not be subleased to parties having pecuniary interest in the railroad company. The three members of the state railroad commission were given greatly expanded supervisory powers and required to make regular inspections of the camps of lessees and sublessees. The statute also charged the commissioners with responsibility for preparing "a practical and comprehensive plan" by which the state might "exercise direct control and exclusive management of the Penitentiary and convicts at the earliest possible date."[7]

The penitentiary act of 1886 forged a marriage of convenience, a union of supply and demand, between convicts and Bourbon railroad interests via the state railroad commission. It was, moreover, cleverly done, the best for which the leasing interests could hope, and the compromise won the support of disinterested men as the lesser of evils.[8]

A Thickening Political Plot

The first decision of the beneficiaries of the new act was to leave the convict concession in the hands of Hamilton, Allen, and Company until the end of the year. That decision, which was apparently influenced by the complexity of Hamilton's remaining contracts with sublessees, did nothing to enhance the popularity of the new arrangement. Meanwhile, the Agrarians consolidated their strength, agreed on a plan of battle, and sought to take the offensive. Contemplating the railroad commission's charge to prepare a scheme by which the state could regain control of its convicts, they moved forward in August 1886, advancing a blueprint for an alternative scheme of penal administration.

The plan, which was unveiled in a letter from Senator George C. Dillard to the editor of the *Vicksburg Post*, rejected every assumption underlying existing policy. It propounded the long-forgotten principle that the primary purpose of the penal law was to punish criminals, not to exploit their labor for pecuniary gain. Pecuniary gain might well be forthcoming; but if it were, surely the state and not private interests should realize it. Long experience had shown that the notion of deterring crime and defraying expenses via an industrial prison in Jackson was chimerical. Hence it would be far better to relocate the penitentiary on a large plot of good farm land, as far away from Jackson and every other population center as possible, and to commence agricultural operations utilizing convict labor. Such a scheme would allow the state to punish felons through hard labor on a self-sustaining penal farm supervised by state employees. During the next four years, Dillard concluded, Mississippi should amass a fund of $150,000 for the purchase of the required acreage.[9]

Dillard's plan, which was modeled on similar schemes then under consideration in a number of other Southern states, was soon endorsed by Ethelbert Barksdale, who only recently had split with Bourbon leaders after failing in a bid for the gubernatorial nomination. On December 1, 1886, the editor resumed his attack on the inhumanity of the convict lease system, and afterward the widely read Jackson *Clarion* emerged as a vehement critic of leasing and as a strong advocate of state-administered penal farming.

Other influential journalists joined the attack. Roderick Gambrell of the Clinton *Sword and Shield* had become a harsh critic of convict leasing during the legislative investigation of prison finances in the spring of 1886, and John Martin of the Jackson *The New Mississippian* had entered the fray later in the year. Both editors propounded humanitarian principles, endorsing the Dillard plan as well as other far reaching penal reforms and printing defamatory accusations against those prominent Bourbons involved in the manipulation of the penal system.[10] Barksdale, Gambrell, and Martin were supported by the editors of a number of smaller newspapers throughout the state. By the end of 1886 the press had become a major element in the attack on leasing.

With the state's convict concession firmly in hand, the directors of the Gulf and Ship Island Railroad Company were seemingly oblivious to such criticism, and during the last week of December they met in Jackson to make final arrangements for the disposition of some seven hundred convict laborers. From Hattiesburg came company president William H. Hardy, a man of immense personal fortune and political influence. He was joined by company vice-president W. C. Faulkner of Oxford, planter, land speculator, and emerging railroad magnate. In Jackson to meet them was Jones S. Hamilton, consummate manipulator of the legislature and general manager of the firm.

They made short work of it. Hamilton took charge of fifty convicts and the penitentiary in Jackson, the receiving station and distribution center for laborers; from that strategic point he could negotiate advantageously with subcontractors while keeping a close eye on the legislature. Faulkner, directing the construction of the rail line from New Albany southward to Hattiesburg, drew two hundred convicts for his northern division, while Hardy received three hundred for the southern division, extending from Hattiesburg to the Gulf of Mexico. The remaining convicts, some 150 in number, were subleased to levee contractors in the Delta and to J. P. McDonald and Company for labor on the Kansas City, Memphis, and Birmingham Railroad in Monroe County.[11]

On January 1, 1887, Hamilton, Allen, and Company officially transferred the convict lease to the Gulf and Ship Island Railroad Company, and convicts from across the state began to converge on Jackson. They came in straggling procession, a virtual army of pathetic, manacled souls. Hamilton, engaged in the dubious act of relinquishing convicts on behalf of one firm while receiving them for another, was understandably eager to complete the redistribution as rapidly as possible.

He was thwarted by the railroad commissioners, who displayed that they meant to pursue their duties as a penitentiary board of control very zealously. The commissioners ordered a physical examination of every convict so as "to prevent, if possible, weak and feeble persons from being put to work which they were physically unable to perform." As Hamilton waited, physicians examined the convicts and issued certificates defining the type of labor for which each was qualified.[12]

After the convicts had been distributed, the commissioners hounded the lessee and the subcontractors. They popped up at Coahoma Station and interviewed convicts apart from their keepers, attempting to confirm a report that subleased convicts were suffering from frostbite. Later reports of abuse led the commissioners to the railroad camps of the sublessee J. P. McDonald. They found horrid conditions, ordered the withdrawal of McDonald's convicts, and delivered their evidence to the grand jury of Monroe County.

The investigation in Coahoma County was thwarted by conflicting testimony given by terrified convicts. The grand jury of Monroe County refused to return a bill of indictment, and McDonald delayed the return of his convicts for months before sending them to Jackson in dreadful condition. The two cases confirmed, however, that a conspiracy of silence, rooted in local self-interest and apathy and upheld through the suppression by terror of convict testimony, rendered legal safeguards inconsequential. One state legislator, who had supported the penitentiary act of 1886, was led to the conclusion that the visits of state officials were "usually anticipated and prepared for; and if the wretched victims opened their mouths at all, the dread of the lash inspired them to sound the praises of their taskmasters."[13]

Hostility between the railroad commissioners and the lessee worsened almost daily, and in early 1887 the board brought suit against Hamilton, Allen, and Company for the recovery of $18,800 in delinquent payments. Meanwhile, the Agrarian press stepped up the attack. Roderick Gambrell led the charge, denouncing Hamilton in a series of stinging editorials in his *Sword and Shield*, and in the spring of the year, when a movement was launched to return Hamilton to the state senate, the editor printed a "scathing denunciation" of the candidate. The upshot was a confrontation between Gambrell and Hamilton on the night of May 5, 1887. A gunfight ensued on the streets of Jackson, resulting in the death of Gambrell, one of the most celebrated criminal trials in Mississippi history, and the eventual highly controversial acquittal of Hamilton.[14]

The death of Gambrell fueled even greater criticism of the lessee by editors Barksdale and Martin, and soon the commissioners resumed their attack. After conducting an inspection of the railroad camps, they lodged a vigorous complaint with President Hardy, pointing to numerous transgressions of the law and to blatant violations of the rules governing the treatment of prisoners. Representatives of the railroad company met with the commissioners in Jackson on June 30 and pledged greater vigor in enforcing the rules.[15] Shortly after the meeting, however, yet another scandal erupted.

While making a routine inspection of the penitentiary, members of the grand jury of Hinds County wandered into the makeshift infirmary. Before them lay twenty-six convicts recently returned from plantations and railroad camps. Their plight was graphically revealed in the grand jury's presentment:

> Most of them have their backs cut in great wales, scars and blisters, some with the skin peeling off in pieces as the result of severe beatings. Their feet and hands in some instances show signs of frostbite and all of them with the stamp of manhood almost blotted out of their faces, which shows that they have been treated more cruelly and brutally than a nation of savages ought to permit inflicted upon its convicts. They are lying there dying, some of them on bare boards, so poor and emaciated that their bones come through their skin, many complaining for the want of food.

While being hesitant to condemn "the lessees in person," foreman J. M. Gray was unequivocal in his condemnation of "the principle and system of this great State taking a poor creature's liberty and turn[ing] him over to one who's [*sic*] interest is to coin his blood into money." "God," the foreman concluded, "would never smile upon a State that treats her convicts as Mississippi does."[16]

The grand jury's presentment inspired a public hearing in the Jackson offices of the commissioners on July 15. There, in the presence of journalists, Superintendent Johnson admitted failure. During the past six months he had traveled "over four thousand miles by railroad, five hundred by land, and two hundred by water" in an attempt to police the far-flung camps, but he could not stop the abuses.[17]

Such an admission, coming on the heels of Gambrell's death and the grand jury's galling presentment, was most damaging to the railroad company. It came, moreover, on the eve of the hotly contested legislative elections of 1887, and Agrarian candidates exploited the mounting difficulties of the Bourbon lessees to the fullest. Country folk flocked to the hustings. They heard appeals to class hatred and outrageous promises, and through it all the leasing interests were the whipping boys. The *Clarion* went so far as to denounce the lessees as "murderers with the stains of hundreds of slow pitiless murders resting upon them." The unmistakable drift of the campaign led to important defections, most notably that of former state attorney general Frank Johnson, who in October penned a remarkably effective argument against the convict lease system and submitted it for publication in Martin's *The New Mississippian*.[18]

After the Agrarians scored resounding victories at the polls, the leasing interests sought to bolster their threatened position. On December 13, a letter to the editor from William Hardy appeared in the Jackson *Clarion*. The president of the railroad company professed disenchantment with the terms of the existing lease and proposed several remedial innovations in convict discipline, including the initiation of an incentive program.

Shortly thereafter, the newly constituted board of control, fulfilling the obligation mandated by statute in 1886, submitted a plan for the reversion of the penal system to state control. In striking contrast to their predecessors, the Lowery-appointed members of the board were essentially happy with existing arrangements. The governor quite agreed, and in his opening address to the 1888 legislature, Lowery praised the existing lease and denounced what he described as excessive "maudlin sentiment" for convicted felons.[19]

These tactics found little support. The Agrarian press countered with a demand for a total abandonment of leasing and, as a first step, the repeal of the convict-generating Pig law. Within days the new Agrarian majority in the legislature set out to destroy the Bourbon lessees. The house penitentiary committee initiated "a thorough investigation of the alleged cruel treatment" of convicts, while the senate committee on penitentiary and prisons inquired into the possession and control of state convicts since the spring of 1884.[20]

The Overthrow of the Bourbon Lessees

The reports of the legislative committees must be interpreted with reference to the political animosities of the time; clearly, both committees were stacked with Agrarians who sought to discredit their Bourbon adversaries.[21] As the reports stand on the public record today, however, they constitute one of the most shocking revelations in American penal history.

Drawing on a voluminous body of evidence, including testimony by the railroad company's own employees, the report of the house committee described conditions that defy the imagination. Convicts were poorly shod and clothed, even in winter, and their rations of food were meager. They were confined at night in cages and forced to labor seven days a week. Each morning they were roused by blows, set to work before dawn, and kept at it so long as there was "light enough for a guard to see how to shoot." During the day, callous sergeants beat them, sometimes for no apparent reason, with an assortment of clubs and whips. If exhaustion overtook a prisoner, he was flogged as he lay senseless on the ground, and there were numerous incidences of homicide.

The report named names. Four of Hardy's camp sergeants were portrayed as beasts. The sublessee J. P. McDonald was labeled "a brute in human form." The account of an eyewitness related how Hardy, on a winter morning, had turned away from an unshod convict who was standing in the frost begging for shoes, and all the company's directors were judged guilty of presiding over gross violations of the law, of blatant subterfuge in their dealings with the commissioners, and of a failure to take remedial measures when ordered to do so. The report recommended not only the termination of the railroad lease, but also the abandonment of all forms of convict leasing. The system was "a state of servitude worse than slavery," and subleasing was "doubly" injurious.[22]

The report of the senate committee described persistent and determined resistance, obfuscation, and apparent perjury by the directors of the railroad company during the course of the investigation, but still the investigators had found numerous incidences of breach of contract. Hamilton, Allen, and Company and the Gulf and Ship Island Railroad Company were in effect the same firm. Jones S. Hamilton straddled them, keeping two sets of books. An inner circle of shareholders consisting of Hamilton, Hardy, Faulkner, Wirt Adams of Natchez, and attorney William L. Nugent appeared to dominate the railroad company. That firm, while officially holding the convict concession, looked to Hamilton, Allen, and Company for the management of the penitentiary and the assignment of convict labor. Business operations were haphazard and highly irregular. Contracts for the subletting of convicts, from which Hamilton in particular had derived immense profits, had been mere verbal agreements perfunctorily approved by the governor, and neither the amount nor the disposition of monies could be determined.[23]

Collectively, the two legislative reports portrayed the directors of the railroad company as men who cared about nothing but the rich rewards to be gained upon the completion of their railroad. They expected to receive the option to purchase hundreds of thousands of acres for as little as two cents per acre. Moreover, as directors and shareholders of other lines expected to intersect with the Gulf and

Ship Island Railroad, Hardy and his colleagues stood to reap substantial profits from the commerce and development almost certain to follow completion of the project.

But the critical first step, the completion of the principal line through Hattiesburg to the Gulf of Mexico, was pivotal to the realization of those plans. It had become increasingly clear that mounting public hostility to the lease system and imminent Agrarian control of the legislature might lead to abrogation of the lease. That possibility had threatened disaster because there was no affordable substitute for convict labor. The directors, then, had been engaged in a race against time, one in which they had spared neither the general welfare nor the very lives of their convict laborers.[24]

The failure of the railroad company to meet its financial obligation to the state darkened the picture considerably; a semiannual payment due on January 1, 1888, was already several months in arrears. That omission, combined with the shocking revelations of the two legislative committees, immediately fueled a successful attack on the jugular of the convict lease system, the felon-generating Pig law; its repeal occasioned a dramatic decline in the state convict population from 833 to 447 in a single year.[25]

Meanwhile the Agrarian press roundly abused the retreating directors. On May 1, 1888, several weeks after the legislature adjourned, Wirt Adams, incensed by a critical editorial in *The New Mississippian*, shot and killed John Martin on the streets of Jackson before being mortally wounded himself by the dying man's return fire. The death of Martin at the hands of a prominent lessee, following that of Gambrell by roughly a year, completed the disgrace of the railroad company, and the board of control immediately set out to strengthen its case against the surviving directors. Later inspections revealed continuing abuses in the railroad camps, and on December 3, 1888, after President Hardy had defied a direct order to discharge two company sergeants accused of mistreating prisoners, the railroad commissioners revoked the existing lease on grounds of deliberate and repeated breach of contract.[26]

By January 1889 every state convict had been returned to Jackson, and the railroad commissioners, at last exercising direct control over a diminished yet substantial number of felons, were scrambling to accommodate them. The old penitentiary could confine only about one-third of the convicts, so the commissioners made it a maximum security unit, a place of confinement for those convicted of heinous offenses. An approximately equal number of sickly and decrepit prisoners were assigned to two leased farms near Jackson, the Porter and Belhaven places; there, the state of Mississippi launched an initial, modest experiment with penal farming. The remaining convicts, nearly two hundred in number, were disposed of through several short-term leases with private planters, but in all cases state employees supervised labor. In late 1889 the commissioners reported dramatic improvements in the health and general well-being of the convicts but stressed the pressing demand for a comprehensive legislative package, one placing all convicts on state lands.[27]

Constitutional Reform

The assault of the Farmer's Alliance gained steam during the legislative session of 1890. Partisan committees sniffed out political indiscretions; statutes sought to dismantle the machinery of Bourbon rule. Through it all, Agrarian leaders exploited the documented iniquities of lessees to great advantage. The membership of the board of commissioners was expanded to include the governor and the attorney general, thereby adding two popularly elected officials to a closed circle of political appointees.[28] That reform later would figure prominently in penitentiary politics, but it was largely overshadowed by a much more significant Agrarian victory, a successful crusade for a state constitutional convention.

Held in Jackson during the autumn of 1890, the Agrarian-dominated constitutional convention resulted in a new charter of government that practically disfranchised Negroes and mandated legislative reapportionment transferring voting strength from predominantly black counties to predominantly white ones. Those constitutional provisions, which dramatically weakened the fount of Bourbon power in the Delta, framed all the other work of the delegates. Legislative reapportionment, notes one historian, was "crucial to the fate of the penitentiary."[29]

Also crucial was Article 10 of the new constitution. When the delegates to the constitutional convention gathered in Jackson, the old Dillard plan for penal farming had been endorsed by Governor Stone and recommended strongly by penal authorities in the recently published penitentiary report, and the only real issue was whether, and to what extent, convicts would continue to be employed at public works outside the penitentiary.[30]

That question was resolved very quickly via a concession delivering convict labor to levee commissioners, and afterward the delegates approved provisions of great significance. The most important banned the leasing of convicts effective December 31, 1894—earlier if possible—and instructed the legislature to purchase land, to place all state convicts on it, and to engage them "under state supervision exclusively, in tilling the soil or manufacturing, or both."

Other tactics that had been employed by the Agrarians to discredit the Bourbon leasing interests received constitutional mandate as well. The plight of children in the clutches of lessees had made for good political capital, as had the occasional association of the races and sexes in the camps. The Agrarian attack had also bemoaned the absence of religious training and the failure of lessees to hold out hope to their convicts through a program that rewarded hard work and good behavior with early releases. The new constitution accordingly provided for the establishment of a juvenile reformatory, for the classification of state prisoners by race and gender, for places of worship on the penal farms, and for the implementation of a scheme for the commutation of sentences.[31] When the delegates left Jackson, the termination of the long reign of the convict lease system was a matter of constitutional law, and the legal foundations of the state's penal policy of the twentieth century had been laid.

Policy in a Vacuum

In the years immediately following the constitutional convention of 1890, Agrarian leaders entered into a political union with the national Populist party. Populism never caught on in the state, Agrarian political strength eroded steadily, and every conceivable legislative tactic was employed to delay or subvert Article 10 of the new state constitution.[32]

Among the several provisions of that article, only the segregation of convicts by race and gender was achieved immediately. Special arrangements for minors were delayed, and in 1906 a journalist found children "crowded in with the old and hardened criminals." Three years later, a scheme segregating youthful white convicts was implemented but quickly discontinued. In 1916, when an industrial training school for young white offenders was at last established near Columbia, the legislature failed to provide for black minors. Thereafter, until 1942, Mississippi's political establishment heeded the words of Governor Anselm McLaurin, who remarked in 1897 that there was "no use trying to reform a negro"; black children continued to be quartered with adult felons of their race.[33]

Nor did the constitutional provisions lead to the establishment of places of worship for convicts. Legislators pleased their religiously inclined constituents with rhetoric about the inculcation of morality in felons and enacted several statutes mandating religious activities, but no state penal institution was equipped with a chapel for convicts until the sixth decade of the twentieth century. Much the same was true of the constitutional mandate for the implementation of a program for the commutation of sentences. A "good-time" policy, which enabled convicts to reduce the length of their sentences by 36 to 120 days each year, was functioning by 1903, and seven years later Governor Edmond Noel used the clemency powers of his office to grant conditional pardons to well-behaved convicts. Not until 1916, however, did the legislature establish a formal mechanism for early releases, and the board of pardons created in that year functioned merely to advise the chief executive in clemency proceedings.[34]

Opposition to the placement of all convicts on state lands was far more vociferous. Between 1890 and 1894 little effort was made to purchase penal farms, and the wholesale leasing of convicts to private business interests continued. But the constitutional mandate to terminate leasing and to place all convicts on state lands was unavoidable, so despite considerable opposition the 1894 legislature enacted a bill "to establish a penitentiary farm, to appropriate money to pay therefor, and to authorize the employment of State convicts."[35]

A specially appointed commission purchased Mississippi's first penal farms in the summer of 1894. The largest tract was the Hunter and Stevens farm consisting of 3,207 acres and located six miles south of Jackson in Rankin County; thereafter it was known as the Rankin County farm. The others were the Oakley farm, a 2,725-acre tract located about twenty-one miles southwest of Jackson in Hinds County, and the Belmont farm, a tract of 2,005 acres situated roughly sixty miles north of the capital in Holmes County. On December 31,

1894, the board of control terminated all leasing agreements, thereby ending the long reign of the convict lease system.[36]

But the purchase of penal farms was one thing, the implementation of penal farming quite another; and for some six years the resurgent Bourbon interests of the Mississippi Delta thwarted every effort to terminate the exploitation of convict labor by the private sector. Dating from 1890 the membership of the board of control included the three railroad commissioners, the governor, and the state attorney general. Railroad commissioners were normally drawn from the ranks of the railroad interests, and they often came to office with financial and social ties that conflicted with their official charge. Much the same was true of attorneys general; their political fortunes depended on the favor of the Bourbon chieftains who controlled the nominating conventions of the state Democratic party. And beginning in 1892 three successive chief executives—Stone, McLaurin, and A. H. Longino—aligned themselves very closely with the state's monied interests, including those who sought to exploit convict labor.[37]

After January 1, 1895, Mississippi's convicts were distributed among private interests by leases of land and "share" agreements—arrangements through which the state and a private contractor collectively exploited the fruits of convict labor without technically violating the constitutional provision. In most cases the convicts were used to clear malarial swamps in the state's northern river counties, a type of employment that decimated their ranks no less than had labor in the railroad camps of Hamilton, Hardy, and their associates.[38]

The availability of such contracts inspired competition among planters, and political influence was used to distribute convicts behind closed doors. With convict labor continuing to be a chip on the table of state politics, vested interests hyped the pecuniary advantages accruing to the state through share contracts. Income was reported as $56,000 in 1896 and as $150,000 two years later. While even the black editor of the Macon *Beacon* praised existing arrangements, the Oakley, Belmont, and Rankin County farms went largely undeveloped, the old penitentiary in Jackson was allowed to decay, and convict leasing was perpetuated in substance, if not by name.[39]

As in the days of leasing, the state's trial judges satisfied the demand for labor; there were nearly a thousand convicts working on ten private plantations by 1896. Three years later the convict spoils were spread among eleven prominent planters, and promises of convict labor reportedly bought the support of powerful men at the 1899 state nominating convention. In 1900 Longino emerged as chief executive with the support of McLaurin, his predecessor. Along with other well-placed parties, McLaurin's brother, state senator Henry McLaurin, secured convicts for his Sandy Bayou Plantation, as he had done for a number of years.[40]

The Purchase of the Parchman Farm

A number of factors combined to renew interest in penal farming at the turn of the century. Jacksonians embraced the idea by default. The capital press had advocated the destruction of "The Walls" for years, and by 1900 the citizenry was growing tired of a ramshackle penitentiary in their midst. A year earlier the grand jury of Hinds County had described the old prison as a "public disgrace" and an "insult to the City of Jackson." Largely abandoned and neglected by the board, its walls were collapsing, its buildings rotting. Cattle, horses, and swine now made up most of the inmate population. The odor was overpowering; the citizenry complained of the leakage of kitchen slops and animal waste into the adjoining streets.[41]

The disgust of Jacksonians with the old penitentiary roughly paralleled the displeasure of legislators with the old state capitol. The statehouse was becoming an eyesore. It was, moreover, uncomfortable, incapable of accommodating the increased number of politicians manufactured by legislative reapportionment. In 1892 and 1896 bills calling for the razing of the penitentiary and the construction of a new state capitol on the grounds had progressed from committee to the floor of the house before being abandoned. Now a growing number of politicians cast covetous eyes toward the choice lots occupied by the penitentiary. Such views added a new ingredient to the traditional debate on criminal policy. Even the senate, where the strength of McLaurin and Longino was concentrated, expressed interest.[42]

The termination of the disastrous Agrarian alliance with the Populist party swelled the ranks of those favoring change. By 1900 the Agrarian minority in the legislature was again a force to be reckoned with, and party leaders, consulting the tactics of their predecessors, rightly regarded the exploitation of convict labor by the McLaurin-Longino faction as a point of political vulnerability.

The popularity of the old Agrarian plan for penal farming was enhanced by successes in Mississippi and other Southern states. Despite the policies of the penitentiary board, the public record confirmed astonishingly remunerative operations on the state's three penal farms, and the immense profits turned by the convict farms of North and South Carolina between 1895 and 1900 equipped reformers with an instructive example.[43]

In all probability scholars will never know the motives that led the McLaurin-Longino interests to agree to an expansion of penal farming. They controlled the executive branch of state government and dominated the legislature, the state supreme court, and the penitentiary board in 1900; clearly they were in a position to thwart reform. On the other hand, by all appearances they genuinely supported the construction of a new state capitol. So perhaps their very political supremacy, or maybe the prospect of a lucrative land deal, motivated them. At all events, the 1900 legislature mandated the razing of the old penitentiary and the construction of a new state capitol on the grounds. And despite the availability of the nearly eight thousand acres of largely undeveloped land comprising the Oakley, Belmont, and Rankin County farms, an accompanying statute sanctioned the purchase of "an additional penitentiary farm or farms" consisting of up to fifteen thousand acres.[44]

Between December 31, 1900, and January 17, 1901, a board dominated by McLaurin-Longino interests concluded fourteen separate contracts delivering 13,789.32 acres in northern Sunflower County. Another transaction with the Ohio Hardwood Lumber Company brought the state that firm's well-developed headquarters at Gordon Station on the Yazoo and Mississippi Delta Railroad roughly thirty miles south of Clarksdale. Gordon Station was located on the eastern fringe of the lands purchased. It boasted the rail line, a fully equipped sawmill, a headquarters building, a large hotel, a barn, a storage warehouse, several farm vehicles, numerous livestock, roughly twenty thousand feet of cut lumber, and other useful equipment. Of the lands purchased, a tract of some 8,375 acres was obtained from the Iowa Land Company. The prominent Parchman clan of Sunflower County had once owned the tract, which was known locally as the "Parchman place," and J. M. Parchman evidently came in the deal as the penal farm's first warden. Soon state officials were referring to their future penal farm as "Parchman."[45]

Circumstances suggest that it was a dubious beginning. Nearly fifty years later, Senator Oscar O. Wolfe, Jr., a Delta planter, remarked that Parchman was "the sorriest 17,000 acres of land in the delta area." There were, according to Wolfe, only 600 acres on the whole farm that would grow cotton.[46] But the nail was driven. Here, amid cutover timberland, a clogged bayou that transformed the flatlands into stinking mud flats during the rainy season, and an equally smelly series of land deals, was the Mississippi penitentiary of the twentieth century.

The Final Push

After the 1901 legislative session the penitentiary board, with over twenty-one thousand acres of state land at its disposal, continued to place hundreds of convicts on private plantations. That policy, of course, retarded the development of the state farms. Parchman was a miserably drained tangle of cutover timberland at the time of its purchase, but only a relatively small percentage of the state's convicts were sent to develop it. Furthermore, nobody kept an eye on the early operations of penal authorities in Sunflower County, and later reports by legislative committees confirm a maze of shady transactions.

Private firms exploited the facilities at Gordon Station. Over two hundred convicts were set to work on the road bed of the Yazoo Delta Railroad. Others labored on nearby private plantations, including properties owned by the warden's family. Meanwhile, large amounts of agricultural produce vanished, virtually no records were kept, and little money was receipted.

Similar activities reportedly thwarted the other state farms. Oakley was a fine farm, one with great potential, but only a handful of convicts were assigned to it. Perhaps it was just as well; the sergeant worked the convicts on his own adjacent farm, presided over a number of other shady deals and atrocities, and sent gifts to Anselm McLaurin and board members when someone blew the whistle. The sergeant at the Rankin County farm probably did better for himself; he made off with wagon loads of state property on a weekly basis. The state farms accordingly lost a great deal of money, remained largely undeveloped, offered convicts no improvement in living conditions, and thus seemed to confirm the comparative superiority of "share" agreements.[47]

Increasing Agrarian representation in the legislature assured that the operations of the penitentiary board were exposed to increasing scrutiny. In 1900, the decision to purchase additional lands for the penal system had led to the adoption of two joint resolutions, one "requesting the board of control to report to the legislature a detailed statement of receipts and expenditures," the other calling for an investigation of the "management and control of the State Penitentiary." At the time they were enacted these resolutions posed no great threat to the board, but a continuing shift in the balance of power in the lower house of the legislature rocked the boat considerably. An Agrarian-stacked legislative committee launched its investigation with predictable vigilance, and after September 1901, when the Jackson *Clarion-Ledger* predicted that the investigation would place the board in a tenuous position, rumors flew in the capital.[48]

The committee's report, which went back as far as 1894, was another chronicle of brutality, graft, and embezzlement. Indeed, it included evidence of indictable transgressions by board members and employees of the penal system, and governors Stone, McLaurin, and Longino were implicated in the charges leveled. The Vicksburg *Herald* regarded the disclosures as the worst scandal in state history.[49]

The combined forces of McLaurin and Longino still held sway in the senate, a fact that apparently facilitated a number of important compromises. The investigating committee was sent back to try again, ostensibly for the purpose of clarifying its hair-raising allegations, and a second report, less critical of personages than the first, was forthcoming. Still, the second report presented a strong argument for sweeping reform, actually observing that "a dishonest Warden may, if he so chooses, safely, and without fear of detection annually rob the State of thousands of dollars." That prospect led to legislative action that terminated the fiscal autonomy of the penitentiary board. After February 1902 penal authorities were required to transfer all monies into the state treasury immediately upon receipt and to disburse monies only upon the issuance of warrants by the state auditor.[50]

More important was a statute that replaced state nominating conventions, the last bastion of Bourbon power, with statewide primary elections. Afterward populism flowered on the hustings, the class and racial hatred of white dirt farmers emerged as common denominators in state politics, and a silver-tongued demagogue, James Kimble Vardaman, rode the prejudices of the "redneck" into the governor's mansion in the elections of 1903.[51]

Vardaman was a curious man. His career, like that of many other

Mississippi politicians, is marred by the tactic of political negativism, always successful among deprived and illiterate constituents. No state politician since Albert Gallatin Brown, the backwoods demagogue who led the radical Jacksonian Democrats during the antebellum era, equaled his vicious attacks on wealth and influence; perhaps no man in Mississippi history has been a more accomplished Negro-baiter on the hustings. Yet within Vardaman was genuine empathy for the plight of Mississippi's depressed farmers, white and black, who had been pawns on the board of state politics since Appomattox. More than one historian has labeled the so-called "White Chief" the most progressive Southern politician of his age.[52]

Among Vardaman's progressive credits, perhaps none affected Mississippi more profoundly than his contribution to penology. His interest in penal policy, at least at the outset, was probably tactical; the Bourbon leasing interests were on the run by the time he entered the fray, and surely he was influenced by the effectiveness of Agrarian political tactics during the 1880s. However, as editor of the Greenwood *Enterprise*, and later of the Greenwood *Commonwealth*, Vardaman had emerged as one of the state's most passionate advocates of penal reform after the Constitutional Convention of 1890. His editorials, especially a series written in April 1894, had protested the brutality of leasing, reminded Mississippians of their Christian principles, and asserted that a penitentiary should function to prepare convicts for later social respectability.[53] Now, in January 1904, when the governor assumed the chairmanship of the penitentiary board, he invaded the closed circle of interested men who alone thwarted the placement of convicts on state lands.

Vardaman displayed extraordinary personal interest in the penal system from the first. Often accompanied by Albert H. Whitfield, his sole ally on the bench of the state supreme court, the governor went for long rides before breakfast. On a number of occasions the staff at the Rankin County farm, which in those days housed the penal system's kennel, were snapped to attention by the unexpected appearance of the chief executive and the eminent jurist. Once at the farm, Vardaman and Whitfield sometimes lingered for a "hunt." Substituting for foxes, convicts fled into the woods and were pursued by sniffing, slobbering bloodhounds. The governor, Whitfield, and the camp sergeant followed the baying hounds on horseback until their prey were duly treed, then culminated the hunt with a picnic attended by the captured convicts. All the while Vardaman displayed genuine compassion for the inmates, listening to their tales of woe and effecting a dramatic improvement in their stark standard of living.[54]

The governor's involvement with the penal system, however, went far beyond frolic and humanitarian gestures at the Rankin County farm. Indeed, almost from the day he took office there was a discernible improvement on all the state penal farms. Oakley became a productive ranch, raising and slaughtering large amounts of livestock; Belmont emerged as a considerable producer of food crops; and the Rankin County farm, cursed with poor soil, at least stopped recording financial losses. Meanwhile, Parchman, the apple of Vardaman's eye, began to emerge as a great plantation. Clearing operations proceeded at a lightening pace, cotton acreage rolled westward, the sawmill at Gordon Station operated day and night, and the locomotives, pulling cars stuffed with cotton and timber to market, disturbed the quiet lifestyles of local sharecroppers. On September 30, 1905, the penal system reported a fiscal year profit of nearly $185,000.[55]

But still the governor was thwarted by the policies of the board of control, and one must suspect that his long rides with Justice Whitfield featured discussions of what was one of his first priorities as chief executive—the abolition of the penitentiary board, the concentration of all convicts on state lands, and the development of the Parchman farm. Vardaman was repeatedly outvoted in board meetings, where the majority continued to place convicts on Henry McLaurin's Sandy Bayou plantation. He sought redress through the judiciary and gained injunctive relief in the lower courts, but Whitfield was invariably outvoted by McLaurin's two appointees on the bench of the state supreme court.[56]

By early 1906 Vardaman's hold on the lower house of the legislature was firm, and it was there that he resolved to offer battle to his faltering adversaries. Much of the governor's legislative message of January was devoted to the evils of the penal system. He recounted historical developments and spoke of the enormous profits being earned by Henry McLaurin and others through the exploitation of the state's convict labor. He related how "distinguished gentlemen, prominent in politics," bought votes with the nasty bribe of delivering convicts to "some political dictator's Delta plantation." He told of acts "rivalling in brutality and fiendishness, the atrocities of . . . Torquemada."[57]

Then, following the successful Agrarian tactics of earlier days, a house committee once again set out to humiliate the penitentiary board and the beneficiaries of its policies. The report of the committee was indeed humiliating and delivered what Vardaman wanted: recommendations for the abolition of the board and for the placement of all convicts on state lands.[58]

The McLaurin-Longino faction had been in retreat since 1902, but the old guard, still powerful in the senate, had not struck their colors. Now, however, it was clear, even to the truculent and infuriated McLaurins, that eventually Vardaman would have his way, so the protectors of the status quo gave ground, bent on securing what they could. The result, effected through much logrolling, was the enactment of statutes banning "the working of the State's convicts on lands other than that owned by the State of Mississippi," abolishing the board of control, and providing for a superintendent to replace the warden at Parchman.[59]

Vardaman was now virtually sovereign over state penal policy. The new superintendent was to be appointed by the governor for a four-year term; a popularly elected board of trustees composed of three members was to replace the board of control; the governor was to appoint interim trustees to serve until the elections of late 1907. In the aftermath of victory, Vardaman stacked the board with some of his most loyal lieutenants and set his political machine to work on the upcoming election of trustees. He refused to rehire Warden John J. Henry, who had close ties with the McLaurin faction, instead appointing C. H. Neyland, a farmer from Wilkinson County, to the superintendency. Then the governor stepped up the assault on the wilderness of Sunflower County. Nearly three-quarters of a century later, an old-timer, with eyes gleaming, spoke of the old days when he and his convicts had stood waist-deep in brackish water, fought off the dreaded cottonmouth moccasin, and brought "Mr. Vardaman's farm" to fruition.[60]

4

Mr. Vardaman's Farm

with R. E. Cooley

The gravel road running south from Clarksdale to the state penal farm in Sunflower County invaded some of the richest cotton land in the world. Along the way one observed the unpainted shacks of black sharecroppers dotting the flatlands of the Yazoo Delta and realized that here, despoiled by neither Appomattox nor almost four decades of sweeping national change, was a culture of bygone days. At journey's end was old Gordon Station, now dubbed "Front Camp" by the rough men in charge; beyond, fanning out westward toward the great Mississippi River, lay the Parchman farm.

In 1904, while Vardaman and his legislative allies were preparing for their final battle with Anselm McLaurin's faltering political machine, Henry B. Lacey, collecting information for the state's *Statistical Register*, undertook the long trek from Jackson to Sunflower County. Amid yellow dust and sweating men at Front Camp, Lacey concluded that Mississippi, keeping step "with the progress of advanced thought," was "evolving a system of control for its penal institution, that, whilst protecting society and punishing the criminal with hard labor, leaves open to him the door of hope."[1]

Lacey observed an awe-inspiring spectacle, but one that was only beginning to take form. Vardaman and his allies would pay scant attention to the smaller penal farms; their eyes were fixed on the great plantation in the Delta, and the law soon reflected their vision. The Mississippi Code of 1906 defined the penal system as "the plantation known as Parchman . . . in Sunflower County, and such other places . . . owned or operated by the state in the enforcement of penal servitude."[2]

The Agenda

Vardaman was not only the political architect of Mississippi's penal farm system; he was also its philosophical architect, the "founding father" of all that followed. None of the state's governors has come to office with a firmer grasp of criminological theory. None of them has more successfully incorporated such theory within a broader scheme of polity.

Vardaman was evidently influenced by the recently propounded theories of the Italian Positivists, Cesare Lombroso, Enrico Ferri, and Rafaele Garofalo. He did not believe that mankind possessed complete freedom of will and found it "quite probable" that the behavior of humans was "determined by countless causes over which they have no control." The biological determinism of Lombroso and the environmental determinism of Ferri were especially popular with the governor; man, he once remarked, was a "creature of heredity and environment," an animal whose acts were "often the result of influence set in motion by the unconscious deeds of some forgotten ancestor." But Vardaman leaned more heavily on Garofalo, whose published works had attributed crime, in part at least, to "moral anomaly" among certain groups within the community. Criminals, the governor maintained, were "moral cripples."[3]

Such a view of criminality conditioned Vardaman's penal philosophy. He argued that the old and revered Babylonian adage of "an eye for an eye" was nonsense, a reflection of ignorance and ill-breeding, and he asserted that capital punishment was no more justifiable than lynch law. Nor did the governor think that vicious secondary punishments served the interests of the state. Legal punishment was not "inflicted in the spirit of revenge, but rather for correction—in love rather than hate."[4]

His concept of "correction" centered on the pragmatic fact—so troublesome within the deterrence theory of the early classicists—that eventually the great bulk of convicts would reenter society. Discipline, he stressed, could not be allowed to embitter an inmate. The interests of the state dictated that all convicts, but especially one who was a "low-bred, vulgar creature, congenitally corrupt, [and] inured to physical and moral filth," should receive "kindly treatment, a decent bed to sleep on . . . sanitary surrounding," and management by an "upright, honorable, intelligent and just man."[5]

The governor also placed great emphasis on the tactics of convict indoctrination that had been pursued by the early Victorians. Remunerative labor was an essential component of his plan, but the primary purpose of labor, he emphasized, was convict remission. The ethic of work could be instilled in convicts only through a comprehensive and systematically pursued program of incentives, he thought, and other social instincts might be inculcated by the influence of Christian doctrine. Penitentiaries should be "moral hospitals," institutions that treated "patients" and released them whenever they displayed signs of complete "recovery."[6]

Vardaman considered the tribulations awaiting released convicts as well. Despite whatever constructive influence the penal system might have on an inmate, a convicted felon had a "brand" on him when he returned to society. Consequently, the opportunities offered to a released convict by illegal behavior often eclipsed those offered by legal behavior, and further criminality was normally the result. The remedy, Vardaman concluded, was to make the penitentiary a "school," an institution that provided vocational training and thus equipped convicts for successful social reentry. A percentage of the penitentiary's profits, he added, should be allocated either to the families of convicts or to the convicts themselves at the time of their release. "I am more interested in the salvation of man," the governor assured the legislature in 1906, "than I am in hoarding gold."[7]

If evaluated in an intellectual vacuum, Vardaman's opinions seem incredibly progressive for a Mississippi politician of his time; but the governor did not advance them in a vacuum. His staunch determinism contemplated inescapable facts peculiar to Mississippi. His plan for the penitentiary was clearly tactical. Both were products of his broader concept of politics.

The axis around which the political creed of the "White Chief" turned, and the fount of his strength on the hustings, was a defense of white rule. Nobody believed more earnestly in the innate inferiority of the Negro race. No politician exploited the Negrophobia of the state's downtrodden white electorate more successfully. No man defended the racial status quo more zealously. But Vardaman saw widening cracks in the foundations of white rule. The "criminal tendencies" of blacks troubled him deeply, and he warned of impending disaster. The great number of "criminal negroes" who were migrating to the state's cities, he told Mississippi's peace officers in 1905, sought "a way to live without honest toil" and menaced "the safety of the white man's home."[8]

The question was how to counter the threat. Here, Vardaman accepted Garofalo's thesis that crime often arose among "certain inferior races" and embraced the paternalistic view of the underclass so common among the most thoughtful members of ruling oligarchies everywhere. While championing, and even wishing to expand, the numerous provisions in the state's constitutional and statutory law that impeded the advancement of blacks, Vardaman also thought that the privileged status of the white man brought with it social responsibilities. Blacks, he felt, were as children, wards of the state doomed by genetic inferiority. He therefore wished them no harm, treated them respectfully, and actively sought to protect and improve the lot of blacks within the confines of their subordinate status.[9]

Vardaman attempted to instill his tactical paternalism within the institutions that propped the unequal social order. The church, which functioned to preserve established values rather than to create new ones, and the schools, no less valuable as tools of indoctrination, constituted the first line of defense. So while steadfastly defending white rule, Vardaman encouraged his constituents to consult their Christian principles when dealing with blacks and meddled in the state's "separate but equal" educational system with uncommon vigor, always drawing a clear line between the type of education required for the respective races.[10]

If religion and education were proactive tools supporting the prevailing social order, criminal process was a reactive one, the last line of defense. The law was stacked against the black man; the state's entire apparatus of force was vested in the hands of the white establishment. It was hardly surprising that the convict population had been roughly 80 percent black since the forced termination of slavery forty-two years earlier.[11] Mississippi's penal policy, therefore, was a vital component of a broader political agenda, a sphere of public administration that must be handled with great care; for the state penitentiary was essentially an institution for the wayward members of the black underclass.

What to do with them? The pivotal issue was not one of racial inequity; inequity was the essence of the social system. Rather, it was one of iniquity, the manner in which power should be wielded. Vardaman saw grave problems in the manner in which his political predecessors had employed their police powers. Their shortsighted policies, always justified by hollow appeals to the tenets of legal retributivism, had rendered legal punishment nothing more than an instrument of exploitation and brute force. The state had forgotten the first principle of social control and, indeed, the nexus of classical retributivism itself. The preservation of white rule necessitated policies of moral suasion and social indoctrination in all branches of public administration, but especially in the administration of legal punishment.

Vardaman accepted the thesis advanced by Marx and Engels some fifty years earlier that law was the exclusive domain of those who controlled the means of production. He carried that thesis to its logical conclusion, rationally viewing criminal process as a mechanism of social control. And in the fashion of the "enlightened" eighteenth century English aristocrats who had pioneered the penitentiary movement, he felt that the word was more effective than the sword in the management of an increasingly troublesome underclass.[12]

The governor's quest to protect white rule narrowed the scope of his reformative penal philosophy. His political rhetoric repeatedly emphasized the absurdity of attempts to educate the Negro. The black man was a common laborer; he must never be allowed to rise above that station in life. Education could only breed rising expectations, dissatisfaction, and misery among blacks; a literate black man in white-ruled Mississippi, he once remarked, was inclined to criminality. Vardaman, therefore, steadfastly opposed education in letters at the penitentiary. Vocational training, though, especially in agriculture, promised to perpetuate the traditional role of the black man. Such training, moreover, could enhance the living conditions of the underclass, breed greater happiness among its members, and thereby strengthen the foundations of white rule.[13]

The organizational and administrative schemes endorsed by Vardaman were perfectly consistent with his measured philosophy. Available assets included a huge expanse of fertile Delta land and a large labor force consisting primarily of black convicts of agrarian origins. Inevitably, the governor adopted a blueprint of antebellum vintage.

The first principle was centralization: the entire convict population would be concentrated in Sunflower County and placed under unitary management. The second principle was self-sufficiency: the penitentiary would be an island, a fortress altogether removed from the capricious private sector.

Parchman's Front Camp would be the hub. From there the central administration would coordinate purchasing, allocate labor and other resources, receive and process raw cotton, and preside over sales. Convict laborers would be distributed among overseers on a number of "working plantations" or field camps, each growing its own food and raising the cash crop. The field camps would be widely dispersed over Parchman's acreage, thus facilitating proper inmate classification and confining possible riots to defensible space. Several specialized units would house carpenters, brick masons, and others capable of performing services for the whole. Until the primary plantation was developed, the three smaller state farms would provide support services; afterward, they would be phased out.[14]

The scheme also sought to screen the penal system from the pitfalls of a large, publicly administered business. Auditing procedures were stringent. The central administration was required to transfer all monies to the state treasurer immediately upon receipt and to rely on legislative appropriations for maintenance. All disbursements were to be made on the warrants of the state auditor.

The popularly elected members of the board of trustees were to be the watchdogs. Responsible only to their constituents, the trustees formed a political entity that was independent of the executive and legislative branches of state government. A division of the penitentiary's patronage between governors and the board was designed to check the abuses inherent in the political spoils system. The trustees' charge was to represent all facets of the penitentiary's operations. They would counterbalance the cupidity and fickleness of a republican political process serving a market economy. They would represent a constituency of felons that was otherwise unrepresented. They would keep a close eye on financial operations, venture periodically to the far-flung field camps, and seek to protect convicts from the inevitable abuses of their taskmasters.

Implementation

All three members of the interim board of trustees, as well as those who were elected to the board in late 1907, belonged to Vardaman's political faction. The lower house of the legislature was no less devoted to the governor, and Vardaman, later one of Mississippi's United States senators, would continue to exert powerful influence on state politics until 1914. Hence a political vacuum existed when the trustees got down to work in 1907, and the continuing dominance of the Vardaman faction provided them and their successors with an uncommon reprieve from many of the vicissitudes of partisan politics. The result was a rarity in American public administration: the systematic pursuit of a well-reasoned policy for a considerable number of years.

Working closely with the governor, the interim trustees got things moving during 1907. The Rankin County farm was made the primary residence of white male convicts. Oakley became the sole residence of all females, the temporary site of the penal system's major medical facility, and a holding station for convalescents. Old and infirm black male convicts were dispatched to the Belmont farm, while the younger and healthier black men were placed at Parchman.

During 1907 roughly eighty white men at the Rankin County farm raised livestock and grew truck crops while Oakley accommodated female and sickly male convicts. The women were lodged at what was known as the Oakley Walls. There, with their virtue ostensibly protected from the nearby men by a towering fence, they produced clothing and other domestic articles for the entire penal system. Oakley's hospital, which remained a "shack" despite a number of renovations, cared for convicts from all the farms. After being released from the hospital, convicts convalesced at the Oakley farm, where animal husbandry was the chief occupation. Meanwhile, approximately 120 black male convicts worked at Belmont, no doubt thankful that poor health or advancing years screened them from the far more rigorous regimen in Sunflower County.

At Parchman the younger black men were initially distributed among nine field camps, a sawmill camp, and a carpenters' camp. Operations at the sawmill required a degree of skill unavailable among the black convicts, so thirty white men were brought up from the Rankin County farm. At Parchman's sawmill they worked alongside six blacks, representing the only Caucasians on the plantation except overseers and others in managerial positions. Seventeen black carpenters were on hand, however, and they manned the carpenters' camp. While the saws hummed and the carpenters transformed the raw wood into permanent buildings, nearly 850 black men in the field camps cleared land, hauled wood to the sawmill, prepared the alluvial soil for cultivation, and left cash crops behind them.[15]

In 1910 penal authorities increased acreage in Sunflower County with three separate acquisitions. The first, a 222-acre tract bordering Parchman to the south, was purchased in June. In September another 320 acres south of the plantation were obtained, and in October 1,358 acres adjoining Parchman to the north were added. Dating from October 1910, the holdings of the penal system in Sunflower County stood at 15,689 acres.[16]

The inmate population grew in almost direct proportion to the demand for labor and the capacity of the penal farms to accommodate convicts. On October 1, 1907, there were 1,337 prisoners on hand. Two years later the work force stood at 1,628, and in June 1911 at 1,843. The trustees shifted a larger percentage of convicts to Parchman each year. In October 1909 some 69 percent of them were in Sunflower County, by July 1915 nearly 80 percent. The laborers were exploited to the fullest. As early as 1905 rail spurs had begun to reach into the plantation; now they reached further, accelerating clearing operations and bringing the wilderness to heel.

Operations on the smaller farms were scaled down as the trustees diverted a greater percentage of their resources to Parchman. In 1908 the female convicts were transferred from Oakley to Sunflower County. About three years later, when a new medical facility opened at Parchman, Oakley was reduced to a small contingent of convicts engaged in animal husbandry.[17]

The early operations of the penal farm system paid extraordinary dividends. While the produce of the satellite farms fed and clothed the convicts, Parchman's surplus lumber commanded a hefty price, and the cotton market was strong. A modest net profit of $24,606.84 was reported for fiscal year 1906-07. But during the 1907-09 biennium profits leaped to over $176,000, and in 1913 the trustees reported an incredible profit of nearly $937,000 for the most recent biennium.[18]

In 1912 the members of a legislative committee visited Parchman and voiced astonishment. "Think of 16,000 acres of land stretching out before us as level as a floor and as fertile as the Valley of the Nile, in the very finest state of cultivation," the chairman wrote in his official report. The farm was "a very monument to labor that our state can boast of, and one of which we might well be proud." Indeed, it was impossible to doubt that Mississippi now had "one of the best, if not the best, Penitentiary systems in the United States."[19]

Further expansion ensued. In 1914 the board purchased two small tracts of land—one near Okalona and one near Waynesboro—and established limestone-crushing plants at both locations. Two years later the legislature created a commission and authorized it to obtain additional acreage for the penal system. The resulting acquisition of the five-thousand-acre O'Keefe plantation in Quitman County—afterward dubbed "Lambert" due to the close proximity of the Lambert community—carried the land holdings of the penal system to 28,910 acres.[20]

The Emerging Penal Farm System

By 1917 clearing operations at Parchman were virtually complete, and the farm was organized along lines that would remain largely unchanged until the eighth decade of the twentieth century. Outside the front gate were warehouses, a large gin, and a railroad depot. One crossed the tracks to approach the gate. Armed guards perfunctorily waved visitors through, and the gate seemed unnecessary because neither fence nor wall was connected to it. Once beyond the gatekeepers, one entered Front Camp, which seemed to be a "little city." It consisted of a barn-like administration building, a guest house, a number of staff houses, a small church for employees, a post office, and the hospital. Rising above everything was a new house for the "super," a two-story mansion rendered pretentious by the spindles, gables, and other hallmarks of Victorian architecture.[21]

Beyond Front Camp were twelve widely spaced field camps housing male convicts, ten for blacks and two for whites; more would be established in succeeding years. The major function of the field camps was the production of cotton, but all of them were required to maintain a garden and to raise livestock for the sustenance of their inmates.

Each field camp was equipped with a long, one-story dormitory known as a cage. The windows of the cages were barred, and most of the units were subdivided into three sections—a dining room with a connected kitchen, a small room for convict trusties, and a large room for "gunmen"—convicts under the gun. A corridor intersected the room appropriated to gunmen; on each side of it were approximately fifty beds some two feet apart, each equipped with a footlocker. A door led from the central corridor into the dining room, where there were a number of four-by-four tables. Initially the cages were made of wood, but by the 1930s convict labor had transformed most of them into brick, and by then all cages were equipped with electric lights, running water, and bathrooms.[22]

Parchman's other units had a unitary function. There was a wide range of such units on a plantation that strove for self-sufficiency, but the largest of them were the women's camp, the hospital, the brickyard, the sawmill, and the carpenters' camp. The women's camp was equipped with sewing machines. There, like pupils aligned at desks, sweating women produced all of the bedding, curtains, and linens utilized by the entire penal system as well as the striped uniforms and the crude suits of clothing allocated to prisoners on the day of their release.

Considering the small number of females within the penal system during the early years of the century, the women's camp was remarkably productive. In June 1917 only twenty-six females were under sentence, but their numbers increased over the years; between 1923 and 1933 an average of sixty-two women were at Parchman. Negro and Caucasian women were said to share a single dormitory subdivided into two wards. But in all probability few, if any, white females resided at the women's camp. There were no white women under sentence in June 1915, and records indicate that no more than two were at Parchman at one time up to 1933. A small number of women, white and black, were quartered at places other than the women's camp: reportedly at Front Camp, at the Governor's Mansion, and at state institutions for the insane and feebleminded. Judging by the sexual and racial mores of the time, there can be little doubt that those favored few included the white women. The women's camp at Parchman, then, served principally, and probably exclusively, as a unit for black females.[23]

Parchman's hospital was divided into wards with patients segregated by race, gender, and malady as much as space would permit. Farming and the raising of livestock were conducted on a small scale so as to occupy the patients' time, to contribute to the maintenance of patients, and to discourage malingering. The brickyard produced bricks, not only for the penal farms, but also for other state institutions, and the convicts there raised food crops on roughly sixty acres of land. The sawmill was located on the northeastern part of the plantation; its crew, housed nearby at Camp Ten, was excused from farming because of the time required to produce lumber and shingles for the entire penal system. Camp Six, which housed the subunit known as the carpenters' camp, accommodated thirty carpenters who served the needs of the plantation when they were not employed in the fields.[24]

Compared to Parchman, the penal system's other units were minor operations. The only producers of revenue were Belmont and Lambert. Belmont continued to house old and infirm black males. They raised various breeds of livestock for the benefit of the other penal farms, and agriculture, most notably the growing of food crops, was conducted on a surprisingly large scale. Between 1908 and 1934 the farm had an average of about seventy convicts on hand.

With five thousand acres of fertile, if often flooded, bottom land, Lambert was said to have great potential at the time of its purchase. In developing it penal authorities followed the same principles of organization and management that had worked so well in the development of Parchman a decade or so earlier. In 1917, 104 convicts, including a sawmill gang and a crew of carpenters, were put to work clearing land and constructing buildings. In 1922 the farm was divided into two separate camps, and in 1930, when a third camp was added, operations expanded. Between 1923 and 1930 an average of some 170 convicts were at Lambert, but in 1931, when a dramatic increase in commitments caused overcrowding in Parchman's cages, the plantation in Quitman County absorbed the overflow. In 1931 the convict population increased to 360, and two years later it stood at 386.

The two limestone-crushing plants, the Rankin County farm, and the Oakley farm recorded financial losses each year, but they met demands that the revenue-producing units could not supply. The two lime plants employed from fifteen to thirty convicts between them, produced lime for all the penal farms, and sold surpluses to the state's farmers at cost. The Rankin County farm was a white man's Belmont—a low-key institution for white males whose age, health, or social status disqualified them from the rigors of labor at Parchman. Fifty-seven prisoners were there in June 1917, but the population decreased steadily through the years. The farm averaged about thirty-five inmates during the twenties, and only thirty men were there in 1927 when the board abandoned it.

Most of Oakley's 2,740 acres stood barren. After the transfer of the women's camp and the opening of the hospital at Parchman, the unit was an unproductive farm inhabited chiefly by convalescents who raised livestock and piddled in a vegetable garden. Housing an average of about seventy convicts, Oakley was a large and unjustifiable financial drain until 1925, when overcrowding in the two white camps at Parchman led to an accession of seventy-five white convicts between the ages of fourteen and twenty-one. Thereafter serving as an institution for young white felons, Oakley remained a financial drain, though perhaps a more justifiable one.[25]

The penal system also maintained a number of road camps around the state. From them, manacled men under armed guard ventured forth for labor on public highways and levees. Occasionally the road camps were reinforced by gunmen from Parchman and Lambert, especially when the spring rains caused flooding in the Delta. But relatively few convicts were assigned to the road camps. Vardaman and his allies on the board frowned on any labor that carried convicts off state lands, and besides, penal farming was too remunerative. Mississippi thus rejected the "good roads movement" so common among other Southern states in the early twentieth century, and few of the state's convicts were links in a chain gang.[26]

The Organization of Labor

A convict's involvement with the state penal system began when the judge of a trial court notified the superintendent that a felon was lodged in a county jail awaiting his order. The superintendent, in turn, ordered the penitentiary's "traveling sergeant" to proceed to the jail, to collect the prisoner, and to transport him or her to Parchman's Front Camp. Upon arrival the convict was conveyed to the hospital, where fingerprints, photographs, and Bertillon measurements (of primary physical characteristics) were taken. The convict was then given a physical examination and either assigned to the hospital for medical treatment or released for a work assignment.

After being released for labor, male convicts were issued ten-ounce duck trousers and seven-ounce duck shirts with horizonal black and white stripes, known as "ring-arounds" in prison jargon. Female convicts were given dresses with vertical stripes—"up-and-downs." Identification numbers were stamped on the front and back of uniforms. Printed copies of the rules and regulations governing the penitentiary were then distributed among the prisoners. Because few of them could read, a staff member normally explained the rules point by point.[27]

Work assignments contemplated neither a convict's crime of conviction nor the mitigating or aggravating circumstances surrounding the transgression; prevailing wisdom held that the association of prisoners by "criminal tendency" could only result in the reinforcement of deviant behavior. Instead, the penitentiary's classification system was based on race, gender, healthfulness, age, and vocation. The camp structure at Parchman and the operations of the smaller farms took everyone into account except black minors, who were housed with adults of their race.[28]

Every camp was commanded by a sergeant who reported directly to the superintendent. In the larger camps—those with one hundred or more convicts in residence—the sergeant was normally assisted by two assistant sergeants. Smaller camps were usually staffed with one assistant sergeant, and the smallest had no assistant.

The convicts in the field camps were roused well before dawn. A small number of prisoners remained near the cage, working in the garden, and a few proceeded to the kitchen, subject to the cook's orders for the day. But at dawn's first light the great mass formed up outside the cage, underwent something akin to a military "morning call," and then followed their sergeant to the cotton fields.

In planting season the convicts rode mules to the fields, and upon arriving at their destination they dismounted, harnessed the beasts for the work at hand, and undertook their assigned duties as members of either the hoe gang or the plow gang. In picking season the convicts normally walked to the fields and, again divided into two groups, set about picking their daily quota of two hundred pounds per man. Regardless of the season, the convicts worked under the supervision of the sergeant and his assistants, who were known to the prisoners as "drivers," and they labored in close, tight files that came to be called the "long line."

At sunset the convicts were marched back to their cages and fed supper. The sergeants and their assistants set out for their homes at Front Camp, leaving the convicts under the supervision of salaried night watchmen known as "night-shooters." Throughout the hours of darkness convicts were forbidden from venturing outside their cages, and the night-shooters were authorized to open fire upon observing any movement whatsoever. Next morning the sergeant and his assistants returned, relieved the night-shooters, and again led their charges to the fields.[29]

Labor on Mississippi's penal farms was hard, especially at Parchman and Lambert during the months of summer. With temperatures hovering near the century mark, the drivers pushed the shuffling long line ever forward. The Delta sun bore down relentlessly, the pounding hoes raised the choking yellow dust, and the "mercy man" with his wagon load of water seemed to appear all too infrequently. But as the perspiring gunmen neared the limits of endurance, most of them were kept at it by a great number of incentives.

The scheme of behavioral reinforcement that evolved during the early years of penal farming in Mississippi leaned heavily on what modern behavioral scientists term operant-based learning theory.[30] Simple, explicit rules of behavior, complemented by equally simplistic positive and negative discriminative stimuli, were held out to convicts. A reasonable schedule of behavioral consequences was followed. And convicts were given models—living examples of the results of positive and negative behavior.

The Trusty System

The penitentiary's scheme of behavioral reinforcement centered on the trusty system, which elevated some 14 percent of the convict population to privileged positions during the first three decades of the twentieth century. Apparently the state's version of the system was an outgrowth of antebellum days, when slaves generally worked in one of four capacities—as field hands, drivers, artisans, or house servants—and were allowed to improve their lot through promotion.

Like female inmates, all male trusties wore up-and-downs, but trusty-servants were the penitentiary's crème de la crème. The envy of all other convicts, they earned and maintained their positions by good manners, docility, and superior domestic skills. They worked as domestic "help" in the superintendent's mansion or in the homes of other employees, as cooks and janitors, and in a variety of other positions that lightened the workload of the penitentiary's staff. Convicts panted for such assignments. The staff panted as well; the number of trusty-servants assigned to an employee was a reflection of status. In 1924 a joint legislative committee was astonished and appalled by the number of trusty-servants assigned to the homes of Parchman's employees.[31]

Below the trusty-servants in the convict pecking order were the trusty-artisans. A disproportionately large number of them were white men. Superior vocational skills helped Caucasians escape from the field camps, as did the lingering notion among sergeants that labor in the fields was "niggers' work." The best and most senior of the trusty-artisans served in middle management positions within the penitentiary's support services, often supervising convict-apprentices. Perhaps the most notable among them were those who managed the penitentiary's kennel. They trained bloodhounds, beagles, and German shepherds; they followed the baying hounds in pursuit of escaping convicts, all the while restraining the muzzled "kill dogs"; they chaperoned the beagles on private hunting expeditions; and they frequently presided over dog shows, to the delight of the superintendent's guests.[32]

Then there were the trusty-shooters, who lived within the cages, and who were the only armed men on the penal farms. Frequently drawn from the ranks of long-term convicts, usually convicted murderers, trusty-shooters were appointed by camp sergeants only after years of trouble-free service. Thereafter under strict orders to avoid familiarity with gunmen, they slept apart and stood apart from their former peers, representing law and order in a society of felons.

The rooms within the cages allocated to trusty-shooters resembled the quarters of a sergeant in a traditional military barrack. They contained storerooms filled with supplies; under lock and key were .30-.30 Winchester rifles and carefully rationed ammunition.

Each morning the shooters were the first to rise. Dressed in their up-and-downs, and with their rifles pointed skyward from the hip, they roused the sleeping gunmen with shouts, organized them for the work of the day, and reported to the arriving sergeants. As the troop of sleepy-eyed gunmen proceeded to the fields, the shooters rode ominously to the flanks, always with the Winchesters exhibited prominently. As the drivers set the gunmen to work on the long line, the shooters drew the "gun line," a mark in the dirt that surrounded the working convicts. Beyond the gun line was no-man's-land; there, the shooters' Winchesters had license.

Such duties, of course, earned trusty-shooters the envy and contempt of the gunmen, who derisively labeled them "headhunters," and with good reason. The shooters were usually desperate men serving life sentences, and efficiency on the job alone offered them hope. They drew the gun line meticulously and watched the working gunmen like a hawk views its prey. If a gunman dared to cross the line, the shooter was required to shout a warning. Failing there—and policy apparently said nothing about the interval—the shooter was under orders to open fire. They were, by and large, expert marksmen, and their lethal efficiency often earned them the ultimate reward. Shooters performing "conspicuous meritorious service" were recommended for a discharge or a pardon; many of them were deemed conspicuously meritorious after dropping a gunman in his tracks.[33]

The trusty-shooter system was the centerpiece of Parchman's incentive program. As in the free world, status and power had their liabilities; nothing haunted a shooter more than the prospect of running afoul of his sergeant and being returned to the ranks of the gunmen over whom he held sway. For themselves, the lowly gunmen harbored hopes of one day wearing the up-and-downs of the shooters. With the zebra-like garments came not only status and power, but also greater freedom of movement, better quarters, the possibility of being reassigned to one of the cushy jobs at Front Camp, and a better chance of an early release.[34]

The efficiency of the shooter system was displayed graphically in the years immediately following 1922. In that year a number of reported abuses led the legislature to prohibit discharges and pardons for trusty-shooters who meritoriously slaughtered a fellow inmate. Attempted escapes more than doubled during the next three years. Governors, collaborating with penal authorities, granted enormously increased numbers of suspended sentences, and the 1928 legislature allowed meritorious trusties to discard their up-and-downs in favor of blue denim uniforms. But the shooters regarded mere suspensions with disdain, and the new dress code facilitated a rash of escapes. So the denim uniforms were discarded, the legislature backed off, and the old scheme was restored with a number of advertised safeguards. Thereafter, escape rates declined markedly.[35]

Executive Clemency

Trusty-shooters were not the only convicts who stood to gain a pardon or a suspended sentence. Along with trusty-servant status came accessibility to the throne, so to speak; thus assignments to the homes of the superintendent and his principal underlings, and more notably to the Governor's Mansion, were coveted. As had been the case of domestic "servants" in the days of slavery, long and faithful service in the home of the master offered the prospect of freedom.[36]

Voluntary participation in medical experiments afforded convicts an avenue out of the penitentiary as well. In 1915 twelve inmates at the Rankin County farm participated in a pellagra experiment, survived six months of dietary deprivation, and obtained pardons from Governor Earl Brewer. In 1933 another ten convicts were granted executive clemency after participating in an encephalitis experiment.[37]

Professed humanitarian motives also led to the granting of executive clemency. The legislature's failure to provide suitable institutions for young criminals led Governor Brewer to pardon or suspend the sentences of many minors he deemed worthy of a second chance. Governor Mike Conner established a "mercy court" with himself as "judge." Accompanied by two colleagues, he traveled periodically to the various farms, interviewed convicts, studied case histories, and granted pardons or suspensions to those he called "forgotten men." Subsequent governors followed his precedent.[38]

The moods of chief executives, too, opened the doors of the penitentiary. Governors tended to be especially generous on their last day in office and on holidays, especially Christmas, Thanksgiving, New Year's Day, and the Fourth of July. Such generosity sometimes diminished the convict population substantially. Depending on one's point of view, Governor Theodore Bilbo was famous, or infamous, for his propensity to pardon and to suspend sentences. During the Christmas season of 1931 he raised the ire of conservatives by granting a staggering 536 early releases.[39]

Excluding only the years 1916 to 1924, when the controversial board of pardons advised governors on petitions, the granting of executive clemency was essentially left to the discretion of superintendents.[40] In their hands, of course, clemency was a carrot on a stick that dangled just above the extended hands of the convicts. But influence in the granting of clemency also gave superintendents a means of controlling the size of their work force—a flexible tool capable of countering the effects of sentences by the independent judiciary, keeping overhead expenses somewhat consistent with the appropriations of an undependable legislature, and navigating through the ebb and flow of the market economy. Mississippi's system of pardons and suspensions produced about the same number of early releases per capita as did parole boards in other states. An average of over 205 convicts—nearly 13 percent of the population—obtained some form of executive clemency each year between 1907 and 1933.[41]

The Blessed Sabbath

The penitentiary's scheme of behavioral reinforcement extended to virtually every facet of convict life. The rigorous work schedule stole leisure six days a week, and the Sabbath, the one day of rest, was treasured by the gunmen. On Sunday mornings large numbers of prisoners attended religious services, normally presided over by a felon with evangelical talents. Within the cages radios blared while the more energetic convicts engaged in "horsing around" to the chagrin of those trying to sleep. There was considerable interest in football, baseball, and boxing broadcasts, and sports betting, accompanied by regular games of craps, emerged as hallmarks of convict life. "Hell," remembered a former employee, "we let 'em do anything they wanted on their time so long as they did what we wanted on state time." But even on Sundays there was work to be done; and if "state time" was wasted by a convict's truculence or by violations of the rules, the Sabbath could be taken away by any number of disgusting work details.[42]

Camp sergeants also exploited the penitentiary's single organized recreational activity: well-behaved and productive convicts were allowed to play baseball on Sunday afternoons and on holidays. The state provided no monetary support but, as in prisons everywhere, an ample supply of bats, balls, and gloves somehow found their way into the camps. Each of the field camps had a curiously named team, and competition between the black camps was lively. One of Parchman's former employees, recalling the booming home runs of an otherwise forgotten inmate-catcher from Drew, the flashing spikes of "Snowflake Harper," and the exploits of other champions of the diamond, remembered that "The cons worked hard 'cause they knew they couldn't play ball if they didn't."[43]

The pursuit of the national pastime was no more vigorous than the pursuit of women by the black inmates. The facts surrounding the advent of "conjugal visitation" at Parchman are cloudy, but it seems safe to say that the practice was not conjugally motivated. Indeed, everything suggests that penal authorities viewed sexual favors by prostitutes as a valuable tool in the management of black field hands.[44]

One old-timer, grinning sheepishly and understandably insisting on remaining anonymous, assessed the logic behind the practice in the following manner:

> Hell, nobody knows when it started. It just started. You gotta understand, mister, that back in them days niggers were pretty simple creatures. Give a nigger some pork, some greens, some cornbread and some poontang ever now and then and he would work for you. And workin' was what it was all about back then. I never saw it, but I heard tell of truckloads of whores bein' brought up from Cleveland at dusk. The cons who had a good day got to get 'em some right there between the rows. In my day we got civilized—put 'em in little houses and told everybody that them whores was wives. That kept the Baptists off our backs.[45]

During the thirties an employee at Parchman confirmed that sexual privileges were restricted to black male convicts without reference to marital status, that black prostitutes were actually quartered in the central administrative building during the day, and that they moved freely between the field camps at night. Some years later, Professor Columbus B. Hopper explained that "the white sergeants of the Negro camps simply 'looked the other way' in accommodating what they considered to be natural among Negroes."[46] Presumably the "moral superiority" of the white male convicts explains their exclusion from all the sexual promiscuity; certainly the capacity to bear unwanted children excluded the female inmates. Nobody seems to be altogether certain of how the prostitutes were paid.

The penitentiary's visitation policy was also a managerial tool. The families of convicts were allowed to enter the penal farms on the fifth Sunday of months that had more than four Sabbaths; and dating from about 1920 the lonesome wail of the fabled "Midnight Special," churning at dawn on the railroad tracks bordering Parchman to the east, announced the eagerly anticipated arrival of spouses:

> Heah comes yo' woman, a pardon in her han'
> Gonna say to de boss, I wants mah man,
> Let the Midnight Special shine its light on me.[47]

Many of the convicts could think of nothing else. They sang of their women while working in the fields, often gazing toward faraway Front Camp and the blessed depot, and many of the gunmen, especially the older ones, began to prepare for the arrival of "mama" after "weighin' up" on Saturday evening. On Saturday night they reclined listlessly in their bunks, wishing away the time; before dawn on Sunday one could see the forms of their pathetic faces through the barred windows of the cages; and as the sun rose higher and higher over the flat landscape of the Delta, they strained their ears, trying to hear the sweet sound of the locomotive's whistle.

At last the train would arrive at the depot, with "mama" in her Sunday best, stretching and yawning amid warehouses stuffed with cotton. The convict-husbands who had reached their quota and who had played by the sergeant's rules were brought up by wagon. The male convicts and their spouses reportedly shared intimate moments in designated rooms at Front Camp. They stood in long lines leading to tables heaped with fried chicken and all the trimmings. They wandered aimlessly hand-in-hand; they cheered wildly at the baseball games. At dusk, when the women boarded the train with streaked faces, the camp sergeants could reasonably anticipate a manageable labor force during the weeks ahead.[48]

Black Annie

Despite the considerable number of incentives held out to them, some members of the inmate subculture refused to respond. In such cases, the only official sanction available to camp sergeants was "Black Annie," a heavy leather strap of antebellum vintage that was four inches wide, a quarter of an inch thick, and three feet long. Although by policy the sergeants could inflict no more than fifteen lashes per day, as had been the case by law in the days of slavery, the strap was sovereign on the penal farms, the sergeants' sole means of effecting what modern behavioral scientists label "positive punishment."[49]

Critics heard no apologies. In 1909 Superintendent Neyland emphasized that it was "absolutely necessary to whip a convict" when incentives failed to make him behave himself and "earn his salt." A year later Parchman's physician, Dr. A. M. M'Callum, told the American Prison Association that whipping was "the only effective method of punishing the class of criminals in the Mississippi penitentiary and keep[ing] them at the labor required of them."[50]

At the time M'Callum referred to the presence of a unique "class of criminals" in the Mississippi penal system, he was describing a convict population that several months later was composed of 1,843 felons, 509 or 28 percent of whom had been convicted of murder and 749 or over 40 percent of whom had been convicted of other heinous crimes against the person. Those statistics held firm until 1929. Between 1911 and 1929 roughly 32 percent of the convicts admitted to the penal system were murderers, and some 34 percent were under sentence for other grave crimes against the person.[51] After 1929 the penitentiary housed a steadily increasing number of property offenders, but the percentage of malefactors remained extraordinarily high. Perhaps Dr. M'Callum's assessment was correct. The Mississippi penal system had more than its share of long-term convicts whose crimes illustrated dire social depravity, and the penitentiary had neither fences, walls, nor maximum security unit.

Successes and Failures

Vardaman's goals for the penal system were pursued with a degree of success between 1906 and 1934. Financial productivity easily constituted the most tangible victory. During those years, while prisons elsewhere were recording mounting deficits, the receipts of Mississippi's penal farms exceeded disbursements by well over $4.2 million.[52]

The financial success of the penitentiary is easily explained. Whereas remunerative prison labor to the North, and even in other Southern states, was undone by the opposition of the private sector, Mississippi's dominant planter class never seemed to be worried about a few thousand bales being produced on the penal farms. Apparently they agreed with Governor Edmond Noel, who told the legislature in 1910 that the cotton grown at the penitentiary did not have "the slightest effect on the general market nor would any less be grown if the state would dispose of its lands to individuals." Furthermore, an agrarian economy, and the virtual political disfranchisement of nearly half the proletariat, assured that the labor movement, with its rational opposition to competing convict labor, never got off the ground in Mississippi. The result was a penal system that Superintendent L. T. Fox once described quite accurately as a "profit-making machine."[53]

A number of Vardaman's other goals were also realized. Absolutely nothing about the operations of the penitentiary threatened the foundations of white rule; if a Negro felon got an education in letters, he got it somewhere else. The ideal of vocational training was promoted by the diversified operations of a large, self-supporting plantation system that relied exclusively on convict labor and employed many inmates in key middle management positions. After visiting the penitentiary in 1914, the editor of the Memphis *Scimitar* reported that Parchman was "a school within itself."[54]

Excepting only the worst years of the Great Depression, housing, culinary arrangements, medical services, and the other essentials of life were evidently adequate by the standards of the time. The minute books of the board of trustees and the biennial penitentiary reports, which were extraordinarily candid due to the political independence of the elected trustees, generally project a healthy convict population.

There is no reason to conclude that the heavy workload of convicts was any more taxing than the workload on Delta plantations employing free labor. Alan Lomax, a seemingly impartial observer who visited Parchman in the early thirties, wrote:

> Only a few strands of wire separated the prison from adjoining plantations. . . . Only the sight of an occasional armed guard or a barred window in one of the farm dormitories made one realize that this was a prison. The land produced the same crop; there was the same work for the Negroes to do on both sides of the fence.[55]

Nor did retributivists and advocates of deterrence have reason to be displeased. Felons were punished by the denial of freedom and by an exacting regimen of discipline, and the hallmarks of convict life were unpleasant enough to discourage recidivism in rational beings. While records are scanty for the early years of the century, available commentary suggests that few convicts offered themselves for recommitment.[56]

The free citizens of the state, if not necessarily deterred from criminality by the example of Parchman, were certainly aware of the perils attending felony convictions. Then, as now, released convicts related harrowing tales of their hardships, and their stories were enhanced by the contributions of musicians. Among the many work chants emanating from the penitentiary, none is more famous than the "Parchman Farm Blues," which was composed early in the century by a forgotten gunman. In the 1950s Mose Allison sang his version of the old ballad:

> Well, I'm sitting over here on the Parchman Farm,
> And I ain't never done no man no harm,
> Well, I'm putting that cotton in a 'leven foot sack,
> With a twelve-gauge shotgun at my back.

The published works of novelists were no less influential. William Faulkner's *The Mansion*, for example, related the "doom" of the murderer Mink Snopes, who did not "even count off the years as they accomplished" on the great plantation. Snopes trod the passing days "behind him into oblivion beneath the heavy brogan shoes in the cotton middles behind the mule which drew the plow and then the sweep, then with the chopping and thinning hoe and at last with the long dragging sack."[57]

The public's perception of the penitentiary developed accordingly. In the early years of the century, no less than today, people whispered about the unmarked graves in the penitentiary's orchard, all the while forgetting that every prison had its share of inmates whose remains went unclaimed.[58]

Black parents, seeking to influence the behavior of their offspring, told hair-raising tales of murderous trusty-shooters and of white sergeants who whipped "bad little niggers" on the cold floors of the cages. White boys and girls, too, were intimidated by the specter of the penitentiary. A judge told one youngster, guilty of a juvenile offense, that next time he transgressed he would find himself hoeing cotton at Camp Five with a Winchester at his back. The rare glimpses the citizenry got of the remote penitentiary fed the legend. Early-rising hunters and fishermen, unhappily trapped at railroad crossings, saw the forlorn faces of black women who boarded the Midnight Special in the lazy little towns of the Delta. Occasional convict labor outside the penitentiary also had effect. Motorists grimaced as they passed the sweating road gangs, always attended by the stalking shooters, and even today the older residents of the Delta enliven after-dinner conversation with stories of manacled convicts, guarded by hard men with shotguns, singing their soulful blues as they hoisted sandbags onto the threatened levees.[59]

The legend that came to surround Parchman was undoubtedly bigger than life itself, a mesh of fact and fiction, but it was pervasive among Mississippians, and by the 1930s the stories that were told of the great prison in the wilderness constituted a major focus of local folklore. The legend, and the evident gulf between realities and appearances within it, constituted the realization of a vital component of the old doctrine of general deterrence—Bentham's emphasis on the necessity of a penitentiary projecting an appearance of punishment that was more severe than its reality.

Planters whose properties abutted Parchman complained that their laborers refused to work the acreage near "the line." "Them black folks was scared to death of the farm," remembered an employee of the penitentiary. "Most of their stories were bullshit, but I reckon that's what a prison is all about."[60] If any scheme of legal punishment is capable of influencing the behavior of the general population, surely the grim legend that came to surround "Mr. Vardaman's farm" gave would-be felons ample reason to pause and reflect.

Credit for most of the early successes of the penal farm system must be assigned to Vardaman himself. He kept an eye on things, visiting the farms regularly, studying the appointment of every employee closely, and his benevolent philosophy was realized in many instances. The historian Albert D. Kirwan observes with much justification that Vardaman generally appointed able and humane administrators "who seemed to see the penal institution as a hospital for the morally sick."[61]

Vardaman's political successors assured that his principles enjoyed many successes after he had passed from the stage of politics. Governor Noel, who succeeded Vardaman, displayed great interest in the penal farms and consistently advocated better arrangements for minors and the creation of a formal mechanism for early releases. Governor Brewer also showed great interest in the plight of young felons and rooted out graft at the penitentiary with a vigilance that alienated all political factions. Governor Henry L. Whitfield, one of Vardaman's most intimate friends, sought to bolster the "moral hospital" and reminded an obstinate legislature that Vardaman had hoped to make the agricultural operations of the penitentiary a model for the state's farmers. Theodore Bilbo, who rode the old Vardaman horse to two terms in the Governor's Mansion and to a seat in the United States Senate, regarded Parchman as "the greatest of the State's institutions" and pursued most of his colleague's principles throughout a long career.[62]

The minute books of the penitentiary's board of trustees suggest that Vardaman's philosophy prevailed among many of its elected members as well. Lawrence Yerger, who served as president of the board until 1914, was a steady advocate of benevolence in convict discipline. James F. Thames, a future superintendent who was president of the board during the twenties, often propounded an almost philanthropic concept of penology. Colonel Will Montgomery, who sat on the board for the central district until his death in the mid-twenties, was a close friend of Vardaman and his personal representative on the board.[63]

Montgomery's efforts on behalf of the convicts were eclipsed by those of his widow, Betsy, who was appointed to the board to complete her deceased husband's unexpired term. She was elected trustee in her own right in both 1927 and 1931, and served as president of the board between 1932 and 1935. According to one observer, her terms displayed "a record of . . . endeavor to make life for the state's unfortunates just a little of brightness in knowing someone was interested in them as human beings."[64]

Betsy Montgomery was fully cognizant that she was a "bleeding heart" in a sphere of public administration where few hearts bled. She was, moreover, no blushing belle in temperament, and she regarded her office as a sacred trust. The penitentiary was "one institution that should not be run in the dark," she stressed; "the authority to rule over human beings placed absolutely under their control" often led even competent penal authorities "to blow up completely." More than a few administrators on the farms felt "Miss Betsy's" lash, and the minute books of the trustees abound with examples of her efforts to improve the lot of the convicts.[65]

Available evidence also suggests that superintendents generally followed Vardamanite principles of convict discipline until the early 1930s. The precedents established during the long, successful tenure of the benevolent planter C. H. Neyland, Vardaman's handpicked "super," were apparently enduring. Jim Williamson, who served as superintendent during both of Bilbo's stints as chief executive, was a stout defender of his convicts and a consistent advocate of formal religious programming. Superintendent Fox, who presided during the twenties, scolded the legislature with reckless abandon and lobbied passionately for rehabilitative services that went far beyond those championed by Vardaman himself.[66]

The penitentiary had failures, of course. A widely publicized scandal transpired during 1913–14, when several highly placed penal authorities, among them Trustee Yerger and another of Vardaman's faction, were convicted on charges ranging from embezzlement to the misappropriation of public funds. Shortly thereafter, "gross negligence" by Superintendent J. C. Gathings resulted in a fire at Oakley in which thirty-five convicts, trapped on the upper floor of a burning building, perished in screaming agony.[67]

The minute books of the board of trustees confirm the dismissal of a number of employees for unacceptable behavior. The trusty-shooter system bred abuses flagrant enough to occasion repeated remonstrances. Despite the evident vigilance of the board, surely there were unreported atrocities at a remote penitentiary that housed a predominantly black convict population, employed white men of modest class origins, and operated in the heyday of Jim Crow.[68]

Other failures of the penitentiary were rooted in the inability of Vardaman and his disciples to impose their views on the legislature, where there was truculence even during the gubernatorial term of the "White Chief." Vardaman sought to establish separate institutions for young convicts of both races and to terminate a trusty-shooter system that tempted a man "to do wrong to his fellow prisoner." But his passionate pleas for legislation capable of "preventing criminals" and for the employment of civilian guards failed to mobilize even his own followers behind the reforms. So the dreaded shooters continued to stalk the fields, and in June 1929, when there were 302 minors housed with adults in the black camps, critics labeled the penitentiary a "school for vice."[69]

Apparently a great deal of "vice" resulted from the presence of women at the penitentiary as well, notwithstanding their separate camp. In 1925 Trustee Thames told delegates to the annual meeting of the American Prison Association that the women's camp was a "little bit closer" to the men's quarters than was desirable. It was, in fact, "not more than three or four hundred yards from one of the men's rooms." The transfer of the women's camp to a more isolated part of the plantation followed shortly, but the presence of women remained a source of difficulty. According to a former employee, the male and female convicts "stopped at nothing in trying to get at each other." Sometimes, he recalled, "we would just turn our heads and pray for all that sowing of oats to end up with a crop failure."[70]

The weakening hold of the Vardaman faction on state politics assured further compromises of the philosophy that launched the penal farm system. There were spirited religious services in Parchman's black camps featuring much "howling and squealing," but the ideal of a "moral hospital" was crippled by the absence of a place of worship for convicts on the penal farms. Although convicts received a degree of vocational training, the notion that the penitentiary should be a "school" preparing released convicts for successful social reentry suffered in the absence of formal programming.[71]

Vardaman's recommendation that a percentage of the penitentiary's profits be allocated to convicts and their spouses was also rejected by the legislature. One prison official thought that paying wages to convicts would be counterproductive; the wives of shiftless black men, he speculated, would scheme to get their spouses in the penitentiary so as to make them breadwinners. But racial considerations aside, it is safe to say that opposition to paying wages came primarily from the legislature's reluctance to increase the overhead expenses of the penal system.[72]

The fact is that virtually every facet of the penitentiary's operations deteriorated more or less after about 1914, when the Vardaman faction was eclipsed in the state political arena. The 1914 conviction of the two Vardamanite penal authorities on charges of embezzlement, and the subsequent sentence of one of them to an extraordinary five-year term, coincided with Vardaman's political demise and was accompanied by attacks on other vestiges of his rule.[73] The purchase of the Lambert plantation in Quitman County—a flagrant violation of Vardaman's principle of centralization at Parchman—followed in 1916, and thereafter the structure of penal administration that Vardaman willed Mississippi rendered the penitentiary a bleeding sore on the body politic.

The front line of conflict pitted the elected board of trustees against the lower house of the legislature, which controlled the penitentiary's purse strings. But skirmishes, often rising to the size of pitched battles, erupted between chief executives and trustees as well, and frequent fights between governors and legislators and among the trustees themselves were no less hot. Such conflict, of course, was the inevitable result of a functional system of checks and balances. However, the allure of convict labor, the profitability of penal farming, and the coveted patronage of the penitentiary carried tensions to alarming levels.

To some extent, the problem stemmed from a fundamental flaw in Vardaman's system of checks and balances. Trustees, like chief executives, were required to stand election every four years. After Vardaman's day, that statutory requirement—so harmless during the reign of a political strongmen—occasioned vicious infighting and assured that the entire staff of the penitentiary normally turned over every four years.[74]

The result was fluctuating priorities, inconsistent farm management, and declining revenues. Declining revenues, in turn, led to smaller legislative appropriations, and dating from about 1917 the penitentiary operated with insufficient capital. Afterward, as the physical plant and the general standard of living on the penal farms degenerated, governors, trustees, and superintendents virtually begged the legislature for catch up funds. Sufficient monies were not forthcoming, however, and the standoff between the trustees and the legislators at last culminated amid the litter of the Great Depression. By 1933 the convicts were living in squalor, deficits were mounting, and a majority of legislators were convinced that Mr. Vardaman's scheme had run its course.[75]

"The Walls": The Mississippi State Penitentiary at Jackson, ca. 1880. Courtesy of the Mississippi Department of Corrections (hereafter cited as MDOC).

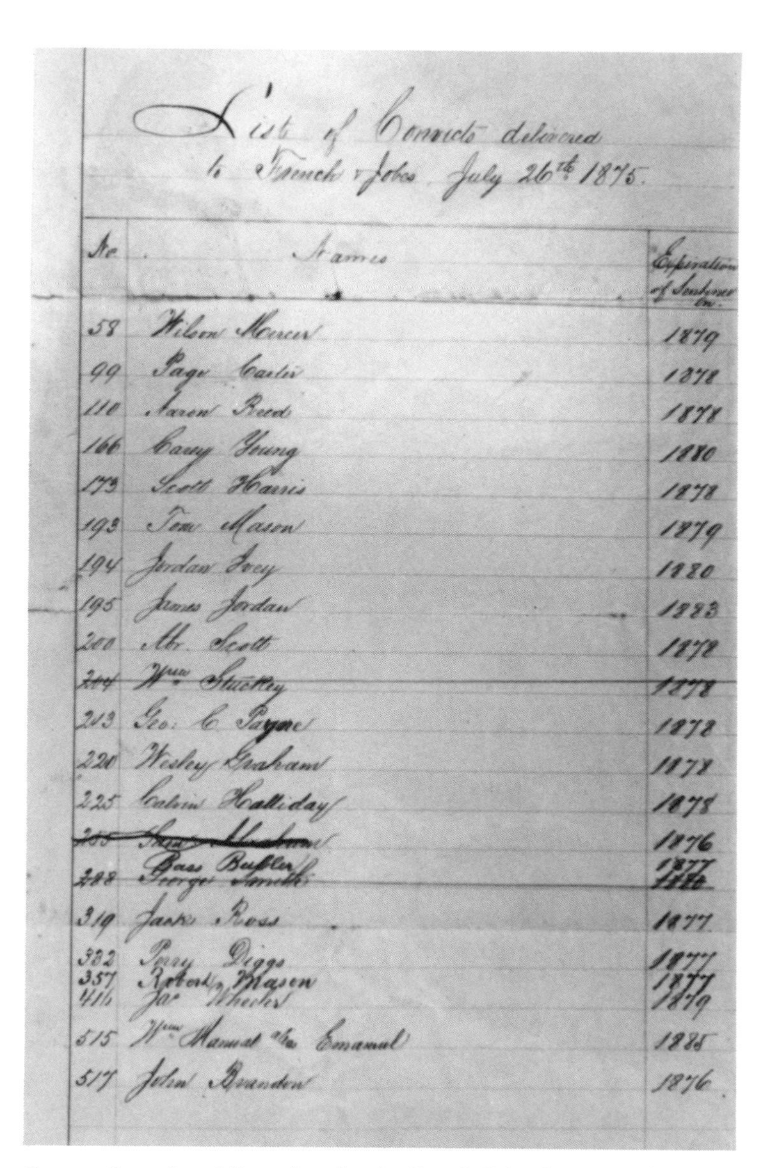

List of Convicts delivered to French & Jobes July 26th 1875.

No.	Names	Expiration of Sentence on
58	Wilson Mercer	1879
99	Page Carter	1878
110	Aaron Reed	1878
166	Carey Young	1880
173	Scott Harris	1878
193	Tom Mason	1879
194	Jordan Ivey	1880
195	James Jordan	1883
200	Abr. Scott	1878
204	Wm. Stuckey	1878
213	Geo. C. Payne	1878
220	Wesley Graham	1878
225	Calvin Halliday	1878
[illegible]	[illegible]	1876
	Bass Butler	1877
288	George Smith	1876
319	Jack Ross	1877
332	Perry Diggs	1877
357	Robert Mason	1877
416	Jas. Wheeler	1879
515	Wm. Manuel alias Emanuel	1885
517	John Brandon	1876

Roster of convicts delivered under the French-Jobes lease, 1875. Courtesy of Lonnie L. Herring, Jr. (hereafter cited as LLH).

Ethelbert Barksdale, editor of the Jackson *Clarion* and a leading opponent of Mississippi's convict lease system. Courtesy of the Mississippi Department of Archives and History (hereafter cited as MDAH).

Governor James Kimble Vardaman, principal architect of the Mississippi penal farm system. MDAH.

Superintendent's home at Parchman, ca. 1916. MDAH.

Interior of a Negro cage, ca. 1940. LLH.

Sewing room at Parchman, ca. 1950. LLH.

Laundry day at a Negro camp, ca. 1940. LLH.

Negro gunmen preparing to ride to the fields, ca. 1920. MDAH.

The long line, ca. 1940. LLH.

A mercy man and his wagon, preparing to transport water to the long line, ca. 1950. LLH.

Convict dog-handlers, ca. 1940. LLH.

Trusty-shooters in their up-and-downs, ca. 1940. LLH.

Convict baseball team, ca. 1950. LLH.

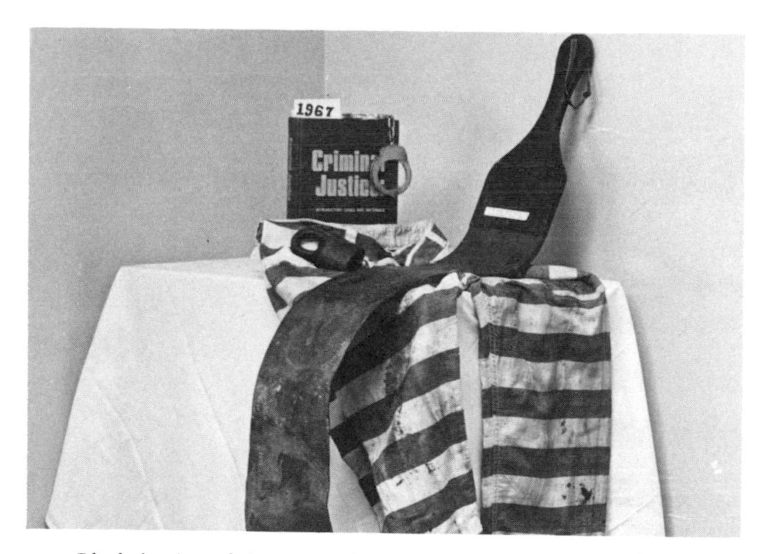

Black Annie and ring-arounds in a sadistic display, 1967. LLH.

Mrs. W. A. "Betsy" Montgomery, chairwoman of the penitentiary board of trustees, 1932–36. MDAH.

Photo gallery continued following p. 232.

5

Conflicting Goals amid Prosperity

In January 1934 the state of Mississippi was in the worst throes of the Great Depression. Nowhere were the ramifications of the crash more evident than at the penitentiary. The convict population had climbed to above twenty-six hundred, but for two years the legislature had failed to allocate a cent for permanent improvements, and a Spartan appropriation for mere maintenance had amounted to only $32.21 per inmate during 1932 and 1933. The physical plant was a wreck. The convicts in the overcrowded cages were hungry, sickly, and in rags. Medical services were virtually nonexistent. Farm operations were at a low ebb.[1]

The financial accounts included in the biennial penitentiary report released in early 1934 confirmed that the problems were of long duration, merely brought to a head by the current economic dilemma. About 40 percent of the net profits reported for the period 1906-33 had been generated between 1906 and 1913, when Vardaman's political machine had held sway. After July 1, 1913, and continuing until June 30, 1933, the business affairs of the penitentiary had degenerated steadily, and a combined deficit of over $707,000 had been reported between 1929 and 1933.[2]

Governor Mike Conner thought the penitentiary could do better if only the operations of the institution could be emancipated from the awkward system of checks and balances imposed by Vardaman some twenty-eight years earlier. Since coming to office in 1932, Conner had been engaged in an increasingly bitter struggle over the penitentiary's patronage with Betsy Montgomery, president of the board of trustees, and her ally, Trustee Thad Ellzey of the southern district. Mounting difficulties at Parchman had placed the trustees in a no-win situation, and the governor had maneuvered to exploit the vulnerability of his adversaries. Now, in early 1934, Conner garnered support in the legislature and "attacked from ambush." In February a legislative committee confirmed "evidence of a lack of business judgment and economy" at the penitentiary, and in March the legislature stunned political observers by rushing through a sweeping reform package purporting to place the penitentiary on a "practical business basis."[3]

The Penitentiary Act of 1934

The penitentiary act of 1934 abolished the elected board of trustees effective January 1, 1936, created a board of commissioners composed of three gubernatorial appointees, and delivered all the penitentiary's patronage to the office of the governor.[4] At a stroke, the safeguards so essential to Vardaman's old scheme ceased to exist.

The announced goal of the reformers was retrenchment; the act declared that the penitentiary would punish felons at no cost to the state, and at a profit if possible. That priority led not only to political consolidation but to physical consolidation as well. The offices of the new board of commissioners would be at Parchman, not in Jackson, as had been the case of the meddling trustees. The lime plant at Okalona and the Oakley farm would be leased to private parties. Five thousand acres adjoining Lambert would be purchased.

A number of the statute's provisions brought its sponsors crucial support in the legislature. The old administrative structure had divided the penitentiary's patronage among trustees and governors, thereby spreading the spoils so thinly that powerful elements in the statehouse had been denied their share. Now legislators got their share, if indirectly. Concentrated in the hands of chief executives, the penitentiary's patronage became a tool in the governor's necessary task of legislative management, and Conner soon exploited it.[5]

Apparently the mandate to lease the Oakley farm and to purchase land adjoining Lambert was also part of the deal. For years Lambert had been plagued by chronic flooding, yet nobody asked questions when Trustee Montgomery expressed doubt about the motives behind the purchase of additional land in what she described quite accurately as "an overflow drainage district." Nor did anybody respond to

Montgomery's queries about the curious decision to lease the fertile lands comprising Oakley. Soon the 2,725-acre tract would be delivered to a private party for $651.25 per annum.[6]

The governor and a considerable number of interested parties also had reason to be pleased by a provision of the act that required "annually all of the able-bodied male convicts over the age of 21 years and under the age of 50 years . . . to work for a period of six days on the public roads in the counties in which the . . . farms are situated." That provision, complemented by an earlier political trade-off—the constitutional requirement that convict labor would be employed to maintain levees—facilitated two practices of consequence. First, it assured that chief executives could please politicians in the Delta, the cradle of political power in Mississippi, by delivering to them manacled convicts for labor on public works. Secondly, it opened the door to the private exploitation of convict labor. Long experience confirmed that the employment of convicts outside the penitentiary led inevitably to cupidity. Now, in the absence of independent inspectors, convicts could be distributed far and wide.

Other than Montgomery and Ellzey, a handful of legislators, and fifty or so deposed employees at the penitentiary, everyone seemed pleased with the new arrangements. Conner came calling at Parchman in July, slapping backs at Front Camp, touring the wretched cages with his handpicked superintendent, Oliver Tann, a former camp sergeant and the brother of the governor's campaign manager. Two weeks later Conner entertained more than five hundred legislators, county agents, and other public officials at a barbeque on the grounds of the penitentiary.[7] All in all, it was a masterpiece of political maneuver.

The New Context of Penitentiary Politics

The demise of the board of trustees removed one of three players from the game of penitentiary politics. Remaining were the chief executive and the legislature. The governor held all the patronage formerly possessed by the trustees as well as that created by the new statute; the legislature continued to hold the purse strings. The politics of the thing, therefore, revolved around the ability of chief executives to manage the legislature.

There were three common denominators for success. First, governors had to assure that their principal appointees at Parchman were loyal, trustworthy, politically adept, prudent, and cooperative. Under the provisions of the new statute, the primary function of the commissioners was to look after the political interests of chief executives. They were brokers for the spoils of the penitentiary, men who negotiated contracts with the private sector and distributed staff positions, commodities, and convict labor. One imprudent appointment to the board could undo a governor.

So could the wrong superintendent. Chief executives and commissioners had to balance the demands of politics with the essential interests of penal farming, which were defined by the "super." In the absence of an independent board of inspectors, superintendents held great authority and responsibility. They were, in fact, virtual feudal barons who enjoyed sovereignty in the day-to-day operations of the penitentiary. The convicts were at their mercy. Commissioners merely rubber-stamped their purchase requisitions. In most cases it was necessary to heed the advice of superintendents in every staff appointment and in negotiating every contract. Perhaps no appointment in state government demanded more gubernatorial scrutiny. Chief executives simply had to employ superintendents possessed of great expertise in large-scale agriculture, considerable managerial skills, and a degree of political savvy and influence.

Secondly, the cotton market had to improve. Cotton was almost worthless in 1934, and Parchman's warehouses were stuffed with dusty bales. No matter how expertly a superintendent managed farm operations, and no matter how shrewdly patronage might be distributed, continuing deficits would upset the political apple cart.

Finally, a smoke screen had to envelop the penal farms. Control of the penitentiary brought governors incalculable political sweets, but control had its liabilities. State history confirmed that the penal system provided political detractors with a splendid avenue of attack, and Conner's own success in deposing the board of trustees was a recent case in point.

Conner and his immediate successors understood these facts of political life and successfully exploited their opportunities. Loyal, discreet chums of governors manned the board of commissioners and conducted their wheeling and dealing without fanfare. A new breed of superintendent also emerged. Prior to 1934 Parchman's superintendents had been farmers, men on the right side of politics to be sure, but not one among them had enjoyed a statewide political reputation. After the departure of Oliver Tann in early 1936, planter-politicians found their way to the superintendency.

Tann was a dray, a loyal workhorse appointed as a component of Conner's attack on the board of trustees, and he was retained in the wake of victory to look after things until Montgomery and Ellzey vanished from the political scene some twenty-two months later. He was succeeded in early 1936 by Governor Hugh White's appointee, James F. Thames of Mendenhall, formerly chancery clerk of Simpson County, penitentiary trustee for the southern district from 1913 to 1930, and afterward state highway commissioner.

There followed the instructive eight-month superintendency of J. H. Reed, a Delta planter with but modest political influence who resigned after finding himself altogether incapable of combating the currents around him. In November 1940 an embarrassed Governor Paul B. Johnson replaced Reed with his hometown crony, Lowery Love of Hattiesburg. Love was a planter, a former state senator, an unsuccessful candidate for lieutenant-governor, and a leading figure in the powerful Mississippi Baptist Convention. He moved on to the secretaryship of the state eleemosynary board in the spring of 1944 and was succeeded by Marvin E. Wiggins. Like his predecessor, Wiggins was an experienced planter, a former state senator, and an unsuccessful candidate for lieutenant-governor.

The selection of such chief administrators put the first piece of the puzzle in place, but neither governors nor superintendents could control the state of the cotton market. Here, Lady Luck came to the rescue. In 1936 the penitentiary sold cotton at prices ranging from about twelve cents to fourteen cents per pound, and a year later one consignment drew only 8.43 cents per pound. But mobilization in Europe led to a steady appreciation in the value of cotton dating from 1938, and prices mounted substantially between 1940 and 1945 due to the war. Then, following a brief postwar slump, the value of cotton rose to unprecedented heights. By October 1950 it was selling at more than forty cents per pound on the New York market.[8]

Governors were also quite successful in screening the penal farms from political detractors. In January 1936 a curtain fell around a penitentiary that was a pork barrel of gubernatorial patronage, and one that was fraught with potential for graft and human abuse. The federal government posed no threat, for the doctrine of states' rights extended to the administration of criminal justice, and the federal judiciary studiously avoided involvement in state penal institutions. The same was true of the state judiciary; never did the Mississippi bench do anything that might have compromised the sovereignty of chief executives or their appointees at the penitentiary.[9]

The legislative branch of state government was equally pliable. The distribution of the penitentiary's patronage among the oligarchy of the Delta bought the support of all the right men in the statehouse. The penitentiary committees of the house and senate, whose members conducted inspections and penned potentially damaging reports each year, were courted by governors, and superintendents entertained the committeemen lavishly at Parchman.

Feasts were laid out on the dining tables of the guest house or, in fair weather, on tables placed on the front lawn of the superintendent's mansion. Grinning, shuffling trusties served prime beef and mounds of vegetables on massive platters, told of their contentment, and wondered if they would be remembered by the governor. At the kennel the politicians marveled as the dogs performed. A dove hunt, with convicts sometimes substituting for retrievers, was often on the agenda. Later the politicians conducted a cursory inspection of the superintendent's favorite units, where the convicts virtually stood on their heads to display productivity and delight with their taskmasters. Then it was back to Front Camp, where a generous superintendent distributed the penitentiary's produce among the supposed inquisitors.[10]

The commissioners, operating from Front Camp, neutralized potential threats posed by local politicians. Among the local folk requiring constant attention were the members of the Sunflower County Board of Supervisors, who found their way to Parchman frequently, and the county district attorney, whose grand juries held jurisdiction over the penitentiary. The supervisors were content so long as they were given a little produce, allowed to place a worthless nephew or a "kissin' cousin" on the payroll from time to time, and allocated a few convict laborers for both public and private work projects. District attorneys, too, took their share of the penitentiary's fruits, and the members of the grand jury enjoyed themselves immensely during their cursory inspections of the penitentiary, often departing with everything from bags of vegetables to choice cuts of beef.[11]

Only the general public and journalists threatened to rock the boat. The public was uninformed and generally indifferent. Hazy accounts of backbreaking labor, of Black Annie, and of the deadly shooters continued to circulate among Mississippians, but the penal farms were well off the beaten path and shrouded in mystery. In 1934 Trustee Montgomery found it "surprising to know how few people understand, or in fact, have ever thought about . . . what the penitentiary is, or how it is operated."[12]

The "team" running the penitentiary made great efforts to assure that the mystery lingered. The tone of the biennial penitentiary reports changed dramatically. Earlier reports had been remarkably candid, a reflection of the conflict inherent in a functional system of checks and balances. After 1936 there was a degree of candor, but only when superintendents and commissioners tried to justify larger appropriations.

Governors and superintendents engaged in fulsome mutual flattery. Conner and Tann, ever dwelling on the proverbial bottom line, could not say enough nice things about each other. Thames was a capable superintendent but not the wizard Governor White said he was. Love talked frequently about the big money he was generating, always taking care to mention the many paths of righteousness he was blazing at the penitentiary; and Governor Johnson, a great fan of the gridiron, once told the press that Love was a "triple-threat back doing three things at once: managing a big farm, managing a big business, and . . . [being] warden for 2,600 convicts." Wiggins spoke a great deal, if none too articulately, about the good morale of his convicts, and three successive governors described him as God's gift to Mississippi.[13]

A trusting press printed all the platitudes and defended the penitentiary passionately. On July 17, 1932, during a period when convict life on the penal farms was galling, the Jackson *Daily Clarion-Ledger* argued that "Very few states give their prisoners more humane treatment or keep them in healthier environment." Official reports of overcrowding, starvation, and sickness failed to alter that editorial opinion. "The more we study conditions elsewhere," another staff writer observed on October 29, 1933, "the greater is our respect for the Mississippi system." The executive branch of government managed the press very effectively in later years. None of the state's leading newspapers questioned the operations of the penitentiary with any consistency until well into the 1940s.

Two instances illustrate the almost inevitable result of the strong-governor scheme of penal administration. In early 1935 Trustee Montgomery charged that convicts had been denied the essentials of life and worked on private plantations in violation of the law. Those allegations, lodged by the most experienced penal administrator in Mississippi, were ignored by the legislature, the grand jury, and the press. Roughly five years later, when the besieged Superintendent Reed made a number of unsettling public statements about the penitentiary, Governor Johnson denied any knowledge of the problem. Then, after a legislative committee confirmed inexplicable financial losses and open warfare between factions at Parchman, the governor defused the budding scandal by simply changing superintendents. Then, when the new superintendent, Lowery Love, reported that everything at the penitentiary was "proceeding smoothly" due to "splendid organization," everyone was quite satisfied.[14] Such was the nature of penitentiary politics in the absence of an independent board of inspectors.

Riding Mr. Conner's Horse

Operating behind closed doors and blessed with a rallying cotton market, superintendents Tann, Thames, and Love carried the penitentiary out of the bog of the Great Depression between 1934 and 1944. Tann's official report for fiscal year 1934–35 would have one believe that he presided over a renaissance at the penitentiary. Nothing resembling a renaissance transpired, but the superintendent did renovate the sawmill and the brickyard, keep the trusty-artisans busy, and begin a campaign to refurbish the physical plant.

Otherwise Tann's time was devoted to politics. He simply had to show a profit and, by hook and crook, he did it. Cotton acreage was expanded, and observers noted that farm buildings were being erected as fast as the sawmill could produce lumber. Tann sold the increased yield of the cash crop, along with the numerous bales that had been produced and stored by his predecessor, in the glutted market. He also reduced operating expenses, most notably in the line items of kitchen supplies, medical services, and electricity. In preparing his financial statement for the fiscal year, the superintendent seemingly deferred payment on a number of expenses, thereby willing red ink to his successor.[15]

These tactics enabled him to show a misleading but politically fortuitous "profit" of nearly $142,000. "Waving a typed statement triumphantly at a press conference" on January 30, 1935, Governor Conner represented the penitentiary's financial recovery as "just another example of savings that can be realized through a reorganization of government along business lines." The grand jury of Sunflower County said much the same thing in its presentment of March, and later in the year Tann's biennial report hailed the superior wisdom of the governor and the legislature.[16]

A substantial deficit for the 1935–36 fiscal year made all the boasting seem ridiculous, but Conner and Tann were long gone by the time the bad news broke. On January 1, 1936, they had the satisfaction of witnessing the statutory death of the board of trustees. Conner turned the executive office over to his successor, Hugh White, boasting to the end that his administration had placed the penitentiary on a sound financial footing, and Tann resigned in triumph.[17]

The superintendency of Jim Thames produced more substantive results. Thames increased brick production and, capitalizing on Tann's renovations at Parchman's sawmill, led the carpenters and bricklayers to impressive levels of production. Between 1937 and 1941 the convicts produced 650,000 bricks and 1.35 million feet of rough lumber. Those materials were used to renovate cages and other buildings and to construct an enlarged cold storage plant, an ice plant, a bigger woodworking shop, a small canning factory, a mattress factory, and a new sewing room for the female convicts.[18]

Animal husbandry improved with the expansion of the corn and oat crops, milk and meat production mounted steadily, and by 1941 the dairy and beef herds had been restored to pre-Depression levels. Cotton production also increased. In March 1937 the grand jury noted that the superintendent's "scheme of soil fertilization and improvement as well as conservation is among the best . . . in Mississippi." There was a 25 percent increase in the 1936 cotton yield to 4,324 bales, and the 1937 crop yielded 5,863 bales. The next two years brought further increases, and the steady appreciation in cotton prices enabled the superintendent to turn very real profits. For the four-year period that began on July 1, 1936, and ended on June 30, 1940, the penitentiary reported net profits of almost $400,000. Thames boasted of his accomplishments a great deal, and with some justification; when he left Sunflower County in the spring of 1940, Parchman was reportedly "the only profit-making prison in the country."[19]

Following J. H. Reed's brief, unhappy superintendency, and a substantial deficit for fiscal year 1940, the energetic Lowery Love arrived at Parchman with a number of his friends from south Mississippi in tow. After reflecting on the rising value of cotton and the cost of provisions in the inflationary economy, the new superintendent launched a campaign to render the penitentiary entirely self-sufficient. He promptly reduced cotton acreage and increased acreage in food and feed crops in a like amount. Some months later Love released word that the penitentiary had produced enough meat, vegetables, and feed to supply itself during the winter of 1941. There would be a profit of about $325,000 for fiscal year 1941, he reckoned; returns would be better if only the penitentiary had access to more operating capital.[20]

Love's tactics produced grumbling among a number of Delta politicians, but nobody could doubt his success. The Jackson press described the superintendent's accomplishments as a model for the state's farmers. Governor Johnson hailed his superintendent as a magician. The 1941 legislature hesitated but eventually approved an increase of nearly 61 percent in the penitentiary's appropriation.[21]

The following year brought the two master strokes of Love's administration—the construction of a new canning factory and the establishment of a centralized dairy. During 1942 some one hundred thousand gallons of vegetables were canned. The dairy began operations with 275 cows, grew rapidly, and so impressed the governor that he represented it to the press as a major accomplishment of his administration.[22]

Superintendent Love's successes unfolded almost daily. Cotton sales for fiscal year 1941 totaled nearly $500,000, and the next year cotton and cotton seed sales catapulted to over $885,000.[23] Love continued to exploit the inflationary economy, capitalizing on rising cotton prices while simultaneously reducing the penitentiary's dependence on the private sector. But Love was doing considerably more than manipulating the wave of inflation; he was getting much greater production from much less acreage.

According to his press release of December 1943, 5,700 bales had been ginned, and a net profit of some $358,000 could be expected for fiscal year 1943. The superintendent, though, was far more pleased with other statistics. Between July and December 1943 the penitentiary had canned eighty thousand gallons of vegetables and stored large amounts of food and feed. The livestock inventory listed 3,800 hogs, 250 milk cows, 850 head of beef cattle, and 825 mules and horses. Meat consumption, the superintendent added, had been almost halved to twenty thousand pounds per month; the penitentiary had not been forced to purchase beef from the private sector in two years.[24]

In June 1944 the penitentiary recorded in excess of $586,000 in cotton sales, nearly $118,000 in cotton seed sales, and well over $595,000 through the sale of surplus food and feed crops, thereby concluding a three-year financial recovery that produced an impressive net profit of $1,123,223.58. More important for the future, however, were Superintendent Love's additions to the penitentiary's physical plant. By the summer of 1944 the "triple-threat back" had begun construction on a machine shop, a shoe shop, a modern slaughter house, a large implement shed, and an addition to the cold storage plant that would double its capacity.[25]

By 1944 Mike Conner's goals had been realized. Parchman was a plantation operating on a "practical business basis," pumping exorbitant revenues into the state treasury, and figuring ever more prominently in the distribution of sweets among those on the right side of politics.

A Fly in the Ointment

Vardaman was largely forgotten amid the clatter of construction that characterized Lowery Love's Parchman, but the penal philosophy of the "White Chief," if not the political motives underlying it, emerged anew during the late thirties and early forties. This time the notion that the state penitentiary should seek to redress the underlying causes of criminality emanated from the North, arising from realities peculiar to that section of the country.

The dire social manifestations of urbanization and of a maturing market economy manufactured convicts at an alarming rate in the industrialized Northern states, and the increasing strength of organized labor continued to erode productive work by convicts. Seeing nothing but evil in their explosive, overcrowded cellblock prisons, Yankee "liberals" soured on the old penology and began to seek solutions to a problem of serious and worsening dimensions. In time they came to see much virtue in the theories of social and behavioral scientists who argued that it no longer sufficed merely to deter crime through the certainty of punishment afforded by evenly applied custodial sentences.

The old guard fell back before the onslaught. The advent of probation and parole, which reflected a headlong retreat from the thought that had launched the penitentiary movement over a century earlier, altered the profiles of prison populations substantially. Those felons remaining behind bars came under the scrutiny of experts who attempted to "diagnose" and "treat" the factors that "determined" criminality. Earlier emphasis on incapacitation, deterrence, and retributive punishment slowly faded. The new rage, propelled by behaviorism and an undertow of New Testament Christianity, became convict rehabilitation.[26]

Such thought was generally confined to the wealthier states of the North until the thirties. But the leveling influence of the Great Depression and the pragmatic federalism born of it opened the floodgates. The Federal Bureau of Prisons, motivated by chronic overcrowding, undertook a massive campaign designed to reduce its convict population and to provide better organization and management in its penal institutions.

In 1930 the federal parole system was created. Four years later the federal penal system initiated a comprehensive program of inmate classification. "Scientific" researches were conducted on behalf of each commitment by classification committees. Personality traits, work skills, and educational needs were tabulated by the committees for the purpose of determining the type of penal environment to which convicts should be assigned. Options for commitment included the old cellblock prisons of the federal system, which were labeled "maximum security," and a number of recently acquired buildings and camps, which were designated as "medium security" and "minimum security" institutions.

These changes were advertised as "progressive" steps toward the individualization of convict treatment, and the example of the Federal Bureau of Prisons was embraced by many state penal systems, including those of Georgia, North Carolina, and Texas. Soon a rebirth of idealism, fed by the pervasive spirit of the New Deal, came to characterize an increasing number of penal administrators across the nation.[27]

Meanwhile, Mississippi was headed in the other direction, back to the "sound business principles" of early nineteenth-century penology, via the penitentiary act of 1934. In both 1929 and 1933 penologists surveying the penal systems of the separate states commented on the total absence of the "paraphernalia of reform" in Sunflower County, and the program of development pursued at the penitentiary during the following decade altogether eschewed the Yankee innovations.[28]

The status quo was defended zealously. On March, 3, 1934, the Jackson *Daily Clarion-Ledger* warned that it was "dangerous for society to fall into the error [of thinking] that science can, through a little remodeling, make model citizens of all hardened criminals." That opinion commanded almost universal support in Mississippi. Seldom did the Jackson press fail to defend the increasingly peculiar hallmarks of the state penal system.[29]

Yet new ideas began to infiltrate Mississippi during the late thirties, most notably among the emerging middle classes of Jackson and the relatively cosmopolitan coastal counties, and the leading features of Parchman's system became ever more contentious, notwithstanding the cloak of mystery that shrouded the penitentiary. Black Annie, of course, was an Achilles heel; despite official policy, the characters of the inmates and their keepers rendered abuses inevitable. In March 1937 the penitentiary received bad press when an escapee, apprehended in Virginia, fought extradition and charged that he and five other convicts had been given "80 lashes on their bare backs for failing to give alarm when another prisoner escaped." The allegations were fended off by Governor White and Superintendent Thames, but similar reports surfaced more frequently in future years.[30]

The trusty-shooter system was also an Achilles heel. The shooters had been controversial since Vardaman's day, but rarely had the iniquities of the now legendary "headhunters" been assessed with any specificity by journalists or legislative committees. During the late thirties, however, reports of a number of chilling scandals involving trusties began to appear in the state's newspapers.[31]

Superintendent Reed's difficulties at Parchman in 1940 also gave the public a rare glimpse of the dark side of penitentiary politics. A legislative probe resulted in a report that revealed ruinous factionalism among the staff, financial irregularities, and other failings that cast odium on the entire structure of penal administration.[32]

By the late thirties and early forties, a number of journalists, professional organizations, and influential public figures were endorsing new goals for the penitentiary. In September 1938 an editorial in the Jackson *Daily Clarion-Ledger* argued that "the cost of maintaining prisons is a great waste unless some of the money spent is devoted to the rehabilitation of the inmates." By 1940 the Mississippi Bar Association was coming around to a reformative concept of penology, and in early 1941 the Mississippi Conference on Social Work endorsed a resolution maintaining that convict rehabilitation was the sole purpose of legal incarceration.[33]

Such views found support among a handful of legislators. Their leader was Representative Howard A. McDonnell of Biloxi, a gutsy New Deal Democrat who was beginning a long career in the statehouse that would earn him a degree of respect among even Mississippi's conservative majority. McDonnell's attacks were radical. In 1941 he laid out his creed in the house of representatives:

> The sooner the public realizes that crime and criminals are the natural results of a given cause, rather than a vicious and willful surrendering to the evil, the sooner will safe and humane legislation be enacted to cope with the problem scientifically, rather than vindictively.[34]

McDonnell's language was far too extreme for the average Mississippian to stomach; somehow it seemed ridiculous to believe that the age-old concept of criminal guilt should be thrown over so unceremoniously. But the times were changing, and by the early forties the notion of reforming "fallen" men and women at the penitentiary, if not that of reforming society itself, had a nice ring to it.

A Crippled Chief Executive

The first statutory manifestations of changing criminological thought in Mississippi came in 1940, when the gallows were abolished in favor of the "more humane" electric chair, and in 1942, when the legislature at last provided for the establishment of an institution for delinquent and dependent black children at the old Oakley farm.[35] Those reforms had no great impact on the penitentiary, but they reflected important shifts in public opinion and portended of things to come.

The concept of parole was the first great cause of those who advocated reforms in the adult penal system. As early as 1936 a bill calling for a politically independent board of pardons and paroles drew surprising support. Similar measures were introduced and debated extensively during subsequent legislative sessions, and in late 1939 Superintendent Thames endorsed parole in his biennial report. In the spring of 1940 Howard McDonnell hosted the annual meeting of the Southeastern States Probation and Parole Conference in Biloxi. There, a number of eminent speakers joined the crusade for parole, and thereafter the reformers lobbied extensively among state legislators.[36]

Still, the idea of an independent parole board remained unpopular in the statehouse. The old suspension system had been a vital cog in the wheels of the penitentiary for many years; it continued to work perfectly well, said its defenders; and legislators, always suspicious of heady abstractions emanating from the North, saw no reason to fix something that was not broken. In the summer of 1940, however, Governor Johnson grew quite ill. He remained more or less incapacitated until his death in December 1943, and in the process demonstrated a number of liabilities within the state's system of penal administration.

From the first, Johnson had guarded his clemency powers very closely, exercising them only after careful deliberation, and thereby breaking with the long-standing precedent that gave Parchman's superintendents a virtual free hand in awarding pardons and suspended sentences to their charges. Superintendent Love was perfectly content with the governor's desire to assure fair play, and even applauded his vigilance; but illness progressively forced Johnson to cut back in clemency proceedings. For some reason Acting Governor Dennis Murphree refused to pick up the slack, and he was none too eager to allow Love greater latitude. The result was unfortunate: daily, the incentives that motivated senior trusties at the penitentiary were compromised.[37]

Swamped with applications for executive clemency and responding to Love's pleas for assistance, Johnson and Murphree supported the establishment of "some kind of investigating agency, parole board, or pardon board to assist the governor in determining which of these cases are meritorious." Such a plea opened the door to reform and sent McDonnell's hopes soaring, but the 1942 legislature stopped short of embracing parole, instead resurrecting the old board of pardons. That compromise equipped the chief executive with a three-member advisory body, yet Johnson's continuing sickness and Murphree's curious lethargy handcuffed the board, creating a large backlog of petitions and breeding truculence among trusties at Parchman.[38]

The situation had Love in a box by 1943. The inmates did not like the superintendent. His first principle of management was that a tired convict was a manageable convict, and he admittedly worked his charges to the limits of physical endurance. Love had also launched a campaign to stop all the whoring and gambling at the penitentiary, and that departure from traditional policy had alienated the gunmen still further. Now the trusties, especially the shooters, were upset by the interrupted flow of suspensions and pardons, and the superintendent was experiencing terrible problems. As early as February 1942 Love had told a reporter that the situation at Parchman was grave and that the attitude of the convicts had him "sitting on a keg of dynamite." By 1943 he was frantic.[39]

Love's anxiety was compounded by political problems. The strong-governor scheme of penal administration assured that Governor Johnson's extended illness created a vacuum in penitentiary politics. The vacuum appeared, moreover, at a time when Parchman was producing massive profits, and a number of legislators and Sunflower County politicians, all jockeying for a greater share of the spoils, posed a problem of great proportions. Superintendent Reed's difficulties in 1940 had been the first manifestation of the problem; "eaten alive" by Delta politics, he had resigned upon failing to get the support he thought he needed from the chief executive. Love had tougher skin than his predecessor, and was much better equipped for a knock-down Delta brawl; but he was forced to go toe-to-toe with political detractors from the day he arrived at Parchman, and by 1943 he was overmatched.

The superintendent's woes began with an issue of political geography. He, like Governor Johnson, was from south Mississippi. That fact in itself was offensive among the closed society of the Delta, and the Deltans were all the more outraged by the inevitable result of the political spoils system, which had fashioned a staff at the penitentiary composed of south Mississippi "rednecks" to the virtual exclusion of the local folk. Nor did Love fawn in the presence of the local aristocracy; he was an outsider, and he despised the Delta nabobs no less than they despised him.

The superintendent's crusade for self-sufficiency at the penitentiary, which cut out local contractors, also produced umbrage, as did his decision to sell huge amounts of surplus food crops and other produce on the open market. And Love simply refused to sanction the graft and other illegalities that kept the local boys happy; on one occasion a well-connected local bumpkin threatened "to git yo' Goddamn job" when the superintendent refused to give him his standard ration of beef.[40] All this, combined with the complaints of overworked, sex-starved, dice-robbed gunmen and the truculence of uninspired shooters, added up to trouble.

As early as 1941 the grand jury of Sunflower County, traditionally Parchman's stoutest defender, had reported evidence of excessive flagellation at Camp Five, and further criticism of Love's regime was forthcoming the next year. The district attorney, it seems, was on the warpath, and the 1943 presentment of the grand jury went so far as to assert that convict welfare was being sacrificed for money-making. The dying governor emphatically denied the charge, assuring everyone that he was "more concerned with the welfare of the inmates than with making a lot of money" at Parchman. Love, resisting the temptation to publicly lambast local politicians, also refuted the findings of the grand jury. Feeling a tightening noose, however, the superintendent broke for daylight, advocating the abolition of the trusty-shooter system, the hiring of civilian guards, and the construction of a maximum security unit. Love put his convicts to work on a special camp for "hardened criminals" almost immediately and later endorsed parole and a "very definite and well balanced Rehabilitation Program" as the only solution to his problems.[41]

The attack on the superintendent continued. Two Delta senators with enormous influence, Oscar Wolfe, Jr., and Fred Jones, expressed grave, if remarkably well-timed, concern about conditions at Parchman. They were supported by McDonnell and his small band of followers in the legislature, and in January 1944, to the surprise of nobody, the newly inaugurated governor, Tom Bailey, called for sweeping reforms at the penitentiary.

The Compromises of 1944

Bailey's inaugural address to the legislature expressed displeasure with the penitentiary, advocated new programs for the reformation of convicts, and endorsed a parole system patterned after "that adopted by the Federal government and most of the states of the Union." Shortly, a special legislative committee headed by Senator Wolfe and including Senator Jones departed for Parchman. Meanwhile, a bill calling for an independent parole board was introduced in the senate and assigned to the judiciary committee. While Bailey and the beleaguered Love gave the bill public support, William Keady of Greenville, chairman of the senate judiciary committee and a man destined for bigger things, guided the legislation through stormy sessions.[42]

The report of Senator Wolfe's committee, which included many tales of woe emanating from convicts, was released with great effect in the midst of the debates on parole. It was a remarkable document, one that criticized almost every facet of operations at the penitentiary without directly censuring Superintendent Love. The committee endorsed a politically independent parole board and in effect called for the repeal of Mike Conner's strong-governor scheme of penal administration. Discovering conflict between farm operations and convict welfare, the committee members advocated the creation of a powerful, independent board of commissioners and a division of the penitentiary's operations between two independent administrators—a superintendent or manager with expertise in agriculture and a warden educated and experienced in penology, both to report as equals to the board.[43]

On February 21, 1944, two days after the committee's report was made public, the senate voted 38-5 to abolish the board of pardons and to create a parole board patterned after the one employed by the federal penal system, and the lower house followed suit in mid-March. Legislation designed to implement the Wolfe committee's other recommendations ran into "well-organized and persistent opposition" on the floor of the senate. Fully fifty amendments were proposed before the senators could reach agreement, and then the lower house did not like the senate bill. While the two chambers maneuvered to reach accord, a Jackson newsman, evidently understanding the currents beneath all the political rhetoric, bemoaned the "farcical and hypocritical" behavior of the politicians and contended that the public demanded better care, recreation, religious instruction, and "rehabilitation" for the convicts.[44] At last a heavily compromised reform package limped through the legislature.

The statute added the chief executive, sitting in an ex officio capacity, to the three gubernatorial appointees who already constituted the board of commissioners and made the board sovereign over all purchases exceeding $100. The law also stipulated that the commissioners, not the governor, would employ the superintendent, the physician, the dentist, and the head bookkeeper. With the concurrence of the commissioners, the superintendent was to make all other appointments, including those who would occupy the new positions of farm manager, husbandman, and assistant chaplain.[45]

There was not much reform here. The strong-governor scheme remained intact, and now the chief executive was to attend the meetings of the board. Despite all the sound and fury about convict rehabilitation, the legislature mandated nothing resembling such a program, instead focusing on staff positions and money bills capable of enhancing agriculture. In the final analysis, only one change of any consequence was effected by the 1944 legislature. The creation of a parole board, positioned squarely between the governor and the superintendent, stripped the penitentiary's chief administrator of his traditional influence in the granting of early releases. That reform ended the superintendent's ability to control the size and makeup of the convict population, threatened the trusty system around which middle management and security turned, and compromised the most vital component of the penitentiary's internal incentive program.

Thus fell the second major facet of Governor Vardaman's old scheme. The 1934 legislature had opened the door to countless abuses by abolishing the independent board of trustees. Now, in 1944, political jockeying and legislative compromise penetrated the heart of Parchman's system. Nobody paid much attention to the minority report submitted by the five senators who voted against the parole bill. They represented the old suspension system as the axis around which the penitentiary's operations turned and predicted that parole would cause insurmountable problems. Senator McDonnell quite agreed. Raising the bloody stick, he represented the triumph of parole as the entering wedge of a penal reform movement that would eventually terminate the reign of "the old antiquated maxim of 'an eye for an eye and a tooth for a tooth'" and usher in the scientific methodology of the new "corrections."[46]

When the smoke cleared, Governor Bailey reflected on the problems of the penitentiary and took stock of his resources. His predecessors had laid the foundation for bigger and better agricultural operations. The 1944 legislature had bestowed on the penitentiary a biennial appropriation of some $1.2 million, as well as a hefty special appropriation earmarked for the renovation of the physical plant. Concluding that he had the resources to please everyone if only he could bring proper leadership to the penitentiary, Bailey stacked the board with his most trusted supporters, moved Superintendent Love to the state eleemosynary board, and appointed Marvin Wiggins to the superintendency.[47]

Governor Bailey displayed uncommon perspicacity in the appointment of Wiggins. The new superintendent was the consummate farmer, a man who brought with him the dirty fingernails of thirty years' experience in large-scale Delta agriculture. Wiggins also had considerable powers of judgment and good business sense, and he was adept at surrounding himself with competent underlings. He was not afraid to delegate responsibilities to his staff, he fought hard for their welfare, and he got production from them.[48]

He got production from the convicts as well. In managing them, the superintendent was a hard man but, by most accounts, a fair one. Wiggins understood convicts, convicts understood Wiggins. All were agreed that convicts were convicts and that Wiggins was boss.[49]

There was something unsettling about the superintendent. Like most Mississippians of his generation, he had known hard times, and hard times had left a mark. He could smile, jaw, and slap backs with the best of the Delta boys, but beneath it all, one sensed, was the temperament of a rattlesnake. Neutralizing the serpent, in the best of Southern tradition, was wife Pauline, a sweet, caring woman whose presence softened the superintendent. Pauline, however, knew her place; the word in Jackson was that a prudent man would keep out of Marvin's way.[50]

Whenever Wiggins's powers of intimidation failed him, he could turn for support to the ruling oligarchy of the Mississippi Delta, in whose company he had moved for years. Fred Jones was his ally, as was Oscar Wolfe, Jr. Allied with his native shrewdness and years of experience in Magnolia politics, those connections made the superintendent an extraordinarily gifted political navigator. Wiggins would carry Parchman to what is remembered as its "golden age," all the while attempting to reconcile the old and the new at the penitentiary. And with detractors biting at his heels every step of the way, he would hold the line until advancing years and the politics of civil rights at last banished him to the obscurity of retirement.

Governor Bailey's "Reformed" Penitentiary

Bailey gave Wiggins a charge much like that which Vardaman had given Superintendent Neyland some forty years earlier—to make the penitentiary both a money-maker and a vehicle for the social improvement of convicts. Wiggins accepted the challenge. He appointed his old friend, C. E. Breazeale, to the new position of farm manager and exploited Breazeale's considerable talents to develop a comprehensive scheme for the enhancement of agriculture. Meanwhile, Wiggins made plans to attend the annual meeting of the American Prison Association in New York City, and in the autumn of 1944 the superintendent probably squirmed uncomfortably as he was introduced to the litany of the new "corrections" in the Big Apple.[51] Shortly after his return, the popular Methodist minister A. R. Beasley arrived at Parchman and, in the capacity of chaplain, began to formulate plans for a "rehabilitation program" with the assistance of the new assistant chaplain, George H. Skutt.

Wiggins profited from the strength of Mississippi's postwar economy. The cotton market was strong, the state treasurer raked in huge tax revenues, and the future looked rosy. Often in the company of the governor, and always with his political cronies from the Delta in tow, the superintendent made the rounds in Jackson, lobbying in his quiet, almost sinister manner, and headed back to Sunflower County with more than his share.[52]

He exploited it to the fullest. The dust of construction always hovered over Wiggins's penitentiary, but it was never more noticeable than during his early years. A new gin, farm buildings, new staff cottages, new cages, a slaughterhouse, a lard plant, a machine shop, a shoe shop, and an addition to the cold storage plant appeared very quickly. New wells began to cough up more of the precious, rust-colored water, and brick water towers soon rose over the various camps. The superintendent's emphasis on the production of food and feed crops and his success in improving the beef, swine, and dairy herds made the penitentiary a horn of plenty. Parchman's dairy herd, in fact, became the talk of the Delta, Wiggins's pride and joy, but improvements at the canning plant, which enabled the penitentiary to ship large consignments of canned goods to other state institutions, towered among his earliest political triumphs.[53]

Wiggins also laid the foundation for greater cotton production. Supported by experts on loan from the Cooperative Extension Service of Mississippi State College, he slowly introduced scientific techniques of farming. Legislators, seemingly forgetting the primary function of a penal farm, helped the superintendent displace convict laborers with tractors and combines. After wrangling proper equipment from his friends in Jackson, Wiggins assaulted the tangled swamps flanking Black Bayou, the key to Parchman's drainage system, and upgraded the penitentiary's sadly deficient twenty-mile road net.[54]

Simultaneously, the superintendent slowly implemented the "paraphernalia of reform." He did it for two reasons, the first of which was political. The state's penal reformers, with whom Governor Bailey sympathized more or less, kept a close eye on the penitentiary after Wiggins's arrival and continued the attack under the banner of Howard McDonnell, now a member of the state senate. McDonnell headed the Mississippi Association of Crime and Delinquency, an organization boasting an impressive roster of members, principally judges, defense attorneys, journalists, and criminal and juvenile justice practitioners. Their primary goal was to root out abuses in the state's systems of juvenile and criminal justice and to encourage reforms.

The activities of the association were anchored on specially appointed committees chaired by eminent personages. The various committees visited institutions, collected evidence supporting a preconceived hypothesis, prepared printed reports, and distributed them widely on the eves of legislative sessions. During Wiggins's early years the association conducted studies of the abuses inherent in "the patronage system of the state penitentiary appointments," the omissions of the penal system in convict rehabilitation, and the need for a system of adult probation. Meanwhile, McDonnell railed against capital punishment in the senate and drew surprising support in an attempt to outlaw Black Annie.[55]

Wiggins did not like the criticism and despised the snooping committees that popped up at Parchman, but the mounting strength of McDonnell and his collaborators made him a model of accommodation. He frankly admitted the penitentiary's shortcomings, pleaded for patience, and encouraged the reformers to lobby legislators for funds and staff positions commensurate with their goals.[56]

Wiggins's sympathy with the "paraphernalia of reform" was also inspired by a lucid perception of the effects of the recently enacted parole statute. He worried a great deal about the eventual effect of parole on the convict profile generally, and on his trusty system in particular. The only solution, he felt, was to bolster the penitentiary's system of internal incentives and to implement programs capable of improving the morale of convicts.[57]

The superintendent took the offensive almost immediately. In late 1944 Chaplain Beasley initiated a modest elementary education program in the three R's for a handful of convicts, and an expanded version of the program, formulated with the assistance of the state department of education, was put into effect on September 26, 1946.

It was designed to provide adult elementary education to the roughly nine hundred convicts who had less than a fourth-grade education. Classes were taught by literate convicts; the chaplain and his assistant provided supervision; consultants included the superintendents of two local school districts.[58]

One-hour classes were offered during the lunch break three times each week, and supervised study periods were held every evening after the convicts returned from the fields. By most accounts the first pupils were enthusiastic, and the "separate but equal" racial division of the program produced interesting comparisons. An unidentified convict-teacher spoke of the "enthusiasm and quickness" with which his Caucasian pupils learned; by January 1947 one class was clamoring for a course in algebra. A group of black gunmen learned basic mathematics by way of very unique methodology. The teacher, life-term preacher Marion Enochs, taught his students to chant the multiplication tables in the fashion of black spirituals. A visiting journalist reported:

> Negroes in prison stripes chanting the multiplication tables in the rhythm of their beloved spirituals heralds a new policy trend. . . . "Five times five is twenty-five, five times six is thirty, five times seven is thirty-five and five times eight is forty," they sing-song as they tend to their fields under the sole guard of "trusties."[59]

It was indeed a new policy trend, a stunning departure from the traditional racial parameters of state penal policy. Wiggins, however, supported the classes as boosters of morale, and an amused reporter observed that the prisoners "read with obvious pride in their new ability to pronounce the printed words." A black inmate ridiculed that view of the education program, remembering instead that none of his peers "gave a damn about education" but participated "because we had to and because we wanted out of the joint." Whatever the case, by June 30, 1947, a reported six hundred convicts had enrolled in the program, and it was said that over half of them had learned to read and write.[60]

Chaplain Beasley also implemented a comprehensive religious program. In 1945 the board of commissioners authorized religious services in the camp dining halls, approved the purchase of a number of pianos, and mandated that all convicts attend Sunday morning services. Thereby blessed with a captive flock, and advising the parole board on all petitions, Beasley held the cards necessary for success.

Soon a multitude of preachers representing various denominations descended on Parchman. Often they delivered sermons that inspired the black convicts to the point of either real or calculated delirium. The chaplain was impressed; the camp sergeants were not. The inmates, according to witnesses, enjoyed the singing, pleased the chaplain with frequent "amens," and hoped for parole.[61]

In January 1946 Beasley organized "The Inmates' Gospel Service of Camp 6," a group of evangelical convicts bound together by a written constitution. The pious members of the group, who numbered fifty-three by August, held spirited services on Sunday mornings. A visitor found the spectacle amusing. "There is no church or chapel and guards stand by with guns, but the spirit of the service is good," he wrote. "The leader, a prisoner, is an ordained Baptist minister, and a rather forceful, spirited preacher, oddly enough."

In May 1946 Beasley convinced Dr. D. A. McCall, the executive secretary of the board of the Mississippi Baptist Convention, to stage a revival at Parchman. McCall stayed a week, preaching fire and brimstone whenever Wiggins could spare a detachment of field hands, and in the end seven convicts claimed to be converted. Several months later Dr. McCall was authorized by Jackson's Calvary Baptist Church to return to Parchman and baptize the seven convicts along with one more who had come to see the light since the departure of the evangelist. The eight men, dressed in their ring-arounds, waded into a small stock pond and were dunked in its muddy waters under the watchful eyes of Winchester-brandishing trusty-shooters.[62]

By June 1947 Chaplain Beasley had established Sunday schools at every camp, conducted 949 services attended by a total of 37,622 convicts and visitors, and accumulated mountains of religious literature. "If part of our job is to rehabilitate the prisoners for a return to the outside world, it seems to me we ought to try to educate them," Beasley told a reporter. Such talk made for good press, but there is reason to believe that not all the inmates profited. "C'mon man, you don't really believe that any of us read that Jesus shit?" asked a beneficiary of Beasley's reading program.[63]

If the inmates were unimpressed by the advent of educational and religious programming at Parchman, they were surely pleased with the many indulgences held out by Wiggins. In December 1944 the superintendent initiated a program of Christmas furloughs that allowed well-behaved convicts to leave the penitentiary for a period of ten days. After March 1946 the immediate family members of convicts were allowed to visit every Sunday for two hours, and for the entire afternoon every third Sunday, while other relatives and friends could visit once every six months. In 1947 penal administrators purchased a portable projector and began showing motion pictures at each camp twice monthly. Wiggins also implemented a system that allowed convicts to bypass their sergeants and to "convey suggestions and express grievances [directly] to the prison administration."[64]

The Unholy "Correctional" Alliance

Despite these innovations, Wiggins's worst fears were realized between 1945 and 1948: his penitentiary was progressively undermined by the advent of parole. After a number of early problems, the parole board began to process applications very rapidly in 1946, and the board's success in identifying and paroling the best of the penitentiary's long-term convicts was confirmed in 1947, when Mississippi achieved the lowest parole revocation rate in the thirteen-state Southeastern States Probation and Parole Conference.[65]

The effects of parole began to be felt at the penitentiary in early 1946, when a large group of trusty-artisans and shooters bid adieu at Front Camp. Their departure signaled the first stage of the erosion of middle management and security at Parchman. In March a troubled board of commissioners compounded the penitentiary's problems by adopting policies upgrading the qualifications for trusty status and restricting the mobility of all trusties.[66]

By early 1947 the ranks of Wiggins's veteran shooters and trusty-artisans were decimated, management and security were compromised, and the demise of the penitentiary's well-oiled scheme of behavioral reinforcement was breeding increasing truculence among the gunmen. The camp sergeants fell back on their last line of defense, employing Black Annie on the recalcitrants, but some of them apparently went too far, for a widely reported scandal alleging excessive flagellation erupted in May. Wiggins moved decisively to mend his fences, and a period of relative tranquility ensued. In December, though, trusty Edmund Perry ran amok, stabbed the wife of a night-shooter, fatally wounded a camp sergeant, and then committed suicide.[67]

The widening cracks in the foundations of Parchman's system suggested that perhaps the state had been a little hasty in abandoning the old suspension system, which after all had been the fulcrum of the penitentiary's scheme of convict management. But there was also the argument, propounded by Senator McDonnell and his noisy followers, that the parole statute had been merely the first act of the piece, and that difficulties would continue so long as the state operated a labor-intensive cotton plantation with little or no regard for the ideals of modern "corrections."

McDonnell's notion of "corrections" translated into more staff positions and larger appropriations for the penitentiary. That, if not his medical model for Parchman, found support among Delta politicians who, as in 1944, sensed an opportunity to increase the flow of money to their section of the state. For his part, Wiggins thought McDonnell's views hilarious, and doubled up with laughter at the thought of Negro gunmen being diagnosed and treated by a battery of psychiatrists; but he, too, sensed opportunity and was willing enough to play along.[68]

The unholy alliance was promoted by gubernatorial politics. Governor Bailey's death in November 1946 had elevated his lieutenant-governor, Fielding L. Wright, to the office of chief executive. An ambitious man who coveted the governorship in the upcoming election, Wright sorely needed to broaden his political base within the state. By all appearances he broadened it, in part at least, by supporting far-reaching changes at the penitentiary. At all events, Wright's successful gubernatorial campaign attracted support among key Delta politicians, and once elected he emerged as an ardent supporter of a sweeping penal reform package that, while pleasing McDonnell and his "corrections" lobby, delivered a huge increase in jobs and money to Sunflower County.[69]

A great deal of behind-the-scenes jockeying concerning the terms of a comprehensive penal reform package transpired during the early months of the 1948 legislative session, but the magnitude of the measure promoted by the governor and the senate leadership kept the issue in doubt until the early spring. In March, however, the penitentiary's most celebrated inmate, the charming murderer Kennie Wagner, walked out of Parchman's front gate with a .45-caliber machine gun and successfully evaded the bloodhounds he had trained as trusty-dog-handler.

"The notorious Kennie Wagner 'walk-away' from the Mississippi penitentiary," noted an editorialist, "could not have been timed better to increase legislative support of pending bills instituting reforms in prison administration." So it would appear. One legislator remarked that the parole board allowed "the cream of the crop" to leave the penitentiary. Another observed that the parole system had spread the trusty-shooter system "as thinly as warm butter may be spread on a crisp cracker." In bed with the reformers, Wiggins stoked the fire, stressing that he and his staff were incapable of combating the effects of parole and lobbying successfully for a legislative package of unprecedented scope.[70]

The penitentiary act of 1948 authorized the employment of fifty civilian guards, thereby increasing the Sunflower County tax base by some $120,000 per annum, pleasing those who sought to terminate the trusty-shooter system, enhancing the governor's patronage, and adding to the size of Wiggins's staff. The same interests were promoted by provisions that added an educational director, a vocational director, a classification officer, and a classification records clerk to Wiggins's stable and granted across-the-board salary increases to all existing employees.

The statute also reflected a number of trade-offs. One of them, a token concession to be sure, authorized the superintendent to spend up to $3,000 annually on psychiatric treatment for convicts. Another, which repealed a plum bestowed on local government by the penitentiary act of 1934, banned convict labor on the roads of Sunflower and Quitman counties. Yet another authorized an almost predictable land deal—the sale of half of Lambert's acreage—but nobody complained about the curious decision to unload the same floodplain that Mike Conner's cronies had hyped as an agricultural bonanza only fourteen years earlier. The central thrust of the penitentiary act of 1948, though, was a new commitment to remunerative plantation agriculture, and the delivery of immense resources to Wiggins's farm manager.[71]

The thinking of the reformers was explained by McDonnell's surly Delta ally, Senator Fred Jones who, not incidentally, represented Sunflower County. There was a pressing need to supplement the convict constabulary with civilian guards, he pointed out. Across-the-board salary increases would attract "higher-type" employees, he theorized optimistically, ignoring the political context of all penitentiary appointments. And since the absence of a modern classification system was "one of the worst evils of our present penal system," the addition of classification specialists would solve a maze of problems, allowing the penitentiary to segregate convicts "according to criminal tendencies."

Jones also found great wisdom in mitigating the "back-breaking" labor required of convicts; it "degraded" and made them despair, he observed sympathetically. So it was time to withdraw at least half the gunmen from the fields, to replace them with machines, and to embrace the scientific methods of modern agriculture. Hence Wiggins would be provided with a professional agronomist, bigger and better machinery, the assistance of publicly paid technicians, and seed money to finance major farm improvements.

All this was consistent with not only the principles of business, but also with those of modern correctional administration, Jones emphasized. For increased mechanization and the advent of scientific farming techniques would allow Mississippi to pursue the correctional philosophy of the Federal Bureau of Prisons. The penitentiary would establish industries, employ the displaced gunmen within them, produce goods that could be distributed among public institutions via the state-use system, and thereby provide vocational training for convicts while also promoting the public interest. Thus came the justification for a vocational director.

Vocational training, however, could not possibly occupy all the time of the convicts if intensive human labor were to be reduced by 50 percent. Hence the need for an educational director; education, Senator Jones explained, was the very essence of convict rehabilitation. All the philosophy confused Superintendent Wiggins, but the politics of the thing were impeccable, and he thought he could pull it off so long as the politicians kept the money coming. The key to everything, he felt, was the mechanization of farm operations.[72]

Parchman at High Tide

The penitentiary act of 1948 came at the outset of Governor Wright's own term of office. Perhaps no chief executive in state history has enjoyed a more tranquil administration. Wright became the darling of Mississippians when the Southern Democrats, incensed by the civil rights platform of Harry Truman and the national Democratic party, forged the Dixiecrat party and nominated him as Strom Thurman's running mate in the presidential election. The failure of the Dixiecrats had no apparent effect on the governor's statewide popularity. After all, Germany, Japan, and Italy lay in ruins, and in Mississippi, as elsewhere in the country, peace had brought prosperity.

The cotton market, yet to feel the pinch of the new synthetic fibers, boomed. State tax revenues, still dependent on the produce of planters, soared. Enjoying a happy relationship with legislative leaders, Governor Wright smiled a great deal, said all the right things, and appeared to get along with everyone. In this climate, Marvin Wiggins carried Parchman to its zenith.

The superintendent's chums in the legislature made it all possible. In the smoky antechambers of the statehouse they had bought Wiggins's support for the recently enacted penitentiary bill with a number of promises. The provisions of the statute that banned convict labor on the roads of Sunflower and Quitman counties not only pleased McDonnell, but also ended countless problems with local politicians. The sale of roughly half of Lambert's flooded acreage removed an albatross from Wiggins's back.[73]

The politicians had also promised heftier appropriations. Now they delivered. During fiscal year 1948 Parchman got a new administration building, a new hospital, a new and "splendidly equipped" canning plant, forty new cottages for employees, and a number of new barns. The following biennium brought the construction of a tuberculosis unit, a new steam laundry replacing "the old wash-tub method," a new dairy, and a "pure dairy barn" to house Wiggins's prized herd.[74]

During fiscal year 1947 the penitentiary produced six hundred thousand pounds of beef and pork, and soon a poultry unit was added. D. L. Edson, the agronomist Wiggins hired in 1948, immediately undertook soil surveys in league with experts from the Mississippi Cooperative Extension Service. Next year, after Wiggins's dragline had transformed Black Bayou's tangled, snake-infested waters into a placid irrigation canal, Edson's scheme of land use enabled the farm manager to exploit the new drainage patterns and all available farm machinery. By June 1951 the penitentiary boasted a fleet of thirty-four all-purpose tractors, more on order, and a modern machine shop to maintain them.[75]

Soon Parchman's fields flowered as never before. Food crop production was prodigious, easily doubling the needs of the penitentiary. By July 1949 the new canning plant was producing between three thousand and five thousand gallons of canned goods daily. Production increased later in the year when an artesian well was dug, and the penitentiary's shipments of canned goods to other state institutions reached new heights.[76] Meanwhile, truck after truck conveyed raw cotton to Front Camp. The gin hummed, buyers gathered around the administration building, and stuffed boxcars swayed as they lumbered toward the processing plants of Memphis, New Orleans, and the Mississippi Delta.

The convicts, along with the state treasury, profited from the penitentiary's mounting prosperity. In February 1944, shortly before Wiggins arrived at Parchman, a number of convicts had complained about a daily ration that consisted of three-tenths of an ounce of coffee, nine-tenths of an ounce of sugar, over one and one-half ounces of lard, a bountiful serving of vegetables, and 3.2 ounces of meat.[77] Compared to the diets of most free Mississippians, that ration was hardly mean, but the penitentiary's culinary arrangements improved dramatically after Wiggins took the helm.

As early as April 1945 every convict received a daily ration of a quart of milk and an ounce of butter, and afterward a much wider variety of dairy products appeared on the menu. By the summer of 1949 convicts were being allocated all the fruit and vegetables they wanted, and later in the year the meat ration was increased to a half-pound daily. The meals enjoyed by the inmates on holidays, especially on Christmas Day, were nothing short of feasts, and after 1948 a professional dietician coordinated all culinary arrangements at Parchman.[78]

Ever-improving food services were complemented by ever-improving health care. The new hospital was said to be "commodious; well planned and a credit to the State." The superintendent experienced difficulty in hiring and retaining competent medical personnel, but between 1948 and 1952, when the inmate population averaged about two thousand, only a reported ten or so convicts died each year. In January 1951 the chaplain contended that "the physical care provided for inmates at Parchman equals, if indeed it does not exceed, that to which the average Mississippian has access."[79]

The improvement of the physical plant also accrued to the advantage of the convicts. One member of Wiggins's staff insisted that the brick cages were infinitely superior to those housing enlisted personnel in the United States armed forces. Furthermore, if the coming of parole diminished the incentives inherent in trusty status, working conditions in the penitentiary's many new shops partially compensated. Trusty-artisans competed for the more favorable assignments—the shoe shop, the dairy camp, and the new steam laundry.[80]

Wiggins also sought to bolster the penitentiary's sagging system of internal incentives by holding out a considerable number of indulgences to the convicts. The Christmas furlough program begun in 1944 is a notable example. By January 1951 more than two thousand convicts had spent a part of the Christmas season in the company of their families, with only twelve failing to abide by the rules.[81]

Journalism made its debut in 1949 when a shoddy, mimeographed inmate publication dubbed *Inside World* was distributed among the camps. The quality of the little magazine improved with the purchase of an electric mimeograph machine in 1950, and in its second year of operation *Inside World* received awards from the National Association of the Penal Press for being the most improved prison newspaper and for having the best inside coverage.[82]

Organized musical activities got underway about the same time. In early 1951 Chaplain S. B. Harrington procured musical instruments, opened a "music school," and formed a fifteen-piece orchestra. The blacks tended to hang back, preferring instead their own sessions in and near their cages.[83] But Harrington's program started organized music at Parchman; the black musicians would come around later.

Following the terms of the agreement he struck with legislative leaders in 1948, Wiggins withdrew increasing numbers of gunmen from the fields and engaged them in "rehabilitation programs" as more and more farm machinery arrived. In May 1948 one W. R. Burrus of Greenwood, a veteran rehabilitation counselor for the state department of education, was appointed educational director. His school graduated 308 convicts on March 31, and Burrus reported that the average convict-student had advanced from a first-grade to a fifth-grade level during the term.[84]

The energetic R. L. Patterson, who replaced Burrus as educational director in the summer of 1950, carried Parchman's education program to new heights in a very short period of time. During biennium 1949–51 the penitentiary maintained elementary schools in eighteen camps employing 112 convict teachers and serving 1,142 convict-students. Of those, only eighty-one failed to complete their classes, and seventy-eight pupils earned fourth-grade certificates. In addition, Patterson organized a special advanced class providing instruction through the twelfth grade for twenty-six convicts and a typing class utilizing reconditioned typewriters obtained from the Veterans Administration. Supported by the chaplain's distribution of some forty thousand pieces of literature between 1949 and 1951, the adult education program had progressed to a point far beyond the most optimistic projections of its founders by the summer of 1952.[85]

The classification of convicts "by criminal tendencies" began in July 1948, when W. D. Durrett was appointed classification officer. Durrett replaced Parchman's "outmoded method of registrar's records" with what he described as "a modern and adequate system." By the summer of 1949 two camps had been designated for inmates who were physically or mentally incapable of regular duties—Camp Four for white men and the old hospital for black men. Collaboration between the classification officer and the educational director had led to reported improvement in the penitentiary's "rehabilitation program" by the summer of 1951. Work assignments and placement in the educational program were being determined by a block of tests, and ongoing study was resulting in a considerable number of reassignments.[86]

Durrett described the classification system as "a model of efficient organization," but the camp sergeants were displeased. "Wiggins let the convicts run the farm," remembered one malcontent. "I suppose he had to please McDonnell and the other shysters in the legislature, but he sho' did it at our expense. Any con who could convince the chaplain he had found religion, or convince that damned Durrett he was too good for nigger work, got re-classified." A black convict agreed. "Sure," he recalled, "we did whatever it took to get outta dem cotton fields. Wouldn't you?"[87]

Less dependent on field hands due to farm mechanization, Wiggins issued a new policy in 1951 allowing two-hour lunch breaks Monday through Friday and terminating all labor at noon on Saturdays. To occupy the increasingly idle convicts, the superintendent established an intercamp basketball program and allocated state monies for the purchase of sports equipment.[88]

Perhaps the superintendent's crusade to bolster convict morale explains the penitentiary's ever-diminishing escape rate; certainly that was the official explanation. Or perhaps would-be escapees were deterred by Wiggins's legendary bloodhounds. Whatever the case, attempted escapes, which had averaged slightly more than seventy-three annually during Love's superintendency, decreased to thirty-six during Wiggins's first year and averaged fewer than sixteen per annum between 1948 and 1952.[89]

All this pleased the politicians. In February 1952 Howard McDonnell told a reporter that no superintendent had "made more physical improvements and other progress" than Wiggins. Governor Hugh White, who wisely decided to retain the superintendent during his second term as chief executive, told reporters several months later that Wiggins was "one of the most valuable men who ever worked for the state."[90]

By 1952 Parchman was at high tide, a curious admixture of remunerative farming and the forms of convict rehabilitation. But Wiggins saw problems beneath the surface. Parole continued to steal the best of his long-timers, to erode middle management and security. Recently, unsmiling agents of the Federal Bureau of Investigation had begun to poke around the black camps looking into allegations of what they called "civil rights violations," and the black gunmen seemed restless. Trouble was also brewing in the white camps. The penitentiary was now admitting more Caucasian felons than ever before, and most of them were of a new breed—"lazy, smart-assed city boys who respected nothin' or nobody." How long, the aging superintendent wondered, could he and his sergeants continue to hold the line?[91]

6

The Great Tactical Offensive

On January 16, 1952, W. B. Alexander, chairman of the senate penitentiary committee, delivered a stinging denunciation of the state penal system on the floor of the senate. Alexander was a native of Cleveland, a little town just down the road from Parchman. He did not get along with Superintendent Wiggins, and rumor held that his reforming zeal was born of rancor. But Alexander's hostile view of the penitentiary, while perhaps conditioned by personal feelings and the vicissitudes of Delta politics, was inspired primarily by the gathering storm clouds of the national civil rights movement.[1]

Difficulties had begun to unfold in 1950. First there had been serious problems with the state of California in the extradition of an escaped black convict. Then several reports of racial iniquity at the penitentiary had popped up, and the appearance of FBI agents at Parchman had sparked unsettling speculation. Late in the year a terrible indictment of the penitentiary written by former Jackson newsman Craddock Goins had appeared in *True Detective* magazine.[2]

All this had occasioned outrage among most white Mississippians, but Alexander, an experienced attorney, perceived a dangerous undertow at Parchman, a broadening of the traditional scope of penitentiary politics. The federal agents who snooped around the black camps, the senator warned privately, were the advance elements of an army of conquest, one threatening the entire superstructure of Mississippi's institutionalized racial caste system. Bill Alexander was among the first of a new breed of state politician, a breed of tactical reformers who saw the writing on the wall and advocated remedial measures. One conservative, recalling those native sons who had cooperated with the hated Republicans during the Reconstruction era, labeled Alexander and those of his ilk "scalawags."[3]

The Old Versus the New

Alexander emerged as an outspoken critic of the penitentiary during the 1952 legislative session. Referring repeatedly to the results of his recently concluded survey of 250 "correctional experts" across the nation, he belittled the professional qualifications of Wiggins and his staff and wanted to clip the superintendent's wings through the creation of a Jackson-based department of corrections. Alexander also advocated an adult probation system, pointing out that Mississippi was one of only three states without this "progressive correctional tool," and he wanted rehabilitation programs to supplant farming at the penitentiary. With "better corrective measures," he insisted, "we could greatly cut down on repeaters, and the savings would be equal or better [than] the financial gains of the state by the forced labor system."[4]

Although he appreciated the many triumphs of Wiggins's administration, Howard McDonnell found much virtue in Alexander's view of affairs. In late February the two senators sponsored a bill calling for 25 percent of the penitentiary's annual profits to be set aside for "the correction, welfare, rehabilitation, recreation and health of the inmates including vocational training." The measure stipulated further that 10 percent of annual profits would go to the development of a religious program, and that the remaining 65 percent would be earmarked for construction and mechanization.[5]

The revolutionary bill failed, but the reformers certainly had their say, and their attacks went to the very core of existing policy. The "present set-up gave nothing to the convict who did not come from a farming area," McDonnell argued, and such a convict was "not a bit better able to make an honest living when he gets out of the penitentiary [than] he was before his conviction and incarceration." It was "a well established fact among penologists that no correctional institution should operate for profit."[6]

Alexander and McDonnell grounded their attack on the most vulnerable aspects of Parchman's system. Exploiting the debilitating effects of parole on middle management and security, they reopened the debate on the trusty-shooters. There had been "suspicions of certain unnecessary shootings" for several years, Alexander contended, and in the spring and early summer he protested vehemently when several prisoners crossed the gun line and fell prey to Wiggins's shooters.[7]

The reformers were even more adamant in their attacks on Black Annie. Alexander printed a booklet decrying the evils of the lash, distributed it among legislators and journalists, and actually carried one of the sergeant's straps into the senate chambers, waving it with great effect in the faces of his detractors. He continued to hit hard throughout the 1952 legislative session, all the while utilizing the considerable skills he had acquired in a successful career as a trial lawyer. On one occasion he asked: "If a man were spread-eagle, stripped and placed stomach down on the cold concrete floor, with four other prisoners holding him fast as the lash was applied, slave-fashion, and Jesus walked in, do you think he would approve?"[8]

The senator and his supporters offered alternatives. The strap and the trusty-shooters would be unnecessary, they stressed, if only a maximum security unit could be made available to penal administrators. "Progressive correctional experts" everywhere, said Alexander, favored solitary confinement over corporal punishment.[9]

The reformers gained ground during 1952. The upper house of the legislature was especially sympathetic. There, the concept of an adult probation system was popular, and a bill calling for the abolition of corporal punishment passed the senate by an astonishing 30-6 vote, only to be killed by the house penitentiary committee.[10]

The notion of reforming the penitentiary also attracted powerful support outside the legislature. The Mississippi Bar Association was brought around to liberal views, and several influential journalists joined the attack. Oliver Emmerich, editor of the McComb *Enterprise-Journal* and an active member of the Mississippi Association of Crime and Delinquency, came to regard Parchman as an eleemosynary institution. Hodding Carter, the Pulitzer Prize-winning owner of the Greenville *Delta Democrat-Times*, began to train his guns on the penitentiary. Even Jackson's powerful Hederman press moved to the left.

Marvin Wiggins observed these developments with consternation. The prospect of having the penitentiary administered from Jackson by a bureau within state government was unthinkable. There were already too many political chefs in the penitentiary's kitchen; the addition of a group of Jackson bureaucrats would be downright intolerable. A probation system was no less threatening. Parole was stealing the best of the penitentiary's long-timers; probation promised to remove the best of the short-timers, and Wiggins was haunted by the prospect. Nor could the superintendent think about the demise of his trusty-shooters or the abolition of the strap without despair. The new civilian guards were woefully incompetent, the shooters alone held the lid on the penitentiary, and Black Annie was his sergeants' sole means of maintaining order in the camps. The advertised panacea of a maximum security unit, he remarked privately, sounded like something a "shyster lawyer" would propose.[11]

Since becoming superintendent in 1944, Wiggins had played politics behind closed doors, prudently avoiding public combat with legislators who attacked his penitentiary. Now, however, it was becoming increasingly clear that his detractors were scoring points, so in early February he publicly refuted Alexander. Well might solitary confinement suit the failed cellblock prisons of the North, but it was anathema to the successful, labor-intensive Mississippi penitentiary, he told a journalist. It allowed inmates to malinger, thereby threatening the very existence of penal farming. Besides, placing a human being in a dark hole was inhumane, notwithstanding the notions of "progressive" wardens in other parts of the country. The convicts themselves preferred flagellation, he asserted.[12]

The superintendent "called in all his political debts and played all his political chips" in contesting the proposed reforms. Alexander and McDonnell were opposed stoutly in the legislature, Wiggins's staff supported their boss, and "numerous prisoners" interviewed by lawmakers endorsed the superintendent's negative view of solitary confinement. Alexander and his supporters were beaten back in the state house, but the reformers would not go away. Wiggins was troubled by the hostile attitude of the senate and fearful that his strength in the lower house would erode due to a strong legislative initiative to build a maximum security unit at Parchman capable of housing a gas chamber.[13]

All the while, the superintendent pondered the worsening business affairs of the penitentiary. Inflation had been rampant since the war; reforms had necessitated the purchase of much expensive equipment and the hiring of many new employees; annual operating expenses had increased from $374,288 in fiscal year 1942–43 to $1,005,377 in fiscal year 1952–53.[14] Wiggins was painfully aware that the financial health of the penitentiary demanded ever-increasing cash crop production and the maintenance of high cotton prices. Heretofore fortune had smiled on the superintendent; but now the introduction of synthetic fibers was beginning to be felt in the cotton market, and in

May a terrible drought struck the Delta. By the early summer of 1952 Wiggins could see that his sparkling record of production was in dire jeopardy.

The superintendent grew depressed. He was having trouble enough coping with the crippling effects of earlier reforms. Now it seemed clear that eventually the legislature would "put the cart before the horse." Governor White was sympathetic but none too eager to do battle with the senate, so on August 23, 1952, Wiggins abruptly resigned the superintendency. The governor encouraged reconsideration and apparently made a number of promises. Reluctantly, the superintendent agreed to stay on.[15]

The Politics of Appeasement

Wiggins was besieged on all fronts in the months that followed. The long drought of 1952 was among the worst in Mississippi history. Black Bayou ran "flat dry," the penitentiary's wells coughed up diminishing amounts of the precious water, and every attempt to irrigate the vast acreage proved desultory. Through it all, the farm manager slept on his feet, attempting to save what he could, while old Wiggins, bareheaded, perspiring profusely, and with sleeves rolled above the elbow, joined his sergeants and their gunmen in the fields.[16]

Governor White attempted to reduce overhead expenses by granting large numbers of suspensions and pardons while Wiggins and his staff tried to cope with the worsening problems spawned by Parchman's sagging security system. Both efforts came to naught. In April 1953 the governor suffered a torrent of abuse from conservatives for turning malefactors loose on society.[17] Several days later Wiggins was sent reeling when a youthful white prisoner had his throat cut within days of being admitted to the penitentiary.

Hodding Carter's Greenville *Delta Democrat-Times*, which learned of the homicide before penal authorities released official word of it, accused the superintendent of a cover-up and demanded official inquiry. Such "irresponsible" reporting made Wiggins furious; he commenced sulking, his mood worsened as the newspaper continued its sniping, and in June he got a measure of revenge by denying Tom Karsell, the tabloid's managing editor, passage through Parchman's front gate. Karsell screamed to the heavens through the medium of his newspaper, alleging in the process that Governor White had not been to the penitentiary in several years. White told reporters "off the record" that Karsell was a "dirty liar," but the Associated Press printed the comment anyway. Senator McDonnell called for Wiggins to be replaced by a "trained prison administrator." Senator Alexander criticized the superintendent for failing to hire a psychiatrist and a black chaplain, and announced that he would personally escort journalists to the penitentiary.[18]

Word broke almost simultaneously that the long drought had proved more damaging than had been expected. With gross income diminished by some $328,000, the penitentiary recorded a deficit of more than $295,000 for fiscal year 1952–53.[19] The deficit was a bitter disappointment for Wiggins; it was his first.

Then the Mississippi Bar Association adopted a resolution calling for the employment of trained "correctional administrators" and a "qualified" superintendent. This was too much. Governor White angrily called a press conference at which he defended farmer Wiggins. The bar was unaware of the type of convicts who were incarcerated at Parchman, he told newsmen. "I don't understand what those fellows could be thinking about. When the day comes that we have to go around powder-puffing hardened criminals, then God help the country."[20]

Yet the appearance of such powerful opposition caused White to reconsider. He closeted with Wiggins, emphasized the necessity of compromise, and afterward endorsed a probation system, a maximum security unit, and a new policy on the use of the strap. Wiggins jockeyed behind the scenes to head off a probation statute but otherwise followed the governor's plan of appeasement. He told journalists that henceforth Black Annie would be utilized only as a "last resort" in disciplining unruly convicts and begrudgingly accepted the maximum security unit. Ninety percent of his difficulties at Parchman were attributable to some two hundred white prisoners, he explained to a journalist. A maximum security unit was not the solution; indeed, the construction of such a facility would be a "mistake," but he would not actively oppose it.[21]

Governor White attempted to bolster his position at a press conference, where he outlined his superintendent's virtues and accomplishments, refuted the "gross misrepresentations" of the *Delta Democrat-Times*, and invited journalists to inspect the penitentiary. Soon a number of newsmen were knocking at Parchman's front gate.

Among them were Kenneth Toler of the Memphis *Commercial Appeal* and Wilbur Minor of the New Orleans *Times Picayune*. They were greeted by a congenial Wiggins, who "literally handed the penitentiary keys" to Toler. Following an extensive tour of Parchman, both journalists penned favorable reports and contended that they had investigated "all there was to be seen."[22]

Wiggins exploited the opening. On June 29 he announced that, effective immediately, the maximum number of lashes allowed at the penitentiary was reduced from fifteen to ten. "Spankings," the superintendent assured the press, were never allowed to draw blood; they were a means of discipline to which the sergeants seldom resorted, and never were they administered without his express permission. Reports that convicts were being abused were blown out of proportion, he insisted. To the contrary, Mississippi's convicts enjoyed a large number of uncommon privileges.[23]

The *Delta Democrat-Times* continued to snipe, and in early July Tom Karsell attacked the penitentiary in a speech delivered to the Brookhaven Lion's Club. Soon Karsell was supported by an anonymous "young convict," recently released from Parchman, who told a Memphis *Commercial Appeal* reporter that the role of vocational and religious opportunities at the penitentiary was "greatly exaggerated," that "the main interest" was raising cotton, and that beatings were common.[24]

White and Wiggins remained on the offensive. After a "shakedown" of several camps produced a large assortment of grisly weapons, the *Commercial Appeal* observed that there were "two sides to the situation" at Parchman. Wiggins then invited relatives of convicts to a gala "open house." His stated motive was to "relieve some of the tension." The event attracted an estimated one thousand guests—"the largest crowd ever to visit the inmates"—and many visitors gave reporters favorable accounts of life at Parchman.[25]

On July 10 Governor White traveled up to Sunflower County in the company of a host of journalists. White made no pretenses. The inspection was being conducted "to throw open the doors . . . in an effort to refute some of the charges of recent days." All of the journalists were impressed, and Gene Roper of the Jackson *Clarion-Ledger* wrote an almost idyllic account of convict life, complete with a reminder that felons were felons after all. Governor White scolded the penitentiary's critics and remarked that the state was not "running a Y.M.C.A." at Parchman. Former superintendent Tann, interviewed in Memphis, told a reporter that those who criticized the penitentiary were ignorant. "Loving kindness and entertainment programs," he observed, "will never replace the lash as a means of controlling the prisoners." The penitentiary's personable educational director, Bob Patterson, took to the speaker's circuit during the late summer and early fall. In September he gave the McComb Lion's Club a heady account of classification, education, and recreation at Parchman.[26]

The penitentiary's detractors attempted to regain lost ground. The Greenville *Delta Democrat-Times* continued its criticism during the final six months of 1953, and Oliver Emmerich's McComb *Enterprise-Journal* asserted that the penitentiary was "an institution of blame and punishment rather than diagnosis and therapy." Meanwhile, Parchman's legislative critics rattled their sabers, all the while laying plans for the upcoming session. In October 1953 the Jackson *Clarion-Ledger* sized up matters very well. All the squabbling of the spring and summer, a staff writer observed, had assured that "any angle of interest that is raised in connection with the institution attracts more than usual interest."[27]

In February 1954 Alfred C. Schnur, professor of criminology at the University of Mississippi, told reporters that Parchman was a "wonderful training ground for criminals." Wiggins, the professor added, was "just a good farmer"; he and his staff were unqualified to administer a modern penal institution, and their professional shortcomings precluded the rehabilitation of convicts.[28]

Shortly one of the professor's students, Dick Anderson, was invited by Hodding Carter himself to speak before a Greenville civic group. On March 10 Anderson lambasted the penitentiary, reportedly basing his negative comments on data drawn from the files of the FBI, the results of Schnur's research, and personal observations he had made during several visits to Parchman. Governor White was angered to the point of imprudence by the remarks of Schnur and Anderson. He stated publicly that the professor should be fired; and a day later, when a journalism class from Ole Miss visited the governor's mansion, White told the students that "officials of one state institution should not publicly make derogatory remarks about another." That statement, of course, offended the interested protectors of the First

Amendment; within days the Ole Miss public relations office received copies of ten editorials from major daily newspapers defending Schnur's right to voice professional opinions.[29]

The Politics of Capital Punishment

All the controversy was shortly obscured by weightier matters. The 1954 session of the legislature was most notable for an emotional debate on how and where Mississippi should execute those convicted of capital crimes. It was clear from the first that the state would abandon legal electrocution, universally acknowledged as a humane method of inflicting legal death only several years earlier, and adopt lethal gas, now regarded as a more humane substitute. There was a glitch, however: no legislator wanted a gas chamber in his own constituency.

The issue was nothing new. In 1940, when the state had abandoned the gallows in favor of electrocution, the only real point of dispute had been the place of execution. On that occasion political compromise had distributed the burden equally, for after 1940 a curious portable electric chair, hauled around in a truck, had enabled the state to execute criminals in counties of conviction.[30] Now compromise was impossible. Experts advised that gas chambers could not be made portable, and county governments could not afford to purchase and maintain their own chambers. Not surprisingly, the politicians decided to foist the problem on state government.

Among the possible sites was Parchman's maximum security unit. Wiggins had begun construction in September 1953. It was a grim structure patterned after "Little Shamrock," the unit employed by the Texas penal system, and the convict-laborers, troubled by the introduction of real cages at Parchman, had dubbed the ugly building "Little Alcatraz." Wiggins hated the thing, and built it only because of his earlier agreement with Governor White; but the agreement had not stipulated the addition of a gas chamber, and the superintendent was enraged that anyone would even suggest the gassing of convicts on his plantation. He leaned on political cronies, and gained the support of an impressive array of Delta politicians led by Senator P. G. Batson and Representative Wilma Sledge of Sunflower County. "Place that thing at Parchman and you will have riots and a wholesale breakout to descend hundreds of criminals down upon our people," warned Sledge.[31]

Wiggins and the Delta politicians scored first, shrewdly inducing the legislature to establish a "death chamber" in the newly constructed headquarters building of the Mississippi Highway Patrol in Jackson. The capital city's mayor, Allen Thompson, promptly threatened legal action, rightly claiming that the measure placed the gas chamber within a stone's throw of a heavy concentration of schools and hospitals in violation of city zoning ordinances. Soon other alternatives were being considered. Predictably enough, someone suggested placing the thing at Oakley, the Negro reformatory, but Governor White, referring to the recent interest of the federal judiciary in racial matters, squashed the idea with the comment that "we have enough Negro problems already." Thereafter the original plan of locating the chamber in Parchman's maximum security unit gained ground by default, and on September 22, 1954, during a special session of the legislature, a bill to that effect was enacted over the vehement protests of Delta politicians.[32]

Superintendent Wiggins took the news very hard. Several days after the enactment of the "gas chamber bill," he accompanied staff writer Charles M. Hills of the *Clarion-Ledger* to the site of Little Alcatraz. There, while watching his convicts work, he expressed disillusionment. "I hope we never have to use these cells," he told Hills. "They are ten times worse than the strap." Wiggins was even more concerned about the prospect of executing criminals on the grounds of the penitentiary. One member of his staff recalled that the superintendent "felt betrayed by the governor and had the look of a beaten old man." A convict-editorialist, writing in the *Inside World*, stressed that capital punishment was "a legalized form of murder, contrary to the teachings of Christianity." Parchman's employees were equally disturbed, if for different reasons. "Politics, politics, politics; nobody wanted the thing [the gas chamber], so the bastards stuck it up here," remembered a staff officer. "The last thing we needed was something sensational to upset the prisoners and attract more bleeding-heart reporters."[33]

Journalists descended on the penitentiary. The Jackson *Clarion-Ledger* ran a lengthy story on the new chamber, and morbid speculation on the identity of the first victim filled the newspapers. The two likeliest candidates, murderers Minor Sorber and Gerald Gallego, granted interviews from their cells in the Hinds County jail. After both expressed relief that they would not be "fried" in an electric chair, a newsman performed the curious, heartrending journalistic ritual so customary in the reporting of death row interviews—a before-the-fact eulogy. Both Sorber and Gallego had served their country as soldiers; both of them wanted to atone for their crimes by donating their eyes to the blind; both of them, but especially "family man" Sorber, were good chaps gone wrong.[34]

On February 25, 1955, as Gallego's date of execution neared, Wiggins expressed grave reservations, telling a reporter that the condemned man had been a "model prisoner," that he had been converted to Christianity, and that he now saw "the error of his ways." These were strange words—the words of a farmer and not those of a professional prison man—and on the morning of March 3, as Gallego took his last meal and was read the last rites, Wiggins was visibly upset.[35]

Journalists crowded into the death cell's antechamber, positioning themselves so as to see the "death seat" through the heavy glass, while many of their colleagues, denied entry due to overcrowding, chattered nervously outside, glancing occasionally at the ominous guard towers above them. The victim disappointed nobody. As four condemned black convicts sobbed, and as the strains of *Up Above There's A Heaven Bright* "sounded through the grim corridors," Gerald Gallego walked the "last mile." He stood erect and smiled as he passed the distraught convicts. He encouraged them to keep singing. He seated himself in the chair and cooperated as leather straps were fastened around his wrists and ankles. As the lethal gas rose from beneath the chair, he chanted the Lord's Prayer, jerked violently, lingered for fully twenty minutes due to miscalculations by the executioner, and at last died. Convict Allen Donaldson followed Gallego a day later; and in April, when only one journalist showed up for the third execution, an editorialist quipped that the gas chamber "wore out its popularity in a hurry."[36]

The End of the Wiggins Era

Although Superintendent Wiggins disapproved of this grisly business, he could at least find satisfaction in the fact that his critics broke off their attack after the execution of Gallego. The explanation, according to one former politician, was the threatening attitude of the Warren court on the "Negro question," which "tended to make all [white] Mississippians . . . pull together."[37]

So it would appear. The landmark decision of the United States Supreme Court in the case of *Brown v. the Board of Education of Topeka, Kansas*, which knocked the legal props from under the state's segregated public schools, struck Mississippi like a bomb. Virtually every decision made by Governor White during his last two years in office was conditioned by the "Negro question," and everything suggests that White and the state's legislative leadership came to appreciate Senator Alexander's opinion that the penitentiary was no less vulnerable than the segregated public school system. "Scalawag" tactics, therefore, conditioned Marvin Wiggins's last years as superintendent.

The public relations of the penitentiary were entrusted to Patterson, the capable director of education, and thereafter the successes of inmate-students emerged as the focal point of a spirited publicity campaign. Patterson added a sixth-grade class to his educational program, organized a gala graduation ceremony labeled "End of School Follies," and heaped lavish praise on his successes. Wiggins, recalling that the penitentiary had housed some seven hundred illiterate convicts when education was first introduced in 1944, claimed that there were now "very few prisoners who can't write their own letters."[38]

The penitentiary's official reports also advertised an expanded program of vocational education, which included formal instruction in the maintenance and operation of farm machinery. The farm manager observed that the program went "a long way towards preparing [convicts] for better jobs when they leave here." Official word also held that prisoners learned marketable skills by working in the various shops and plants of the penitentiary. The new laundry, for instance, employed twenty-five men, operated in "free world" fashion, and was said to qualify a convict for "a skilled position in an outside laundry upon his release."[39]

A shortening of the long line was noted as well. Official records indicated that of some 1,900 convicts on hand in September 1953, 789 were no longer in the fields. Afterward, increasing mechanization and a "steadily improving" classification system reportedly withdrew even more, and the field hands were given a three-hour lunch break each weekday. By 1955 Patterson was championing the "moral" betterment and "rehabilitation" of convicts. He called on the legislature to finance a modern vocational training facility of adequate size and design "to provide working space for students who are studying radio repair, electricity, carpentry and other technical subjects."[40]

An expansion of the penitentiary's recreational activities was also hyped. By 1955 Parchman's music program had begun to establish a reputation in the Delta. The black prisoners still wanted nothing to do with organized music, instead carrying on as always in or near their cages, but a band composed of seven white convicts performed regularly, often for large numbers of visitors at Front Camp. The music program was advertised as a rehabilitative tool, as was the penitentiary's livestock field day, which would evolve over the years into the celebrated Parchman rodeo. Begun on a small scale in 1951, the field day was staged every October. The animal husbandman presided over the event, camp was pitted against camp, and exhibits featuring beef cattle, work stock, and horses were grouped and judged at the dairy. By 1955 competition was lively.[41]

Another widely publicized event was Pauline Wiggins's hobby contest. The event grew from a very modest beginning in 1950, but on April 8, 1956, it featured six hundred contestants and drew "wide interest in the Delta area." Entries included leather goods, cabinet works, pottery, paintings, and embroidery. Exhibits were displayed in a newly constructed community house at Front Camp and judged by local civic leaders and clergymen. The contest gave convicts an opportunity to earn money through prizes and sales to visitors. Business was so brisk that the superintendent opened a prison bank for the convict-artisans.[42]

The publicity campaign was enhanced by the reported success of Wiggins's Christmas furlough program. In December 1954 the superintendent furloughed his three-thousandth prisoner. Of that number, only a reported fourteen had failed to return to the penitentiary since the program's inception in 1944, and but two of the delinquents remained at large. If those statistics are accurate, the furlough program stands as a huge tribute to the penitentiary's screening process, perhaps as the most successful program of its type in history. In late 1954 an editorialist contended that it had "contributed to the rehabilitation of many discharged convicts."[43]

Official records also indicated improved medical services. For biennium 1953–55 the penitentiary reported not one case of heat exhaustion, not one death attributable to tuberculosis, and only sixteen deaths among its convicts. "The health of the inmates," wrote physician Thomas A. Robinson in the summer of 1955, "has been well above the average of the outside person."[44]

In April 1955 the warden of the Illinois penitentiary, who had visited Parchman in 1944, came again with three of his subordinates. He reportedly found convict morale to be "the finest we have seen in a state prison" and "expressed himself as amazed at the tremendous improvements in the Mississippi prison." Governor White, whose opinion was perhaps less objective, claimed in June, following an inspection of Parchman, that the morale of prisoners was "higher than I have ever seen it."[45]

Of all the penitentiary's reported triumphs, however, nothing was more stunning than Superintendent Wiggins's successes in agriculture. He did it with blood in his eye, ever remembering the embarrassing deficit of 1952-53, and he did it despite unfavorable market and climatic conditions that crippled neighboring plantations. During 1953 he planted 5,895 acres in cotton, produced 6,238 bales, and brought home a net profit of $268,080. In the following spring he fell prey to another debilitating drought but surprised everyone by recording a deficit of only $11,601. A year later he planted his cash crop on 5,365 acres and had the satisfaction of seeing the penitentiary record an astonishing profit of more than $525,000.[46]

In February 1956, however, when the house penitentiary committee concluded a meeting with a standing ovation honoring the veteran superintendent, Wiggins knew that his days at Parchman were numbered. The new governor, J. P. Coleman, was a staunch advocate of an adult probation system, and Wiggins realized that it was only a matter of time before the legislature gave the chief executive his way. Coleman also wanted Wiggins to de-emphasize agricultural operations, to implement more vocational programs, and to spruce up the penitentiary's image even more. The governor was, moreover, a stickler for propriety, a man who had little patience with the petty graft that fed the engines of Parchman's system. In early 1956 Coleman had discovered financial irregularities, had sent his "snooping henchmen" up to Parchman, and Wiggins knew full well that he could not continue to function under such conditions.[47]

The superintendent stood by silently as Coleman's probation bill progressed through the legislature, all the while wondering why nobody seemed to understand the devastating effect that a probation board would have on the composition of an already difficult convict population. The passage of the bill in the spring distressed Wiggins, and about the same time Coleman demanded the dismissal of the penitentiary's chaplain. The superintendent protested vehemently, a period of cool relations followed, and Wiggins resigned in early May 1956.[48]

"WE OWE WIGGINS OUR THANKS," pronounced a leader in the *Clarion-Ledger*. The old farmer, a journalist observed, had "undoubtedly compiled one of the best records of any penal official in the entire South, or even the nation for that matter."[49] Perhaps the journalist went overboard, although the confused goals that characterized the administration of legal punishment in the United States during Wiggins's tenure render comparative analysis virtually impossible. Clearly, however, Wiggins had presided over an impressive transformation at the penitentiary, and between 1944 and 1956 the penal system had recorded net profits amounting to some $2,709,000.[50] On July 1, 1956, when the old man bid adieu at Front Camp and drove out the gate with Pauline, he left behind him a fine stand of cotton, one that would deliver Mississippi's labor-intensive penitentiary its last fiscal year profit.

A Changing of the Guard

Generally regarded as one of the shrewdest, most competent chief executives in state history, J. P. Coleman came to office in the midst of the rapidly evolving civil rights movement, which by 1956 was targeting Mississippi's racial caste system for destruction. The governor saw that his state could not hope to combat the judicial activism of the Warren court, that substantive reform was the only way to mitigate the approaching convulsion, and that appearances would be no less important than realities in the years ahead. Coleman was the greatest of Mississippi's latter-day "scalawags." He heard a clock ticking, and, like Bill Alexander, he saw trouble in Sunflower County.[51]

Great pressure was placed on the governor to appoint Wiggins's understudy, Aubrey Reed, to the superintendency. Instead, Coleman appointed Bill Harpole, a comparatively obscure identification officer employed by the state highway patrol. Harpole was the penitentiary's first superintendent lacking experience in agriculture. That fact was exploited to the fullest by those who "hated to see the team . . . operating Parchman broken up," but even Harpole's numerous critics could not impeach his credentials as an enforcer of the law.

Prior to his most recent five-month stint with the highway patrol, Harpole had worked for four years as a patrolman and had served Oktibbeha County as sheriff and deputy. As deputy he had been employed by his wife, Mary, a gifted administrator who had been elected sheriff in a county included in Coleman's old judicial district. She and her husband had impressed the future governor; Mary had followed Coleman to Jackson in a highly visible position on his personal staff. Now the governor sent the young couple up to Parchman with orders to render the penitentiary's image more compatible with modern political reality. To facilitate a smooth transition, the Harpoles took up residence in May, nearly two months before Wiggins's departure. With them came the Reverend Roscoe Hicks of Calhoun County and E. E. Lacey of Wier, who replaced the disappointed Reed.[52]

Harpole began his superintendency with vigor, almost immediately granting the convicts permission to install television sets in their cages, and Director Patterson, who wisely had been allowed to stay on after Wiggins's departure, called on the media to encourage public contributions. Several sets were donated immediately, public officials spearheaded drives to obtain more, and merchants in nearby Drew allowed convicts to purchase sets through special time-payment schemes. By December antennas towered over most of the cages.[53]

Harpole and his staff made a great production of the advent of television. Patterson announced that television viewing strengthened the penitentiary's "Rehabilitation Program" by serving as a "pre-release orientation project." The grand jury of Sunflower County praised the television sets as "a morale builder for prisoners." Journalists were also impressed. Even Emmerich's McComb *Enterprise-Journal* conceded that television viewing enhanced convict rehabilitation.[54]

Coinciding with the introduction of this "pre-release orientation project" was enormously increased emphasis on religious activities. Harpole believed, or at least said he believed, that "a consciously religious person, one who is active in the church, is incapable of criminal acts."[55] He certainly acted on that hypothesis as superintendent. Upon arriving at Parchman he let the convicts know that he smiled on the religiously inclined and worked with Chaplain Hicks to organize activities through which felons might display devotion to their maker.

On July 20, 1956, Hicks and two inmate-preachers presided over Parchman's second mass baptism. Five white men, thirty-six black men, and eight black women waded into one of the penitentiary's irrigation ponds. The blacks "broke into religious songs, halting only to listen to the prayers of the chaplain as he performed his duties." The event, wrote an observer, "was carried out in a religious atmosphere, despite the presence of armed guards and trusties who discreetly, yet nevertheless watchfully, encircled the area with readied rifles and revolvers, but well to the background." By October 3, 1956, when fifty-four convicts were baptized "while other prisoners in choral groups sang softly," Chaplain Hicks had presided over four mass baptisms involving a total of 244 convicts. In the meantime Harpole had converted a watering trough into a more commodious baptismal site. The trough was enclosed by "white-painted brick and surrounded by carefully-tended lawn."[56]

The religious crusade was enhanced by literary contributions from the Mississippi Baptist Convention, the Salvation Army, the Gideons, the Volunteers of America, and a number of independent philanthropists. A virtual revival was staged on Christmas Day, 1956, and the convicts were showered with yuletide cheer. Harpole continued his predecessor's Christmas furlough program, every inmate received a present on Christmas morning, and the convicts were dazzled by a holiday feast. Enraptured by these events, an editorialist writing for the *Inside World* unsuccessfully called on the governor to bestow suspensions and pardons as Christmas gifts.[57]

Harpole also advocated other "progressive" innovations during his first six months on the job. In July 1956, amid all the hoopla surrounding his first mass baptism, the superintendent told reporters that he favored the establishment of a "first offenders' ward" in which young, reclaimable convicts could be removed from the baneful influence of hardened criminals. Notwithstanding the fact that probation was diverting young, reclaimable offenders from the penitentiary already, the proposal earned Harpole much praise. The Sunflower County grand jury endorsed the idea in September, and later the *Clarion-Ledger* contended that the "creation of such a camp for young prisoners . . . would help salvage and reform an increasing number of them."[58] Thereafter the superintendent raised the question on numerous occasions, and even made preliminary moves to establish such a camp, but he somehow never got around to making it a reality.

No less newsworthy was Harpole's promotion of Parchman's recreational and vocational programs. White musicians enjoyed new visibility. In July 1956 "The Insiders" made their debut, its members boasting all the markings of the beat generation. Member Clarence Ruelson had the Lord's Prayer tattooed on his stomach, another musician had a string of beads and the words "cut on the dotted line" tattooed on his neck, and all but one member of the band had the word "love" tattooed on their fingers—one letter per finger. Dressed in their convict stripes, The Insiders were quite a spectacle. Only days after taking office, Harpole arranged for five local radio stations to broadcast the band's performances. Soon the musicians were drawing much attention.[59]

Another of Harpole's tactics that earned the penitentiary favorable publicity was his promotion of the convict-printed newspaper. The *Inside World* had initially operated on a shoestring budget out of a small room in the old hospital, and later the editor's office had been moved to a trusty's room at Camp Five. Under the publicity conscious Harpole, however, the newspaper was given higher priority, and its content broadened considerably.

By August 1956 the *Inside World* was a thirty-page mimeographed magazine being distributed on a regular basis to sixty-eight prisons in the United States and Canada. It was, moreover, no longer a hand-to-mouth operation. Editor Donald F. Morgan, who once had worked on the newspaper staff of Michigan's penitentiary at Jackson, operated out of a newly constructed brick cubicle at Camp Five and received copy from convict-correspondents in all of the penitentiary's eighteen camps. Morgan's paper carried penitentiary news, general news, sports, religion, cartoons, comment on movies, and editorials described by *Clarion-Ledger* staff writer Phil Stroupe as "punchy . . . [and] mostly aimed at matters pertaining to prison politics and laws, but keenly aware of the 'free world'."[60]

Cognizant of the newspaper's potential as a bridge between the penitentiary and the Fourth Estate, Harpole allowed his convict-editor remarkable latitude. Newsman Stroupe, who personified the success of the superintendent's tactics, concluded that the *Inside World* got "a healthy peep through the physical bars of confinement to tell its story to the free world." During the second half of 1956 the convict newspaper emerged as an advocate of many penal reforms, and a number of its articles were either reprinted or paraphrased in newspapers across the state.[61]

Harpole's relatively liberal policy on the printing of the *Inside World* was but one component of his broader public relations effort. He actively encouraged tours by students and teachers of state government, journalists, legislators, law enforcement officials, church and civic groups, penologists from other states, and anyone else who could be lured to remote Sunflower County. To lure them, the superintendent staged interesting events. In the autumn of 1956 he organized a cotton-picking contest that attracted many spectators, and in December he promoted Pauline Wiggins's old hobby contest to such an extent that the event set records for convict entries and visitors. Wife Mary, whose charm remains a subject of Delta conversation even today, dazzled visitors with her hospitality and devotion to the convicts, while Patterson, his vitality undiminished, took to the road, speaking to civic, educational, and religious groups throughout the state.[62]

In September 1956 the Sunflower County Grand Jury complimented Harpole for his "devotion to duty and his eagerness to do a good job." Such praise was richly deserved, commented the *Clarion-Ledger*; recent reports from the penitentiary indicated "that most of the prisoners would applaud and endorse the grand jury's compliment to the . . . superintendent." This was the reaction J. P. Coleman had wanted. On December 7 the governor pointed to "remarkable progress . . . being made at the penitentiary under Supt. Bill Harpole" and announced that soon he would visit the institution. Following Hugh White's happy precedent, Coleman invited journalists to accompany him.[63]

On December 14, 1956, the governor led a number of newsmen to Parchman. Waiting on the entourage was a delegation of Sunflower County politicians; they were there to tell everyone how much they appreciated Harpole. Their plaudits were echoed by numerous prisoners, who were "loud in their praise of improvements in physical facilities and in treatment since Harpole [had] taken over." In the presence of the journalists, Coleman questioned Harpole on the status of Black Annie. There was now little need for the strap, the superintendent replied. The new maximum security unit had proved to be "a great deterrent to prison troubles"; no more than four or five convicts were being disciplined under close supervision each month.

Then the governor turned to the philosophy that was to guide the penitentiary in the years ahead. Money, he said, was not "the prime purpose of the operation." Rather, his administration was committed "to the rehabilitation of prisoners, the protection of society, and the welfare of prisoners who are returned to society." The executive branch of government, however, could not realize those objectives without the support of the legislature, stressed the governor. Agriculture simply had to be balanced with industry. Factories had to be established, and a much more extensive state-use system distributing convict-manufactured goods among state institutions had to be implemented. Furthermore, the superintendent, who was "having great difficulty keeping qualified employees," had to be given more latitude in hiring and setting the salaries of needed technicians.[64]

It was a good plan, a reasoned compromise with economic realities at home and political developments outside the state; but as the governor spoke, those around him saw little more than vestiges of the old plantation system and realized that change would not come easily. A faltering agricultural economy was, as always, causing state legislators to contract, to look suspiciously on money bills promising to change any feature of the status quo, and conservatism was being compounded by an uneasiness bred by the emerging civil rights movement. White Mississippians had been on the defensive since the days of secession. They were inclined to build barricades, to reject even a tactical offensive when threatened by outsiders. That inertia confronted Coleman's criminal policy.

Toward "Progressive" Ways

The governor's visit to Parchman in December 1956 was quite successful. Among the impressed was Charles Hills of the *Clarion-Ledger*, who afterward emerged as a stout defender of Harpole and the penitentiary. Upon returning to Jackson, the journalist reported that the superintendent, "tall, quietspoken and determined, is today racking up a record . . . as a humanitarian as well as a firm administrator." A week later Hills again praised the improvements at Parchman and hailed the governor's plans for the future, not only at the penitentiary, but also in the other components of the state's criminal process.[65] Even Hills, however, could not comprehend the magnitude of the changes projected by Coleman and Harpole. Their plan was to proceed with reform within the parameters of executive discretion, all the while pushing for the legislative support without which comprehensive change was impossible.

The superintendent moved forward in the spring of 1957. In March he collaborated with the state employment security commission to establish a program designed to help convicts secure gainful employment upon release. Beginning on April 1, dossiers were sent to the employment security commission thirty days before a convict was to be released, and an active campaign to overcome the fears of prospective employers was initiated. Harpole claimed that the federally inspired innovation was "an outgrowth of the prison's accelerated rehabilitation program." Ninety-six convicts reportedly secured jobs during the next two years, and in April 1958 Senator Alexander advocated the creation of a job placement bureau at the penitentiary.[66]

Simultaneously, Harpole made the boldest stroke of his entire administration, the *official* establishment of Parchman's famous conjugal visitation program. It was risky business. Sexual relations at the penitentiary were nothing new, of course. However, as reflected by the state's hypocritical policy on the sale and consumption of alcoholic beverages, which were illegal but subject to taxation, it was one thing to be naughty in Mississippi's Bible Belt, quite another to openly admit it. The central thrust of J. P. Coleman's public policy, though, was the introduction of measures that, while being politically dangerous in Mississippi, were calculated to impress outsiders, to protect Mississippians from themselves. The official introduction of conjugal visitation portrayed that shaky tactic to the letter.

In early 1957 Harpole ordered the construction of a number of modest, one-room buildings, allowed spouses to visit the penitentiary for "family day" on Sundays, and made the so-called "red houses" available to couples of all races for designated periods. That gutsy innovation was accompanied by another, initiated in June 1956, that extended "annual vacations" to deserving convicts who wished to visit their families.

In April 1957 the superintendent traveled to Oklahoma City for the purpose of attending the joint meeting of the Southern States Prison Association and the Southern States Probation and Parole Association. He told the delegates of his innovative annual vacations, noting proudly that only one convict had failed to return to the penitentiary since the inception of the program. He said less about the conjugal visits, perhaps because they were only then getting underway, perhaps because he feared the reaction back home; but his language reflected the new image he and Coleman sought for Parchman and the state of Mississippi. "If you place a little confidence in prisoners, they hate to betray it," he reportedly told the delegates. "After all, they are folks just like the rest of us."[67]

There is little reliable information about the formative period of

Harpole's conjugal visitation program. The press had little comment, and neither the superintendent nor his department heads mentioned it in the biennial report submitted in 1957. But in the spring of 1959, when the program was established and functioning smoothly, Harpole displayed no timidity in describing his family day activities before the Southern Conference on Corrections in Tallahassee, Florida.[68] Shortly thereafter, Ernest A. Mitler, a New York attorney who recently had concluded a celebrated study of the nation's juvenile institutions, gave Parchman's conjugal visitation program national exposure with an article featured by *Parade* magazine.

Family day began at 11:30 A.M. on Sundays, when wives and children were allowed to pass through Parchman's front gate. After being searched and having their identities verified, the visitors proceeded to the administration building, where they met their convict-husbands and fathers. The families strolled and talked at Front Camp, fathers played with their children, and many attended religious services. Couples were free to go to "specially designed cottages for complete privacy as husband and wife." Unmarried prisoners often helped their married colleagues by baby-sitting; one convict worked in a commissary and frequently made children his "store assistants."

Mitler was astonished by the lack of an "air of derision or ridicule . . . [among] unmarried prisoners," and also by the absence of the "undercurrent of tension and frustration" so characteristic of prisons elsewhere. It was difficult, he observed, "to see dozens of families coming together in warm affection without some of the warmth permeating the entire feeling of the place." That warmth, he added, was partly owing to "the sympathetic administration and understanding of Harpole."[69]

The author failed to point out that family days, with almost identical activities, had existed at the penitentiary for decades. He was correct, however, in observing that no other American penal institution had a program quite like this one, and his article was distributed to a nation of incredulous readers, many of whom otherwise believed the worst about Mississippi.

Soon the nation heard more. Newspapers everywhere carried stories describing the "Mississippi experiment." *Cosmopolitan* published Charles Knight's positive article entitled "Family Prison: Parchman Penitentiary" in March 1960. Columbus Hopper, the Ole Miss sociologist, initiated research that soon would earn him a considerable professional reputation and focus the attention of the academic world on Parchman's conjugal visits.[70]

The publicity, it seems, caught most Mississippians by surprise. At all events, there was little or no talk of coddling criminals with sexual privileges, and indeed the conjugal visits became a source of state pride. On June 19, 1959, after a St. Louis newspaper had encouraged the governor of Missouri to consider implementing the Mississippi experiment, the *Clarion-Ledger* noted that "our Mississippi experiment may well become a national mode in this key area of prison reform." Coleman and Harpole had followed a risky, if well-plotted, course; Harpole had managed the thing brilliantly; and by late 1959, when the state needed a victory very badly, it had one.

Although nothing could outstrip the public relations coup of family day, Harpole promoted other reforms that bolstered the image of his penitentiary. For years black convicts had competed for what they regarded as favorable work assignments in Parchman's dairy, and a degree of elitism had come to characterize the black dairymen. Harpole built on that foundation, representing the dairy as an "honor camp" for exemplary black convicts, and created, with great ceremony, an "honor camp" for white males at Camp Nine.[71]

The superintendent's emphasis on religious activities never diminished, and during 1959 and early 1960 he butted heads with the legislature in attempting to secure funds for the construction of chapels at the penitentiary. Senator Alexander's penitentiary committee reported favorably on a bill to that effect in February 1958; but the legislature refused to enact it, and the best Alexander could do was to secure the passage of legislation allowing private donations to a chapel-building fund. In October 1959 a Jackson-based citizens' group was formed for the purpose of soliciting donations. Harpole spoke at their first meeting, where he harrangued legislators for their shortsightedness. Such criticism won him few friends in the statehouse, but by February 20, 1960, private pledges totaled $10,000, plans for the construction of the first chapel were advanced, and the superintendent was calling on the legislators for matching funds.[72]

Nor did Harpole neglect the penitentiary's educational program. In the summer of 1958 Patterson added four levels to his adult education program, thus enabling convicts to complete a junior high school education at the penitentiary. In addition, the educational director made arrangements enabling convicts to take correspondence courses through local high schools, the University of Mississippi, and Mississippi Southern College. By the summer of 1959 Patterson was bragging of "a remarkable degree of advancement" and "an increasing amount of success." In February 1960 Harpole unsuccessfully called on the legislature to establish an accredited high school at Parchman.[73]

The Failure of the "Scalawags"

Harpole's triumphs were impressive indeed, but none of them accomplished the first priority of the Coleman administration's penal policy—the balancing of agriculture with industry at the penitentiary and the establishment of an expanded state-use system of convict labor. That priority was born of two crucial facts. First, Mississippi could not continue indefinitely to operate a plantation system employing mostly black field hands in the face of a pervasive national movement for Negro equality. Secondly, a severe glut in the cotton market, accompanied by a sharp decline in prices, coincided roughly with Coleman's inauguration.

Upon coming to office in early 1956, Coleman found allies among legislators who were concerned about the penitentiary's competition with private agriculturalists in a tightening marketplace. That concern led the legislature, on March 31, 1956, to enact a measure authorizing the penitentiary to establish a metalworking plant, to contract for the sale of metal signs to municipalities, counties, and other departments of state government, and to distribute unsalable goods among public institutions. But the statute was heavily compromised. It contained no provision granting the penitentiary a monopoly over the supply of any commodity to a public institution, it made no special appropriation, and thus it fell far short of what Coleman desired. Late in the year the governor called for appropriations to establish shops at Parchman capable of supplying state institutions with paint, disinfectants, and soap.[74]

The governor's plan was opposed by four identifiable groups. There was a sizeable body of hardliners in the legislature who thought Coleman timid, even traitorous, in his reaction to the civil rights movement; they could be counted on to oppose almost anything emanating from the Governor's Mansion. There were legal retributivists who frowned on any attempt to mitigate hard labor at the penitentiary. There were those representing private interests who stood to lose valuable state contracts if a state-use system triumphed. But above all else, the cotton glut had given rise to a crusade, supported strongly by Coleman himself, to balance agriculture with industry throughout Mississippi, and many of those favoring industrial development in the private sector questioned the wisdom of establishing state supported industries at Parchman.[75]

All this added up to a standoff in the legislature, one that left the penitentiary in a most unbecoming position. Harpole, facing imminent financial collapse, could ill afford to wait on feuding politicians. In 1956 he reduced cotton acreage by 425 acres and began beating the drum of prison industry and vocational training.

Superintendent Wiggins had stressed to his critics that the old plantation system provided training in numerous vocations other than agriculture due to the presence of the many shops that made the penitentiary self-sufficient. Harpole made the same point, in March 1957 emphasizing that over half the convicts worked in the penitentiary's numerous shops. Such assignments, he noted, were a valuable part of an "accelerated rehabilitation program in which prisoners learn useful trades, hobbies, occupations and skills."[76]

That was true—convicts *were* learning trades under the old plantation system, always had, and critics needed to know it; but the shops at the penitentiary generated precious little revenue, and that fact was a political liability within Mississippi.

As for the cash crop, Harpole was helpless owing to the demise of the cotton market. In 1957 the penitentiary participated in the federal soil bank program, planting only 3,834.6 acres in return for a federal allowance of $71,000. That income, however, did not arrest the steady erosion of the penitentiary's financial structure. Wiggins's last crop had produced 7,487 bales and generated a net profit of well over a half million dollars. Harpole's first crop of 1956–57 yielded 4,527 bales and an operating deficit of $109,016. The balance sheet for the 1957–58 fiscal year was much worse, depicting an institutional deficit of $355,252.[77]

Harpole, Coleman, and their political allies broke for daylight in early 1958. The biennial penitentiary report submitted in late 1957 pleaded for legislative assistance in convict "rehabilitation," which was essentially defined as vocational training via prison industry. Then, in February 1958, Alexander's senate penitentiary committee reported favorably on a bill calling for the establishment of a soapmaking plant, a mattress factory, and a metal plant capable of producing furniture, highway signs, and other equipment for use by state institutions. The bill met with strong opposition on the floor of the senate. Debate dwelling on the form of prison labor that would be least ruinous to the private sector raged for two hours. At last, after a worthwhile compromise was rejected, the opponents of the bill had their way by a narrow, two-vote margin.[78]

Afterward, as the penitentiary's financial crisis worsened, Harpole concerned himself more and more with occupying the time of his increasingly idle convicts. This he did well, taking care in the process to promote the image of the penitentiary. He created a radio, television, and electronics shop. He expanded Pauline Wiggins's old hobby contest, renaming it a "hobby craft program." He established an Alcoholics Anonymous program through which many free members attended meetings at the penitentiary.[79] All the while, the hopelessly trapped superintendent, ever bemoaning the intransigence of the legislature, watched Parchman's fiscal status degenerate.

In 1958 the penitentiary planted some 4,619 acres in cotton and increased yield-per-acre to such an extent that 6,144 bales were produced, but it fell prey to the lean market and reported a deficit of $307,792.20 for the 1959 fiscal year. On balance, then, Harpole planted four crops and recorded an operating deficit of over $1,104,787 during his superintendency.[80]

In 1959 the superintendent actively supported Lieutenant-Governor Carrol Gartin in the Democratic gubernatorial primary election against winner Ross Barnett, and on January 10, 1960, the *Clarion-Ledger* observed that "The head of one of Mississippi's ablest state officials is on the political chopping block." The ax fell shortly thereafter when Barnett announced that his campaign manager, none other than former state senator Fred Jones, would replace Harpole in March. In February, amid mounting attacks on his financial record at the penitentiary, the lame duck superintendent told several visiting members of the house penitentiary committee that he had "no apologies to make for what we've tried to do here." And later in the month, shortly before leaving Parchman, he again emphasized that at some point Mississippi would be forced to "balance agriculture with industry" at the penitentiary.[81]

Harpole thus ended his superintendency uttering the same language with which he had begun it, a testimony to his failure to achieve his primary goal. He had achieved a great deal, but the penitentiary was adrift and entering stormy seas when he and Mary departed. The Greenville *Delta Democrat-Times*, which had tempered its traditional critical view of Parchman during the Coleman years, expressed astonishment at the dismissal of Harpole. It was, an editorialist concluded, "another example of the stupidity of the spoils system in Mississippi."[82] The journalist failed to note that the spoils system had brought Harpole to Parchman in the first place.

7

Failed Statesmanship and Collapse

During the early months of 1960, the national civil rights movement gained ground rapidly, Mississippi's racially segregated institutions came under ever more determined attack, and groups of bus-riding zealots styling themselves "freedom riders" prepared to descend on Jackson from the North. Within the state, the reforming scalawags virtually disappeared, moderates changed colors, and right wing reactionaries built barricades. The spirit of the times resembled that which had swept Mississippi a century earlier, when fire-eaters had led the state toward ruin on related grounds.

Ross Barnett was ill-equipped to cope with the crisis; he, in fact, was more responsible than any Mississippian for creating it. At a time when moderation and compromise had been demanded, Barnett had drummed up enthusiasm among the white electorate by scorning federal authority, by championing the sagging doctrine of states' rights, and by rattling the bones of the Confederate dead. Now, as promised, he came to office as a defender of the faith. There was pugnacity in his rhetoric; like his antebellum ancestors before him, he was fully prepared to fight the federal host.

Barnett was an accomplished lawyer and a skilled campaigner; but he did not always surround himself with competent lieutenants, and he had never learned that in politics, as in war, frontal assaults against superior force are rarely successful. The traumatic events of Barnett's administration would shake Parchman's foundations, and eight subsequent years of failed statesmanship would bring the old plantation down.

The "Noble Experiment"

Governor Barnett's decision to entrust the state penal system to Fred Jones seemed to be a good one. Jones boasted a solid record as a penal reformer. As a state senator between 1943 and 1953 he had played an active role in the formulation of criminal policy, and as chairman of the senate penitentiary committee he had been largely responsible for the sweeping reform package of 1948. But the sixty-five-year-old Jones contrasted strikingly with Harpole, just as Barnett contrasted strikingly with Coleman; his background, his appearance, his language, and his priorities smacked of the old days.

Jones was a gray-haired, cigar-chewing Delta planter who, at the time of his appointment, was president of the Sunflower County Board of Supervisors. He was a powerful man up Parchman way, a political power broker who combined the best and worst features of the class of men who ruled the Mississippi Delta. His stint in the senate had proved him to be a cunning political infighter, but he had left many enemies behind him in the theater of state politics, and his association with Barnett had created new ones.

Jones had opposed Harpole's policies vociferously; now he wanted to turn back the clock. In one of his first public statements after becoming superintendent, he announced that he would restore the penitentiary as a "money-making proposition." He saw "plenty of land and labor"; with "proper utilization of what we have," he asserted, "we can make money."[1]

The superintendent was extremely critical of his predecessor. "This is a big plantation and the man in charge should know about farming," he proclaimed in June. "The penitentiary lost more than a million dollars during the last four years. Properly managed, it should show a financial profit." To make his point, he ridiculed the condition of farm machinery, contending that he had farmed "30 years ago like they have been farming here." He also announced that the production of food crops had been abysmal, that the dairy and the meat-processing plant had been improperly managed, and that the hospital had been operating without trained or experienced personnel.[2]

In November the superintendent displayed an incredible disregard for the legal and political currents of the day, telling journalists he had found "bad conditions" caused by "too much whipping" when he arrived at the penitentiary. The strap, he alleged, "may have been used . . . last year more than the public realized, especially in August of

1959, when inmates staged two sit down strikes." According to Jones, Harpole's staff "took matters into their own hands," shooters "fired into the cages," and convicts were whipped "for refusing to come out of the cages, for talking loudly in the dining hall and for other reasons." Later, the superintendent reported in an official document that "by and large the inmates are housed in buildings over 50 years old with inadequate heating, toilet or bathing facilities [with] the appearance of not having been painted in years."[3]

Jones's campaign to restore the Parchman of "the good old days" began well enough. He fired fifty employees, replacing them with Barnett folk, and planted a huge cotton crop on 6,423 acres. He lobbied the legislature for more financial latitude, advocated incentive pay for his convicts, relaxed discipline, and asked the inmates to join him in working hard for a better future. In time, Jones promised his work force in the June 1960 issue of the *Inside World*, there would be "trades to learn, progressive farming, better and more schooling and [an] all-around rehabilitation program."[4]

Jones continued the conjugal visits and allowed Patterson, who somehow survived the political turnover, to introduce the Laubach literacy system, a new technique of teaching illiterates to read and write. While the director of education reported "seemingly fantastic results," the superintendent helped convince the legislature to formalize the penitentiary's chapel-building fund and successfully solicited public donations. Jones even promoted a short "hypnosis rehabilitation experiment"; it failed miserably but constituted the penitentiary's first attempt at psychiatric treatment.[5]

In April 1960 Wendell Cannon, who had toured the state with his band as part of Barnett's gubernatorial campaign, was appointed the penitentiary's first director of music. Promises of travel lured several of the formerly reluctant black musicians away from their cages, and by November Parchman had professional and amateur bands for both races as well as a quartet composed of black women. The white professional band, The Insiders, and its black counterpart, The Stardusters, were allowed to go on the road in a bus beginning in June 1960. Between August and November The Insiders logged a reported three thousand miles, appeared on television frequently, and recorded one of Cannon's compositions. By November both bands were scheduled to perform somewhere every weekend.[6]

While Cannon and his bands traveled, Jones followed Marvin

Wiggins's old and revered blueprint. In the autumn of 1960 he concluded a deal with his Delta crony, Robert Crook, the state director of civil defense, through which the penitentiary made a token payment and initiated the manufacture of mattresses for use at times of natural disaster in return for surplus farm machinery valued at more than $100,000. The transaction, Jones announced optimistically, gave him "sufficient heavy equipment to throw up drainage works that make available for plantings hitherto untenable bottom lands."[7]

Impressed by the drift of events at the penitentiary, staff writer Bob Pittman of the Jackson *Clarion-Ledger* reported in November 1960 that Jones's "noble experiment" was "reversing the situation" at Parchman. In early January 1961, the popularity of the noble experiment reached a crescendo when the superintendent reported a "record crop."[8] It appeared, for a fleeting moment, that Jones would realize his boastful predictions.

Cracks in the Armor

The superintendent's experiment began to seem less noble when Austin MacCormick, the former assistant director of the federal penal system, visited Parchman for the third time in early 1961 and issued a report criticizing virtually every facet of the penitentiary's operations. The central problem, MacCormick noted, was the political spoils system. Mississippi needed a politically independent penitentiary board. The challenge for the state was "to get the prison out of politics."[9]

MacCormick's observations were ignored by state officials, who preferred talk of money. In February the governor announced proudly that already the penitentiary's transfers to the state treasury were over $250,000 more than had been projected by the state budget commission. What Barnett failed to announce was the fact that disbursements were running well ahead of receipts, that the penitentiary was en route to a fiscal year deficit of over $336,000, and that Jones and the board of commissioners were fighting like cats and dogs.[10]

The conflict between the superintendent and the board revolved around the very thing Austin MacCormick had observed during his recent visit—the political spoils system. The commissioners were concluding a number of dubious contracts with the private sector. As always, graft was diminishing productivity, but now there was apparently more of it. Meanwhile, Jones's furious attempt to revive agriculture was an expensive proposition. All these factors combined to carry disbursements to an appalling level.

A standoff between politics and penal farming was also discernible in staff appointments. Unlike his predecessors, Governor Barnett did not seem to understand that remunerative operations at Parchman required a degree of competency among staff members. Responding to the wishes of his cronies, he foisted an unprecedented number of political appointees on the penitentiary, thereby heightening conflict about leftover patronage among the penitentiary's administrators. All this undermined the delicate balance of power between the board and the superintendent. The commissioners blamed Jones; Jones blamed the commissioners; matters heated up daily.

In late March a trusty sent on an out-of-state mission for the penitentiary drove a truck to Texas, turned right, and went home to Montana. There was not much anybody could do about it, and great embarrassment resulted. The *Delta Democrat-Times* called for a "new attitude" at Parchman, and the political opponents of the governor seized the opportunity to heap ridicule on his administration. According to Cliff Sessions of United Press International, a rumor circulated in Jackson that hundreds of persons had applied for admission to the penitentiary because "convicts are treated so nicely."[11]

Barnett, who had a wonderful sense of humor, brushed off the incident with a glib question—"If you can't trust a trusty, who can you trust?"—but the escape brought the conflict between Jones and the commissioners to a head. The commissioners demanded a curtailment of Jones's liberal policy on leaves from the penitentiary. The superintendent recoiled like a rattler, things went from bad to worse, and on April 18, 1961, apparently without first conferring with the governor, the commissioners fired Jones.

Barnett issued a vague statement promising to "straighten things out." A joint legislative committee departed for Parchman. Letters from the Delta supporting the ousted Jones swamped legislators. The *Delta Democrat-Times* called for the reinstatement of a superintendent with "a long background in penal reform." With the integration melee heating up daily, many powerful state politicians thought it unwise to change horses in midstream, so great pressure was placed on the commissioners to reconsider. Following much wrangling, the board reluctantly agreed to reinstate Jones as superintendent.[12]

Jones came back with a flourish, expanding Harpole's old job-placement program and renewing his plea for incentive pay for convicts. His attitude impressed the *Delta Democrat-Times*, which featured a story hailing the superintendent's many accomplishments, but Jones's honeymoon was short-lived.[13]

On May 31, 1961, lethal gas at Little Alcatraz martyred the much-litigated Robert Lee Goldsby, a black murderer whose case had been exploited by civil rights advocates to challenge policies that excluded blacks from state voter registration lists, and thus from trial juries.[14] Only days later, freedom riders appeared at Jackson's bus stations, resulting in mass arrests and yet another unsettling collision between the emerging principle of Negro equality and Mississippi's constitutional and statutory law.

Under the provisions of the state code, the freedom riders were guilty of misdemeanors, so they were quickly dispatched to the Hinds County penal farm, where problems ensued. By June 12, 1961, the county penal farm had admitted eighty-four of them and overcrowding was acute.[15] Furthermore, the young activists had come to Mississippi seeking to challenge the authority of a racist regime, and had succeeded in provoking a reaction. Now the question for state officials was what to do with them. The passions of most white Mississippians had been aroused; there was reason to fear that the incarcerated zealots would be abused, even murdered, and thus martyred, like Goldsby, in the eyes of the nation.

The attitude of the civilian guards at the county penal farm was bad enough, but it was nothing when compared to the hostility of the convicts. Trusties grumbled about favored treatment afforded the riders. Other prisoners refused to associate with them. Tensions mounted daily. It was a sticky issue, and the solution that was adopted only made matters worse. In mid-June the Hinds County Board of Supervisors succeeded in foisting their problem on the state penitentiary. Buses began to transport the unmanageable riders to Sunflower County. By June 24 sixty-six of them, including twenty-three women, were at the penitentiary; by August 5 Parchman housed one hundred, with more on the way.[16]

The transfer of these misdemeanants to a statutorily defined institution for felons placed Superintendent Jones and his staff in an unbecoming position. There were, of course, legal problems. While increasing numbers of FBI agents descended on the penitentiary, the American Civil Liberties Union filed a petition for a writ of habeas corpus on behalf of the riders. Justice Hugo Black denied the petition to the delight of state officials, but in the aftermath of Black's holding it was clear to everyone that the state's case would fall apart if the misdemeanants were abused.[17]

That possibility was very real. James Hendricks, editor of the *Inside World*, attacked the freedom riders as fools "suckered into coming down here to disturb the peace." They were hypocrites who did not care about the Negroes of Mississippi, wrote Hendricks, and their time would be more wisely spent if they directed their efforts toward Northerners who labeled blacks "spooks, smokes, boogies, grease-balls" and the like instead of toward those who labeled them "niggers." The editor evidently spoke for a large number of Parchman's inmates. A former white inmate recalls that "we wanted to kick their asses," and a black one remembers that "we [the black convicts] were really pretty ignorant about things back then and weren't especially fond of them [the freedom riders]." Governor Barnett, realizing that the riders were "looking for trouble," cautioned Superintendent Jones to avoid incidents at all costs, and the commissioners ordered a tightening of managerial procedure.[18] The scenario that had haunted Governor Coleman was unfolding: the eyes of the nation were fixed on the state penitentiary.

Jones placed the unwanted intruders in the maximum security unit and in the yet-unoccupied first offenders' camp, thus shielding them from the wrath of his other convicts. The superintendent was, however, in a no-win situation. The stark, sweltering cells of Little Alcatraz did not please the freedom riders. One of them launched a hunger strike, reportedly losing forty pounds in twenty-three days, and another, James Farmer, a founder of the Congress of Racial Equality, claimed that Jones's policy was "the dehumanization of the riders to make us as animals." Jones refuted the charges and did everything imaginable to keep the lid on, but shortly he and the Barnett administration were sent reeling by a scandal of major proportions.[19]

The Kimble Berry Scandal

In December 1961, Kimble Berry of Greenville, a furloughed convict who had fled to Lynn, Massachusetts, told a *Boston Globe* reporter an incredible story. He had been given leave and supplied with a car, a pistol, and power of attorney to open a safe deposit box in an Arkansas bank. His instructions had been to go to the bank, to retrieve stolen currency and negotiable securities, and to deliver the loot to several friends of the governor, who had promised to reward him with a pardon.

Later reports, among which were a number of unsubstantiated rumors, painted an even darker picture. Berry, it was said, had secured a furlough not on merit, but instead at the request of Lieutenant-Governor Paul B. Johnson, Jr., a native of Hattiesburg. The money and the securities in question had been stolen in a recent robbery in Hattiesburg. Five men had been convicted and sentenced to Parchman for the robbery. Parties close to the governor had conferred with one of the convicted men only days before Berry's release, had provided Berry with the car, had left the penitentiary with Berry, and had been seen with him in Greenville.[20]

The reports were given credence by the behavior of the implicated parties, who made public remarks casting odium on the Barnett administration. The governor sought to deflate the mushrooming scandal through an in-house investigation, afterward announcing that everything was exaggerated, but the *Delta Democrat-Times* ridiculed Barnett's effort as a "maneuver . . . to keep the press off his back." Legislative leaders agreed, and in late January appointed a special nine-man investigating committee composed of members from both chambers. The committee elected Senator W. B. Lucas of Macon chairman. Lucas, the dean of the senate who was said to be "as mean as a yard dog," led his committee to Parchman on January 29 and began to review personnel records as well as documents relating to paroles, suspensions, and furloughs. Next day word broke that Superintendent Jones had fired his music director, Wendell Cannon, for stirring up trouble among the prisoners and the staff.[21]

After the state of Massachusetts granted Berry asylum, Barnett ordered Jones to tighten his leave policies and asked the legislative committee to include the organization and management of the penitentiary in its investigation. Heeding the earlier advice of Austin MacCormick, the governor suggested the creation of "a constitutional, staggered board, with authority to select the Superintendent and other specified administrative personnel."[22]

On April 3, 1962, the Lucas committee released the first of three separate reports. It addressed the bizarre events surrounding Berry's release, explained that a "veil of mystery hung over the entire investigation," noted the impropriety of pursuing a criminal prosecution based on inmate testimony, and cleared Lieutenant-Governor Johnson. Next day the committee released its second report, this one addressing the issue of leaves, suspensions, and furloughs. The problem, found the committee, was attributable neither to the governor nor to his appointees at Parchman, but instead to a "faulty system." That interpretation was supported by a lengthy account of how the system had failed, concluding with a harmless proposal for the creation of a five-man board, much like the old board of pardons, to assist the governor in the granting of leaves and suspensions.[23]

So far, so good; actors in state government, it seems, were giving and taking with a spirit of compromise. However, between April 4, when the second report was made public, and April 19, when the committee's third and final report was released, something transpired that dramatically altered the attitudes of the "yard dog" and his colleagues on the committee.

The third report contended that the penitentiary was a "mess because of politics, illegalities and conflicts." Everything was "conducted in an air of uncertainty and confusion due to conflicts over the exercise of authority between the Governor, the penitentiary commissioners and the superintendent." Indeed, "Every phase of the operation . . . [was] controversial, including the hiring and firing of personnel, the granting of leaves and suspensions, the operation of the various departments of the penitentiary, including purchases of supplies, and the supervision and control of the prisoners." Purchases had been made "in an irregular, unusual, and oft-times illegal manner." Due to the conflict of authority, "cross-currents of dissension, discordance and disagreement [filled] the atmosphere."[24]

Prior to the release of the committee's third report, the governor, the commissioners, and the superintendent—all at daggers drawn but in it together—had managed with difficulty to present a united front. Now Lucas's committee produced correspondence and testimony revealing the hostile currents beneath the surface, and the actors aired their dirty laundry with a vengeance produced by long-repressed frustrations.

"If I had a governor like White or Wright or Bailey, it would be all right," said Jones. But it was impossible for a superintendent to administer the penitentiary properly when a governor constantly foisted incompetent political cronies on him. On a "good many" occasions, claimed Jones, he had fired employees on grounds of incompetence, only to have Barnett force him to rehire them, and on one occasion the governor had sent a private investigator to Parchman because he "wanted some records swiped . . . at the hospital."

The superintendent was even more adamant in his attack on the commissioners. Supplies for the penitentiary, he charged, were bought from a supply company partly owned by a son of Commissioner Tom Ross. Most of Parchman's groceries were bought from a firm in which Commissioner Walter Scruggs was a principal stockholder. Over 50 percent of the cotton produced at the penitentiary in 1961 had been delivered to a company Scruggs directed. Furthermore, all the commissioners, especially Ross, said Jones, had "agitated among convicts and other people and I am certain that they have been promised better jobs if I leave here."

The commissioners met fire with fire, denying Jones's allegations and attacking him for lax discipline, a dangerous leave policy, failure to follow rules, incompetent farm management, and gross financial mismanagement. They charged further that the Berry scandal never would have occurred had not Barnett, house speaker Walter Sillers, and other politicians forced them to rehire Jones. That, however, had been nothing new. Politicians constantly exerted pressure for the hiring of favored parties; indeed, the influence of the governor and various legislators accounted for the presence of every employee at the penitentiary.[25]

Barnett delayed his formal reply until the afternoon of April 23. Then, characteristically peering over his eyeglasses at anxious reporters, he unblushingly defended his exploitation of the penitentiary's patronage and dismissed the report of Senator Lucas's committee contemptuously. The governor fired Superintendent Jones a day later.[26]

Parchman Adrift

Barnett replaced Jones with Marvin Wiggins's old farm manager, C. E. Breazeale, fended off the former superintendent's continuing attacks, and set out to block several distasteful bills sponsored by his enemies in the legislature. In Breazeale, Barnett chose a superintendent who could follow orders and keep his mouth shut. Jones's mouth, however, was seldom shut, and it was especially active in the weeks following his ouster. "I placed my head on Ross Barnett's chopping block," he cried to reporters. The people and the legislature, he predicted, would "rise up with righteous indignation and demand that this institution be set up on a plan such as most other southern prisons are operated."

Jones did his best to rouse the people. His dismissal, he asserted publicly, had come because of his long-standing opposition to brutality and because of his objections to a system that kept "the worst employees for political reasons." Later, he wrote to a member of the probation and parole board, claimed he had a number of affidavits proving that "good friends of the governor" had offered to arrange paroles for payoffs, and sent a copy of the letter to the press.

Mississippians did not rise up with righteous indignation. Jones, however, was not without his supporters, the reports of the Lucas committee left many questions unanswered, and the governor yet faced an uphill battle. If Jones was regarded as a villain within the Barnett camp, he was seen as a martyr by many of the convicts. They grew extremely restless, even volatile, after the governor fired "the old reformer." The trusty-shooters were disarmed. Deputies and highway patrolmen reinforced the penitentiary's hopelessly outnumbered civilian guards. Barnett alerted the national guard. Order was maintained, but the convicts remained sullenly defiant, and an unidentified employee saw trouble ahead. "Let me tell you something, those prisoners aren't so dumb," he told a reporter. "They'll wait a couple of days 'til the officers quit patrolling so heavily . . . [and] then they'll do something."[27]

More threatening to the governor were the thrusts of his detractors in the legislature and the lingering possibility of criminal proceedings against members of his administration. Barnett moved quickly to squelch both threats, reportedly leaning on legislative allies and demanding that the Lucas committee turn over its records to the grand jury of Sunflower County. On May 2, 1962, the senate constitution committee killed a bill advocating a constitutional board of penitentiary commissioners. A week later the Lucas committee delivered its findings to the grand jury. Not surprisingly, that body found no basis for indictments.[28]

Meanwhile, everything was done to promote the myth that all was well at Parchman. An Associated Press reporter interviewed a number of prisoners and heard not one complaint. The *Inside World* praised virtually every facet of convict life. Assistant Superintendent Minga

Lawrence claimed that most convicts enjoyed a lifestyle "better than it was in the free world." Breazeale remarked that Black Annie had not been used since Jones's departure.[29]

Similar tactics had proved quite successful in fending off the penitentiary's critics on earlier occasions. But this time all the smiles and assurances failed to deceive even the dullest of Mississippians, and there were powerful men in the legislature who thought it unwise to let Barnett and his cronies off so easily. One such man was W. H. Jolly of Columbus, now chairman of the senate penitentiary committee. Concluding that Superintendent Jones had done his best "under the most trying circumstances," Jolly introduced legislation calling for the creation of a powerful board of commissioners composed of five professionally qualified members serving staggered terms. Unlike the earlier bill, which had been squelched by the senate constitution committee, this one was assigned to Jolly's own committee, which was beyond Barnett's reach. Amendments in committee transformed the original measure into a sweeping penal reform package. In the end, four separate bills came to the floor of the senate with powerful backing.[30]

In late May a flurry of escapes threw folks in the Delta into a "tizzy," wrecked Superintendent Breazeale's public relations campaign, and carried the affairs of the penitentiary to the point of absurdity. One journalist satirized the escapes. Less amused, both houses of the legislature passed Jolly's reform package while convicts were yet "running around like rabbits in the fields and woods."[31]

After having recommended most of the proposed reforms himself in February, Governor Barnett now astonished everyone by vetoing the two bills that sought to alter the political structure of the penal system. The vetoes sent legislative leaders into a rage. Jolly and Bob Anderson, the chairman of the house penitentiary committee, lambasted Barnett and his "henchmen" at the penitentiary while the *Delta Democrat-Times* burst forth with lethal invective. At last Barnett had shown "his true political colors," an angry editorial proclaimed. The governor had displayed all too clearly "that he prefers to use the penal farm as a political pork barrel, with employees hired and fired according to his dictates, and with prisoners given lengthy furloughs on the basis of their political connections."[32]

Legislature leaders, incapable of overriding the unpopular vetoes, exacted a degree of revenge by reducing the penitentiary's appropriation by some $150,000 during the last days of the session, but all the turmoil subsided when the legislators left Jackson. The governor then traveled up to Parchman and announced that he had "never seen greater unity" at the penitentiary. Two weeks later, Commissioner Scruggs toured the penitentiary and spoke of a wonderful transformation. He was followed in late July by Barnett's chum, Senator R. D. Everett. The governor, Everett told the press after a tour, had been "wise and courageous" in vetoing the penitentiary reform bills. Since 1934, the senator added, the state of Mississippi had had "about as nearly perfect laws governing the penitentiary as it is possible to make."[33]

The comments of Barnett and his friends were nonsense, political rhetoric calculated to disguise the fact that Superintendent Breazeale was in deep trouble. The reduction in the penitentiary's appropriation came at the worst possible time. Superintendent Jones's first cotton crop had been a good one, but still the penitentiary had recorded a substantial deficit. The 1961 crop was worse. Now operating with insufficient capital and headed toward a fiscal year deficit of nearly $308,000, Breazeale was forced to cut overhead expenses.[34]

Although Superintendent Jones had spoken of the sorry condition of the physical plant in 1961, Breazeale reported no major physical improvements during the 1962 fiscal year and recommended none for the 1963–65 biennium. Typhoid and influenza immunizations were discontinued. The hospital operated with only one qualified nurse, and the state hospital commission voiced grave concern about conditions in the operating room. The penitentiary's director of dentistry admitted that it was "almost impossible to do all the dental work that is necessary." Obsolete and worn equipment allowed the canning plant to operate only "at about fifty percent efficiency." The chaplain complained that his department was not meeting the needs of the convicts. The education program suffered a great blow when Patterson resigned.[35]

In October 1962 Senator Hayden Campbell of Jackson warned of disaster. Twenty-five staff positions were unfilled, and soon insufficient appropriations would force the abandonment "of at least 2,000 acres of cotton-producing land," he told journalists. On a recent visit to Parchman, Campbell added, he had observed a "pressing need" for shoes, boots, and winter underwear. In one cage, most of the 116 convicts were "almost barefooted."[36]

The penitentiary was sliding backward at a most inopportune time, a fact that was perhaps reflected by a significant increase in reported escapes and deaths among convicts. Surely the cutbacks in staffing, food services, medical services, and the other essentials of life figured prominently in both developments, and no doubt the rising escape rate was partly attributable to a substantial reduction in leaves and suspensions. But one must also consider the continuing shift in the profile of the convict population.

Of the prisoners admitted between July 1, 1962, and June 30, 1963, over 40 percent were white, nearly 86 percent were literate, and less than 43 percent were farmers and farm laborers. By comparison, of the convicts admitted during the 1933 fiscal year, less than 24 percent had been white, some 70 percent had claimed literacy, and almost 75 percent had been farmers and farm laborers.[37]

Those changes were of great significance. White men always had constituted the penitentiary's most unmanageable inmates; they remained so, and now there were more of them. Literate convicts had proved to be less willing than illiterates to buckle under to Parchman's labor-intensive regimen. The shift from farmers and farm workers to artisans and skilled laborers, most of them from urban areas, allowed Breazeale to place fewer effective hands in the fields, and many of the black inmates, inspired by the civil rights movement, were less manageable than in the past. Compounding the dilemma was the continuing effect of probation, which diverted the best of the state's felons from the penitentiary, and of parole, which gave early releases to the best of the rest. The hard fact is that Breazeale faced challenges that were unknown to Superintendent Williamson in 1933, and now the stakes were considerably higher.

Yet the governor and the legislature continued their suicidal standoff on penitentiary affairs throughout 1963, Barnett's last year in office. The result was predictable. A large increase in cotton sales was reported, and the chief executive promised a financial recovery in July; but a continuation of the downward spiral of farm operations was obvious by January 1964, and several months later a fiscal year deficit of nearly $300,000 was reported. The governor was no less emphatic in proclaiming Parchman a "model prison" during the summer of 1963. That boast, however, seemed ridiculous later in the year when three shotgun-brandishing trusties escaped, a furloughed murderer passed bad checks in Greenville, and two men broke into the administration building, making off with $2,500. "That's a hell of a way to run a prison," quipped the *Delta Democrat-Times*.[38]

When Barnett left the Governor's Mansion, Parchman was largely undone. Marvin Wiggins would not have recognized the old plantation. All of Bill Harpole's triumphs were now meaningless. And the clock J. P. Coleman had heard in 1956 continued to tick, louder and more ominously than before, for the iniquities of state penitentiaries were beginning to attract the attention of the federal judiciary. Mississippi had less than eight years.

The Smoke Screen of Reform

In January 1964, shortly after Lieutenant-Governor Johnson succeeded Barnett as chief executive, the legislature took up the problems of the penitentiary. Fred Jones was back in the statehouse, now as a member of the lower chamber, and his rough treatment at the hands of Barnett had convinced him that no improvement was possible unless the penal system could be ruled by a nonpartisan board with members serving staggered terms. Others, observing the faltering cotton market, stressed the absurdity of state competition with the private sector and the advantages of instituting vocational training under a state-use system of convict labor.

Still others argued that Parchman's system could never withstand the national civil rights movement. The penitentiary remained racially segregated, and the staff included nothing but Caucasians. Black men continued to shuffle along as members of the long line; Winchester-brandishing shooters continued to stalk them; the strap continued to hang from the belts of the sergeants. In January Senator McDonnell put "the fear of God" in the commissioners by threatening to go into federal court "to stop violation of the civil rights of prisoners," and later he joined Jones, a powerful group in the senate, and the *Delta Democrat-Times* in advocating the statutory abolition of Black Annie.[39]

The debates were unusually hot, and along the way much dirty laundry was hung out for the world to see. Superintendent Breazeale admitted frankly that nothing resembling a rehabilitation program existed. McDonnell accused the Sunflower County legislative delegation of caring nothing about Parchman "as long as they got the [superintendent's] job for their man." Another senator produced written evidence that convicts were buying their way out of the penitentiary. McDonnell, recalling incidences in which convicts had been whipped unmercifully, threatened to report all future abuses to the United States Attorney and to act as "assistant prosecutor" in civil rights litigation.[40]

Through it all, there was a profound absence of leadership, a failure to go to the root of the problem, and in June 1964 a greatly amended bill claiming to reorganize the penitentiary was at last enacted.[41] The old board of commissioners, whose three members were gubernatorial appointees, was replaced by a new board consisting of five gubernatorial appointees. The duties of the commissioners were left somewhat vague. The idea, one must suppose, was to make them inspectors; at any rate, the statute specified that they were to oversee the business affairs of the penitentiary. But there the purview of the commissioners ended and, serving concurrent rather than staggered terms, they remained the animals of the governor who appointed them. So did the superintendent; he was to be appointed by the governor, to hold office at the pleasure of the chief executive, and to have "exclusive management and control of the penal system." Neither the commissioners nor the superintendent were required to have anything resembling professional qualifications.

The statute did not outlaw Black Annie. It left the trusty-shooter system intact. It did not remedy a well-documented degeneration of living conditions at the penitentiary, and it evaded the question of racial inequity altogether. It authorized the penitentiary to establish vocational training programs, but no money was appropriated for this purpose, and nothing was done to effect a viable state-use system of convict labor. In the face of eight consecutive years of deficits, a glutted agricultural marketplace, and a pervasive national crusade for Negro equality, the politicians clung to the old ideal of remunerative plantation agriculture.

The only substantive provisions of the penitentiary act were those that established token qualifications for sergeants, drivers, and guards, and those specifying that released prisoners would receive a little more money and a bus ticket to either the state line or their county of conviction. "Yep," a perceptive journalist had observed amid the debates, "what's wrong with Parchman may well be us . . . [because] we refuse to yield enough money to keep up a good farm and rehabilitation, expect the best from nothing and cuss loud and long when we don't get what we think we deserve."[42]

Meanwhile, Governor Johnson's close ties with the former administration led him to retain Superintendent Breazeale and most of Barnett's other appointees at the penitentiary. Apparently Johnson knew better, because in early February 1964 he went up to Parchman, called all the employees together, and admonished them for their numerous sins. He would not permit "peanut politics to interfere with the job that must be done"; he would fire any employee who sent him a gift; anyone depending on politics for continued employment was "a dead pigeon." If deficits continued, Johnson added, a council of Delta planters would be formed to advise the chief executive.[43]

Then the governor and his appointees on the board, taking stock of the fact that a great deal of federal money was available, began to talk of convict rehabilitation. In July 1965 board chairman Harvey West announced plans to open formal classes in diesel mechanics, automotive mechanics, sheet-metal working, welding, building trades, air conditioning maintenance, and bookbinding. The plan called for the probation and parole board to screen convicts who desired vocational training and for classes to be offered to those whose graduation coincided with their anticipated date of release. The state department of education, in collaboration with federal agencies, would provide aptitude tests for "prospective convict-students" so as "to ascertain to what employment a prisoner is best suited." Initially the program would operate in temporary facilities, but soon construction would begin on a large educational complex.[44]

In October 1965 Superintendent Breazeale got the program underway on a small scale. By January 1966 "quite a lot of personnel" had been transferred into the training program, and by April sixty-two inmates were at work in a "real life laboratory" consisting of classes in the various trades. The book bindery opened on May 18, 1966, under the supervision of an "expert" from Pennsylvania. Soon the facility was restoring, renewing, and rebinding an average of fourteen hundred textbooks daily at a cost of roughly one dollar per book. By August 1966 the bindery had restored a reported forty thousand books, and the entire vocational training program was employing 190 "students."[45]

In October 1967 the *Clarion-Ledger* hailed the dedication of Parchman's new vocational training facility as a "major breakthrough in the history of inmate rehabilitation in Mississippi." Governor Johnson, a host of journalists, and a number of elected state officials went up for the ceremony and toured the huge building. It consisted of seventy-five thousand square feet of floor space capable of accommodating three hundred convict-students.[46]

After the opening of the facility, the curriculum was expanded. By the summer of 1969 fifteen courses were being offered, and the vocational training program was operating on a $375,000 annual budget. Paul Mellenger, the new director of the school, reported that only 6 percent of his graduates were committing crimes that sent them back to Parchman.[47]

The Johnson administration complemented the vocational training program with other newsworthy innovations. The board adopted a policy banning the use of Black Annie. On May 25, 1965, formal dedication ceremonies marked the opening of what was advertised as the penitentiary's first comprehensive library system. On Christmas Eve, 1966, the convicts were at last taken out of their striped uniforms and issued new outfits consisting of trousers with white drill stripes and blue denim shirts. In 1968 a grant from the new Law Enforcement Assistance Administration facilitated the creation of a reception center and a diagnostic clinic. Next year a similar grant led to the opening of a prerelease center that was said to be racially integrated, and about the same time Camp Seven was converted into an "inpatient clinic."[48]

All the reforms made for good press and tended to obscure the fact that the first priority of the Johnson administration was the restoration of remunerative agricultural operations at the penitentiary. In July 1964 the board of commissioners reduced cotton acreage by sixteen hundred acres, ordered the expansion of soybean and truck crop production, and announced that the penitentiary would no longer ship surplus canned fruits and vegetables to other state institutions. Then the governor and the board lobbied vigorously for special appropriations to purchase modern machinery and for the technical assistance of the Cooperative Extension Service of Mississippi State University.[49]

Their efforts were enhanced by the perception of prosperity spawned by President Lyndon B. Johnson's domestic and foreign policies. Beginning in 1965, the legislature heaped lavish appropriations earmarked for machinery and other agricultural improvements on the penitentiary. As the machinery arrived, Superintendent Breazeale removed increasing numbers of gunmen from the fields, and in 1967 "Progress Through Cooperation" came when the Mississippi Cooperative Extension Service lent the penitentiary its considerable expertise in agriculture and animal husbandry. Improvements in farm operations were noted in 1966, and in late 1967 the mechanized penitentiary reported a very misleading "profit."[50]

Caught in No-Man's-Land

All this resulted in disaster. Johnson had begun his term of office by giving the employees of the penitentiary a tongue-lashing for their ruinous backbiting. Then, amid much publicity, he had backed legislation that addressed neither the source of the backbiting nor the unhappy structure of penal administration. And then, with the penitentiary operating under the same superintendent, the same staff officers, the same sergeants, the same underlings, and the same managerial principles, the governor and the board of commissioners had mandated sweeping changes in Parchman's means of production. They had altered the cash crop, replaced convict labor with machines, exploited the expertise of the Cooperative Extension Service, sold large amounts of cotton, soybeans, vegetables, and fruit on the open market, and reported a profit. But it was a mere "paper" profit, the stuff of politicians, and the tactics that fashioned an improved balance sheet spawned a wide range of other problems.

In 1956 the penitentiary's sale of cotton in a glutted marketplace had excited great criticism. Now the cotton glut was much worse, and as private planters were investing heavily in alternatives to cotton, the state matched them dollar for dollar, all the while exploiting public lands, publicly paid technicians, unpaid laborers, and tax exemptions in the name of penal farming. Understandably, the private sector howled, and the joint legislative penitentiary committee recommended in early 1968 that the state should "avoid unfair competition" with private enterprise.[51]

Johnson's decision to retain Superintendent Breazeale and the bulk of Barnett's employees at the penitentiary also fostered problems. According to several former staff members and convicts, the major weakness of the governor's policy came with the fact that "he left a timid farmer" in charge of a staff that was "a pack of back-biting, corrupt scoundrels." In August 1965 a prison official told a reporter that there were thirty members of one family on the payroll. Several months later the house penitentiary committee, noting that dissension was rife among staff members, recommended a reduction in the number of employees who were related to others employed by the state. In early 1966 yet another scandal involving the penitentiary's leave policy confirmed either graft or sad incompetence among Parchman's staff. While local and state politicians protested vehemently, Senator McDonnell remarked that Superintendent Breazeale was a "good farmer, but we can't legislate him into a warden."[52]

Yet nobody of importance was replaced at the penitentiary, and later the innovations of the Johnson administration exacerbated an already serious problem. Quite simply, old dogs refused to learn new tricks. Increased mechanization, the introduction of scientific farming, and the "meddling of those educated fools from the cow college" (the Cooperative Extension Service of Mississippi State University) did not go down well with many employees.[53]

From the first there was dissension between those who administered farm operations and those who administered the vocational training program and the other innovations that diverted gunmen from the fields. A reporter found Superintendent Breazeale grumbling only weeks after the board announced that the vocational training program would be instituted. He was "much worried about use of a storage house near the administration center for a vocational school." The building afforded great public visibility, and the commissioners liked that, but it could not be guarded properly.[54]

Later, a journalist reported that the penitentiary's employees were divided on the issue of vocational training. One group regarded the program as an important tool in convict rehabilitation; others believed "a crook is a crook and if you teach him to handle a welding torch he will use it to cut the face off a safe." Apparently the latter opinion held the upper hand. "The whole vo-tec thing was bullshit," recalled an employee. "It excited everyone who was ignorant, pissed off everyone who wasn't, and divided the ass-kissers in the administration building from the sergeants."[55]

In early 1968 legislators found unqualified, insecure employees, great bickering among staff members, serious problems in the chain of command, and evidence that visiting politicians were fomenting discontentment. Two years later the house penitentiary committee recommended a study to determine the veracity of recurring reports that the vocational training program was interfering with farm operations.[56]

Many of the problems resulted from a fundamental contradiction in the policies of the Johnson administration, one that revolved around the mission of the penitentiary. Parchman and Lambert were *penal* farms. The idea was to operate them with *convict* labor. But in their haste to make a good financial showing, state officials separated the farm from the prison.

At the base of Johnson's policy was increased mechanization and the removal of progressively larger numbers of convict laborers from the fields. In February 1968 a legislative committee noted that most of the penitentiary's crops were being harvested by machines and, pointing to the greater productivity of mechanized agriculture, predicted that more work would be done by machines in the future. That prediction was sound. In early 1970 Representative Malcolm Mabry was stunned to learn that only some five hundred of the penitentiary's seventeen hundred inmates were available for farm labor. Mabry and his colleagues on the house penitentiary committee were appalled. To them it seemed that penal authorities had lost sight of the primary function of the penitentiary; they strongly recommended that, farm profits or no farm profits, more of the convicts should be engaged in hard labor.[57]

Old principles of convict management supported the views of the committee. In 1943 Superintendent Love had stressed that intensive farm labor was the key to the maintenance of order at the penitentiary. That opinion was not original; it went to the philosophical foundations of the old penal farm system. In 1965 a group of Parchman's older employees told a reporter that cotton was picked by hand because "a tired cotton-picking inmate [was] less likely to promote mischief than one who [stood] around watching a machine do the job."[58] But now machines were doing the job, or at least the better part of it, and increasingly idle inmates posed a problem of no small proportion.

Governor Johnson and the commissioners theorized that the new vocational training program and the many other innovations would fill the void. They were wrong. As late as February 1970 only 165 convicts were involved in vocational training, and the program served only well-behaved inmates who were about to be released. Then, too, somewhere in the shuffle the penitentiary's religious and educational programs fell on hard times. The 1968 joint legislative report on the penitentiary stressed the need to strengthen religious programming and noted critically that an educational director was not on the payroll.[59]

Then there was the dark side of inmate classification. Many nice things could be said about the classification system. There was the reception center, where all sorts of testing went on, and dating from 1968 two psychologists from nearby Delta State College helped assure that convicts were properly assigned.[60] The first offenders were sent to the new first offenders' camp, the physically disabled to the disability camps, the psychologically unbalanced to the inpatient clinic, those with clerical skills to Front Camp, those with medical training to the hospital, and skilled artisans to wherever they could most fruitfully ply their trades. After behaving themselves for a designated period, convicts could apply for the vocational training program. And some three weeks before their scheduled date of release, "short-timers" went to the prerelease center where they ate good food, watched television, enjoyed conjugal pleasures with visiting spouses, and reflected on what awaited them in the free world.

This state-of-the-art system had one notable weakness: it concentrated the worst of the convicts in the farm units, now dubbed "hog camps." There, antisocial tendencies were reinforced by association, and bitterness was engendered by harsh discipline; by the late sixties the farm camps were time bombs. But all things being relative, the commitment of greater numbers of confirmed social deviants, combined with the steady introduction of farm mechanization, dispersed more and more unmanageable convicts among all the camps and subverted the classification process. By the late sixties, recidivists were being assigned to the first offenders' camp.[61]

Toward the Abyss

As early as August 1965 a journalist noted a new tension at Parchman. You could "feel in your bones" that all was not "happiness and sunshine." There were many convicts "who would as soon cut your throat as look at you," and a visitor would be well-advised "not [to] let your pocketbook hang out." The newsman observed, moreover, that greater numbers of convicts were attempting to escape. A recent break had resulted in three deaths; and a prison official led the journalist to Camp Five, pointed to the spot where the corpses had lain, and told of his great relief when he saw "armed guards in charge instead of prisoners." Even the female inmates were becoming unruly. Only recently, several white women working at the canning plant had staged a revolt.

Confronted with these conditions, Superintendent Breazeale was tense, distrustful, and mindful of a need to enclose the cages with fences, while the penitentiary's guards were "pleasant, but never friendly." No longer were visitors simply waved in and out of the front gate. Automobile trunks were opened and searched, and guards maintained that even the governor did not escape their security checks.[62]

The security system of the penitentiary was no better than its trusty-shooters, who continued to hold sway despite the introduction of a number of civilian guards. In October 1965 a reporter found them extraordinarily vigilant at one farm camp. There, four full-blooded Choctaw Indians served as shooters, and the gunmen toiling under their scrutiny showed "genuine respect" for the gun line. "You just can't step an inch over the line around here," said a gunman. "Everyone knows if you do those Indians would pure love to scalp you with that 30-30."

But shooters like those Choctaws were few and far between by the autumn of 1965. Old-timers reiterated the time-honored maxim that long-term convicts made the best trusty-shooters, lamented that parole had stripped the penitentiary of the best long-term men, and expressed grave reservations about the existing convict constabulary, especially the new probationary half-trusties, who so often went "over the hill."[63]

A certain tension existed even among the trusty-servants who worked at the guest house. In former times these grinning, shuffling blacks had charmed most visitors, and nobody had complained about the open violation of the 1934 statute denying trusty status to "conspicuous or notorious criminals." By 1966, however, this crème de la crème of the convict population neither grinned nor shuffled quite as much as they had several years earlier. Indeed, they seemed to be somewhat truculent, scheming, and derisive. In March 1966 a reporter observed murderers serving food in the guest house and expressed alarm. Somehow the face of Parchman had changed utterly; the old plantation was no longer like it had been in the "good old days."[64]

The superintendent had little choice in the matter. He employed "conspicuous and notorious criminals" as trusties because the operation of probation and parole assured that the penitentiary housed little else; because the legislature would not allow him to employ a sufficient number of civilian guards; because low pay, dreadful working conditions, and the penitentiary's isolated location normally rendered the few civilian guards he employed inefficient, corrupt, or both; and because those same factors usually caused the better civilian guards to depart after a short time. Security, then, was a serious and worsening problem, and Parchman's employees, "almost without exception," stressed that order could not be maintained without Black Annie, which was now employed in violation of a toothless board policy. The house penitentiary committee noted the degeneration of the trusty system, decided that it was "financially impossible" to replace trusty-shooters with civilian guards, and concluded in the face of disaster that the old system was generally satisfactory.[65]

On January 25, 1968, while Superintendent Breazeale was away, thirty-nine gunmen at Camp Five, a white hog camp, "bucked the line," ignored the threats of their keepers, and "severely assaulted" three of their fellow inmates who attempted to go to work. Trusty-shooters and drivers stormed the cage, overcame the striking gunmen, and bodily carried the recalcitrant convicts to the maximum security unit. Six days later the penitentiary committees of the house and senate arrived and heard an earful of testimony.

The chaplain told of being offered "as much as $1,000 to get somebody paroled." Kenneth Bagwell, the veteran sergeant at Camp Five, assured the politicians that he had seen problems brewing for a long time. There was a severe shortage of manpower in the fields due to other assignments, the new machinery was not compensating, and convicts in the hog camps resented what they rightly regarded as unequal treatment. J. B. Mabus, sergeant at Camp Eight, agreed with Bagwell, adding that fully 40 percent of his gunmen were homosexuals. Both sergeants criticized the new regime for its declining emphasis on religious training and for its restrictions on the use of the strap.

Those opinions, which attributed all the problems to the recent departure from tried and true principles, were contested by Superintendent Breazeale, who blamed everything on his inability to fully implement the new principles. The sergeants did not need the strap to maintain order, he claimed; they needed more mechanization. A good start had been made, but it had not been followed through, and difficulties were only natural due to a conflict between the old Parchman and the new.

For their part, the convicts did not like anything, old or new. They complained that they were mistreated, overworked, fed terrible food, and forced to endure the advances of pushy homosexuals. They alleged that drivers, shooters, and civilian guards administered "merciless whippings" with a wide belt, that hair was plucked from the faces of convicts as a means of torture, and that drugs were forced down the throats of gunmen. One convict testified that he had turned blue after being denied heating in the maximum security unit. Lifer Lawrence Hessian warned that "Another riot could easily happen anytime." One Bumgardner, a former editor of the *Inside World*, summed up all the complaints with an articulate harangue against the Parchman "system."[66]

An investigative reporter visited the penitentiary after the departure of the legislators and discovered further damaging information. Only days before the riot at Camp Five, a convicted murderer serving a life term had snatched a pistol from a guard and terrorized the inmates of the first offenders' camp. A convict who had been given a Christmas furlough was in police custody in Jefferson Parish, Louisiana, under multiple charges, including the attempted murder of a law enforcement officer. Four other felons granted furloughs had not returned to the penitentiary.[67]

The joint report of the house and senate penitentiary committees did not address the causes of the riot at Camp Five; that matter, legislative leaders decided, would be broached in a later document. Still, the report was hardly an endorsement of the policies pursued by the outgoing Johnson administration. Politicians continued to involve themselves with staff arrangements and day-to-day operations. Management was poor. There were many unqualified employees, staff dissension was rampant, trusties were guilty of abuses, and support services were weak.[68]

The legislative committee's later report on the riot omitted a great deal of evidence that the press had revealed earlier, and shortly after it was released, Theodore Smith of Corinth, a member of the senate penitentiary committee, told journalists that the report was "misleading, incomplete, and did not reflect the consensus of the joint committee." A day later the house indirectly refuted Smith by giving Representative Bob Anderson and his investigating team an extraordinary vote of confidence. Then, however, Senator Corbett Lee Patridge entered the fray. Patridge, who had been stripped of the chairmanship of the senate penitentiary committee in January by Lieutenant-Governor Charles

Sullivan, was not in a cooperative mood. He threatened to "name names" in a penitentiary report of his own. "I can tell you today that there is brutality, insufficient clothes, homosexuality and insufficient food at the penitentiary," he stressed defiantly.[69]

Meanwhile, Governor John Bell Williams succeeded Johnson and replaced Superintendent Breazeale with Tom Cook—a farmer, a college graduate, and a former sheriff of Oktibbeha County. Shortly after Cook arrived at Parchman, the Sunflower County Grand Jury attacked the trusty system, labeled the meat-processing plant a health hazard, complained about the presence of hardened felons in the first offenders' camp, and criticized state officials for pursuing financial profit instead of convict rehabilitation.[70]

Cook sought to make amends, but within days Parchman was criticized along with the penitentiaries of Louisiana and Arkansas in a report released by the Atlanta-based Southern Regional Council. A biracial, nonprofit research group actively involved in the disclosure of civil rights violations, the SRC found that prison administrators in the three southern states were "without funds," a shortcoming that left their convicts "without hope." In all three states, the report added, "archaic and brutal instruments" were used to exact labor and maintain discipline amid alarming racial discrimination. Following on the heels of the SRC report was yet another scandal, this one involving the discovery of a counterfeiting ring at Parchman by federal agents. While that investigation continued, a female convict working in the Governor's Mansion murdered one of the other trusties.[71]

As these events rocked the penitentiary, Rex Jones of Hattiesburg, the archconservative chairman of the house subcommittee on paroles and probation, proceeded with another investigation of leaves, furloughs, paroles, and pardons. Jones produced a galling report, and in April 1968 the house passed a measure restricting the terms upon which repeat offenders could be granted parole. Two months later the house constitution committee reported favorably on a resolution to vest the pardoning power of the governor in a three-member panel of state judges. Both pieces of legislation failed; but the debates on them exposed the state's criminal policy to a bitter tug-of-war, and in November the parole system became even more suspect when criminal proceedings were initiated against Martin Fraley, the former chairman of the probation and parole board, for allegedly selling a parole.[72]

In early 1970 Senator Patridge, now restored to the chairmanship of the senate penitentiary committee, introduced legislation calling for the termination of farm operations at Parchman and Lambert.[73] Patridge's colleagues rejected his proposal, but soon the death of Danny Calhoun Bennett sent the protectors of the status quo reeling.

At Parchman, as at other penal institutions, inmates disappeared or died under suspicious circumstances without exciting any great interest by the public. Not so with the death of Bennett. He was young, he had received a light sentence, he had predicted that he would be murdered only days before his death, and there was, to say the very least, confusion surrounding the cause of his death.

Preliminary official reports attributed death to heatstroke, but an undertaker from Ripley, Mississippi, noticing that the body was badly bruised, suspected foul play and alerted authorities outside the penitentiary. A subsequent investigation revealed that Bennett had been beaten savagely with an ax handle and a rubber hose by trusties, that he had been tossed in a bus to die, that several hours had passed before the corpse had been taken to the hospital, and that there was reason to suspect a cover-up by penal authorities. In the end, two trusties were convicted of murder, a civilian guard was dismissed, and citizens far and wide began to suspect that the homicide was but the tip of an iceberg at the penitentiary. A composer from Tupelo actually wrote and recorded a song about the death of Bennett.[74]

The 1970 report of the house penitentiary committee reflected unprecedented disillusionment. Inspecting Parchman in February, the legislators found that supervision was lax, that too few of the convicts were involved in manual labor, that conflicts between supervisors continued, and that dire financial irregularities recommended the institution of a daily audit. So serious were the problems that the committee actually endorsed Senator Patridge's earlier recommendation, suggesting a feasibility study to determine whether the penitentiary's lands should be leased to private planters. One veteran legislator saw no hope for Parchman. "I've concluded after years of service . . . that we will never straighten Parchman out until it is taken out of politics," he wrote. "I don't intend to worry myself about it any more because there isn't anything we can do."[75]

With no meaningful reforms enacted during the 1970 legislative session, Parchman and Lambert drifted toward the federal litigation that J. P. Coleman had foreseen years earlier. And the penal farms drifted most unbecomingly, directionless, scandal-ridden, the victims of failed statesmanship. "Parchman has always been an embarrassing subject to discuss with an official," a *Clarion-Ledger* editorialist had written on February 6, 1966. "Usually the response to a Parchman question is a sad shake of the head and a vague statement to the effect that things are bad at Parchman but that it is an impossible situation." That was a fair assessment. By 1971 the penitentiary stood as a monument to confused thinking, poor planning, and inept public administration. It was the victim of a ruinous political stalemate, an institution caught squarely between the past and the future.

8

The First Stage of Federal Intervention

with R. G. Marquardt

By the early 1970s Parchman was a failed penal institution by any standard of measurement. The old plantation was, in fact, a festering sore on the body politic; and the would-be political physicians who gathered in Mississippi's pretentious statehouse, well above the foundations of the old antebellum penitentiary, were certain of neither diagnosis nor cure. It was clear to everyone, though, that something had gone terribly amiss along the way, and that the proud institution of Marvin Wiggins's day had been brought to the ground by some sort of fundamental miscalculation. Worse still, now the thing was mired in the unhappy politics of the civil rights movement.

But what to do? J. P. Coleman had been right; the time to get cracking had come and gone years ago. Yet even now, as the seventh decade of the twentieth century dawned, Mississippi's political establishment remained moribund, incapable of breaking out of the defensive mind-set and suicidal inertia that had throttled all public policy for some twenty years.

A considerable number of state politicians, reflecting on the awesome power of their colleagues from the Delta, threw their hands in the air, convinced that discretion was the better part of valor. Whistling in the dark was also quite popular; there were, to be sure, more than a few ostriches in the statehouse. One also discerned a great deal of romanticism among the legislators; everything would be alright, the romantic observed with numbing earnestness, if only the state could carry Parchman back to the tried and true principles of better days.

Others thought a little tinkering, a facelift of sorts, would set things right; a few black employees, perhaps some new paint, and a better public relations campaign might work wonders. And of course many politicos, among them the interests who were doing quite well under existing arrangements, damned the federal menace and insisted that a bit of political jockeying, a stroke here, a rub there, would ward off the threat.[1]

So the warnings of "alarmists" like Bill Alexander and his old "scalawag" friends were dismissed, as they had been since the early fifties. The state of Mississippi would stand pat, clinging to a sickly Jim Crow, satisfying the voracious appetites of the Delta boys, and presiding over a perfectly ridiculous quagmire in Sunflower County until 1972, when the federal judiciary lowered the boom.

The Evolving Federal Threat

Prior to the 1960s, both state and federal courts bowed before a "hands-off" doctrine in cases touching on penal administration. Two theories supported that doctrine. First, jurists deferred, owing to the powers reserved to the separate states by the United States Constitution, to the expertise supposedly possessed by state penal authorities. Secondly, the bench was concerned that judicial intervention might have a negative effect on prison discipline.

Two decisions handed down by the Mississippi Supreme Court as late as 1969 and 1970 illustrate the application of the hands-off doctrine. The deference-to-expertise argument appeared in *Morgan v. Cook.* The high court, wrote Chief Justice W. N. Etheridge, would intervene on behalf of state prisoners only when there was clear evidence that a prisoner had been deprived of a fundamental constitutional right. That holding followed on the heels of the court's decision in *Love v. State,* which upheld state action in segregating prisoners on the basis of race for the sake of security and order. Federal courts also used the principle of comity to support nonintervention in state prison disputes, and they leaned on the separation-of-powers doctrine in avoiding cases arising in the federal prisons.[2]

The posture of the bench was well-reasoned from an interpretation of the United States Constitution that emphasized the structural integrity and republican foundations of American government. But the hands-off doctrine virtually negated the civil rights of convicts. In essence they were "slaves of the state" without benefit of the protections afforded by the Bill of Rights,[3] and such a construction ran afoul of the philosophy of libertarian justice propounded by the Warren and Burger courts.

The breakdown of judicial abstention in prison matters began with three federal cases that did not specifically address the rights of prisoners. *Trop v. Dulles* concerned the revocation of Trop's United States citizenship, which the United States Supreme Court held to be a violation of the Eighth Amendment's provision against cruel and unusual punishment. Significant in the decision, handed down in 1958, was the court's recognition of an "evolving standard of decency" relating to this important clause of the Eighth Amendment.[4]

Four years later, in the case of *Robinson v. California*, the United States Supreme Court broadened its definition of "cruel and unusual punishment" still more, actually creating a sliding scale for determining the constitutionality of state action.[5] Such flexibility had great impact on litigation involving the rights of the legally incarcerated. After *Robinson*, the Eighth Amendment's ban on "cruel and unusual punishment" became a string on the fiddles of prisoner-plaintiffs.

Just as significant was the United States Supreme Court's resurrection of an 1871 civil rights statute in *Monroe v. Pape*. That decision, handed down in 1961, turned on the legality of state action in search and seizure, and the court held that state officials acting under color of state law could be held personally liable for the violation of an individual's constitutional rights. Sovereign immunity, the court ruled, could not serve as a shield, even for those holding police powers under state law. *Monroe v. Pape* spawned an avalanche of what were known as "1983 cases" in the federal courts. Prisoners constituted a large proportion of the plaintiffs.[6]

Another hole in the dike of the hands-off doctrine appeared in *Johnson v. Avery*, a 1969 case that pitted a Tennessee regulation against the federal right of habeas corpus. In its decision the United States Supreme Court championed the constitutional rights of the legally incarcerated, thereby indicating clearly that traditional judicial deference could be overcome.[7]

Less than two years later, Judge J. Smith Henley of the Eastern District Court of Arkansas displayed how far the hole had been widened by issuing a far-reaching decision in *Holt v. Sarver*. Finding conditions at Arkansas's Cummins penal farm to be "shocking or disgusting to people of reasonable sensitivity," Henley judged the prisoner-plaintiffs' allegation of unconstitutional treatment by evaluating the penal farm on the basis of a "totality of conditions." The application of that vastly broadened standard to prisoners' suits constituted a virtual revolution in litigation involving the fundamental rights of the legally incarcerated. Heretofore the federal bench had been generally unwilling to abandon its traditional deference to the expertise of state penal authorities on the basis of a single issue. Given the breadth of a class action and the plaintiffs' presentation of a wide range of relevant circumstances, however, Judge Henley elected to step into the breach. Subsequently the Cummins penal farm was forced to operate under the scrutiny of a federal district judge defining constitutionally acceptable conditions and posing as an inquisitor.[8]

Complementing the judicial activism of the late sixties and early seventies was the enactment by the United States Congress of the Omnibus Crime Control and Safe Streets Act of 1968 and the establishment of the privately financed Lawyers Committee for Civil Rights Under Law. The federal statute allocated huge amounts of money to the administration of criminal justice in the separate states via the Law Enforcement Assistance Administration, thus extending the principle of federalism to a sphere of state affairs formerly shielded from federal encroachment. The creation of the Lawyers Committee for Civil Rights Under Law was no less important. Formerly, civil rights activists had been largely dependent on local legal counsel, a fact that often precluded competent representation. Now private funds from national sources such as the Catholic Campaign for Human Development and the Clark Foundation allowed a battery of attorneys to work free of local constraints.

All these developments, but especially Judge Henley's 1970 opinion in *Holt v. Sarver*, boded ill for Mississippi's troubled penitentiary; there was, to be sure, no appreciable difference between conditions at Cummins and those at Parchman. That fact was revealed very clearly by the astonishingly frank report of the house penitentiary committee in 1970, and by an uncommonly critical section on the penitentiary included in the October 1970 presentment of the Sunflower County grand jury. Then, in 1971, the vulnerability of the penitentiary was underscored when the United States Fifth Circuit Court of Appeals, reviewing the case of 250 civil rights demonstrators who had been arrested and shipped from Natchez to Parchman in 1965, held in *Anderson v. Nosser* that state and local officials had acted in violation of state and federal law. Indeed, the court stated in the opinion that the treatment of the demonstrators was so horrendous that state officials should be mindful that "we deal with human beings, not dumb driven cattle."[9]

That devastating indictment, as well as the implications of the dilemma faced by the Arkansas penal system in the aftermath of *Holt v. Sarver*, convinced Mississippi's legislative leadership that perhaps a little reform was necessary after all. The penitentiary act of 1971 stipulated that, beginning in January 1972, the five members of the penitentiary board, still appointed by the governor, would serve staggered, six-year terms. The statute also mandated that a board-appointed superintendent would "possess qualifications and training which suit him to manage the affairs of a modern penal system," and that the board could choose a superintendent who was not a native Mississippian. That provision was vague—purposely so, one must suspect—but at least it raised the possibility that someone other than a political hack might superintend the penitentiary.

The legislature bit the bullet on the trusty-shooters as well; the much-maligned "headhunters" were to be disbanded by July 1, 1974. But the statute neither created nor financed staff positions to replace the convict constabulary, it did not ban the lash, and it altogether ignored the threatening question of racial inequity.[10] The penitentiary act of 1971, therefore, was modest work, the stuff of reluctant, backpedaling politicians, and it displayed appalling shortsightedness.

The executive response was no less shortsighted. In January 1972, when William Waller succeeded John Bell Williams as governor, the penitentiary board demonstrated the weaknesses of the 1971 statute by appointing an untrained, inexperienced kinsman of Waller's wife, John Allen Collier, to the superintendency. That ill-advised appointment was followed roughly a month later by a warning from the state board of health that Parchman might have to be closed because of an obsolete water system, an inadequate sewage system, an improper system of waste disposal, dubious fire protection, and violations of state milk-processing regulations. Almost simultaneously, several convicts overpowered and killed a trusty-shooter, commandeered a bus filled with other convicts, and headed for the nearby town of Drew brandishing firearms.[11]

The Inevitable Lawsuit

By early 1972 the Mississippi penal system was vulnerable indeed, essentially a sitting duck, and it was hardly surprising that Parchman inmates Nazareth Gates, Willie Holmes, Hal Zackery, and Mathew Winters brought suit in federal court against the state penitentiary. Into the case of *Gates v. Collier* stepped attorney Roy Haber and United States District Judge William Keady, two men who would revolutionize the terms on which the state of Mississippi formulated and administered the provisions of penal law.

Haber, employed by the Lawyers Committee for Civil Rights Under Law, was a divorce lawyer from New York who had grown tired of his work and migrated to Mississippi.[12] He had few roots in the state and little in common with Mississippians. Shortly after the initial holding in *Gates*, he would leave the state and transfer subsequent litigation to David Lipman, who in turn would pass the mantle to Ron Welch. All three attorneys would bear the brunt of fighting the case in future years, but it was Haber upon whom responsibility for the first and most crucial battle fell. The New Yorker came prepared.

Keady was a native of the Mississippi Delta. Before ascending to the federal bench, he had been a member of both the Delta Council and the Mississippi Economic Council, a director of the Greenville Chamber of Commerce, a state legislator, and president-elect of the Mississippi Bar Association. Keady had been championed by both of Mississippi's United States senators, James Eastland and John Stennis, for the newly created judicial position in the northern federal court district. It seemed hardly likely that such a man could pose a threat to Mississippi or its penitentiary.

On the other hand, while Keady was a political insider, he was also an independent thinker who bowed before no local gods. According to a boyhood friend, "Billy Keady was born an adult and did everything well."[13] He certainly did well enough to gain admission to the Washington University School of Law. That achievement said less for his academic record than for his independence of spirit; in the Mississippi of the early twentieth century, a Delta youngster who opted against the Ole Miss law school was independent indeed. Young Keady's professional perspective had been broadened by association with professors and students at Washington University, and his achievements there had led to his selection for membership in the prestigious Order of the Coif.

After returning to Mississippi, Keady had come up through the professional ranks amid incessant embarrassing disclosures about operations at Parchman, all of which had been reported indignantly by his hometown newspaper, the Greenville *Delta Democrat-Times.* As a young state senator, Keady had chaired the judiciary committee, had steered the state's first parole statute through the legislature, and had often found himself in agreement with Bill Alexander, Howard McDonnell, and other "radical" penal reformers. Such a background made Keady a potentially dangerous man. He was fully aware of the penitentiary's iniquities, of the factors that spawned them, and of the interests that perpetuated them.

Still, there was the troublesome question of civil rights, which had led more than one enlightened Mississippian to shrink in the estimation of the nation. If there were such skeletons in Keady's closet, the American Bar Association's Committee on the Federal Judiciary could not find them. That body, which studied Keady's fitness for appointment to the federal bench, had given the nominee its highest assessment, deeming him exceptionally well qualified for the post.

Once on the bench, Keady had displayed a degree of sympathy for plaintiffs who brought civil liberties claims before his court. The *New York Times* went so far as to say he was "friendly to Negroes."[14] That was probably an overstatement, but clearly Keady's decisions during the four years he served on the court prior to *Gates* suggested that racial prejudice played little part in his thinking. During that period he had ruled in favor of plaintiffs in cases involving school desegregation, racial gerrymandering, and freedom of speech. There were exceptions to that trend in his judicial record, most notably his refusal to enjoin racially segregated private academies from participating in the state's textbook rental program.[15] In twelve key cases prior to *Gates*, however, Judge Keady had supported civil rights plaintiffs in six.

In backing Keady's nomination to the federal judiciary, attorney Charles Clark had described his fellow Mississippian as a "fair man whose life attests that each matter which comes before him will be judged on its merits without regard to the nature of its causes or the personality of the parties."[16] By 1972 history suggested that Clark had known his colleague very well.

All this added up not only to a fair trial, but also to a degree of judicial sensitivity that allowed Keady to "follow the law" in a manner harmonious with political reality. The judge determined early on that the case qualified as a class action under rule twenty-three of the federal rules of civil procedure. The two classes recognized by the court as seeking injunctive and declaratory relief included, first, all present and future persons incarcerated at the state penitentiary, and, secondly, all present and future black inmates. Those decisions struck at the jugular of the penitentiary. While wedding state penal policy with the constitutional issue of Negro equality, they assured that the case would never die for want of a plaintiff and opened the door to the imposition of broad remedies affecting each member of the recognized classes.

Keady's determination that the case qualified as a class action set the stage for a protracted series of legal skirmishes, but legal skirmishing was costly, prohibitively so for the classes recognized by the court. Hence, while the orders for substantive penal reform contained in the initial ruling would be of the first importance, a second spate of decisions revolving around whether the Eleventh Amendment prohibited the district court from awarding attorneys' fees to successful plaintiffs was crucial to the future of the case.

The matter of legal fees for plaintiffs alleging civil rights violations would be resolved in 1976 with the passage of the Civil Rights Attorney's Fees Act, but in the early rounds of *Gates* the state's attorney argued that the Eleventh Amendment prohibited such raids on the state treasury. Both the District Court and the Fifth Circuit Court of Appeals disagreed, holding that state actors had been unreasonably obstinate, and that attorneys for the plaintiffs would be paid from funds regularly appropriated for the operation of the penitentiary.[17] That decision gave real meaning to Keady's earlier determination that *Gates* qualified as a class action: it assured that present and future plaintiffs would be undeterred by pecuniary considerations. Initially the state was ordered to pay $52,736.05 in attorney's fees; that sum would mount significantly in the years ahead.

The early tactics of the courtroom adversaries also had great bearing on the future of the case. The definition of clearly identifiable rights in the plaintiffs' pleadings was absolutely essential in such momentous litigation. Haber skillfully delivered those definitions, thereby allowing the judge to shift the focus of the case away from traditional considerations of pragmatism and federalism to humanistic concerns.[18] Keady shifted shrewdly, dressing his opinions in respected First Amendment, Eighth Amendment, and "equal protection" clothing.

No less important in the pretrial skirmishing was an extensive discovery process that led the state to confess constitutional fault in open court. Governor Waller, recognizing the strength of the plaintiffs' case, stated: "We are, in effect, your Honor, admitting that the constitutional provisions have been violated."[19] The governor's open-court confession probably enhanced his rapport with the court and shielded the state from prolonged, unfavorable publicity. It was, however, a questionable legal tactic, one that dashed the state's chance for a successful appeal and placed all of Mississippi's eggs in the basket of the District Court.

The Initial Ruling of the District Court

Keady's initial finding of fact was handed down on October 20, 1972.[20] The judge began with a nod to the hands-off doctrine but quickly dashed it with the observation that the United States Constitution protected persons rather than considerations of professional expertise and federalism. He then concluded that Mississippi was in violation of the First, Eighth, and Fourteenth amendments as well as of several provisions of its own code relating to standards of food and medical care at the penitentiary.

The Fourteenth Amendment violations centered on infringements of the equal protection and due process clauses. The penitentiary remained racially segregated. Considerations of race not only dictated housing and work assignments, but also figured prominently in vocational training opportunities and the delivery of medical services. Black convicts received a disproportionately small share of resources, and racial discrimination was evident in staff arrangements. Although some two-thirds of the convicts were black, only two recently hired African Americans were on the payroll.

Nor was it difficult to find violations of due process. Disciplinary procedures, to say the least, were on an ad hoc basis. Trusty-shooters often terrorized other convicts by firing around or at them. One prisoner had been shot because he was slow to "get up." Others were chained to fences, forced to stand barefoot on soft drink cases for long periods of time, and beaten. Even statutorily recognized disciplinary procedures were being implemented in violation of inmates' rights to due process. Black Annie had been banned by board policy, if not by statute, in 1965, but the strap remained a hallmark of life at the penitentiary. Assignments to the maximum security unit were being made in violation of the due process requirements of notice and an impartial hearing.

Keady leaned on Judge Henley's standard of a "totality of conditions" in citing infringements of the Eighth Amendment. His investigation had carried him into a "world turned upside down," one in which armed felons often controlled the environment. Damaging indeed had been the admission of former Superintendent Cook that "when the lights go out, there is not much we can do to protect the prisoners from other prisoners." Some camps had cages that were unfit for human habitation. Recently, sewage and waste disposal facilities had been condemned without result by the state's own regulatory agency. These and many other facets of convict life at the penitentiary constituted a "totality of conditions" that violated the Eighth Amendment's clause proscribing "cruel and unusual punishment."

Perhaps the court's findings on solitary confinement portrayed the cruelest, if not the most unusual, transgression. State law prohibited the placement of convicts in the "dark hole" for more than twenty-four hours, but testimony revealed that naked men were being locked in the dark, tiny cells of Little Alcatraz without adequate bedding, heating, food, or hygienic materials for periods of up to seventy-two hours. In itself, solitary confinement was not unconstitutional, ruled Keady, but the circumstances under which it was administered at Parchman violated "human decency."

When compared to the court's other findings, Judge Keady's injunction against the censorship of convicts' mail on the basis of the First Amendment seems relatively unimportant. It was not. Finding that penal authorities exercised undue control over the outgoing mail of convicts, the judge enjoined against the opening, tampering, or restricting of letters addressed by prisoners to state and federal officials, to members of the state probation and parole board, and to attorneys of record. That enjoinment unleashed a steady flow of complaints that revealed, perhaps for the first time, the convicts' version of life within the penitentiary.[21]

Judge Keady's initial ruling was marked by prudential draftsmanship. There was a solid reliance on precedent, a careful portrayal of the state's violations of its own statutes, and, whenever possible, an inclusion of incriminating findings by state regulatory agencies supporting the court's conclusions. All in all it was an overpowering opinion characterized by an extraordinary grasp of facts, and it prefaced an order for immediate relief: the termination of mail censorship, of the improper utilization of solitary confinement, of corporal punishment, and of racial discrimination. In addition, the state was directed to establish proper administrative procedures for the penitentiary, to develop a plan for the proper classification of inmates, to phase out the trusty-shooters, to improve physical facilities, and to provide better protection for prisoners.

These requirements for immediate relief, while of the first importance, were not earthshaking; in essence they called for change within the context of existing operations. But Judge Keady's orders for long-range relief made it all too clear that he meant business, that his real target was Parchman's *system*, and that he was fully prepared to wage protracted warfare with state officials. Under the category of long-range relief were orders for the state to investigate means of improving medical, water, and sewage facilities, of constructing additional housing, of reducing the convict population, and of terminating forced labor.

Understanding the enormity of the task at hand, and no doubt the thinking of state politicians, the judge set the first of what would become many deadlines. He wanted written plans for the termination of all specified unconstitutional conditions by December 20, 1972. Boding of a more comprehensive assault to come, he reserved the power to issue further orders. Like Judge Henley before him, Keady would pose as an inquisitor.

The "Cosmetic" State Response

Political pragmatism shaped the state's initial response to *Gates*. Given the implications of the decision, the Waller administration had little choice but to appeal, despite the hole that had been punched in the state's case by the governor's earlier courtroom admission that constitutional provisions were being violated. An appeal also promised to buy time. As matters stood, the penitentiary was legally indefensible, but the context of Mississippi politics made sweeping reform an impossibility. Delay would enable the state to effect modest remedial measures displaying good faith. Even if such tactics proved unsuccessful, continuing litigation would at least blunt the force of the blow. So the state went forward with a plea to the United States Fifth Circuit Court of Appeals, arguing that the District Court's finding imposed unreasonable expense on the public treasury and constituted an excessive degree of intervention by a federal court in a state-operated institution.[22]

The campaign to show good faith had begun during 1972, shortly before the ruling of the District Court, with the creation of a department of mental health services and an "official" adult education program at Parchman. Both innovations were tactics designed to patch holes in the state's case, and in September 1972, just before Keady's ax fell, an embarrassing murder by a half-trusty at Parchman had inspired a concerned governor to appoint a special investigatory commission headed by a prominent member of the state bench.[23]

In the wake of Judge Keady's ruling, however, the state's attorneys were undermined by continuing political inertia within Mississippi and by yet another spate of penitentiary-related scandals. Astonishingly, convicts continued to keep the penitentiary's financial records until well after the initial ruling in *Gates.* Professional audits later disclosed great humor on the part of the convict-accountants. Twenty-one new tires installed on the same vehicle in a single week? An automobile engine mounted on a commode?[24]

All the while, little effort was made to hide petty graft by state employees. New suits were purchased for board and staff members under the guise of "uniforms." A commissioner's insurance company handled the workman's compensation account of the penitentiary. And shortly after Judge Keady's initial ruling in October 1972, a story broke that a member of the board had purchased 208 pounds of beef and pork from the penitentiary for $48.90. Questioned about the transaction, the man explained lamely that such favored purchases constituted a privilege that had been "passed along."[25]

Also difficult for the state was the fact that an unqualified in-law of the governor superintended the penitentiary. That, in itself, was bad enough, but in early December 1972 word broke that Collier had spent $15,000 out of what the state was representing as an austere penitentiary budget to purchase office furniture from a firm that was owned by another kinsman of the governor. A few years earlier the transaction would not have caused so much as a ripple on the surface of state politics, and Collier was correct in thinking that such things were among the traditional "perks" of the "super." Now, though, it simply would not do. Waller directed the superintendent to return the furniture. Collier submitted a letter of resignation.[26]

The unfortunate Collier was replaced on an interim basis by Bill Hollowell, chief of police at Indianola, while the board initiated a national search for a superintendent. But the legislature refused to approve a competitive salary; given the many "perks" of the job, $17,000 per annum was enough. Hence everyone who was interviewed left with the impression that inadequate remuneration, the horrid condition of the penitentiary, and a political quagmire rendered the superintendency untenable. One candidate, a native Mississippian employed by the Colorado penal system, declined the job with the comment that Parchman was the worst prison he had ever seen.[27]

As applicants came and went during the first half of 1973, the Waller administration sought to redress the problem of overcrowding at the penitentiary. Here, too, the legislature refused to cooperate, balking at the idea of major construction and renovation at Parchman, opposing early-release schemes, and absolutely nixing a proposal to foist satellite units on local government. So Waller went, hat in hand, to hostile local officials, beseeching them with only modest success to retain state prisoners in county jails until the state could remedy the housing shortage at Parchman and Lambert. Meanwhile, the Lawyers Committee for Civil Rights Under Law, now assisted by several prisoners' rights groups based within Mississippi, kept state authorities reeling by introducing additional litigation. In rapid succession, prisoner-plaintiffs won suits forcing the state to establish a law library at Parchman and giving Muslim convicts the right to worship.[28]

Waller had run out of rope by the summer of 1973. The inmate population was increasing, matters were not going well in the appellate court, neither the legislature nor local politicians were cooperating, and Hollowell hardly conformed to the District Court's notion of a qualified chief administrator. Keady nudged matters forward in August by ordering an increase of $15,000 in the annual salary of the superintendent. Legislators fumed and cursed about this attack on their sovereignty, swearing to resist it at all cost; but the court order allowed the besieged Waller to secure the extra money from the Law Enforcement Assistance Administration. The penitentiary got a federally financed superintendent some three months later.[29]

The Short Career of the "Hit Man"

Jack Reed was the only viable candidate willing to accept the job. He was an intelligent, energetic prison man from California with a wealth of professional experience. He came to Mississippi knowing that the legal and political parameters of his job made him a "hit man" for the hated federal judiciary, a scapegoat for a hopelessly trapped governor, and in many ways he was well-equipped for the task at hand.

Formerly a lumberjack, a Marine, and a combat veteran of Korea, Reed had thick skin and the disposition of a warrior; he quickly identified the enemy and attacked with vigor. Surrounded by uncooperative staff members, he placed "Yankee bastards"—colleagues from California—in key staff positions. He brazenly sought to terminate entrenched local influence in penitentiary affairs without so much as a tactical smile. He refused to wink at the misappropriation of penitentiary lands, the private exploitation of convict labor, and the larceny and petty graft that were inseparable aspects of the old system. For all the world, this man seemed to embody the hated encroachments of liberal federalism in Mississippi; the lips of the local people curled whenever they uttered his name.[30]

The superintendent's popularity was hardly enhanced when he abruptly dismantled the foundations of the old penal farm system. He removed the gunmen from the fields. He relieved the shooters and persuaded the governor to replace them with unhappy state highway patrolmen until the legislature could be induced to appropriate monies for civilian guards. He ordered racial integration within the camps and attempted to redress racial imbalance among his staff. Legal tokenism had led to the appointment of two black staff officers, including a camp sergeant, in 1972. Now Reed made a black man, the Reverend James T. McGlowan, one of his principal assistants and promoted the cause of Eddie Holloway, who later would become Mississippi's first black warden.[31]

Reed also caught the brunt of the criticism arising from increased legislative appropriations and the termination of penal farming. Distressed legislators, acting with a federal gun at their backs, coughed up an unprecedented $3 million for renovations, including $875,000 for the sweltering maximum security unit. Such a financial outlay was deeply resented, and resentment increased in May 1974 when the Mississippi Cooperative Extension Service assumed total control of all agricultural operations at the penitentiary, thereby divorcing the farm from the prison and exploding the hallowed, if long-sagging, ideal of remunerative convict labor.[32]

The reforms implemented by Reed, especially the integration of the races, bred unprecedented security and disciplinary problems at Parchman, and the superintendent was also hampered by scheming staff members. As early as January 1974 he was locked in bitter conflict with a number of his own subordinates who reportedly plotted with hostile local politicians, and in Jackson a powerful anti-Reed lobby was emerging. The difficulties, Reed snapped condescendingly, were caused by the "blood-sucking good ole boys" who encircled Parchman "like vultures," by the very iniquities that had undermined the state's case in *Gates*.[33]

The superintendent's position was weakened by his poorly developed social skills and general lifestyle. Reed, like Lowery Love before him, was altogether incapable of maneuvering in the closed society of the Mississippi Delta. A touch of humility, an occasional joke, an understanding word, a slap on the back—any of those tactics could have won him friends. But he either would not or could not do it. He was at war, he refused to be intimidated by the enemy, and his hard, indifferent glare alienated more than one would-be peacemaker.

Reed also liked a good drink; alcohol sometimes made him say and do very dubious things, and that personal failing left him vulnerable to attack. In the spring of 1974 twenty-five of the penitentiary's employees signed a notarized statement alleging that the superintendent often drove state vehicles while under the influence of alcohol. Reed brushed off the allegation, but subsequent incidents led to widespread gossip that a brutish alcoholic was running the penitentiary. Of those incidents, the most spectacular was Reed's fall from a tree while demonstrating his prowess as a lumberjack in the front yard of the superintendent's home at Parchman.[34]

All this added up to a political tug-of-war. Reed's strongest supporter was Tyler Fletcher, chairman of the penitentiary board, who almost begged the superintendent to clean up his behavior, only to be embarrassed on numerous occasions. Two members of Fletcher's five-man board were adamantly opposed to the confirmation of Reed's appointment, and, despite intensive lobbying by Fletcher, the senate penitentiary committee voted five-to-four against confirmation in the spring of 1974. With the support of the governor and a shaky majority of one on the penitentiary board, though, the superintendent agreed to carry on, never knowing at dawn if he would have a job at dusk.[35]

Again the federal bench nudged the state forward. On September 24, 1974, the United States Fifth Circuit Court of Appeals rejected Mississippi's fiscal and jurisdictional arguments, holding that the injunctive relief provided by Judge Keady was within the remedial jurisdiction of the District Court.[36] David Lipman, heading the newly formed Mississippi Prisoners' Defense Committee, had contended in a recent number of the *Mississippi Law Journal* that the state's response to the original orders of the District Court had been merely "cosmetic."[37] Now, with the state's appeal laid low, he took the offensive, in late 1974 representing a group of inmate-plaintiffs who contended that the state had failed to comply with the District Court's original order in a number of material respects.

Clearly, state politicians were dragging their feet, continuing to speculate that the replacement of a few urine-soaked mattresses, a little sprucing up, and the addition of several new units at Parchman would suffice; since October 1972 only 368 new beds had been added.[38] But Keady gave his old political colleagues ample reason to rethink matters on January 1, 1975, when he held that Mississippi remained in violation of both the Eighth Amendment and its own code due to insufficient housing and a failure to provide for the physical health and well-being of inmates. Then Keady turned the screws by establishing a schedule for housing relief. Constitutionally insufficient cages would be closed at designated intervals in the future, he warned.[39]

The failure of the state's appeal and Keady's uncompromising order of January 1975 brought penitentiary politics to a new juncture, but even now state politicians displayed alarming truculence. Although Reed was the only qualified superintendent available, and although Keady had praised him in his ruling of January, fifteen senators voted in the minority when Reed was at last confirmed later in the month. Despite Keady's threat to close old units, and despite projections that warned of an approaching deluge of commitments, the legislature appropriated funds for the construction of only two 162-bed units at Parchman. Knowing full well that 324 new beds were insufficient, the legislators bickered about the best way to reduce the convict population, decided that none of the alternatives was feasible, and left the solution of that unhappy problem in the hands of the chief executive.[40]

Caught squarely between a federal judge demanding money bills and a legislature unwilling to deliver them, Governor Waller was incapable of doing much. A number of articles in the January 1975 number of *Inside World* related the problems faced by the chief executive and his superintendent. The roofs of the old cages leaked terribly. The sewage system was awful. Anyone sitting on a commode when it rained was thrilled by a "backup bath." But the "number one problem" at Parchman, an inmate staff writer observed astutely, was inadequate and overcrowded housing.

The "number one problem" worsened daily, and the Mississippi Prisoners' Defense Committee exploited the opening. On August 7, 1975, surely to the surprise of nobody, Judge Keady ordered the closure of several antiquated cages and mandated that henceforth every inmate must be allocated at least fifty square feet of living space.[41]

The ruling of the District Court brought state criminal policy to a point of crisis similar to that which had developed in the years immediately following the War Between the States. An independent, elected, and thus hard-nosed state judiciary was generating inmates without reference to the penal resources of the state. Legislators, reflecting on the views of their constituents, were understandably reluctant to mitigate the severity of the penal law or to allocate scarce resources for the enhancement of convict life. Each legislator, representing a local constituency, was loathe to foist the problem on local jails. Now something had to give. So between July 1, 1975, and June 30, 1976, as legislators engaged in get-tough-on-crime rhetoric, and as the first of Parchman's sagging cages were consumed by flames, records were set as fully 1,202 convicts were dispatched via parole, "emergency" suspensions, and various schemes of work release. During the same period, however, the state's trial courts produced 1,356 new commitments. By June 30, 1976, Parchman's inmate population had grown to 2,509, its highest level since the peak years of the Great Depression.[42]

In the midst of this unfolding dilemma, Jack Reed's native impetuosity and vulnerable lifestyle at last enabled his numerous enemies to get him. On March 17, 1976, Reed fired his well-connected associate superintendent for security during a midnight altercation. The circumstances surrounding the rhubarb cost the beleaguered superintendent the support of his most powerful ally, board chairman Tyler Fletcher, and on Fletcher's recommendation Reed was relieved of his duties almost immediately by the new governor, Cliff Finch.[43]

Breaking for Daylight

The edicts of the District Court and the firing of Reed created a vacuum in penitentiary politics. Something simply had to be done to reverse a deteriorating situation. The governor knew it, the state attorney general knew it, the members of the board knew it; but few members of the legislature wanted even to talk about the problem. The dilemma demanded unity of action, a bold stroke capable of combating the inertia of fragmented legislative governance, but everyone winced when Chairman Fletcher proposed the obvious.

Fletcher was a native of Texas, a former colonel in the United States Army who had commanded military police in Saigon at the height of the "police action" in Vietnam, and more recently he had accepted employment as chairman of the state's first department of criminal justice at the University of Southern Mississippi. Fletcher was shrewd, a calculating man of the first rank, and one to whom people were inclined to listen. Now they listened as he laid out a plan.

Since Judge Keady's initial ruling of October 1972, state officials had been on the defensive, reacting begrudgingly instead of acting constructively to stabilize the worsening drift of the penitentiary. That failing, Fletcher pointed out, was owing largely to the centralization of the penal system in Sunflower County, where local political influence thwarted change and assured continuing difficulty with the federal judiciary. Up to this time the power of Sunflower County legislators had gone unchallenged. Now, however, the lessons of Reed's superintendency, the edicts of the District Court, and overcrowding at the penitentiary opened the door to reforms that might loosen, if not break, the iron grasp of Delta politicians.

Fletcher argued that the state must abandon the defensive, launch an ambitious statewide penal system, and develop a political framework within which competent administrators might operate with effect. With an eye to those goals, the chairman of the board resurrected Bill Alexander's old concept: the creation of a powerful, Jackson-based department of corrections. The existence of such a department, he felt, might shift the political base of the penal system from the Delta to Jackson, facilitate the distribution of the penitentiary's patronage among an expanded number of political constituencies, and shield penal administrators from the pressures of local politics.[44]

The proposal sought to undo the principal provision of the penitentiary act of 1934, to resurrect a major component of Vardaman's old scheme, and that fact assured determined opposition. Old-timers remembered the days when Betsy Montgomery's independent, Jackson-based penitentiary board had caused so much trouble with its meddling at Parchman. They remembered, too, the traumatic duel between Montgomery and Governor Mike Conner, the undoing of the elected board, the centralization of penal administration in Sunflower County, and the "good old days" that had followed.

But it did not take an old-timer to realize that Fletcher's ideas threatened the interests of Sunflower County. Parchman was the county's greatest employer, the pipeline through which state and federal monies flowed into an economically deprived section of the Delta, and the local folk stood to lose a great deal if the penitentiary's patronage were spread around. Fletcher's proposal also promised to make graft—winked at by state officials for three-quarters of a century—much more difficult. Furthermore, everyone had doubts about the efficacy of a Jackson-based bureaucracy that, like all bureaucracies, would surely expand and breed an ever-widening division of authority between practitioners and politically influenced bureaucrats operating from the seat of government. For those reasons Sunflower County politicians mobilized for political combat, called allies to their side, and soon posed formidable strength.

Judge Keady's former rulings and his continuing inquisitorial posture enhanced Fletcher's position. Governor Finch, always keen on any proposal that might increase his patronage, and no great favorite in the Delta, was with him. So, too, were A. F. Summer, the state attorney general, who saw no other game in town; Con Maloney of Jackson, the polished chairman of the newly renamed senate corrections committee; Robert "Bunky" Huggins of Leflore County, an influential member of the lower house who was willing to break with the Delta oligarchy; and Bill Alexander himself, now concluding a distinguished political career as president pro tempore of the senate. Provided with useful "inside information" by supporters at Parchman, Fletcher stirred the political cauldron, and at last a heavily compromised bill creating a state department of corrections was enacted.[45]

The new department, which was authorized to begin operations on July 1, 1976, was to be governed by a lay board consisting of seven members appointed by the governor with the advice and consent of the senate. In addition to setting general policy, the board was to approve new facilities, programs, and operational decisions, to open bids and sanction the sale of all products, and to approve all administrative decisions promulgated by the department. Appointed by the board with the advice and consent of the senate was a commissioner of corrections who was to serve as the department's chief executive officer. Under the commissioner was placed a considerable supporting staff, including a warden who supplanted the superintendent as Parchman's chief administrator.[46]

The new scheme, which was wrapped in a great deal of high-sounding language about "correcting" convicts through "modern" methodology, was launched in the summer of 1976, when Governor Finch appointed the members of the new board and hired an interim commissioner, the much-traveled Ellis McDougall. As trucks transported records from Parchman to a suite of offices near the state capitol in central Jackson, McDougall and a skeleton staff took stock of their resources and began to chart policy. In December 1976 the Finch administration scored what was thought to be a major coup when Dr. Alan Ault, described by McDougall as one of the top three prison administrators in the nation, left the Georgia penal system and became Mississippi's first permanent commissioner of corrections.

Ault set about his duties with vigor, boldly advancing proposals that made everyone wince, and fighting off intrigues in both the legislature and the Governor's Mansion. Attorney General Summer argued with apparent effect before the United States Fifth Circuit Court of Appeals that the creation of the department of corrections enhanced the state's effort to comply with the orders of the District Court.[47] Meanwhile, as the personable Ault moved forward, attempting to build a political constituency, winning dreamers, and mortifying the old guard, and as new and troubling alignments began to appear in the legislature, the framers of the penitentiary act of 1976 looked toward the future with trepidation, fully aware that a new and uncertain era loomed.

Epilogue

Marching to the Beat of a Federal Drum

Dating from the initial ruling in *Gates v. Collier* and continuing through the early months of 1992, the United States District Court for the Northern District of Mississippi has issued in excess of 150 orders relating to the administration of criminal corrections. The orders generally define legal incarceration as the deprivation or restriction of liberty by due process of law and seek to deliver to the imprisoned those protections of the Bill of Rights deemed compatible with the essential interests of discipline and security. The District Court has also bestowed on state inmates a right to a specified standard of living and access to a number of legal, medical, rehabilitative, recreational, and educational services.[1]

Was the intervention of the federal judiciary necessary? Yes. The penitentiary Judge Keady evaluated in 1972 was, indeed, "a world turned upside down," a quagmire of public corruption, racial inequity, and brutality. There was no way to defend the Parchman of John Collier; there was no alternative to an inquisition by the federal judiciary. Almost unbelievable transgressions of legality and morality by state actors demanded the application of the protections of the Bill of Rights, come what may.

Has federal intervention brought improvement? Again, yes, provided one subscribes to the libertarian or "justice model" of criminal corrections. The racial abuses that so influenced Judge Keady's early orders have been addressed. The old Parchman practiced racial segregation; the contemporary penal system is fully integrated. The old had no black employees; the current staff of the MDOC reflects a considerable triumph for Affirmative Action employment. And, of course, while Parchman's old system was designed to manage the black men who composed the bulk of Mississippi's convicts, the new one does not consider the racial or ethnic peculiarities of inmates in matters pertaining to discipline and security.

The "justice model" also affords inmates much more protection from the iniquities of their keepers. Before federal intervention, legal resources were generally not available to convicts; today, inmates are guaranteed access to law libraries, to writ-writers, and to legal counsel at all times. Formerly, inmates enjoyed no First Amendment rights; discipline and security, the argument went, demanded that prison officials inspect and, if necessary, censor incoming and outgoing mail. Today, convicts enjoy written communication with the free world largely free of meddling.

Prisoners had no right to due process before federal intervention; the superintendent and his sergeants served as judge and jury whenever their charges violated rules, and they imposed sanctions, including the lash and solitary confinement, without a mechanism for external review. Today, due process rights are followed to the letter in all disciplinary proceedings.

The libertarian penitentiary also maintains strict culinary, sartorial, and medical standards; and it offers a wide array of educational, vocational, recreational, and religious opportunities. Alcohol and drug treatment programs, psychological services, and counseling programs are available to inmates. Forced labor is out. No longer do inmates reside in shabby, crowded barracks. Modern structures, each conforming to the space requirements of the District Court, now house felons.[2]

Quite another question, however, is whether federal intervention and the forced application of the "justice model" have led to substantive improvement within the broader pail of criminal jurisprudence. Have the reforms brought a dysfunctional state political process nearly right? Have they fostered more efficient prison administration? Have they enhanced efforts to rehabilitate convicts? Have they redressed the racial imbalance of the inmate population? Are convicts, black and white, really better off? Has the libertarian agenda preserved the essential punitive foundations of public law? Have the changes accrued to the advantage of the governed?

A political veteran of Mississippi's penitentiary wars expresses mixed feelings:

> Keady's main focus was the racial issue and the stupidity and corruption of Barnett's and Johnson's and Williams's people up at Parchman. Hell, it was out of hand by the time Waller came on the scene, and Bill [Keady] was right to lower the boom. But he went too far. He forgot the good things that existed at Parchman under Wiggins and Harpole. He forgot the terrible impact of the civil rights movement on Mississippi politics; hell, things weren't normal back then; it was obviously a period of chaotic transition that would pass. He forgot what criminal process was all about too, and he damn sure forgot what a state penitentiary is in business for.
>
> Anyhow, in writing your book, don't assume, like everybody else seems to, that things are necessarily better at Parchman now than they were in Wiggins's last years. They're better than they were when Bill got involved—God, anything would be—but, racism or no racism, I'll put Wiggins's Parchman, and maybe Harpole's too, up against anything in the country, then or now. Bill [Keady] meant well. But like all the lawyers who grew up worshipping that Goddamn Earl Warren, he went overboard with the rights thing and ended up throwing the baby out with the bath water. Never has there been a bigger mess.[3]

Did Judge Keady throw "the baby out with the bath water?" He certainly had second thoughts. In 1986, shortly after his retirement, the judge took stock of the changes wrought by *Gates* and its progeny, hailed the improvements, but concluded despondently that the Mississippi penal system was "an ongoing problem that is going to be with us long after I'm gone."[4] Keady died on May 18, 1989. Well over two years later, when the typescript of this book went to press, the penal system remained an "ongoing problem" with no relief in sight.

An Administrative Quagmire

In late 1976, shortly after the creation of the Mississippi Department of Corrections, Tyler Fletcher assessed the political ramifications of continued intervention by the federal judiciary:

> As things stand, the politics of the thing are impossible. The department of corrections is a vehicle for the formulation and implementation of penal policy, but it has no political constituency within the state and can have neither a policy nor a constituency so long as Keady keeps the state reeling. The governor and the legislature cannot act, only react, because they are caught squarely between the demands of the electorate and the edicts of the federal bench.[5]

Fletcher's assessment was extraordinarily sagacious. Throughout its history the MDOC has been a stepchild within the state's political process, an ever-expanding bureaucracy born of federal pressure and operating in an executive no-man's-land between the United States District Court and the feuding representatives of a hostile state electorate.

Stable leadership has been rare indeed. Frustrated by gubernatorial politics, by the truculence of legislators, and by the limp attitudes of even his own supporters, Commissioner Ault lasted less than a year. He was succeeded by John Watkins, a glib, philosophical Alabamian of considerable administrative ability, but Watkins, too, was undone by the unhappy political parameters of his job and sent packing in 1980 when the Finch administration left office.

A degree of stability came during the subsequent commissionership of Morris Thigpen, a remarkably liberal-minded native Mississippian with a background in juvenile corrections. Thigpen was a plodder, an appeaser; but he necessarily did much more reacting than acting, and from the day of his appointment in 1980 until he departed for the greener pastures of the Alabama penal system in 1987, he was unfairly criticized as a "do-nothing toady who licked the boots of the federal bench." After the interim commissionership of Donald Cabana, Gene Scroggy took the helm. Scroggy licked nobody's boots, minced no words, attempted to fashion a proactive scheme of policy, and failed to gain senate confirmation. There followed the interim commissionership of Charles Jackson. At last glance the educator and veteran prison administrator Lee Roy Black, Mississippi's first African American commissioner, was occupying the office. According to a senior state politician, the hue of Black's skin "gives him a unique if ridiculous advantage, but he can't be expected to last."[6]

A high-level administrator of the MDOC assessed the plight of a continuing succession of commissioners:

> He doesn't know whose ass to kiss—the federal judge's, the governor's, or those of powerful legislators. The fact is, that he must kiss all of them and hope that nobody notices. But they do notice, and everyone knows that the commissioner is a whore. Neither he nor his department stand for anything. It is the most frustrating, thankless job in the world. The man spends half his time either in court or getting ready to go to court and does nothing but react to the conflicting currents around him.[7]

Not surprisingly, the MDOC has been unable to formulate and implement realistic, clearly defined goals and objectives; all too often, no decision has been the decision. "We have no mission," one employee complained. "The court wants one thing and the legislature wants another. . . . [So] we dodge bullets and hope the payroll continues."[8]

Among the employees of the MDOC, nobody has spent more time dodging bullets than wardens. Like commissioners, they have come and gone with alarming frequency, and several have developed serious physiological or behavioral disorders after only a short stint on the job. According to a former state legislator, the position of warden at Parchman is untenable:

> He must straddle an impossible line. Sunflower County politicians have their demands, and he cannot ignore them. The department [of corrections] has its demands . . . and virtually all of them conflict with local politics and the prison business. He is a scapegoat for the department. . . . In the meantime he is trying to appease the District Court, which is outside the world of practical politics. . . . No warden can survive a situation like that very long.[9]

Below wardens, employees voice confusion, negativism, and fear. None of them, it seems, are quite sure of what is expected of them, or if they can depend on the support of their superiors. "Nobody knows what to do," claims one young correctional officer. "They [middle managers] tell you one thing one day, something else the next, and all the while you know they'll cut your balls off and cover their own asses if someone in Jackson gets embarrassed or pissed off by something you do or don't do."[10]

Unprecedented problems with inmates have developed as a direct result of policies implemented by court order. The granting of First Amendment rights to convicts, which facilitated a number of disturbances and mail order scams, proved so unworkable in a prison setting that the federal judiciary was forced to sanction a number of abridgements.[11] Within Mississippi's penal institutions, however, the greatest legacy of federal intervention is a shift in the balance of power between the keepers and the kept.

Those staff members who function in the prison trenches live in fear of their charges. According to one employee, constant inmate access to a law library and writ-writers confounds "every semblance" of prison discipline:

> There is now a class of inmate ambulance-chasers, a virtual gestapo, who . . . intimidate the staff. A convict can spit in your face and [the 'legal experts'] appear, daring you to retaliate, swearing that the spitter was provoked by injustice and threatening legal reprisal. The convicts know that the staff's hands are tied, that they can run to the [law library] if we dare to meet fire with fire. We must treat prisoners, especially the black ones, with kid gloves because every convict is a lawsuit waiting to happen. . . .[12]

The power to intimidate has fostered increasingly aggressive behavior on the part of many inmates. In fiscal year 1990 the emergency room in Parchman's hospital treated 1,136 injuries resulting from inmate assaults on staff members. During the same time frame, the disciplinary department heard 4,492 rules violation reports and conducted 3,084 investigations.[13]

One correctional officer insists that the convicts hold the upper hand:

> . . . I faced the same situation in 'Nam. We went to fight. We had the tools to fight. But orders from above wouldn't let us fight on Charlie's terms. So we hid in our base camps, fought with each other and eventually got our asses kicked. . . . Police officers face the same situation we do. Some of them have been brutal in the past. More of them have simply met fire with fire; it's demanded by the job. Now, though, witch-hunts by journalists and the courts have them intimidated and, just like us, they are getting their asses kicked. . . . [So] we back off and cover our own asses and laugh at people who wonder why there is more crime. Shit, the whole thing is crazy. The assumption is that we are the bad guys.[14]

Not surprisingly, annual staff turnover within the MDOC approaches 20 percent.[15] That rate is substantial in itself, but extraordinarily high for a state plagued by chronic unemployment and for an agency that offers the bulk of its jobs in the most economically deprived sections of it.

The New Lives of Inmates

While breeding halting behavior among MDOC administrators and correctional officers, the "justice model" is also plagued by the fact that it focuses on prisons and prisoners in a vacuum. Nowhere does one discern accompanying emphasis on the socioeconomic structures and processes of the "free world" to which most criminologists attribute criminality, and to which a released felon must return. So despite the federal inquisition, there has not been much change in the demography of the state inmate population. On June 30, 1956, when a hostile and powerful Jim Crow was arming and loading in anticipation of the federal onslaught, 73.6 percent of state convicts were black. On June 30, 1990, Commissioner Black's office reported that 71.2 percent of the inmates were African Americans.[16]

Nor does the "justice model" assign much importance to the unique social structures and processes of prison life. Students of American prisons note that a transition from a common to a divergent value system began to characterize inmate society during the early 1960s. They also observe that since that time, gangs organized on racial and ethnic lines have constituted a dominant feature of prison life, and that these developments have emasculated staff members and revolutionized prison administration. These developments are the inevitable result of court orders forcing the libertarian ideal of equal treatment, and the resulting tactic of social integration, on prison administrators.[17]

The impact of racial integration on the Mississippi penal system has been considerable. Gangs of blacks and whites mobilized almost immediately in Parchman's integrated cages, each with a hierarchy of leadership upheld by intimidation, force, and appeals to racial solidarity. A black former convict asserts that men of his own race, attempting to enforce unity of action behind convict-chieftains, threatened his personal security "a lot more than the staff and the white cons." A young white convict, writing to a friend in late 1975, gave a similar account of the tactics that molded gangs among convicts of his race and told of the ensuing racial warfare. He survived the attacks of gangs of blacks only because "I made me a knife about ten inches long and started cutting people." "People," he added, "get stabbed here all the time." That contention was confirmed by another white convict in the spring of 1976. Writing from Camp Six, "the roughest camp on the farm," he asserted that "All these big spades think they can . . . make me their bitch. . . . I got a black eye and a few knots on my head, but did pretty good to be against seven dudes."[18]

By all appearances, racial tensions have not eased. In 1990 a veteran employee of the MDOC asserted that the demands of "politics and public relations" necessitated silence on the racial context of prison violence. That, he lamented, was ironic because "the inmates are the victims of a social abstraction that hasn't even been achieved in the free world, and a new standard of political correctness keeps us from tackling the problem." After several nudges, and a guarantee of strict confidentiality, the man was induced to elaborate:

> Hey, I support equal opportunities and equal treatment for everybody. But racial integration is one thing in the free world and another thing in a prison. We are not dealing with educated, sensitive, reasonable people. In most cases we are dealing with the damn scum of the earth, and the federal bench doesn't seem to understand the chemistry of our inmate population. Power is the game. It is won in two ways: by physical force and by appeals to the worst prejudices. Power-hungry cons exploit racism to feather their own nests. That builds black and white gangs that stalk each other, do horrible shit to each other and hold together with constant reminders of the blood that flows. I suppose everyone has their own opinion, but for my money the chief result of federal intervention has been the substitution of racially-inspired convict-on-convict brutality for staff-on-convict brutality, and I've got to believe that the inmates are in much more personal danger now than they used to be.[19]

During fiscal year 1990, 1,169 of Parchman's inmates required medical treatment for injuries sustained in assaults by their peers.[20]

Perhaps the evident breakdown of authority within Mississippi's penal institutions explains a number of disappointing failures in key areas of correctional administration. During fiscal year 1990 only 849 inmates, or slightly over 10 percent of the institutionalized population, participated in vocational programs; and of those, merely 101, or about 11.9 percent, achieved certification in a trade. The successes of educational programs were also modest. Unaccountably, precise statistics on the number of inmates who participated in MDOC adult education and junior college programs were not reported. Based on printed estimates, however, a scant 993, or 12 percent of all inmates, pursued education in letters, and but 123 of some 861 participants in adult education programs, or about 14.3 percent, passed the high school equivalency (GED) examination.[21]

The most unnerving fact regarding the contemporary vocational and educational programs of the MDOC is that their successes do not stack up very well against those of the penitentiary during biennium 1955–57. Bill Harpole and his staff did not present a precise headcount of inmates involved in vocational education, but they did mention the operation of a thriving program that included woodworking, mechanical and electrical arts, painting, plumbing, carpentry, handicrafts, and numerous other marketable skills. Then, too, an astonishing 47 percent of the inmate population were said to have participated in two "highly competitive" hobby shows in which a "considerable amount of creative ability was observed in all entries ranging from leathercraft and ceramic molding to wood-working, plastics, needle-work, and hundreds of general handicraft items." And one must remember that those were the days when the penitentiary strove for self-sufficiency. Inmates were employed regularly in the myriad support services of a huge business enterprise.

A comparison of the reported educational statistics of 1955–57 and 1989–90 is no less troubling. Harpole's educational director reported that about 20 percent of the convict population had participated in the penitentiary's voluntary, state-certified adult education program, that 74.8 percent of them attended regularly, and that 23.2 percent of the participants were awarded promotion certificates. Those statistics did not take into account "hundreds of men not assigned to regular classes because of their jobs, who have been issued materials with which to study in their spare time," or an unidentified number of inmates pursuing correspondence courses offered by the state's institutions of higher learning.[22]

It also seems that the inmates of the old penitentiary enjoyed greater healthfulness, notwithstanding a comparative dearth of medical services and the great advances in medical technology that have occurred since the mid-fifties. Harpole reported an average of 3.60 sick calls per inmate; the MDOC reported an average of 3.97 at Parchman in fiscal year 1990.[23]

One must suspect that the regular physical exertion demanded of inmates at the old penitentiary promoted healthfulness; but so, too, did a diet featuring unlimited amounts of farm-grown vegetables, frequent rations of chicken and turkey, and sparse servings of red meat. One elderly convict, who holds the dubious distinction of serving time under both the old and new regimes, insists that "there ain't no comparison" between the old food and the new:

> Back in the old days they worked us like dogs, sun-up to sundown, and whipped us like mules if we gave 'em any trouble, but they Goddamn sure fed us. Good shit, too—better than grandma made. The food now ain't bad, but it ain't good neither. Reminds me of the high school cafeteria.[24]

Other significant data also figure in the comparison. In fiscal year 1957, 40 percent of commitments were recidivists; in 1990, 49 percent. And surely cost is a legitimate standard of evaluation in correctional administration. In fiscal year 1955, Marvin Wiggins produced a net profit of $525,440.93, or about $247 per inmate. In fiscal year 1990, the drain of the MDOC on the public purse exceeded $75 million.[25]

The contradiction of all contradictions, though, lies in Parchman's recently instituted Regimented Inmate Discipline (R.I.D.) Program. It is a short "shock probation program" for first-time offenders. It offers "Psychological Intervention, Drug/Alcohol Rehabilitation, Specialized Intervention, and Multiple Assessment Strategies." But the cornerstone of R.I.D. is "discipline therapy." It creates a "boot camp." It is "paramilitary." It features "drill instructors" who teach criminals "that there are certain rules and regulations of society which must be adhered to." And the essence of R.I.D., according to an involved employee, is "to bust young asses enough that they won't come back." Success has been remarkable, and the program has been hailed as a major breakthrough by the national media. Bill Harpole, who supported R.I.D. as a state senator, smiled and changed the subject when asked to comment on the similarities between the program and his old scheme of discipline at Parchman.[26]

Underlying the "ongoing problem" of which Judge Keady spoke in 1986 is a simple truth. While the imposition of the "justice model" was necessary in 1972, and while components of it are essential today, there is much reason to doubt its utility as a permanent nexus of state penal policy. For the libertarian standard places secondary emphasis on every plausible principle of penal jurisprudence and, in Mississippi at least, neither retribution, deterrence, incapacitation, nor rehabilitation has been a high priority of policy makers since 1976. In the words of Tyler Fletcher, the "all-consuming consideration, the thing that has permeated everything, has been the attempt to meet the space requirements of the District Court."[27]

A Matter of Demand and Supply

Throughout Mississippi history, an exacting penal code reflecting the values of the governed has combined with the custodial sentences of an independent, elected judiciary to place great demands on the scarce resources of a poor state. The resulting contest between demand and supply figured prominently in territorial penal policy, in the establishment of the first state penitentiary, in the rise of the convict lease system, and at last in the concentration of all state convicts on penal farms.

After the establishment of penal farming, and the emergence of a system of incentives that allowed superintendents to regulate the size and makeup of the convict population via the clemency powers of chief executives, the pressures created by the exacting penal code and by the independent judiciary were largely neutralized. The coming of parole in 1944, while having a decided impact on the composition of the convict population, had no appreciable effect on its size, and the advent of probation twelve years later had no effect on the supply of custodial sentences either. Excepting only the peak years of the Great Depression, the number of incarcerated state convicts remained remarkably stable at some eighteen hundred between 1920 and the early 1970s.

Coinciding with the imposition of space requirements by the District Court, however, was a substantial increase in the number of felony convictions handed down by the state's trial courts. That increase, which has continued to the present day, has graphically revealed the severity of the conflict between the federal judiciary and the state's political structures and processes. For in the face of a growing number of commitments, and despite the costly space requirements of the District Court, the state legislature, responding to the demands of an outraged electorate, has enacted a number of penal statutes that have increased pressures.

An informed observer of the legislative process notes accurately that

> . . . at the same time the legislature was building more prison beds, it was also enacting tough new sentencing laws. Most noteworthy of these was a mandatory sentence for persons convicted of armed robbery. Legislation was also enacted which provided [tougher penalties] for habitual offenders. . . . Still other legislation was passed which

> eliminated work-release programs and prohibited judges from placing any person convicted of a second felony on probation. . . . While the legislature was busy responding to a constituency that demanded a . . . 'get tough' policy toward criminals, it gave little consideration to how these new statutes would affect the ability of the prison system to house increased numbers of inmates.[28]

Helped along by the dire criminological manifestations of a growing drug culture, the state's inmate population roughly doubled between 1970 and 1980. It almost doubled again during the following decade; and a rising convict population afforded "an evolving standard of decency" has, of course, occasioned a growing political crisis.

On the eve of Judge Keady's initial ruling in *Gates*, the annual appropriation for the support of the penal system was well below a half million dollars. But the intervention of the federal court rendered forced convict labor untenable, and in 1978 the state began to lease the penitentiary's lands to private individuals. By 1980, with a whopping 13,188 acres under lease, the penitentiary had completed the long transition from a once-profitable enterprise to a tax-gobbling eleemosynary institution, and appropriations began a mercurial rise.[29]

Since 1980 the legislature, while declaring that the policy of the state is to make the penal system "self-sustaining and to conserve state general fund revenues," has mandated a number of schemes designed to generate revenue. A 1983 statute, reminiscent of the infamous 1866 law that launched the convict lease system, authorized the MDOC to deliver convict labor to private contractors as part of a correctional industries program, and subsequent legislation has sought to achieve the same end. In 1985, the pending demise of federal programs providing commodities to state penal institutions led the MDOC to launch several other schemes. Small numbers of convicts began to produce fruit and vegetables for their own sustenance while a handful of others manned the old long line, actually producing a few bales of cotton. These expedients have made for good public relations, but they have failed to arrest rising costs. The 1992 budget of the MDOC was $85,552,686, and correctional authorities contended that even that sum was dreadfully inadequate.[30]

The mounting costs of the penal system have forced the state to make painful, contentious, and often ruinous policy decisions. One victim of increased spending on convicts has been public education, a major competitor of the penal system within the state's general fund.[31]

Another has been criminal process. While a trapped legislature has generally refused to diminish the purview of public law or the severity of penal sanctions, a growing supply of convicts and the edicts of an exacting federal judge have combined to occasion many indirect retreats from the rigor of the criminal law. The result has been an ever-widening gulf between the de jure and de facto administration of penal law not unlike that which plagued the state during the early years of the nineteenth century.

Many provisions of the state code go unenforced, or enforced very sporadically by the police community. Pointing to deficient manpower and "blockage" in criminal process caused by "too many convicts," one senior law enforcement official confessed that even several common law felonies, most notably burglary, have become low priorities within his jurisdiction. Another speculates glibly on the crisis that would result from a crusade to enforce the state's expansive sodomy statute, from a decision to rigidly pursue the provisions of law relating to alcoholic beverages, or from a "rational approach" to drug enforcement—one "attacking demand rather than supply." "Hell," he concludes, "we [law enforcement] have too much on our plate now, but every damned legislator has a stupid bill or two in his pocket when he gets to Jackson, and before long we're gonna have to abandon traffic enforcement."[32]

Prosecutors, too, have retreated, bargaining pleas with greater, if largely undeterminable, frequency; trial judges have found the expedients of probationary and concurrent sentencing more appealing; and for some years the vast majority of felons receiving custodial sentences have been able to anticipate an early release. By the end of 1979 the state's probation officers had an unprecedented caseload of 3,707, and the parole population, which included neither 163 convicts involved in work-release programs nor 165 who had been farmed out via a new expedient called "supervised early release," numbered 1,292. But even those compromises failed to screen enough felons from the state's overcrowded penal institutions, and in December 1981 a Governor's Task Force on Corrections submitted a report that recommended nonmonetary bail, new sentencing standards, a pretrial intervention program, public works in lieu of incarceration, expanded shock probation, and no new mandatory sentences.[33]

Subsequent legislation has endorsed several of the recommendations of the Task Force along with a number of other tactics designed to screen or remove felons from penal institutions. Among them, none is more remarkable than the 1985 "Prison Overcrowding Emergency Powers Act" which, in utter defiance of the moral underpinnings of criminal jurisprudence, empowered the chief executive and the parole board to circumvent judicial sentences by granting early releases to felons whenever prison overcrowding, as defined by the District Court, produced an "emergency." Since 1985 the state, always hovering at or near "emergency" status, has released felons wholesale on several occasions, notwithstanding the steady growth of the probation and parole population to 7,653 and 3,144, respectively, by June 30, 1991.[34]

Jails as an Escape Hatch

Despite all the compromises, the number of custodial sentences processed by the MDOC has risen more and more each year since 1976, and the state has been forced to leave no stone unturned in a search for space. Being incapable of immediately meeting the court's space requirements, and balking at the prospect of a grand program of prison construction, the legislature at first opted for the much cheaper expedient of housing its felons in local jails.

That decision had several important ramifications. First, it required the legislature to enter a new and cost-ineffective phase in spending—paying local governments to house prisoners who belonged in state facilities. By July 1977 some six hundred felons were housed in local jails, by January 1979 about 1,100, and the numbers mounted in subsequent years. Initially compensating local governments at a rate of seven dollars per inmate per day, and later at a rate of ten dollars, the state distributed a total of $31 million to sheriffs between 1977 and 1987. In 1987 a chagrined legislature declared that the monies so expended could have constructed over one thousand beds for prisoners on the lands of the state penal system, but the shortsighted expedient continues to be a cornerstone of state penal policy. A sum of $3,887,000 was projected for the reimbursement of counties in fiscal year 1992.[35]

Secondly, local officials have bitterly resented the foisting of state prisoners on their jails. In 1978 Albert Necaise, district attorney for Harrison and Stone counties, cleared his jail of state prisoners, loaded them on a bus, had them driven to Parchman's front gate, and demanded that they be admitted. After being rebuffed by a bewildered warden, the district attorney had the convicts driven back to Gulfport.[36]

Such political showmanship has been less frequent since 1978, but the continuing ire of local officials and the mounting expense of lodging state prisoners in county jails have combined to produce some remarkable legislation. A 1982 statute, reminiscent of a number of antebellum expedients designed to reduce jail expenses, extended "the limits of the place of confinement" and authorized sheriffs to employ county and state prisoners in "work camps" so long as their labor did not displace free laborers, impair existing contracts, or unduly exploit convicts. Later enactments, all of which conjure up thoughts of horrible precedents, expand the principle of dispersing convict-laborers quartered in local jails. Chapter 456 of the Laws of 1987 declared bluntly that the "overcrowding of state prisoners in county jails has plagued the sheriffs, the Mississippi Department of Corrections and the Legislature for a decade." On June 30, 1991, however, 816 state prisoners remained in local lockups amid incessant rumors of hanky-panky by favored parties.[37]

Lastly, in 1977, when large numbers of state prisoners were first assigned to county facilities, most of Mississippi's jails were unfit for long-term habitation. The deplorable condition of the jails was given graphic illustration on December 31, 1979, when the Jackson *Clarion-Ledger* published a tabloid entitled *Jails: Mississippi's Worst Punishment.* Complemented by heartrending photographs, the tabloid disclosed dirt, stench, vermin, skimpy menus, inadequate medical care, poor electrical systems, inadequate plumbing, shoddy construction, and the absence of recreational and educational programs. It also dwelt on the exploitation of convict labor by local authorities, on the abuses of jailers and trusties, on homosexual rapes, and on the presence of women and children in the midst of it all. Finally, the tabloid addressed the core of the problem which, according to a quotation attributed to former United States district judge Frank Johnson of Alabama, was "the punting syndrome"—choosing to let the problem fester "until the federal courts finally step in and order improvements."

The "punting" went on between officials at every level of government. At the federal level, the United States Congress displayed "an apparent unwillingness to tackle the national jail problem." The state legislature, according to state senator Glen Deweese of Meridian, opposed appropriations for jails and the state penitentiary because such spending was "sort of a dead-end street." It was "easier to wait for federal court orders" because it was not "very popular to spend money on criminals." County officials thought that it was "political suicide" to discuss improving jails without pressure from a federal judge, observed attorney Cleve McDowell of Drew. As a result, when county tax dollars were doled out, jails got only the leftovers. Citizens simply did not care about the plight of prisoners lodged in local lockups.

The political football described by the tabloid has been punctured somewhat by the threat of class action lawsuits, by the availability of federal dollars for the renovation and construction of jails, and by the District Court's imposition of standards for the confinement of state prisoners in county facilities. By June 30, 1991, a total of 874 cells in local jails were classified as "approved," but hostilities between state and local officials continued and threatened to worsen. Tempers flared across the state when word broke that the 1991 legislature had adjourned without appropriating a dime for the support of state prisoners lodged in local jails.[38]

Overcrowded jails continue to thwart criminal process, especially in the state's larger municipalities. In October 1990, for example, a felon convicted of burglary in three separate jurisdictions, awaiting transfer to a state penal institution, and released from custody on three occasions due to overcrowding in the city jail of Jackson allegedly committed further burglaries. "Burglary used to be a high priority," noted Hinds County District Attorney Ed Pittman. "Now it's become a low priority because of the lack of jail space."[39]

The Travails of Prison Expansion

The inadequacy of tactics designed to stem the flow of convicts has forced the legislature to expand the housing capacity of the state penal system. Such expansion has required a huge outlay of public funds, and increased spending, of course, has led to political infighting. Following the philosophy of decentralization advanced by Tyler Fletcher in 1976, the executive branch of government and the MDOC have steadfastly advocated the distribution of new units among different political constituencies within the state. That philosophy, though, has run afoul of several weighty political considerations.

The powerful legislative delegations of the Delta counties surrounding Parchman have served their constituents well, stopping at nothing in opposing decentralization and insisting on the allocation of state tax dollars for expansion at the old penitentiary. Their cause has been helped along by the unpopularity of decentralization among most of the state's other political constituencies, whose citizens, failing to comprehend the economics of the prison business, balk at the prospect of having a prison in their midst.[40]

The result has been steady expansion at Parchman, which promises to emerge, notwithstanding Mississippi's relatively small population, as one of the nation's largest state penitentiaries before the end of the century. Between 1974 and January 1990 the state of Mississippi added some 4,000 new beds at the old penal farm in Sunflower County at a cost of roughly $50 million, and on September 4, 1990, yet another new one-thousand bed maximum security unit began to receive felons. Commissioner Black told a journalist that the facility had "enough space to house most of the state's . . . inmates who are in county jails" but said nothing of an anticipated avalanche of new commitments.[41]

Meanwhile, the office of the governor and the MDOC, assisted by the inability of even a growing Parchman to meet rising space demands, have attempted with some success to sell the idea of satellite units to other political constituencies within the state. Initially prison satellites were of two types, restitution centers and community work centers. A number of such units housing low-risk, minimum-security inmates were opened in various locations around the state between 1977 and 1980. They did not meet the housing needs of the penal system, however, and the MDOC—crippled by the legislature's refusal to distribute satellite units unilaterally and equitably throughout the state—launched a frantic effort to persuade reluctant municipal and county officials to share in the decentralization of the state penal system.[42]

On November 1, 1979, a booklet hyping a multimillion dollar campaign to establish "Community Correctional Treatment Centers" emanated from the office of Commissioner Watkins. In less polite terms, such centers were legally dubious, minimum-security satellite prisons housing felons who until only recently had been classified as medium-security.

The booklet contended that the centers provided "a gradual, systematic reintroduction of the offender into full community life," that they offered "alternatives to traditional sentencing dispositions," that they allowed "structured supervision in a community setting," and that they complemented "the impact of other sectors of the criminal justice system." After thus bowing to the litany of the new "corrections," the booklet got down to business. The new centers, it emphasized, saved money for the state while enabling local communities to strengthen their economies. In fact, the existing community-based units promised to pump up to $2,757,000 into local economies while reducing the state's daily expenses from roughly $17.50 to $8.50 per prisoner. Hence the centers were panaceas bringing "benefits to the keeper, the kept and the society at-large." These blessings, the booklet concluded, resulted from the "beneficial" effects of federal intervention in "Mississippi corrections."[43]

The MDOC thus laid out an utterly pragmatic idea, wrapped it in heady philosophical language, and tried to sell it with an unphilosophical bribe of jobs and money. The philosophy won the department few converts, and even the bribe was so unpopular among local constituencies that the 1982 *Progress Report* of the MDOC noted that "It would be difficult to predict the future of Mississippi's prison system."[44] Helped along by the unrelenting District Court, however, prison decentralization became the rage of the 1980s despite the continuing growth of the old penitentiary in the Yazoo Delta.

Between 1983 and 1986 thirteen community work centers providing 975 beds were opened at a cost of $521,400, and by 1991 sixteen were operational. In 1985 a 565-bed satellite prison opened in Rankin County. Two years later a 500-bed unit in remote Greene County admitted its first convicts. And in 1987 the legislature at last declared the obvious—the "need of a comprehensive, long-term construction program."[45]

For Better or for Worse

On June 30, 1991, Mississippi's active offender population consisted of 19,498 felons, 8,701 of whom were serving custodial sentences, and, with official projections promising 12,000 inmates by 1995 and 15,000 by the turn of the century, the crusade for prison decentralization continued. Meanwhile, the MDOC was following a legislative mandate "for a substantial increase in . . . maximum security housing at Parchman," and the penitentiary had taken on an appearance that would have astonished its founders.[46]

Only a shadow of the old Parchman remained. Thousands of the acres that Marvin Wiggins had pampered and brought so far were leased to local planters, and the remaining lands of the penitentiary held but faint resemblance to earlier days. The depot, once the site of humming gins, of bulging cotton houses, and of busy industry, was gone. Upon entering Front Camp, formerly the heart of the great plantation, one felt the bland presence of bureaucracy, so characteristic of prisons everywhere. Driving west, toward the great river, the visitor observed a scarred, eroded landscape, rotting cottages, and at last the chilling monuments to Judge Keady's concept of a "modern operation"—gray, foreboding structures rising ominously from the flatlands. These were real cages, cellblocks of cold steel surrounded by electronically guarded chain-link fences topped by coiled razor-ribbon wire.

Black Annie was now a relic of history, a dinosaur spoken of sheepishly by the new generation of employees and displayed naughtily by old-timers who paid lip service to old ways. Gone, too, was the fabled long line, where the dreaded "headhunters" had held sway with hard eyes and shining Winchesters. Shadowy memories of Jim Thames, of Lowery Love, of old Wiggins, of Bill Harpole, and of Fred Jones lingered. The old-timers spoke longingly of their greatness, of the "golden age" of the Parchman farm when the land had flowered with cotton, but all that was gone, perhaps never to be resurrected.

The farm had gone the way of the nation, for better or for worse; Mississippians were being dragged along slowly, all the while wondering naively why a plantation of over fifteen thousand acres with legions of captive laborers could not feed, clothe, and otherwise support itself. Millions of state tax dollars went to private contractors, the caged convicts were largely idle, and tension was pervasive. The emphasis, disguised by a mountain of litany, remained an unrelenting effort to pass felons through a prison treadmill more rapidly than in 1990, when the MDOC had managed to reduce the average felon's term to two years, two months.[47]

But optimism sprang eternal among many employees. On October 17, 1990, U.S. district judge L. T. Senter had reviewed the accomplishments of the MDOC very favorably and pledged to end the long judicial inquisition born of *Gates* if the state should meet the court's space requirements within two years.[48] Not all administrators, however, saw reason to rejoice. One senior official, recalling the "good ole days," saw nothing in state control that was preferable to a daily judicial audit: "It's damned if you do and damned if you don't. Neither alternative is workable, and one must wonder if anybody can strike an acceptable compromise within the present framework of American government."[49]

So the future of Mississippi's penal policy remains very much in doubt. Legislators, avoiding a problem that threatens the very foundations of government, continue to legislate more and more law, to mandate more and more custodial sanctions, all the while ignoring the financial and systemic cost of it all and the unpleasant economic and social faces of criminality. Elected prosecutors continue to bind accused felons over to the courts of criminal jurisdiction and to lobby for longer sentences. The elected judiciary continues to manufacture convicts. The chief executive continues to squirm, still undone by the offspring of the non-system. And, with a cloudy destination still before them, those who administer the legal threats of the state continue to plod along, like Confederate prisoners of war, to the deadening beat of a federal drum.

Parchman's Camp 8 (Negro), ca. 1950. MDAH.

Parchman's Camp 6 in flush times, ca. 1950. MDAH.

A camp dining hall, ca. 1940. MDAH.

Parchman's brickyard, ca. 1950. MDAH.

Farm buildings at Parchman, ca. 1950. LLH.

Negro cattlemen at Parchman, ca. 1940. MDAH.

Mail call, ca. 1940. MDAH.

Female convicts at the slaughterhouse, ca. 1940. MDAH.

Governor Hugh White and entourage inspecting a hog unit, ca. 1953. MDAH.

"Little Alcatraz," the maximum security unit at Parchman, ca. 1960. LLH.

Death Row at Little Alcatraz, ca. 1976. Courtesy of Tyler H. Fletcher (hereafter cited as THF).

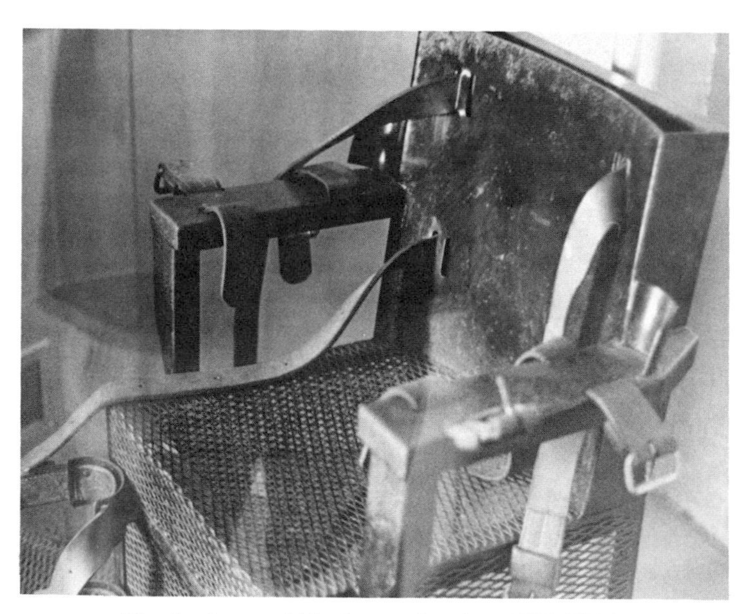

The death seat within the gas chamber, 1975. THF.

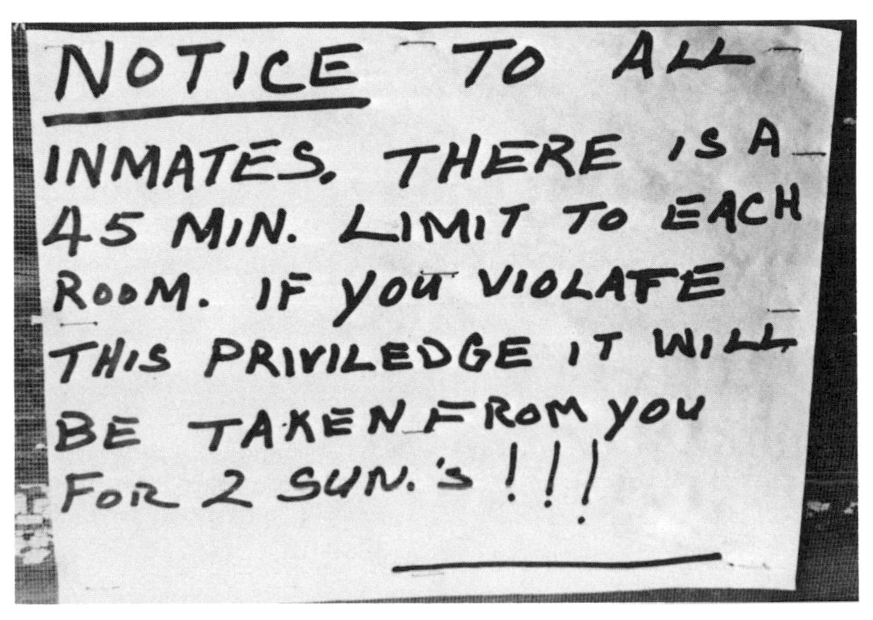

Sign posted on a "red house," ca. 1974. THF.

The Parchman prison band, ca. 1980. MDOC.

Old Camp 10, abandoned and awaiting demolition, ca. 1974. MDOC.

Flames engulf an old cage in the wake of *Gates v. Collier*, ca. 1976. MDOC.

The fruits of federal intervention: the new face of Parchman, ca. 1980. MDOH.

Notes

Chapter 1

1. W. Sargent to T. Pickering, June 16 and Dec. 20, 1798, and Jan. 15, 1799, in *Mississippi Territorial Archives, 1798–1803*, ed. D. Rowland (Nashville, 1905), i. 22, 90, and 104. See also J. Wunder, "American Law and Order Comes to the Mississippi Territory: The Making of Sargent's Code," *Journal of Mississippi History* (hereafter cited as *JMH*), 38 (May 1976), 132.

2. F. E. Devine, "Cesare Beccaria and the Theoretical Foundation of Modern Penal Jurisprudence," in "The Foundation of Modern Penal Practice: A Symposium," comp. W. B. Taylor, *New England Journal on Prison Law*, 7 (Winter 1981), 8–21; and J. Bentham, "The Utilitarian Theory of Punishment," in *Philosophy of Law*, ed. J. Feinberg and H. Gross (Encino and Belmont, Calif., 1975), pp. 523–29. See also W. B. Taylor and R. E. Cooley, "The Emergence of the Penitentiary Concept in Great Britain," in Taylor, "Modern Penal Practice," pp. 22–35.

3. For the original statutes, see *The Historical Records Survey, Sargent's Code. A Collection of the Original Laws of the Mississippi Territory* . . . , ed. P. L. Rainwater (Jackson, 1939), hereafter cited as *Sargent's Code*. For comment and analysis, see Wunder, pp. 142–43; W. B. Hamilton, *Anglo-American Law on the Frontier: Thomas Rodney and His Territorial Cases* (Durham, N.C., 1953), pp. 140–41; J. D. Lynch, *The Bench and Bar of Mississippi* (New York, 1881), pp. 13–17; and D. Rowland, *History of Mississippi: Heart of the South* (Chicago and Jackson, 1925), i. 337–75.

4. Sargent to Peter Walker and Lewis Evans, Nov. 24, 1798, and Sargent to John Girault, Jan. 21, 1801, in *Mississippi Territorial Archives*, i. 84 and 326–27; and Claiborne to Lt. Bowmar, June 27, 1804, *Official Letter Books of W. C. C. Claiborne, 1801–1816*, ed. D. Rowland (Jackson, 1917), ii. 223–25.

5. Business Research Station, Miss. State College, Gen. Bulletin No. 3, *Statistical Abstract of Mississippi 1952* (St. Louis, 1952), p. 3. See also C. D. Lowery, "The Great Migration to the Mississippi Territory, 1798–1819," *JMH*, 30 (Feb.–Nov. 1968), 178–92.

6. For comment on the difficulties of law enforcement, see Wunder, p. 148; J. T. Hartfield, "Governor William Charles Cole Claiborne, Indians, and Outlaws in Frontier Mississippi, 1801–1803," *JMH*, 27 (Nov. 1965), 340–49; M. C. Dunn, "Criminals Along the Natchez Trace," Thesis, Univ. of Southern Miss., 1970, pp. 48–58; and D. C. James, "Municipal Government in Territorial Natchez," *JMH*, 27 (May 1965), 148–51. For evidence of the problems of the judiciary, see Natchez *Mississippi Messenger*, June 17, 1806; Natchez *Mississippi Herald and Natchez Gazette*, Dec. 17, 1807; *Washington Republican* (Washington, Miss.), July 21, 1813, and Nov. 11, 1815; *Washington Republican and Natchez Intelligencer* (Washington, Miss.), Nov. 6, 1816; Natchez *Southern Galaxy*, May 28, 1829, Feb. 11, 1830; and J. A. Quitman to his father, Jan. 16, 1822, *Life and Correspondence of John A. Quitman*, ed. J. F. H. Claiborne (New York, 1860), i. 71. For comment on the general inefficiency of criminal process and the inefficacy of penal law, see the address of Governor R. Williams to the territorial assembly, as reported by the Natchez *Mississippi Herald and Natchez Gazette*, Dec. 17, 1807, and the charge of Judge G. Poindexter to the Adams County grand jury, as reported by the Natchez *Mississippi Republican*, Oct. 27, 1813.

7. E. B. Thompson, "Reforms in the Penal System of Mississippi, 1820–1850," *JMH*, 7 (April 1945), pp. 51–52. For comment on the plight of the Natchez jail, see Claiborne's address of Dec. 9, 1802, to the territorial assembly and the letter of Sheriff W. Brooks to Claiborne, Dec. 11, 1802, in *Claiborne Letter Books*, i. 239–41.

8. *Claiborne Letter Books*, iii. 275–76, and iv. 295–96; *Journal of the Convention of the Western Part of the Mississippi Territory . . . 1817* (1817; rpt. Port Gibson, Miss., 1831), pp. 91 and 95–96; Natchez *Mississippi State Gazette*, Jan. 6, Mar. 13, 1819; Miss. Legislature, *House Journal*, 1827, p. 14, and 1829, p. 14 (hereafter cited as *House Journal*, as the journal of the upper chamber is cited as *Senate Journal*); C. E. Fike, "The Gubernatorial Administrations of Governor Gerard Chittocque Brandon, 1825–1832," *JMH*, 35 (Aug. 1973), 263–64.

9. For information on the construction and inadequacy of the jails of the city of Natchez, see Natchez *Mississippi Herald and Natchez City Gazette*, Jan. 21, 1804, Nov. 18, 1806, and Oct. 6, 1807; Natchez *Mississippi Messenger*, Nov. 11 and Dec. 9, 1806, and Feb. 17, 1807; James, "Municipal Government," p. 158; and D. C. James, *Antebellum Natchez* (Baton Rouge, 1968), p. 81. For information on the construction and early problems of the Adams County jail in Washington, see Natchez *Mississippi Messenger*, July 8, 1806, and Mar. 17, 1808; Natchez *The Weekly Chronicle*, May 27, 1809; *Washington Republican*, April 27, July 21, and Aug. 11, 1813, and May 8, 1814; and J. Foster to the Adams County Courthouse Commissioners, n.d., rec. April 29, 1811, Adams County Courthouse, deed–book F, p. 362. For brief comment on Port Gibson's "mean jail" of the early nineteenth century,

see R. V. Haynes, "Law Enforcement in Frontier Mississippi," *JMH*, 22 (Jan.–Oct. 1960), 38.

10. *Sargent's Code*, pp. 83–87; *The Revised Code of the Laws of Mississippi . . .* , comp. G. Poindexter (Natchez, 1824), p. 82 (hereafter cited as *Poindexter's Code*).

11. Ibid., p. 252; *Laws of . . . Mississippi . . . From . . . 1824 . . . to 1838 . . .*, comp. P. R. R. Pray (Baltimore, 1838), p. 483 (hereafter cited as *Pray's Code*).

12. *Poindexter's Code*, pp. 82–83, 147, and 254–55; Jackson *Southern Sun*, Aug. 4, 1838; Thompson, p. 54.

13. *Sargent's Code*, p. 127.

14. *Claiborne Letter Books*, ii. 251–53, and iv. 295.

15. *Poindexter's Code*, pp. 82, 207, and 311.

16. Ibid., pp. 204 and 396–99; *Laws of the State of Mississippi* (hereafter cited as *Miss. Laws*), 1839, pp. 67–72, and 1840, p. 40. See also D. S. Jennings, *Nine Years of Democratic Rule in Mississippi* (Jackson, 1847), pp. 120–21.

17. *Sargent's Code*, pp. 44–48; *Poindexter's Code*, p. 377; *Pray's Code*, pp. 31 and 183–84. For an account of chain gangs of runaway slaves in antebellum Natchez, see J. H. Ingraham, *The South-West. By a Yankee* (New York, 1835), ii. 185. See also T. B. Rowland, "Legal Status of the Negro in Mississippi, 1832–1860," Thesis, Univ. of Wisconsin, 1933, pp. 38–46.

18. *Woodville Republican*, Aug. 27, 1836.

19. J. Quitman to J. F. H. Claiborne, Oct. 18, 1830, *Quitman*, i. 101.

20. *Poindexter's Code*, pp. 296–309.

21. Hamilton, p. 141; Haynes, p. 39; C. S. Sydnor, *Slavery in Mississippi* (New York, 1933), pp. 80–83; W. L. Baradell, "Runaway Slaves in Mississippi," Thesis, Univ. of Southern Miss., 1974, pp. 77–80.

22. *Poindexter's Code*, pp. 371–90.

23. W. M. Drake, "The Framing of Mississippi's First Constitution," *JMH*, 29 (Nov. 1967), 322; Sydnor, p. 85.

24. Natchez *Mississippi State Gazette*, Aug. 29, 1818; Natchez *Mississippi Republican*, Feb. 16, 1819; Natchez *Southern Galaxy*, Nov. 12, 1829; *Woodville Republican*, Dec. 3, 1831; Thompson, pp. 51–52; R. Holder, "The Autobiography of William Winans," Thesis, Univ. of Miss., 1936, pp. 357–58.

25. T. P. Shenton, *Robert John Walker: A Politician from Jackson to Lincoln* (New York and London, 1961), p. 4; Thompson, pp. 54–59.

26. *Statistical Abstract of Mississippi*, p. 3; James, *Antebellum Natchez*, pp. 259 and 266; W. D. McCain, *The Story of Jackson* (Jackson, 1953), i. 162; J. D. Shields, *The Life and Times of Sargent Smith Prentiss* (Philadelphia, 1883), pp. 84–85.

27. H. S. Foote, *Casket of Reminiscences* (Washington, D.C., 1874), p.

249. See also *Message of the Governor of . . . Mississippi . . . Delivered January 5, 1836* (Jackson, 1936), p. 6.

28. E. A. Miles, *Jacksonian Democracy in Mississippi* (Chapel Hill, N.C., 1960), pp. 33–43; W. B. Taylor, *King Cotton and Old Glory* (Hattiesburg, Miss., 1977), pp. 18–23; J. F. H. Claiborne, *Life and Times of Gen. Sam Dale, The Mississippi Partisan* (New York, 1860), pp. 225–28. For editorial comment on violence and on the passion for firearms, see Natchez *Mississippi Free Trader*, Dec. 8, 1836.

29. Foote, pp. 264–71; Jennings, pp. 244–45; *Quitman*, i. 188.

30. Thompson, p. 52; *Message of the Governor to the Legislature . . . Delivered January 8, 1839* (Jackson, 1839), pp. 7–8 (hereafter cited as *Governor's Message 1839*).

31. Foote, pp. 247–63; Miles, pp. 164–65; James, *Antebellum Natchez*, p. 259; Dunn, p. 63; W. S. Rutledge, "Duelling in Antebellum Mississippi," *JMH*, 26 (Aug. 1964), 181–91.

32. For the best account of the vigilante activity see D. M. Mounger, "Lynching in Mississippi, 1830–1930," Thesis, Miss. State Univ., 1961, pp. 22–49. For proposed reforms in law enforcement, see *Message of the Governor to the Legislature . . . Delivered January 7, 1840* (Jackson, 1840), p. 7 (hereafter cited as *Governor's Message 1840*). For proposed judicial reform, see Shields, p. 85. For emphasis on penal reform, see *Quitman*, i. 101–2.

33. *Poindexter's Code*, p. 83. See also P. B. Foreman and J. R. Tatum, "A Short History of Mississippi's State Penal Systems," *Mississippi Law Journal*, 10 (April 1938), 256.

34. *Poindexter's Code*, p. 253; *Pray's Code*, p. 187; *House Journal*, 1827, p. 14, and 1833, p. 16; Natchez *Southern Galaxy*, Jan. 29, 1829. See also R. T. Dunbar to Gov. Scott, April 23, 1832, and the letters of Scott to Dunbar, J. A. Quitman, R. M. Gaines, and L. Mayhall dated Mar. 14, 1832, in Series E of the Governors Papers, Mississippi Department of Archives and History (hereafter cited as MDAH), p. 23 *et seq*. For general comment, see Thompson, p. 63.

35. W. B. Taylor and R. E. Cooley, "Anglo-American Penology in Transition: The Triumph of the Separate System," in Taylor, "Modern Penal Practice," pp. 40–43; N. K. Teeters and J. D. Shearer, *The Prison at Philadelphia's Cherry Hill: The Separate System of Penal Discipline* (New York, 1957); "Report of William Crawford, Esq., on the Penitentiaries of the United States," House of Commons, Aug. 11, 1834, *British Parliamentary Papers, Crime and Punishment: Prisons* (Dublin, Ireland, 1934), pp. 3–51.

36. Taylor and Cooley, "Anglo–American Penology in Transition," pp. 43–45; H. E. Barnes and N. K. Teeters, *New Horizons in Criminology* (Englewood Cliffs, N.J., 1959), pp. 338–39. See also *The Life of Thomas Eddy*, ed. S. L. Knapp (London, 1836).

37. McKelvey, pp. 15–18, 24–25, 43, 50, 64–66, 73, 89, and 92. See also the first chapter of M. T. Carleton, *Politics and Punishment: The History of the Louisiana Penal System* (Baton Rouge, 1971).

38. Ingraham, ii. 186. See *Poindexter's Code*, pp. 396–99, for the statutory provisions relating to poorhouses and work farms.

39. *Woodville Republican*, Jan. 30, 1836; *Clinton Gazette*, Jan. 9, 23, 1836; Jackson *Mississippian*, June 24 and Dec. 30, 1836; *Pray's Code*, pp. 543–46 and 554–57. See also, in the library of the Mississippi State Penitentiary at Parchman, S. Sullivan's unpublished paper, "Prison Without Walls: A History of Mississippi's Penal System" (1976), pp. 19–20.

40. W. Nichols to Gov. Lynch and the Commissioners of Public Buildings, n.d., MDAH, Governors Papers, Series E, p. 26.

41. *Pray's Code*, p. 826; *Miss. Laws*, 1839, pp. 76–77 and 105–7; *House Journal*, 1840, p. 364; *Columbus Democrat*, Jan. 6, 1838; Jackson *Mississippian*, June 28, 1839, and Jan. 10, 1841. See also D. N. Young, "History of the Construction of State Buildings in Jackson, Mississippi, 1822–1860," Thesis, Miss. College, 1954, pp. 58–60; Thompson, pp. 65–67; and McCain, i. 46. For favorable editorial comment on the new code, see Natchez *Mississippi Free Trader and Natchez Daily Gazette*, Mar. 26, 1839.

42. *House Journal*, 1841, p. 364; McCain, i. 47.

43. *Governor's Message 1839*, pp. 8–9.

44. *Woodville Republican*, Mar. 16, 1839.

45. Jackson *Mississippian*, Mar. 7, 1844, containing the report of the legislature's joint standing committee on the penitentiary submitted in Dec. 1843 (hereafter cited as *Committee Report 1843*).

46. *Miss. Laws*, 1839, pp. 183–85.

47. *Committee Report 1843.*

48. Ibid.; *Miss. Laws*, 1839, pp. 168–69, 177–78, 182–84, 186, and 188, and 1841, p. 90. See also *House Journal*, 1841, p. 364.

49. *Miss. Laws*, 1839, pp. 172–75 and 180–83, and 1840, pp. 177–78. The penitentiary reports were published in the state's *Annual Reports* until 1875, and in the *Biennial Reports* from 1877 until 1963. Hereafter penitentiary reports are cited as *PR*, followed by the year or years encompassed by the report.

50. *Miss. Laws*, 1839, p. 174.

51. Ibid., pp. 172, 175–77, 180, and 183.

52. *Committee Report 1843.*

53. *Governor's Message 1840*, p. 1.

54. *Miss. Laws*, 1840, pp. 177–78, and 1844, p. 370. See also *Governor's Message, Delivered . . . January 2, 1844* (Jackson, 1844), p. 17 (hereafter cited as *Governor's Message 1844*), for comment on the "radically defective" administrative structure. See Jackson *Mississippian*, Dec. 18, 1844, containing the

penitentiary report submitted in Dec. 1844 (hereafter cited as *PR*, 1844), for the superintendent's apparently glib assessment of the prison's fiscal status.

55. *Pray's Code*, p. 545; *Miss. Laws*, 1839, pp. 183–85; McCain, i. 46–47. See *Senate Journal*, 1841, p. 355, for a report on the early forms and productivity of inmate labor, and Young, p. 67, for elaboration.

56. *Miss. Laws*, 1839, pp. 168–69, 183–84, 186, and 188. See also *House Journal*, 1841, p. 364.

57. Ibid., pp. 89–92 and 355; Jackson *Mississippian*, Feb. 23, 1843; Thompson, p. 71; McCain, i. 47; Sullivan, pp. 36–39.

58. *Miss. Laws*, 1842, pp. 105–7.

59. Ibid., 1844, pp. 155–56 and 166–67. For comment on early religious activities at the penitentiary, see Boston Prison Discipline Society, *16th Report* (Boston, 1841), p. 71; *PR*, 1844; Jackson *Mississippian*, April 25, 1851; Jackson *Flag of the Union*, Feb. 27, 1852; and "An Overlooked Source for Mississippi Local History: The Spirit of Missions, 1836–1854," ed. N. K. Burger, *JMH*, 7 (July 1945), 173.

60. McCain, i. 162; J. V. Hawks, "Social Reforms in the Cotton Kingdom, 1830–1860," Diss., Univ. of Miss., 1969, pp. 73–74; Jackson *Mississippian*, May 28, 1845; *PR*, 1844; *Committee Report 1843*. For further editorial criticism, see Jackson *Mississippian*, May 13, 1846.

61. *Senate Journal*, 1842–43, p. 271; *PR*, 1843, appendix; Young, p. 76.

62. *Committee Report 1843*; *PR*, 1844; Jackson *Mississippian*, April 24, 1844, and Jan. 7, 1846, containing the governor's message to the legislature of the previous day (hereafter cited as *Governor's Message 1846*).

63. Jackson *Mississippian*, Aug. 6, 1845.

64. McCain, i. 83.

65. *Committee Report 1843*.

66. *Governor's Message 1844*, p. 17; *The Inaugural Address of . . . A. G. Brown, Governor, . . . Delivered . . . January 10, 1844* (Jackson, 1844), pp. 13–14; *Governor's Message 1846*; Jackson *Mississippian*, Jan. 14, Feb. 4, and Sept. 24, 1846; *Woodville Republican*, Feb. 14, 1846; *Miss. Laws*, 1844, pp. 369–70, and 1846, pp. 237–38.

67. For comment on the advantages of placing the prison in Vicksburg, see *Woodville Republican*, Jan. 30, 1836. For accounts of the shortage of wood and of failed attempts to procure it, see *PR*, 1855, pp. 9–10, and Sullivan, p. 39. For accounts of the continuing shortage of water and the comedy of errors that attended the digging of wells in the prison yard between 1856 and 1859, see *Governor's Message 1844*, p. 17; Jackson *Mississippian*, Aug. 12, 1843, and Aug. 11, 1858; *PR*, 1855, pp. 6, 9, and 26; and Sullivan, p. 55.

68. *PR*, 1843, appendix; Jackson *Mississippian*, July 22, 1846, and Jan. 30, 1852, containing the penitentiary report submitted in Dec. 1851 (hereafter cited as *PR*, 1851); *PR*, 1855, pp. 5, 10, and 25–26.

69. McCain, i. 48–49; *Miss. Laws,* 1857, p. 41. For earlier warnings of fire by the staff, see *PR*, 1848, p. 18, and *PR*, 1851.

70. For accounts of convict labor on the penitentiary and on other public works projects, see Jackson *Mississippian*, Feb. 18, 1846, and Feb. 5, 1847; *PR*, 1848, pp. 17–23 and 38; *PR*, 1851; *PR*, 1855, p. 9; Sullivan, p. 62; and L. G. Shivers, "A History of the Mississippi Penitentiary," Thesis, Univ. of Miss., 1930, pp. 21–22.

71. *Miss. Laws*, 1841, pp. 90–91; *Governor's Message 1844*, p. 17; *PR*, 1848, p. 18; *PR*, 1851; Young, p. 68.

72. Jackson *Mississippian*, Feb. 5, 1847; *PR*, 1851; *PR*, 1855, pp. 5 and 19; McCain, i. 83.

73. Jackson *Mississippian*, Feb. 4, Mar. 3 and 10, 1848.

74. Ibid., April 25, 1851; *PR*, 1851; *Miss. Laws*, 1852, p. 41. See generally the Board of Inspectors Minute Book, 1851–1865, MDAH, r.g. 49, v. 35 (hereafter cited as IMB 1851–65), especially the entries of Jan.–May 1851.

75. *PR*, 1855, pp. 7 and 27; *Miss. Laws*, 1856, pp. 137–39, and 1857, p. 41, and 1858, pp. 131–32.

76. *Governor's Message, Delivered . . . Nov. 1858* (Jackson, 1858), p. 21; *Governor's Message, Delivered . . . Nov. 1859* (Jackson, 1859), p. 24 (hereafter cited as *Governor's Message 1859*); Jackson *Mississippian and State Gazette*, Aug. 11, 1858; Young, p. 69; McCain, i. 49; *Biographical and Historical Memoirs of Mississippi* (1891; rpt. Spartanburg, S.C., 1978), i. 22.

77. *Miss. Laws*, 1863, p. 79; Rowland, *Mississippi*, i. 804–5; Young, p. 70; J. K. Bettersworth, *Confederate Mississippi* (Baton Rouge, 1943), p. 134. For information on the role of the penitentiary in the Confederate war effort, see the entries of 1861–63 in IMB 1851–65.

78. For general information, see Jackson *Mississippian*, April 24, 1844, Feb. 5, 1847, and April 25, 1851; *PR*, 1848, pp. 7 and 17; *PR*, 1851; *PR*, 1855, pp. 8–9; and Shivers, pp. 2 and 14.

79. *PR*, 1846, p. 6; *PR*, 1848, p. 24. See also Hawks, p. 75, and Sullivan, p. 68.

80. *PR*, 1851; Jackson *Mississippian*, April 25, 1851; *Miss. Laws*, 1858, p. 132. See also Shivers, p. 19.

81. *Governor's Message 1859*, pp. 17–24; Jackson *Mississippian and State Gazette*, June 16, 1858.

82. Annual legislative appropriations are depicted in *Miss. Laws.*

83. McCain, i. 47–49.

84. *PR*, 1855, p. 11. For comment on the deplorable jail of Vicksburg, see Boston Prison Discipline Society, *16th Report*, pp. 66–71. For comment on the jail of Woodville, see B. Beaumont, *Twelve Years of My Life* (Philadelphia, 1887), pp. 129–35.

85. Jackson *Mississippian*, Mar. 10, 1848.

86. Statistics on the crimes of conviction and on the states or foreign coun-

tries in which convicts were born were included in the penitentiary reports. Brief comment on the convict profile during the antebellum era is offered by McCain, i. 47–49, and by Sullivan, p. 61. Sydnor, *Slavery*, p. 123, comments on the fact that the penitentiary housed runaway slaves for a fee.

87. *Miss. Laws*, 1850, p. 105; *Governor's Message, Delivered . . . Jan. 1854* (Jackson, 1854), p. 2; *Revised Code of Mississippi*, comp. W. L. Sharkey et al. (Jackson, 1857).

Chapter 2

1. Shivers, pp. 26–27.

2. Ibid., pp. 27–28; Jackson *Daily Clarion*, Nov. 20, 1865; *Senate Journal*, 1865, p. 194; Rowland, *Mississippi*, ii. 385; W. C. Harris, *The Day of the Carpetbagger: Republican Reconstruction in Mississippi* (Baton Rouge and London, 1979), p. 37.

3. R. E. Cooley, "A History of the Mississippi Penal Farm System, 1890–1935: Punishment, Politics and Profit in Penal Affairs," Thesis, Univ. of Southern Miss., 1981, p. 5.

4. *House Journal*, 1865, p. 138; Jackson *Daily Mississippian*, Nov. 9, 1865; Jackson *Daily Clarion*, Nov. 20, 1865; Jackson *Clarion and Standard*, May 30, 1866; Cooley, pp. 7–8.

5. Jackson *Daily Clarion*, Mar. 27 and Aug. 28, 1866; Jackson *Clarion and Standard*, May 30, 1866.

6. *Senate Journal*, 1866–67, pp. 735–36; Rowland, *Mississippi*, ii. 385; K. Lunquist, "The Administration of Benjamin Grubbs Humphreys, Governor of Mississippi, 1865–1868," Thesis, Miss. College, 1962, p. 56.

7. *Miss. Laws*, 1866–67, pp. 212–13; Jackson *Daily Clarion*, Nov. 3, 1866, and Jan. 29, 1867.

8. Foreman and Tatum, p. 259; Jackson *Daily Clarion*, Jan. 29 and Feb. 7, 1867. For the state's contract with Young, see MDAH, r.g. 49, v. 44.

9. *Miss. Laws*, 1866–67, pp. 735–36. For the report of the special committee appointed to consider the revision of the law, see Jackson *Daily Clarion*, Feb. 21, 1867.

10. Ibid., Feb. 1, 1868; Harris, p. 3.

11. Lt. E. T. Wallace to Gov. Humphreys, Mar. 31, 1868, and Lt. J. R. Haynes to Gov. Humphreys, May 27, 1868, MDAH, r.g. 27, v. 69. See also Harris, p. 39.

12. S. Curtis, "Penitentiary Reform in Mississippi, 1875–1906: A Study of Politics in Penal Affairs," Thesis, Miss. College, 1974, p. 10.

13. Ibid.; *Senate Journal*, 1870, *Appendix*, p. 58; Foreman and Tatum, p. 260. For the state's contract with Richardson, see MDAH, r.g. 49, v. 44.

14. Penitentiary Committee to Gov. J. L. Alcorn, June 30, 1870, MDAH, r.g. 27, v. 72.

15. *Biographical and Historical Memoirs*, ii. 666–68.

16. *Senate Journal*, 1870, *Appendix*, pp. 58–59.

17. Jackson *Semi-Weekly Clarion*, Mar. 29, April 15 and 29, May 9, and July 12, 1870; Penitentiary Committee to Gov. Alcorn, June 23, 1870, MDAH, r.g. 27, v. 72; Harris, p. 354; Shivers, p. 30.

18. Jackson *Semi-Weekly Clarion*, April 13, 1871; Shivers, p. 31; Harris, p. 355.

19. Jackson *Semi–Weekly Clarion*, April 7, 1871.

20. Ibid., April 21, 1871; Harris, pp. 356, 493, and 571.

21. Jackson *Semi-Weekly Clarion*, June 15, Sept. 8, 15, and 19, and Nov. 28, 1871; Harris, p. 559.

22. Jackson *Semi-Weekly Clarion*, Sept. 15 and 22, 1871.

23. *House Journal*, 1872, *Appendix*, pp. 9–10; *Senate Journal*, 1872, pp. 24–25; Jackson *Semi-Weekly Clarion*, Jan. 9, 1872; Harris, pp. 433–35.

24. See Jackson *Semi-Weekly Clarion*, Jan. 19 and 30, 1872, for accounts of unsuccessful attempts by prominent black politicians to ban convict leasing during Jan. 1872, and the editions of Feb. 2 and Mar. 1 and 12, 1872, for reports on the tactics of Powers's opponents in the legislature.

25. *Miss. Laws*, 1872, pp. 67–86.

26. Harris, p. 356.

27. *Senate Journal*, 1873, *Appendix*, pp. 556–57, constituting excerpts from *PR*, 1872; *House Journal*, 1873, pp. 1770–77; Jackson *Weekly Clarion*, April 10, 1873.

28. *Senate Journal*, 1873, pp. 21–22; *House Journal*, 1873, pp. 1776–77, and 1874, *Appendix*, pp. 84 and 172.

29. *Senate Journal*, 1873, p. 35; *House Journal*, 1873, pp. 1770–77; Jackson *Weekly Clarion*, Dec. 26, 1872, Jan. 23 and 30, Feb. 6 and 13, Mar. 13 and 20, and April 10, 1873; Harris, p. 423.

30. *PR*, 1873, pp. 84–85, 88, 90–91, and 173–74; *Senate Journal*, 1874, p. 204; *Biographical and Historical Memoirs*, rpt, ii. 668.

31. Harris, pp. 360 and 603.

32. Ibid., pp. 468 and 610–11; *The Testimony in the Impeachment of Adelbert Ames, as Governor of Mississippi* (Jackson, 1877), pp. 27–28, 154–59, and 295–96 (hereafter cited as *Testimony*).

33. Jackson *Weekly Clarion*, Mar. 12, 1874; *Miss. Laws*, 1874, pp. 58–60; Harris, p. 414.

34. *Senate Journal*, 1874, p. 204; *Testimony*, p. 193.

35. Ibid., pp. 193–94 and 197.

36. *PR*, 1874, in *House Journal*, 1875, pp. 102–3.

37. *Testimony*, pp. 126–28 and 155; *House Journal*, 1875, pp. 304–5 and 366–67; Jackson *Weekly Clarion*, Feb. 25, 1875; *Miss. Laws*, 1875, pp. 107–8.

38. *Testimony*, pp. 126–27, 155, 159 and 194; *PR*, 1875, pp. 3 and 5.

39. *House Journal*, 1875, pp. 59 and 366–67; *Miss. Laws*, 1875, pp. 94–96.

40. *Senate Journal*, 1876, pp. 435–38; Harris, pp. 620–21, 694, and 697–98. For other charges of corruption in penal affairs lodged against Republicans, see *Testimony*, pp. 126–28, 155–59, and 193–97; and Jackson *Weekly Clarion*, Mar. 22 and 28, 1876.

41. Ibid., Feb. 9, 12, and 23, and Mar. 8, 1876; *House Journal*, 1876, p. 374.

42. V. L. Wharton, *The Negro in Mississippi, 1865–1890* (Chapel Hill, N.C., 1947), pp. 239–40; Cooley, pp. 16–17. For comment on the racial context of leasing elsewhere in the South, see D. T. Carter, "Prisons, Politics, and Business: The Convict Lease System in the Post-Civil War South," Thesis, Univ. of Wisconsin, 1964, pp. 54 and 107; and B. McKelvey, "Penal Slavery and Southern Reconstruction," *The Journal of Negro History*, 20 (1935), 154.

43. *Miss. Laws*, 1876, pp. 194–203. See also Jackson *Weekly Clarion*, April 26, 1876.

44. *Miss. Laws*, 1876, pp. 51–52; Curtis, p. 21; Wharton, p. 239.

45. The lease was printed in *PR*, 1876, pp. 10–13. For biographical information on Hebron and Hamilton, see Wharton, p. 239; Shivers, p. 45; and *Biographical and Historical Memoirs*, i. 836 and 897.

46. *PR*, 1876, pp. 7–8; *Senate Journal*, 1877, p. 20; Jackson *Weekly Clarion*, Jan. 3, 1877.

47. Ibid., Jan. 31 and Feb. 14, 1877.

48. See the pointed remarks of Rep. W. F. Featherston, as reported in Jackson *Weekly Clarion*, Mar. 10, 1880.

49. *Senate Journal*, 1880, pp. 33–34, containing the message of the governor (hereafter cited as *Governor's Message 1880*).

50. Jackson *Weekly Clarion*, Jan. 21 and 28, Feb. 4, and Mar. 3, 1880.

51. Ibid., Feb. 11 and 18, 1880.

52. *Miss. Laws*, 1880, pp. 183–89; Jackson *Weekly Clarion*, Mar. 3 and 10, 1880.

53. Quoted by Shivers, p. 41.

54. Ibid., pp. 42–44; Jackson *Weekly Clarion*, July 7 and 21, 1880; *Biennial Message of Governor John M. Stone . . . January 4, 1882* (Jackson, 1882), p. 22 (hereafter cited as *Governor's Message 1882*).

55. For reports of the abuse of convicts, see Penitentiary Committee to Gov. Alcorn, June 23, 1870, and N. B. Forrest to Gov. Powers, April 2, 1872, MDAH, r.g. 27. v. 72 and 79; *PR*, 1872, pp. 562–63; *PR*, 1873, pp. 90–91 and 123; *PR*, 1875, p. 3; *PR*, 1877, pp. 4 and 126; *PR*, 1878–79, v; *House Journal*, 1873, p. 1775, and 1875, pp. 521–23; *Senate Journal*, 1874, pp. 203–4, and 1877, p. 20; and Jackson *Weekly Clarion*, May 1, 1873, and Feb.

5, 1874. For Richardson's chilling, matter–of–fact assessment of the political economy of convict leasing, see *Testimony*, pp. 127–28. See also Harris, p. 356, and Wharton, p. 239.

56. For Governor Powers's harangues against leasing, see *Senate Journal*, 1870, *Appendix*, p. 58, and 1872, pp. 24–25. For similar language by inspectors and superintendents, see *PR*, 1874, pp. 85 and 88, and *PR*, 1875, p. 5. For the most passionate and well-reasoned protest against leasing by black legislators, see *House Journal*, 1875, pp. 304–5. For Wines's indictment of Mississippi's criminal policy, see his *The State of Prisons and of Child–Saving Institutions in the Civilized World* (1880; rpt. Montclair, N.J., 1968), pp. 111–12 and 196.

57. Jackson *Weekly Clarion*, Jan. 25 and 31, and Feb. 15, 1882; *Governor's Message 1882*, pp. 21–23.

58. Jackson *Weekly Clarion*, Mar. 1 and 22, 1882.

59. *PR*, 1882–83, pp. 4–5, 10, and 127–28. See also *Biennial Reports of . . . Benevolent Institutions of . . . Mississippi for . . . 1882–83* (Jackson, 1884), p. 16 (hereafter cited as *RBI 1882–83*), and Shivers, p. 62.

60. J. H. Jones, "Penitentiary Reform in Mississippi," *Publications of the Mississippi Historical Society*, 6 (1902), 112; *RBI 1882–83*, pp. 17–19.

61. Jones, pp. 114 and 144.

62. Jackson *Clarion*, Mar. 5, 1884; *RBI 1882–83*, pp. 17–19.

63. For comment on the report of the Wilson committee and its disappearance, see Foreman and Tatum, p. 262, and Shivers, p. 48. For information on the numerous bills for penal reform and Rep. Baker's motion for statistics on convict mortality, see Jackson *Clarion*, Jan. 30, and Feb. 6, 20, and 27, 1884.

64. *Miss. Laws*, 1884, pp. 24–67 and 971–75.

Chapter 3

1. Shivers, p. 49; *Biennial Message of Governor Lowery . . . Delivered . . . January 5, 1886* (Jackson, 1886), pp. 20–21 (hereafter cited as *Governor's Message 1886*).

2. Curtis, pp. 22 and 34–36; C. V. Woodward, *Origins of the New South, 1877–1919* (Baton Rouge, 1951), p. 215. See generally J. S. Ferguson, "Agrarianism in Mississippi, 1871–1900: A Study in Nonconformity," Diss., Univ. of North Carolina, 1953, pp. 304–22.

3. *PR*, 1884–85, iv–vii, pp. 84–87; *Governor's Message 1886*, pp. 20–22. For comment on the allegation that Lowery and other high–ranking state officials were in collusion with Hamilton and his colleagues, see A. D. Kirwan, *Revolt of the Rednecks. Mississippi Politics, 1876–1925* (1951; rpt. New York, 1965), pp. 55–56, 167–68.

4. *Senate Journal*, 1886, *Appendix*, pp. 8–11 and 17–18; *House Journal*, 1886, pp. 592 and 603; Jackson *Clarion*, Jan. 13 and 20, 1886; Curtis, p. 37.

5. Jackson *Clarion*, Jan. 20, Feb. 24, and Mar. 3, 10, and 17, 1886; Curtis, p. 39.

6. Jackson *Clarion*, Feb. 10 and 26, 1886.

7. *Miss. Laws*, 1886, pp. 72–82.

8. Jones, p. 116.

9. Dillard's letter to the *Vicksburg Post* was reprinted by the Jackson *Clarion*, Aug. 18, 1886.

10. Curtis, pp. 41–43.

11. Jackson *Clarion*, Dec. 29, 1886.

12. *PR*, 1886–87, p. 9.

13. Ibid., pp. 9–10 and 18; Jones, p. 116.

14. Curtis, pp. 42–43.

15. Jackson *Clarion*, July 6, 1887.

16. Ibid., July 13, 1887.

17. Ibid., July 20, 1887.

18. Ibid., Oct. 11, 1887; Jackson *The New Mississippian*, Oct. 11, 1887; Curtis, p. 44. For a notable example of the exploitation of the presentment of the Hinds County grand jury by the Agrarian press, see Chickasaw *Messenger*, July 14 and 21, and Oct. 20, 1887. See also Natchez *Democrat*, Jan. 17, 1889, and Kirwan, pp. 168–69.

19. *PR*, 1886–87, pp. 12–13; *Biennial Message of Governor Robert Lowery to the Legislature . . . Delivered . . . January 5, 1888* (Jackson, 1888), pp. 24–26 (hereafter cited as *Governor's Message 1888*).

20. Clinton *Sword and Shield*, Jan. 7, 1888; *Senate Journal*, 1888, *Appendix*, p. 560; Jones, pp. 116–17. For a brief assessment of Agrarian strength in the new legislature, see Curtis, pp. 48–49.

21. See Hardy's two letters defending the railroad lease in Jackson *Clarion–Ledger*, Mar. 15 and Dec. 13, 1888. See also the defense of the lessees in *No Compromise With Principle: Autobiography and Biography of William Harris Hardy*, ed. T. A. Hardy (New York, 1946), pp. 229–34.

22. *House Journal*, 1888, pp. 3–35.

23. *Senate Journal*, 1888, pp. 560–82.

24. See the assessment of J. H. Lemly, *The Gulf, Mobile and Ohio, A Railroad That Had to Expand or Expire* (Homewood, Ill., 1953), pp. 386–87.

25. *Miss. Laws*, 1888, pp. 85–86; *PR*, 1888–89, pp. 3–4 and 13; Jackson *Clarion–Ledger*, Mar. 28 and April 4, 1889.

26. For comment on the double homicide, see Jackson *The New Mississippian*, May 8, 1888, and Lemly, p. 288. For details on the circumstances that led to the abrogation of the lease, see *PR*, 1888–89, pp. 4–6.

27. *PR*, 1888–89, pp. 6–15, 24, 27, and 29–43; Jackson *Clarion-Ledger*, Feb. 27, April 4, May 23, Sept. 12, and Nov. 28, 1889.

28. *Miss. Laws*, 1890, p. 61.

29. Curtis, p. 53. See also F. A. Johnston, "Suffrage and Reconstruction in Mississippi," *Publications of the Mississippi Historical Society* (Oxford, 1898–1914), vi. 237, and Kirwan, pp. 78–79.

30. Jackson *Clarion-Ledger*, Jan. 16, 1890, reporting Gov. Stone's speech. See Jones, p. 119, for comment on the popularity of penal reform at the time of the constitutional convention.

31. *The Constitution of the State of Mississippi, Adopted . . . November 1, 1890*, comp. G. L. Rice (Jackson, 1936), pp. 94–95; Curtis, p. 53. See also *Journal of the Proceedings of the Constitutional Convention* . . . (Jackson, 1890), pp. 123–24, and Jackson *Clarion–Ledger*, Sept. 2, 1890.

32. Curtis, p. 83. See generally, W. D. McCain, "The Populist Party in Mississippi," Thesis, Univ. of Miss., 1931.

33. Jackson *Weekly Clarion-Ledger*, April 1, 1897, Sept. 24, 1906, and July 1 and Aug. 5, 1909. For further comment on the plight of young convicts, see the publication of the Mississippi Juvenile Reformatory Association, *Mississippi Boy Convicts* (Jackson, 1911). For the statute creating the state's first agricultural and industrial training school for white youth, see *Miss. Laws*, 1916, pp. 149–50.

34. *PR*, 1903–05, p. 256; *House Journal*, 1910, p. 59; Jackson *Weekly Clarion-Ledger*, Aug. 4, 1910; *Miss. Laws*, 1916, pp. 138–39. See also *Senate Journal*, 1912, p. 24; M. L. Hutson, "Mississippi's State Penal System," Thesis, Univ. of Miss., 1939, p. 42; L. T. Balsamo, "Theodore G. Bilbo and Mississippi Politics, 1877–1932," Diss., Univ. of Missouri, 1967, pp. 95–96; and W. D. McCain, "The Triumph of Democracy, 1916–1932," in *A History of Mississippi*, ed. R. A. McLemore (Hattiesburg, Miss., 1973), ii. 59–62.

35. *Miss. Laws*, 1894, pp. 65–67. For information on continuing resistance to the purchase of penal farms between 1891 and 1894, see *House Journal*, 1892, pp. 206–7 and 735–36; *Senate Journal*, 1894, p. 51; and L. Q. Stone, "Prison Problems in Mississippi," *Proceedings of the Annual Congress of the American Prison Association . . . 1917* (Indianapolis, n.d.), p. 110 (hereafter cited as *APA 1917*).

36. Jackson *Weekly Clarion-Ledger*, Nov. 29, 1894; *House Journal*, 1896, pp. 44–45; *PR*, 1893–95, pp. 5–6.

37. Kirwan, pp. 171, 174, 308, and 312.

38. See the "share" contract between the state and planter H. C. Watson for the year 1897, MDAH, r.g. 49, v. 3. For a galling report by a medical examiner of the condition of convicts on one privately owned Delta plantation, see R. D. Farish, M.D., to Penitentiary Board of Control, May 23, 1896, MDAH, Governors Papers, series E, p. 110.

39. Macon *Beacon*, Feb. 15, 1896; Kirwan, pp. 169–70; W. F. Holmes, *The White Chief. James Kimble Vardaman* (Baton Rouge, 1970), pp. 151–52. For a vivid picture of Bourbon tactics regarding the award of "share" con-

tracts, see H. J. McLaurin to A. J. McLaurin, Nov. 4, 1895, MDAH, Governors Papers, Series E, p. 99.

40. *PR*, 1895–97, p. 92; *Senate Journal*, 1900, p. 33; Kirwan, p. 170; Holmes, p. 154.

41. Jackson *Clarion-Ledger*, Jan. 26, 1899.

42. *House Journal*, 1892, p. 735, and 1896, p. 704; *Senate Journal*, 1900, p. 34.

43. For statistics and comment evaluating the comparative strengths of convict labor on private and public lands, see penitentiary reports: 1891–92, pp. 1–3; 1892–93, pp. 6–9; 1893–95, p. 49; and 1895–97, pp. 4–5, 8–9, and 92. For further evidence, see generally, "Sergeants' Daily Reports, 1892–1900," MDAH, r.g. 49, v. 25 (hereafter cited as SDR 1892–1900), and *Senate Journal*, 1900, p. 33. See Zimmerman, pp. 251–53, for information on the success of penal farming in the Carolinas.

44. *Miss. Laws*, 1900, pp. 63–65 and 67–69. See also *Senate Journal*, 1900, p. 63, and *House Journal*, 1900, pp. 106 and 178.

45. *PR*, 1899–1901, pp. 3–4; *Senate Journal*, 1902, p. 8; "Works Project Administration: Historical Records Survey," MDAH, r.g. 60, v. 6, 403; "Lands of the Mississippi State Penitentiary," comp. P. J. Townsend, Jr., and E. McBride (Office of the Governor, Sept. 3, 1980), pp. 7–28 (hereafter cited as "Penitentiary Lands").

46. Jackson *Daily Clarion-Ledger*, Nov. 2, 1947. See also "Penitentiary Lands," pp. 71–73, for an analysis of land potential at Parchman.

47. These allegations were advanced in the reports of two subsequent legislative committees. See *House Journal*, 1902, pp. 58–67, and 1906, pp. 615–28, 916–18, and 1328–29. See also Holmes, p. 152, and Kirwan, pp. 170–71. For accounts of the distribution of the convict population during the two years following the purchase of Parchman, see *PR*, 1901–03, p. 4, and the warden's papers for 1901 and 1902, MDAH, r.g. 49, v. 6, 7.

48. *Miss. Laws*, 1900, pp. 245–46; Jackson *Clarion-Ledger*, Sept. 5, 1901.

49. *House Journal*, 1902, pp. 58–67; Vicksburg *Herald*, Jan. 9, 15, and 22, 1902; Kirwan, pp. 170–71. See also Jackson *Clarion-Ledger*, Jan. 16 and Feb. 6 and 20, 1902.

50. Ibid., Jan. 16 and Mar. 6, 1902; *House Journal*, 1902, pp. 146–47 and 451–61; *Senate Journal*, 1902, p. 62; *Miss. Laws*, 1902, p. 54; Kirwan, pp. 173–74.

51. For details of the state's first primary election, see Kirwan's eighth chapter, pp. 144–61.

52. Curtis, p. 83; Holmes, xii; N. P. McLemore, "James K. Vardaman, A Mississippi Progressive," *JMH*, 29 (Feb. 1967), 2; H. Ladner, "James Kimble Vardaman, Governor of Mississippi, 1904–1908," *JMH*, 2 (Oct. 1940), p. 175.

53. Holmes, pp. 31–32.

54. Ibid., p. 150, summarizing articles in the Jackson *Clarion-Ledger*, Nov. 2, 1904, and Brookhaven *Leader*, Dec. 16, 1905, and also drawing on an interview of May 1, 1968, with J. K. Vardaman, Jr.

55. *PR*, 1903–05, v–viii.

56. Kirwan, pp. 171–72; Holmes, pp. 152–54 and 158–59; Curtis, p. 106. For elaboration, see *PR*, 1903–05, v–viii; "State Penitentiary, 1901–06," MDAH, r.g. 49, v. 30, 242–43; Jackson *Clarion-Ledger*, Dec. 7, 9, 14, 20, and 21, 1905, and Jan. 25 and Mar. 8, 1906; and Jackson *Evening News*, Dec. 7, 1905.

57. *House Journal*, 1906, pp. 17–22. See also Kirwan, pp. 172–73, and Holmes, pp. 159–60.

58. *House Journal*, 1906, pp. 615–28, 916–18, and 1328–29. For the minority report, see ibid., pp. 638–44. See also Kirwan, pp. 173–74, and Holmes, pp. 161–63.

59. *Miss. Laws*, 1906, pp. 142–43; *The Mississippi Code of 1906* . . . (Nashville, 1906), p. 1012–13 (hereafter cited as *Code of 1906*). See also Holmes, pp. 165–76, recounting in detail the concessions in educational policy made by Vardaman in return for the package of penitentiary legislation.

60. Interview by W. B. Taylor with a former employee of the Mississippi penal system who requested anonymity, Parchman, Miss., Oct. 1978 (hereafter cited as Interview 1).

Chapter 4

1. H. B. Lacey, "The Mississippi Penitentiary System," in *The Official and Statistical Register of the State of Mississippi 1904*, ed. D. Rowland (Nashville, 1904), p. 302.

2. *Code of 1906*, p. 1012.

3. *House Journal*, 1906, pp. 19–20. See M. E. Wolfgang's chapter on Lombroso, F. A. Allen's chapter on Garofalo, and T. Sellin's chapter on Ferri in *Pioneers in Criminology*, ed. H. Mannheim (1972; 2nd ed., Montclair, N.J., 1973), pp. 232–91, 318–40, and 361–84.

4. Greenwood *Enterprise*, June 19 and Oct. 31, 1890, Mar. 21 and July 4, 1891, July 21, 1893, and June 29, 1894; Holmes, pp. 30–33 and 160. Holmes suggests (pp. 32–33 n.) that Vardaman "may well have been influenced" by the published views of J. P. Altgeld, governor of Illinois. Altgeld's *Our Penal Machinery and Its Victims* (1884) advanced a deterministic view of criminality and a reformative concept of penology. See also R. Ginger, *Altgeld's America: The Lincoln Ideal Versus Changing Realities* (New York, 1958), pp. 65–66.

5. *House Journal*, 1906, pp. 20–22.

6. Ibid., p. 19; Greenwood *Commonwealth*, April 15, May 6 and 20, and Aug. 12, 1897, Sept. 29, 1899, Jan. 19, 1900, and Feb. 22, 1901.

7. *House Journal*, pp. 19–22. For brief summary and analysis of Vardaman's views on criminality and convict discipline, see Kirwan, pp. 172–73, and Holmes, pp. 30–33 and 159–60.

8. Jackson *Clarion-Ledger*, Mar. 16, 1905; Kirwan, p. 163.

9. See, for example, G. Harris, "A Defense of Governor Vardaman," in *Harper's Weekly*, 49 (1905), p. 238.

10. For an account of state educational policy for blacks in the age of Jim Crow, including comment on Vardaman's views, see N. R. McMillen, *Dark Journey: Black Mississippians in the Age of Jim Crow* (Urbana and Chicago, 1989), pp. 72–108. See also J. D. Anderson, *The Education of Blacks in the South* (Chapel Hill, N.C., and London, 1988).

11. See McMillen, pp. 197–223, constituting the chapter entitled "Jim Crow's Courts."

12. Vardaman advanced this philosophy most succinctly in his address to the legislature of Jan. 1906 (*House Journal*, 1906, pp. 17–23). But see also his editorials in the Greenwood *Enterprise*, April 13, 20, and 27, 1894.

13. Holmes, pp. 54–56 and 182.

14. Governor Stone had advocated a similar scheme in 1896 (*Senate Journal*, 1896, p. 46).

15. *PR*, 1905–07, pp. 5–6; Board of Trustees Minute Book, 1906–1916, entries of 1906 and 1907, MDAH, r.g. 49, v. 31 (hereafter cited as TMB 1906–16).

16. *Miss. Laws*, 1910, p. 160; *PR*, 1907–09, p. 15; *PR*, 1909–11, p. 4; "Penitentiary Lands," pp. 32–36.

17. TMB 1906–16, entries of 1907–12, chronicling the tactics of centralization; "Penitentiary Lands," pp. 37–41; *PR*, 1907–09, pp. 4–5.

18. For these and other pertinent statistics, see penitentiary reports: 1905–07, pp. 5, 21, and 52; 1907–09, pp. 3, 51–52, 85, and 88; 1909–11, pp. 3, 21, 28–46, and 49; 1911–13, pp. 3, 35, and 54; 1913–15, p. 5; 1931–33, p. 18.

19. *Senate Journal*, 1912, pp. 348–49.

20. *Miss Laws*, 1914, pp. 176–77, and 1916, pp. 52–53; *House Journal*, 1918, pp. 1642–49; *PR*, 1917–19, p. 21.

21. *PR*, 1915–17, pp. 34–37.

22. Hutson, pp. 5–7.

23. Penitentiary reports: 1913–15, p. 116; 1915–17, pp. 17–19, 194, and 207; 1917–19, pp. 120 and 124; 1919–21, pp. 126, 134, and 136; 1921–23, p. 144; 1923–25, pp. 143 and 146; 1925–27, pp. 139, 148, and 151; 1927–29, pp. 4 and 140; 1929–31, pp. 4, 129–30, and 135; 1931–33, pp. 14 and 26; *APA 1917*, pp. 111–12; *Proceedings of the Annual Congress of the*

American Prison Association . . . 1921 (New York, n.d.), p. 257 (hereafter cited as *APA 1921*); *The Annotated Mississippi Code . . . 1917 . . .*, comp. W. Hemingway (Indianapolis, n.d.), p. 2646 (hereafter cited as *Code of 1917*); *Miss. Laws*, 1934, p. 359. Information amplifying that depicted by the penitentiary reports was obtained in an interview by W. B. Taylor with a former employee of the penal system who requested anonymity, Cleveland, Miss., June 1979 (hereafter cited as Interview 2).

24. *PR*, 1915–17, pp. 36–39 and 61–62; *PR*, 1933–35, p. 6; Hutson, pp. 28–29. For further details on operations, see generally the Board of Trustees Minute Book, 1917–1934, MDAH, r.g. 47. v. 28 (hereafter cited as TMB 1917–34).

25. Interviews 1 and 2; penitentiary reports: 1905–07, p. 5; 1907–09, p. 3; 1915–17, p. 5; 1919–21, pp. 5 and 8; 1921–23, p. 3; 1923–25, pp. 3 and 14; 1925–27, p. 3; 1927–29, pp. 4–5; 1929–31, p. 4; 1931–33, pp. 4 and 16–19; 1933–35, p. 15.

26. Interviews 1 and 2; Zimmerman, p. 322; Hutson, p. 38. For statutes mandating convict labor on the levees, see *Miss. Laws*, 1912, pp. 155–56, and 1916, pp. 625–26, and 1934, p. 569. For specific examples of such labor, see penitentiary reports: 1901–03, p. 7; 1915–17, pp. 40–43; 1927–29, p. 4.

27. *APA 1917*; *Proceedings of the 55th Annual Congress of the American Prison Association . . . 1925* (New York, n.d.), p. 80 (hereafter cited as *APA 1925*); *PR*, 1925–27, p. 24; Interview 1; N. B. Bond, *The Treatment of the Dependent, Defective and Delinquent in Mississippi* (n.c.p., n.d.), pp. 27 and 83. The rules and regulations governing convicts were formulated at least as early as 1890, adopted anew in 1907, and mandated by statute without revision in 1934. See *PR*, 1890–91, p. 32; TMB 1906–16, entry of Feb. 8, 1907; and *Miss. Laws*, 1934, pp. 364–65.

28. Interview 2.

29. Interviews 1 and 2; *APA 1925*, p. 85; Hutson, p. 20.

30. For a good summary of the operant learning theory propounded by B. F. Skinner and more recently given criminological application by C. R. Jeffrey, and of the related "social learning theory" advanced by R. Akers, see F. P. Williams III and M. D. McShane, *Criminological Theory* (Englewood Cliffs, N.J., 1988), pp. 118–27.

31. Interviews 1 and 2; *Senate Journal*, 1924, pp. 888–89.

32. Interview 2.

33. Interviews 1 and 2; *PR*, 1888–89, pp. 11 and 14; *Proceedings of the American Prison Association . . . 1910* (Indianapolis, 1910), pp. 123–24 (hereafter cited as *APA 1910*); Bond, pp. 87–88; Hutson, p. 6.

34. Interviews 1 and 2.

35. *Miss. Laws*, 1922, pp. 323–24, and 1928, p. 216; Interview 2; Bond, p. 87. Between 1907 and 1922 there were 157 discharges for "meritorious

service" and only 123 suspended sentences. Between 1922 and 1929, 294 suspended sentences were granted (see note 41 below). For data depicting the increase in attempted escapes, see *PR*, 1919–21, p. 143, and *PR*, 1923–25, pp. 143 and 145. See also *House Journal*, 1930, p. 12, for comment by the governor.

36. Interview 2.

37. Jackson *Daily Clarion-Ledger*, Nov. 2, 1915, and Oct. 31, 1933; W. F. Minor, "They Ate Their Way to Freedom," *The Times-Picayune New Orleans States Magazine*, Jan. 9, 1949; P. de Kruif, *Hunger Fighters: A Social History of Pellagra in the South* (Westport, Conn., 1972), pp. 92–96.

38. *House Journal*, 1916, p. 47; F. Wallace, "A History of the Conner Administration," Thesis, Miss. College, 1959, pp. 59–60.

39. Jackson *Daily Clarion–Ledger*, Jan. 1 and 20, 1932.

40. Interviews 1 and 2; Foreman and Tatum, p. 271. For evidence of the controversy surrounding the board of pardons, see *Senate Journal*, 1920, pp. 349, 929, 955, and 1595–97. For related statutes, see *Miss. Laws*, 1922, p. 357, and 1924, pp. 222 and 589.

41. Penitentiary reports: 1907–09, p. 88; 1909–11, p. 49; 1911–13, p. 54; 1913–15, p. 116; 1915–17, pp. 194 and 207; 1917–19, pp. 120 and 124; 1919–21, pp. 126 and 133; 1921–23, pp. 143–44; 1923–25, pp. 143 and 145; 1925–27, pp. 148 and 150; 1927–29, p. 140; 1929–31, p. 129; 1931–33, p. 14.

42. Hutson, p. 32; Interview 1.

43. Interview 2.

44. C. B. Hopper, *Sex in Prison: The Mississippi Experiment With Conjugal Visiting* (Baton Rouge, 1969), pp. 52–81.

45. Interview 1.

46. Hopper, pp. 79–80.

47. The passage cited here, as well as other descriptive comment about the state penitentiary, is available in the 1938 W.P.A. publication, *Mississippi: A Guide to the Magnolia State.*

48. Interviews 1 and 2.

49. Hutson, pp. 22–23; Bond, p. 85; Hopper, p. 35.

50. Jackson *Weekly Clarion-Ledger*, Oct. 7, 1909; *APA 1910*, p. 124.

51. Penitentiary reports: 1909–11, p. 51; 1911–13, pp. 54–55; 1913–15, p. 120; 1915–17, p. 196; 1917–19, p. 22; 1919–21, p. 130; 1921–23, p. 147; 1923–25, p. 137; 1925–27, p. 140; 1927–29, p. 141.

52. Penitentiary reports: 1905–07, pp. 21 and 52; 1907–09, pp. 51 and 85; 1909–11, pp. 26 and 46; 1931–33, p. 18, depicting financial accounts from 1911 through 1933.

53. *House Journal*, 1910, p. 20; *PR*, 1923–25, p. 14.

54. Quoted by Jackson *Daily Clarion-Ledger*, June 23, 1914.

55. Quoted from the record jacket of Lomax's album, "Negro Prison Songs from the Mississippi State Penitentiary," released by Tradition Records in 1947.

56. Interviews 1 and 2.

57. Pages 48–49. My co-author and I are indebted to Peggy Whitman Prenshaw, professor of English at Louisiana State University, for allowing us to peruse and follow leads advanced in her yet-unpublished article assessing the role of the state penitentiary in the literary and musical history of Mississippi.

58. For a modern account of this phenomenon, and the resulting unmarked graves at the Louisiana State Penitentiary at Angola, see New Orleans *Times-Picayune*, Oct. 14, 1990.

59. Such stories are widespread among the older residents of the Delta. The specific accounts above are drawn from the personal experiences of W. B. Taylor, who, as a boy residing in the Delta town of Greenwood and later in Jackson, heard the grim threats of black parents and the tales of old-timers, and witnessed the labor of convicts on the levees of the Yazoo River.

60. Interview 1.

61. Kirwan, pp. 174–75.

62. For Noel's efforts, see *Senate Journal*, 1910, p. 18, and 1912, p. 24; *House Journal*, 1910, p. 59; and Jackson *Weekly Clarion-Ledger*, Aug. 4, 1910. For Brewer's efforts, see *Senate Journal*, 1912, p. 124, *House Journal*, 1912, pp. 861–62, and Cooley, pp. 103–5. For Whitfield's efforts, see *Senate Journal*, 1924, pp. 201 and 212–14, and 1926, pp. 295–98. For Bilbo's efforts, see Balsamo, pp. 95–96, McCain, "The Triumph of Democracy," pp. 59–62, and Cooley, pp. 107–9. See also Bilbo's speech to the legislature in *Senate Journal*, 1917, p. 43.

63. For numerous examples of Yerger's, Thames's and Montgomery's efforts on behalf of the convicts, see TMB 1906–16, and the entries of 1917–1930 in TMB 1917–34.

64. Jackson *Daily Clarion-Ledger*, Mar. 15, 1936.

65. For Montgomery's remarks, which were addressed to the senate penitentiary committee in 1934, see Jackson *Daily Clarion-Ledger*, Mar. 13, 1934. For numerous examples of her efforts on behalf of the convicts, see generally the entries of 1926–34 in TMB 1917–34.

66. For examples of Williamson's efforts, see *PR*, 1929–31, p. 22, and *PR*, 1931–33, p. 13. For examples of Fox's criticism of the legislature and recommendations for reform, see *PR*, 1923–25, pp. 14–15, and *PR*, 1925–27, p. 28.

67. For information on the embezzlement scandal, see *Senate Journal*, 1914, pp. 65–66; TMB, 1906–16, pp. 498–500; Balsamo, pp. 80–82; Holmes, pp. 328–29; Kirwan, pp. 237–39; and C. M. Morgan, *Redneck Lib-*

eral: Theodore G. Bilbo and the New Deal (Baton Rouge and London, 1985), p. 36. For information on the official negligence that resulted in the fatal fire at Oakley, see *Senate Journal*, 1914, pp. 1430–31.

68. See generally TMB 1906–16, and TMB 1917–34, for occasional notations concerning abuses by employees.

69. *Senate Journal*, 1908, pp. 27–28 and 32–33; *PR*, 1927–29, p. 143; Bond, p. 9; McKelvey, *Prisons*, p. 85.

70. *APA 1925*, p. 84; Interview 2.

71. Interviews 1 and 2.

72. J. L. Gillem, *Taming the Criminal: Adventures in Penology* (New York, 1931), p. 13; Bond, p. 91.

73. Holmes, pp. 328–30; Kirwan, pp. 237–39.

74. *PR*, 1925–27, p. 28; *Senate Journal*, 1917, p. 43, and 1924, p. 212, and 1930, pp. 12–13; P. W. Garrett and A. H. MacCormick, *Handbook of American Prisons and Reformatories, 1929* (New York, 1929), p. 257.

75. *Proceedings of the Annual Congress of the American Prison Association . . . 1919* (Indianapolis, 1919), p. 210; *House Journal*, 1930, pp. 601–3, and 1932, p. 55; Jackson *Daily Clarion–Ledger*, May 3 and Oct. 24, 1933; and penitentiary reports: 1919–21, p. 5; 1921–23, pp. 3 and 12–20; 1923–25, pp. 12–22; 1925–27, pp. 20–28; 1927–29, pp. 15–18; 1931–33, pp. 3–11.

Chapter 5

1. See generally *PR*, 1931–33. For Trustee Montgomery's assessment, see Jackson *Daily Clarion-Ledger*, Mar. 13, 1936.

2. *PR*, 1931–33, p. 18.

3. For evidence of the unfolding political duel between Conner and Montgomery, see Jackson *Daily Clarion-Ledger*, Nov. 8, 1933, Jan. 6, 16, and 25, Feb. 4, 7, and 27, and Mar. 2 and 4, 1934. For reports of the final deliberations of the legislature, see ibid., Mar. 2, 4, 13, and 23, 1934; *House Journal*, 1934, pp. 433–35; and *Senate Journal*, 1934, pp. 662–64, 686, 693, and 726.

4. *Miss. Laws*, 1934, pp. 347–70. See also Cooley, pp. 140–43; Bond, p. 87; Hutson, p. 6; and R. F. Saucier, "A History of the Mississippi Penal System, 1935–1970," Thesis, Univ. of Southern Miss., 1982, pp. 1–2 and 4–5.

5. Jackson *Daily Clarion-Ledger*, Mar. 23 and June 7, 1934.

6. Ibid., Mar. 13 and April 14, 1934; *PR*, 1933–35, p. 18.

7. Jackson *Daily Clarion-Ledger*, July 5, 6, 20, and 22, 1934.

8. Ibid., Nov. 5, 1936, and Nov. 5, 1937; Board of Commissioners Minute Book, 1944–1959, MDAH, r.g. 49, v. 27, entry of Oct. 4, 1950 (hereafter cited as CMB 1944–59).

9. For elaboration see the first two pages of the Epilogue.

10. Interview 2; interview by W. B. Taylor with a former employee of the penal system who requested anonymity, Clarksdale, Miss., Dec. 1980 (hereafter cited as Interview 3); interview by W. B. Taylor with a former employee of the penal system who requested anonymity, Cleveland, Miss., Dec. 1980 (hereafter cited as Interview 4); interview by W. B. Taylor with a former state legislator who requested anonymity, Jackson, Miss., Feb. 1980 (hereafter cited as Interview 5); interview by W. B. Taylor with a black trusty who worked in the guest house during the forties and requested anonymity, Natchez, Miss., May, 1980 (hereafter cited as Interview 6).

11. Interviews 2, 3, and 4.

12. Jackson *Daily Clarion-Ledger*, Feb. 4, 1934.

13. Ibid., Jan. 27, 1936, Oct. 22, 1937, Jan. 26, 1938, and Jan. 16, 1940; Jackson *Clarion-Ledger*, Nov. 18, 1942, July 1, 1944, Feb. 26, and Aug. 24, 1952.

14. Jackson *Daily Clarion-Ledger*, Mar. 24, 1935, and Nov. 20 and 21, 1940; *PR*, 1939–41, p. 3.

15. *PR*, 1933–35, pp. 3–5, 12, 18–20, 46, and 51.

16. Ibid., p. 3; Jackson *Daily Clarion-Ledger*, Jan. 31 and Mar. 29, 1935.

17. Ibid., Jan. 10 and 23, 1936.

18. *PR*, 1937–39, pp. 3–5; *PR*, 1939–41, pp. 4–6.

19. Jackson *Daily Clarion-Ledger*, April 1, 1937, and Jan. 16, 1940; penitentiary reports: 1935–37, pp. 3 and 22; 1937–39, pp. 3, 20, and 25–26; 1939–41, pp. 16–17.

20. Ibid., p. 3.

21. Jackson *Daily Clarion-Ledger*, Nov. 13 and 14, 1941; *Senate Journal*, 1941, p. 84.

22. *PR*, 1941–43, pp. 4–5; Jackson *Clarion-Ledger*, Oct. 29, 1942.

23. *PR*, 1941–43, pp. 20 and 34.

24. Jackson *Clarion-Ledger*, Dec. 6, 1943.

25. *PR*, 1941–43, pp. 30 and 34; *PR*, 1943–45, pp. 3, 21, and 23; *Senate Journal*, 1944, pp. 15–16.

26. For pithy accounts of the progression of criminological thought, see Williams and McShane, *Criminological Theory*, and W. B. Pelfrey, *The Evolution of Criminology* (Cincinnati, 1980). For an account of related developments that transformed penology into "corrections," see McKelvey, *Prisons*, pp. 34–196 and 234–67.

27. Ibid., pp. 10, 27, 49, 238, 292, and 300–10.

28. Garrett and MacCormick, pp. 527–29. See also Foreman and Tatum, pp. 271–72.

29. For editorials in the Jackson *Daily Clarion-Ledger* and Jackson *Clarion-Ledger* defending corporal punishment, see the editions of Nov. 8, 1934, July 20, 1935, and May 7, 1936. For defenses of the trusty system, see

the editions of July 14 and 16, Aug. 1, and Oct. 19, 1934. For defenses of the suspension system and attacks on the concept of parole, see the editions of Sept. 2, 1934, Jan. 2 and Mar. 28 and 31, 1935, Jan. 7 and Feb. 21, 1937, Sept. 3, 1938, Mar. 19 and April 18, 1939, and Dec. 18, 1940. For criticism of the state–use system of prison labor, see the edition of Mar. 4, 1936. For defenses of the penitentiary's organization and physical arrangements, see the editions of Dec. 22, 1942, and Dec. 6, 1943.

30. Ibid., Mar. 5 and 8, 1937.

31. Ibid., June 25, 1935, May 15 and June 16, 1938, and Nov. 5 and 9, 1940.

32. Ibid., Nov. 17 and 19, 1940.

33. Ibid., Sept. 3, 1938, and Jan. 9, 1941.

34. Ibid., Nov. 26, 1941. See also Howard André McDonnell, *In the Throes of Criminal Justice* (Bryn Mawr, Penn., 1986).

35. *Miss. Laws*, 1940, pp. 73 and 711–13, and 1942, pp. 38 and 384–86. For an account of the state's drift toward the establishment of a reformatory for black youth, see Jackson *Clarion-Ledger*, Jan. 15, 1950.

36. *Senate Journal*, 1938, pp. 891, 912, and 918; *PR*, 1937–39, p. 6; Jackson *Daily Clarion-Ledger*, Nov. 13, 1936, April 12, 1939, May 4, 1940, and Nov. 26, 1941.

37. Interviews 4 and 5.

38. Jackson *Daily Clarion-Ledger*, Aug. 9 and Nov. 10, 1940, Dec. 8, 1941, Mar. 14, May 13 and 16, Sept. 19, 1942, and Jan. 6, 1944; *House Journal*, 1942, pp. 361–63; *Senate Journal*, 1942, pp. 427 and 701; *Miss. Laws*, 1942, pp. 62–63.

39. Interviews 4 and 6; *PR*, 1943–45, p. 5; Jackson *Clarion–Ledger*, Feb. 19, 1942, and Feb. 8, 1944.

40. Interviews 4 and 5.

41. Jackson *Clarion-Ledger*, Sept. 14, 1941, Mar. 10, 11, and 20, and June 20, 1943, and Feb. 8, 1944; *Senate Journal*, 1944, p. 5; *PR*, 1941–43, pp. 6–7.

42. *House Journal*, 1944, pp. 62–63; Jackson *Clarion-Ledger*, Jan. 19, 21, and 22, and Feb. 8, 17, 25, and 27, 1944.

43. Ibid., Feb. 18, 19, and 27, 1944.

44. For reports on the progress of the parole bill and comment by legislators, see Jackson *Clarion-Ledger*, Jan. 21, Feb. 8, 17, and 22, and Mar. 14, 1944. For the parole statute, see *Miss. Laws*, 1944, pp. 574–79. For the debates on the accompanying penitentiary bill, see *Senate Journal*, 1944, pp. 780–81. For the journalistic criticism, see Jackson *Clarion–Ledger*, Mar. 26, 1944.

45. *Miss. Laws*, 1944, pp. 554–71.

46. *Senate Journal*, 1944, pp. 190–91 and 578–83; Jackson *Clarion-Ledger*, Feb. 22, 1944.

47. Ibid., July 1 and 7, 1944.

48. For comment on Wiggins's managerial skills and assessments of the efficiency of his staff, see *PR*, 1947–49, pp. 8–9 and 12; *PR*, 1951–53, p. 21; and Jackson *Clarion-Ledger*, Jan. 2, 1951, and Feb. 26 and Aug. 24, 1952.

49. Interviews 2, 3, 4, 5, and 6.

50. Interviews 2, 3, 4, and 5.

51. Jackson *Clarion-Ledger*, Oct. 7, 1944.

52. Interviews 2, 3, 4, and 5.

53. Interviews 4 and 5; Penitentiary reports: 1943–45, p. 3; 1945–47, pp. 3–4; 1947–49, p. 4; 1949–51, pp. 3 and 15; Jackson *Clarion-Ledger*, Jan. 16 and Sept. 18, 1946, Jan. 19, 1947, July 31 and Nov. 9, 1948, and July 24 and Oct. 14, 1949.

54. Ibid., Dec. 10, 1944, Aug. 30, 1946, Dec. 19, 1947, and Nov. 9, 1948; CMB 1944–59, entry of Jan. 6, 1948; *PR*, 1945–47, pp. 3–5; *PR*, 1947–49, pp. 3 and 7–8.

55. Jackson *Clarion-Ledger*, Jan. 18, Mar. 11, June 30, and Nov. 29, 1946, and Jan. 21 and Dec. 8, 1947; *Senate Journal*, 1946, p. 640.

56. Interview 4; Jackson *Clarion-Ledger*, Jan. 19, 1947, reporting one of several accommodating responses of Wiggins to the criticism of his detractors.

57. Interview 4.

58. Jackson *Clarion-Ledger*, Aug. 8 and Sept. 27, 1946.

59. Ibid., Jan. 19, 1947.

60. *PR*, 1945–47, p. 11; interview by W. B. Taylor with a former inmate whose name is withheld at the discretion of the interviewer, Natchez, Miss., Feb. 1982 (hereafter cited as Interview 7).

61. CMB 1944–59, entries of May 1 and Sept. 4, 1945; Interviews 4 and 7.

62. Jackson *Clarion-Ledger*, Aug. 18, 1946.

63. Ibid., Jan. 19, 1947; *PR*, 1945–47, p. 11; Interview 7.

64. Jackson *Clarion-Ledger*, Dec. 11, 1945, June 14, 1948, and April 19, 1952; CMB 1944–59, entry of Mar. 5, 1946; penitentiary reports: 1945–47, p. 11; 1949–51, p. 25; 1951–53, p. 39.

65. For the progress of the parole board during its first five years of operation, see *First Biennial Report of the State Parole Board . . . From April 15, 1944, Through June 30, 1945* (Jackson, 1945), p. 3 (hereafter cited as *Parole*, 1944–45, as subsequent reports of the parole board are cited as *Parole*, followed by the years encompassed by the biennium); *Parole*, 1945–47, pp. 3–4; *Parole*, 1947–49, p. 2; *PR*, 1943–45, p. 16; *PR*, 1946–47, p. 6; CMB 1944–59, entry of Jan. 2, 1945; and Jackson *Clarion-Ledger*, Jan. 16, July 7, and Dec. 15, 1946, Jan. 19, 1947, and Jan. 9, 1949.

66. Interview 4; CMB 1944–59, entry of Mar. 5, 1946.

67. *Hattiesburg American*, May 3, 1947; Jackson *Clarion-Ledger*, May 4, Dec. 17 and 19, 1947.

68. Interviews 4 and 5.

69. Interview 5.

70. Ibid.; Jackson *Clarion-Ledger*, Mar. 20, 23 and 24, and May 10, 1948.

71. *Miss. Laws*, 1948, pp. 640–65 and 704–7. See *Senate Journal*, 1948, pp. 155, 191, and 381, for accounts of unsuccessful attempts to abolish the strap, to employ a music teacher, and to establish a probation system and an "honor camp" for meritorious convicts.

72. Interviews 4 and 5. Jackson *Clarion-Ledger*, Mar. 23 and 24, 1948.

73. Interview 4; *PR*, 1947–49, p. 7.

74. *Miss. Laws*, 1948, p. 54; Jackson *Clarion-Ledger*, Nov. 28, 1948; penitentiary reports: 1947–49, pp. 4, 5, and 11; 1949–51, pp. 3 and 17–18; 1951–53, pp. 3–4 and 15.

75. Jackson *Clarion-Ledger*, July 31, 1948; *PR*, 1947–49, pp. 3–4, 7–8, and 10; *PR*, 1949–51, p. 13.

76. *PR*, 1947–49, p. 4; Jackson *Clarion-Ledger*, Nov. 9, 1948, and July 24 and Oct. 14, 1949.

77. Ibid., Feb. 19, 1944.

78. Ibid., April 3, 1945, Jan. 16, Sept. 18, and Nov. 27, 1946, Jan. 19 and Nov. 2, 1947, and July 31, 1948; penitentiary reports: 1945–47, p. 4; 1947–49, pp. 4–5 and 10; 1949–51, pp. 3 and 15. See the Christmas day menu in Jackson *Clarion-Ledger*, Dec. 25, 1945.

79. Penitentiary reports: 1943–45, p. 10; 1945–47, pp. 17 and 19; 1947–49, pp. 26 and 29; 1949–51, pp. 30 and 33; 1951–53, pp. 7 and 12; Jackson *Clarion-Ledger*, Jan. 2, 1951.

80. Interviews 4 and 7.

81. *PR*, 1947–49, p. 25; Jackson *Clarion-Ledger*, Dec. 3 and 12, 1946, Dec. 13, 1947, May 10 and 11, and Dec. 2, 1948, Oct. 6, 1950, and Nov. 25, 1952.

82. *PR*, 1947–49, p. 21; *PR*, 1949–51, p. 25; Jackson *Clarion-Ledger*, June 28, 1950.

83. Interviews 1, 4, 6, and 7; *PR*, 1949–51, p. 27.

84. *PR*, 1947–49, p. 20.

85. *PR*, 1949–51, pp. 24 and 26–27; *PR*, 1951–53, p. 41; Jackson *Clarion–Ledger*, Dec. 1, 1949.

86. *PR*, 1947–49, pp. 23–24.; *PR*, 1949–51, p. 25.

87. *PR*, 1951–53, p. 6; Interview 3; and interview by W. B. Taylor with a former inmate whose name is withheld at the discretion of the interviewer, Leland, Miss., April 1982 (hereafter cited as Interview 8).

88. *PR*, 1949–51, pp. 13 and 25; CMB 1944–59, entry of April 5, 1949.

89. For reports on the penitentiary's kennel and the methods employed in the event of escapes, see Jackson *Daily Clarion-Ledger*, May 15, 1938, and Jackson *Clarion-Ledger*, Jan. 26, 1958. For official statistics on escapes, see penitentiary reports: 1939–41, pp. 22 and 27; 1941–43, pp. 9 and 14;

1943–45, pp. 7 and 10; 1945–47, pp. 17 and 19; 1947–49, pp. 26 and 29; 1949–51, pp. 30 and 33; 1951–53, p. 12.

90. Jackson *Clarion-Ledger*, Feb. 26 and Aug. 24, 1952.

91. Interview 4.

Chapter 6

1. Jackson *Clarion-Ledger*, Jan. 17, 1952, reporting Alexander's speech; interview by W. B. Taylor with a former state legislator who requested anonymity, Jackson, Miss., Mar. 1986 (hereafter cited as Interview 9).

2. Jackson *Clarion-Ledger*, May 23, Aug. 6, and Dec. 23, 1950, and Jan. 2 and 20, 1951; *True Detective*, 54 (Dec. 1950), pp. 40–43, 69–71.

3. Interview 9.

4. Jackson *Clarion-Ledger*, Jan. 17, 1952. The proposal to establish a state department of corrections was rooted in northern penal reform and in the propensity for bureaucratic reorganization that swept the country after World War II. Governor Wright's address to the legislature of Jan. 3, 1950, had proposed governmental reorganization, and later in the year a legislative committee had endorsed the amalgamation of all "correctional agencies" under a single department of state government. See *House Journal*, 1950, pp. 30–31, and Jackson *Clarion-Ledger*, Nov. 8, 1950.

5. *Senate Journal*, 1952, p. 217.

6. Jackson *Clarion-Ledger*, Feb. 26, 1952.

7. Ibid., Mar. 15, May 14 and 16, and Aug. 5, 1952.

8. Ibid., Feb. 3 and 22, 1952. See ibid., Feb. 23, 1958, for retrospective comment on Alexander's pamphlet, *The Lash*.

9. Ibid., Jan. 17 and 29, 1952.

10. *Senate Journal*, 1952, pp. 433, 438, 481, and 900; *House Journal*, 1952, pp. 352, 354, 407, and 652; Jackson *Clarion-Ledger*, Feb. 3 and 22, Mar. 2 and 15, April 19, and June 16, 1952.

11. Interviews 4 and 9.

12. Jackson *Clarion-Ledger*, Feb. 3, 1952.

13. *House Journal*, 1952, pp. 204, 244, and 274; Jackson *Clarion-Ledger*, Jan. 29 and Feb. 3 and 22, 1952; Interview 9.

14. *PR*, 1941–43, p. 20; *PR*, 1951–53, p. 5.

15. Interview 4; Jackson *Clarion-Ledger*, Aug. 24, 1952.

16. Interviews 3 and 4.

17. Jackson *Clarion-Ledger*, April 18, 1953.

18. Greenville *Delta Democrat-Times*, April 24 and June 23, 1953; Jackson *Clarion-Ledger*, April 15 and 26, and June 25 and 26, 1953; New Orleans *Times Picayune*, June 26 and July 12, 1953; Memphis *Commercial Appeal*, July 11, 1953.

19. *PR*, 1951–53, pp. 4–5.

20. Jackson *Clarion-Ledger*, June 23, 1953.

21. Ibid., June 30 and July 11, 1953; New Orleans *Times Picayune*, July 5, 1953; Interview 4.

22. Memphis *Commercial Appeal*, June 30, 1953; Jackson *Clarion-Ledger*, June 26 and 30, 1953.

23. Ibid., June 30, 1953; New Orleans *Times Picayune*, July 5, 1953.

24. Memphis *Commercial Appeal*, July 11, 1953; Jackson *Clarion-Ledger*, July 9, 1953.

25. Memphis *Commercial Appeal*, July 5, 1953.

26. Jackson *Clarion-Ledger*, June 26, July 9, 11, 12, and 29, and Oct. 1, 1953.

27. McComb *Enterprise-Journal*, Sept. 30, 1953; Jackson *Clarion-Ledger*, July 21 and Oct. 9, 1953, and Feb. 24, 1954.

28. Ibid., Feb. 24, 1954.

29. Ibid., Mar. 11 and 12, 1954.

30. For reports of the earlier debates, see Jackson *Daily Clarion-Ledger*, Mar. 12, 1936, and Mar. 7 and April 5, 1940.

31. Interview 9; Jackson *Clarion-Ledger*, Sept. 13, 1954. See ibid., July 25 and Aug. 2, 1953, reporting on-site inspections by state officials of the maximum security units at Atmore, Alabama, and Huntsville, Texas, and the resulting decision to adopt the Texas model. For a description of "Little Shamrock," see R. C. Copeland, "The Evolution of the Texas Department of Corrections," Thesis, Sam Houston State University, 1980, pp. 129–32. For a description of "Little Alcatraz," see Jackson *Clarion-Ledger*, Sept. 26, 1954.

32. Ibid., Jan. 20, May 8 and 13, and Sept. 12, 13, 14, 15, 17, 20, 23, 26, and 29, 1954; *Senate Journal*, 1954, pp. 27, 141, 145, and 167, and 1954–55 (Extra Session), pp. 27 and 94; *Miss. Laws*, 1954, pp. 44–46.

33. Jackson *Clarion–Ledger*, Sept. 26, 1954; *Inside World*, Oct. 1954; Interview 4.

34. Jackson *Clarion-Ledger*, Dec. 9 and 12, 1954.

35. Ibid., Feb. 26, 1955; Interviews 4 and 9.

36. Jackson *Clarion-Ledger*, Mar. 4 and May 1, 1954; McDonnell, pp. 256–59; Interviews 4 and 9.

37. Interview 9.

38. Jackson *Clarion-Ledger*, April 3, 1955; *PR*, 1953–55, p. 34.

39. Ibid., pp. 20 and 34–35.

40. Ibid., pp. 7, 20, and 34.

41. Jackson *Clarion-Ledger*, Oct. 23, 1953, and April 3, 1955; Interview 4.

42. McComb *Enterprise-Journal*, Sept. 30, 1953; Jackson *Clarion-Ledger*, Mar. 11 and April 1, 1956. For a description of the handiwork produced by convicts participating in the hobby contest, see D. Evans, "Afro-American

Folk Sculpture from Parchman Penitentiary," *Mississippi Folklore Register*, vi. 4 (Winter 1972), pp. 141–52.

43. *PR*, 1953–55, p. 13; Jackson *Clarion-Ledger*, Dec. 16, 1954.

44. *PR*, 1953–55, pp. 24–30.

45. Jackson *Clarion-Ledger*, May 1 and June 25, 1955.

46. *PR*, 1953–55, pp. 5, 17–18, and 33; *PR*, 1955–57, p. 6.

47. *House Journal*, 1956, p. 417; Interview 4; interview by W. B. Taylor with a state official who requested anonymity, Hattiesburg, Miss., Oct. 1986 (hereafter cited as Interview 10).

48. For reports of the key debates on the probation bill, see *Senate Journal*, 1956, p. 22, and Jackson *Clarion-Ledger*, Jan. 18, Feb. 23, and Mar. 21, 1956. For the statute, see *Miss. Laws*, 1956, pp. 312–18. For Wiggins's letter of resignation, see CMB 1944–59, entry of June 5, 1956.

49. Jackson *Clarion-Ledger*, May 9, 1956.

50. Penitentiary reports: 1943–45, pp. 10, 23, and 27; 1945–47, pp. 17–18 and 21–22; 1947–49, pp. 6, 26, and 29; 1949–51, pp. 4, 30, and 33; 1951–53, pp. 5 and 7; 1953–55, pp. 5, 17–18, and 33; 1955–57, p. 6.

51. For assessment of Coleman's racial strategy and tactics, see N. R. McMillen, "Development of Civil Rights 1956–1970," in McLemore, ii. 158–59; E. Terry Jack, "Racial Policy and Judge J. P. Coleman: A Study in Political-Judicial Linkage," Diss., Univ. of Southern Miss., 1979, pp. 61–94; *Greenwood Commonwealth*, May 10, 1984; and *Life*, April 15, 1957, pp. 93–98.

52. Jackson *Clarion-Ledger*, Mar. 9, June 6, and Aug. 17, 1956; CMB 1944–59, entry of Aug. 7, 1956; Interviews 4 and 9; interview by W. B. Taylor with a former state official who requested anonymity, Jackson, Miss., Jan. 1982 (hereafter cited as Interview 11).

53. Jackson *Clarion-Ledger*, July 15 and Dec. 2, 1956.

54. Ibid., Aug. 2 and Sept. 12, 1956; McComb *Enterprise-Journal*, Aug. 1, 1956; *PR*, 1955–57, p. 37.

55. Jackson *Clarion-Ledger*, Sept. 24, 1958.

56. Ibid., July 22 and Oct. 4, 1956.

57. Ibid., Dec. 20, 1956; *PR*, 1955–57, pp. 38–39; *Inside World*, Dec. 1956.

58. Jackson *Clarion-Ledger*, July 21, Sept. 12, and Dec. 8, 1956.

59. Ibid., Aug. 5, 1956.

60. Ibid.

61. Ibid.; *Inside World*, Sept. and Dec. 1956; *PR*, 1955–57, p. 36.

62. Ibid., pp. 36–38; Jackson *Clarion-Ledger*, Dec. 16, 1956.

63. Ibid., Sept. 12 and Dec. 8, 1956.

64. Ibid., Dec. 16, 1956.

65. Ibid., Dec. 16 and 23, 1956.

66. *PR*, 1957–59, pp. 6–7; *Inside World*, Mar. 1957; Jackson *Clarion-Ledger*, April 8, 1958, and June 28, 1959.

67. Ibid., April 18, 1957.

68. Ibid., May 17, 1959.

69. *Parade*, May 17, 1959. See also Jackson *Clarion-Ledger*, June 19, 1959.

70. Professor Hopper's first article was "The Conjugal Visit at the Mississippi State Penitentiary" (*The Journal of Criminal Law, Criminology and Police Science*, liii. 3 (Sept. 1962), 340–43). It was followed in 1969 by Hopper's celebrated book, *Sex in Prison*.

71. *Inside World*, Sept. 1957; Jackson *Clarion-Ledger*, Oct 6, 1957. See also ibid., June 28, 1959, reporting the favorable opinion of nineteen state circuit judges who inspected the white honor camp.

72. *Senate Journal*, 1958, p. 287; *Miss. Laws*, 1958, p. 246; Jackson *Clarion-Ledger*, Feb. 23, 1958, Oct. 9 and Nov. 13, 1959, and Feb. 21, 1960.

73. Ibid., June 18, 1958, and Feb. 21, 1960; *PR*, 1957–59, p. 35.

74. *House Journal*, 1956, pp. 369, 430, 575, 812, 845, 977, and 1045; *Miss. Laws*, 1956, pp. 325–26; Jackson *Clarion-Ledger*, Feb. 2 and Dec. 16, 1956.

75. Interview 10.

76. Jackson *Clarion-Ledger*, Mar. 10, 1957.

77. *PR*, 1955–57, pp. 6 and 19–21; *PR*, 1957–59, pp. 3, 5, 7–8, and 18.

78. *PR*, 1955–57, pp. 3, 7–8, 21, and 36; *Senate Journal*, 1958, pp. 287, 549, and 578; Jackson *Clarion-Ledger*, Mar. 21, 1958.

79. *PR*, 1957–59, pp. 31 and 36–37; Jackson *Clarion-Ledger*, June 28, 1959.

80. *PR*, 1957–59, p. 21; *PR*, 1959–61, pp. 6 and 23.

81. Jackson *Clarion-Ledger*, Feb. 21 and Mar. 6, 1960; Greenville *Delta Democrat-Times*, Feb. 25, 1960.

82. Ibid., Mar. 28, 1960. The author is indebted to Mr. Harpole, a state senator until his death in the autumn of 1990, for reviewing the portions of this chapter relating to his superintendency. His review focused entirely on matters of fact. Although he expressed no disagreement with the author's interpretations, the author is solely responsible for all interpretations of fact.

Chapter 7

1. Jackson *Clarion-Ledger*, Mar. 24, 1960.
2. Ibid., June 6, 1960.
3. Ibid., Nov. 20, 1960; *PR*, 1959–61, p. 4.
4. Ibid., p. 24; Jackson *Clarion-Ledger*, June 5, 1960.

5. *Miss. Laws,* 1960, pp. 595–96; Greenville *Delta Democrat-Times,* June 19, 1960; Jackson *Clarion–Ledger,* June 10, 1960, and Feb. 21, 1961; *PR,* 1959–61, p. 44.

6. Interview by W. B. Taylor with a former inmate who requested anonymity, Vicksburg, Miss., April 1982 (hereafter cited as Interview 12); Jackson *Clarion–Ledger,* Nov. 20, 1960.

7. *PR,* 1959–61, pp. 5 and 45.

8. Jackson *Clarion-Ledger,* Nov. 20, 1960, and Jan. 10 and Feb. 5, 1961.

9. Ibid., Jan. 25, 1961; Greenville *Delta Democrat-Times,* Jan. 25, 1961.

10. Jackson *Clarion-Ledger,* Feb. 7, 1961; *PR,* 1959–61, p. 6.

11. Greenville *Delta Democrat-Times,* Mar. 28, 1961; Jackson *Clarion-Ledger,* Mar. 26, 1961.

12. Ibid., April 19, 20, and 21, 1961; Greenville *Delta Democrat-Times,* April 21, 1961; Board of Commissioners Minute Book, 1960–1964, MDAH, r.g. 49, v. 40, entry of April 24, 1961 (hereafter cited as CMB 1960–64). See also Saucier, p. 40.

13. Greenville *Delta Democrat-Times,* May 7 and 17, 1961.

14. For accounts of the unfolding case, which featured Ross Barnett as one of the attorneys representing the husband of Goldsby's victim and charges by state officials and journalists that the federal judiciary was thwarting criminal process, see Jackson *Clarion-Ledger,* Feb. 27, June 16, Oct. 13, 18, and 28, Nov. 3, 8, and 25, 1959, and June 1, 1961.

15. Ibid., June 13, 1961.

16. Ibid., Aug. 6, 1961; CMB 1960–64, entry of June 14, 1961.

17. Jackson *Clarion-Ledger,* July 27 and Aug. 6, 1961; Interview 10.

18. *Inside World,* Sept. 1961; Jackson *Clarion-Ledger,* Aug. 6, 1961; Interview 12; interview by W. B. Taylor with a former white inmate who requested anonymity, Jackson, Miss., Mar. 1986 (hereafter cited as interview 13); CMB 1960–64, entry of Nov. 7, 1961. For general comment, see A. Moody, *Coming of Age in Mississippi* (New York, 1968), particularly p. 275, and Saucier, pp. 41–42.

19. Jackson *Clarion-Ledger,* July 5, 6, 8, and 30, and Sept. 30, 1961; interview by W. B. Taylor with a former employee of the penal system who requested anonymity, Greenwood, Miss., Mar. 1982 (hereafter cited as Interview 14).

20. Jackson *Clarion-Ledger,* Jan. 1, 3, 6, and 10, 1962; Greenville *Delta Democrat-Times,* Jan. 4 and 8, 1962.

21. Ibid., Jan. 16, 1962; Jackson *Clarion-Ledger,* Jan. 25, 28, and 30, and Feb. 1, 1962.

22. Ibid., Jan. 31, and Feb. 4, 8, 10, and 15, 1962; Greenville *Delta Democrat-Times,* Feb. 6, 1962.

23. *House Journal*, 1962, p. 47; *Senate Journal*, 1962, p. 38; Jackson *Clarion-Ledger*, April 4 and 5, 1962.

24. *Senate Journal*, 1962, p. 660. A typescript of the official findings of the Lucas committee is at the MDAH, r.g. 49, v. 21.

25. Jackson *Clarion-Ledger*, April 20 and 21, 1962; Greenville *Delta Democrat-Times*, April 20, 1962. For retrospective analysis, see Jackson *Clarion-Ledger*, Dec. 21 and 22, 1967.

26. Greenville *Delta Democrat-Times*, April 25, 1962; Jackson *Clarion-Ledger*, April 24 and 26, 1962.

27. Ibid., April 26 and 28, 1962; Interviews 8, 12, and 13.

28. Interview 4; Jackson *Clarion-Ledger*, April 29 and May 2, 3, and 10, 1962.

29. Ibid., April 29 and May 2, 3, 8, and 10, 1962; *Inside World*, April 1962.

30. Jackson *Clarion-Ledger*, May 2 and 3, 1962; *Senate Journal*, 1962, pp. 136–37, 670, 903, and 1031–32.

31. Jackson *Clarion-Ledger*, May 27, 1962.

32. Ibid, June 2 and 3, 1962; Greenville *Delta Democrat-Times*, June 3, 1962.

33. Jackson *Clarion-Ledger*, June 16 and July 7 and 31, 1962.

34. Ibid., July 31, 1962; *PR*, 1961–63, pp. 3–5.

35. Ibid., pp. 29–30, 39, 41, and 44.

36. Jackson *Clarion-Ledger*, Oct. 14, 1962.

37. *PR*, 1933–35, pp. 46 and 49–50; *PR*, 1961–63, pp. 9, 11, and 13.

38. *PR*, 1963–65, p. 5; Jackson *Clarion-Ledger*, July 10 and Dec. 19, 1963; Greenville *Delta Democrat-Times*, Jan. 27, 1964.

39. Ibid., Feb. 9, 13, and 27, 1964; Jackson *Clarion-Ledger*, April 16, 1964.

40. Ibid., Feb. 14, 16, and 27, Mar. 25, April 16 and 17, and May 27, 1964.

41. *Miss. Laws*, 1964, pp. 519–37. See also Saucier, pp. 47–48.

42. Jackson *Clarion-Ledger*, Feb. 16, 1964.

43. Ibid., Feb. 14, 16, 20, and 27, 1964.

44. Ibid., July 28, 1965.

45. Ibid., Jan. 26, April 17, and Aug. 17 and 30, 1966. For a later report of progress by Commissioner West, see ibid., Jan. 15, 1967. For an editorial praising the progress of the program, see Greenville *Delta Democrat-Times*, Jan. 27, 1967. See also C. A. Jones, "A Survey of Perceived Needs of Adult Education Faculty at the Mississippi State Penitentiary at Parchman," Diss., Univ. of Southern Miss., 1978, pp. 65–68.

46. Jackson *Clarion-Ledger*, Oct. 29, 1967.

47. Ibid., Nov. 19, 1967, May 6, July 20, and Aug. 24, 1969. For financial accounts, see *House Journal*, 1970, p. 503.

48. For accounts of the library and its subsequent progress, see *PR*, 1965–67, p. 47; *Declaration of Library Service* (Parchman, n.d.); *Dedication of Library Program, May 25, 1965* (Parchman, n.d.); and Jackson *Clarion-Ledger*, April 25 and Oct. 22, 1965, and April 20, 1969. See also an undated typescript entitled "Library" in the library of the Mississippi State Penitentiary at Parchman. For a description of the old striped uniforms, see Jackson *Clarion-Ledger*, Oct. 28, 1965. For accounts of the change of uniforms, see ibid., Jan. 15, 1967, and *PR*, 1964–68, pp. 28 and 34. For accounts of the operations of the reception center, the diagnostic clinic, and the prerelease center, see Jackson *Clarion-Ledger*, Aug. 21 and Nov. 23, 1969, and *House Journal*, 1968, pp. 157–58 and 164–65, and 1970, pp. 505–6. Providing general comment is an unpublished paper written in 1973 by Professor C. Quarles of the University of Mississippi entitled "A Study of the Mississippi State Correctional System," p. 21.

49. Jackson *Clarion-Ledger*, Feb. 16 and July 29 and 30, 1964; *PR*, 1963–65, p. 5; CMB 1960–64, entry of Dec. 14, 1964.

50. *Progress Report of the Mississippi State Penitentiary, 1964–1968* (Jackson, Miss., n.d.), (hereafter cited as *PR*, 1964–68); *House Journal*, 1966, pp. 396–403, and 1968, pp. 165–68.

51. Ibid., 1968, p. 170.

52. Interviews 10, 11, and 12; interview by W. B. Taylor with a businessman who hunted dove at Parchman during the years of the Johnson administration and requested anonymity, Jackson, Miss., May 1982; Jackson *Clarion-Ledger*, Oct. 28, 1965, and Mar. 10, 11, 14, 26, and 27, 1966; *House Journal*, 1966, pp. 396–97 and 1099; *Senate Journal*, 1966, p. 502.

53. Interview 14.

54. Jackson *Clarion-Ledger*, July 28, 1965.

55. Ibid., Aug. 1 and Oct. 30, 1965; Interview 14.

56. *House Journal*, 1968, pp. 156 and 170, and 1970, p. 508.

57. Ibid., 1968, p. 167, and 1970, pp. 503–5.

58. Jackson *Clarion-Ledger*, Mar. 11, 1943, and Oct. 28, 1965.

59. *House Journal*, 1968, pp. 157 and 179, and 1970, p. 503.

60. Ibid., 1968, p. 165.

61. Ibid., 1970, pp. 506 and 508.

62. Jackson *Clarion-Ledger*, Aug. 1, 1965.

63. Ibid., Oct. 28, 1965.

64. Ibid., Mar. 14, 1966; Interview 14.

65. *House Journal*, 1968, pp. 161–62.

66. Ibid., pp. 155–56; Jackson *Clarion-Ledger*, Jan. 31 and Feb. 1 and 2, 1968.

67. Ibid., Feb. 10, 1968.

68. *House Journal*, 1968, pp. 155–71.

69. Ibid., pp. 185–87; Jackson *Clarion-Ledger*, Feb. 18 and 23, 1968; Interview 11.

70. Jackson *Clarion-Ledger*, Feb. 15 and 18, 1968.

71. Ibid., Feb. 23, Mar. 14 and 20, and April 5 and 16, 1968.

72. Ibid., Feb. 23 and 28, June 26, July 2, Nov. 19, 20, and 24, and Dec. 13, 1968, and Jan. 25, 1969; Interview 11.

73. Jackson *Clarion-Ledger*, Jan. 16, 1970.

74. Ibid., Feb. 18, 1970.

75. *House Journal*, pp. 502–8.

Chapter 8

1. This account of the attitudes of state legislators is based on a careful perusal of the public record, on the general tenor of the press reports of the time, and on the assessments of all parties interviewed.

2. *Morgan v. Cook*, 236 So. 2d. 749 (1970); *Love v. State*, 221 So. 2d. 92 (1969). For the most commonly cited federal case asserting the hands-off doctrine, see *Price v. Johnston*, 334 U.S. 266 (1948).

3. See *Ruffin v. Commonwealth*, 62 Va 790 at 796 (1871), for the generally accepted judicial opinion that convicts were deserving of treatment no better than that afforded persons held in bondage.

4. 356 U.S. 86 (1958).

5. 370 U.S. 660 (1962).

6. 356 U.S. 167 (1961); K. C. Haas, "Judicial Politics and Correctional Reform," *Detroit Criminal Law Review* (1977), p. 823.

7. 393 U.S. 483 (1969).

8. 309 F. Supp. 362 (E.D. Ark. 1970). For a brief summary of the judicial decisions that overturned the hands-off doctrine, see H. A. Johnson, *History of Criminal Justice* (Cincinnati, 1988), pp. 281–83.

9. Jackson *Clarion-Ledger*, Oct. 15, 1970; 438 F. 2d. 183 (5th Cir. 1971).

10. *Miss. Laws*, 1971, pp. 847–48.

11. Jackson *Clarion-Ledger*, Feb. 22 and 29, 1972.

12. *New York Times*, Sept. 18, 1972.

13. Interview by R. G. Marquardt with A. Sievers, Hattiesburg, Miss., Feb. 1981.

14. Jan. 27, 1973.

15. *Norwood v. Harrison*, 340 F. Supp. 1003 (N.D. Miss. 1972).

16. C. Clark to Sen. J. Eastland, in "Hearings before the Senate Judiciary Committee on the Nomination of William C. Keady," *Congressional Record*, 90th Congress, 2nd. Session, p. 3.

17. 70 F.D.R. 341 (1976).

18. "Transmittal Letter for Law Enforcement Assistance Administration Consultant Committee," *Interim Report on Mississippi State Penitentiary*, p. 2, as quoted by D. Lipman, "Mississippi's Prison Experience," *Mississippi Law Journal*, 45 (1974), pp. 685–755.

19. 501 F. 2d. 1291 at 1295 (5th Cir. 1974).

20. 349 F. Supp. 881 at 889 (1972).

21. Interview by R. G. Marquardt with R. Welch, Jackson, Miss., July 1981.

22. Interview by W. B. Taylor with a highly placed official of the Waller administration who requested anonymity, Jackson, Miss., Feb. 1983 (hereafter cited as Interview 15). For the state's principal arguments, see *Gates v. Collier*, 501 F. 2d. 1291 (5th Cir. 1974).

23. Interview 15; Mississippi Department of Corrections (MDOC), "Department of Treatment, Parchman Facility, Sept. 30, 1976," p. 2; C. A. Jones, pp. 68–73; Jackson *Clarion-Ledger*, Sept. 13, 1972.

24. Interviews by W. B. Taylor with T. H. Fletcher, former chairman of the penitentiary board of commissioners, Hattiesburg, Miss., Jan. and Dec. 1976, Feb. 1982, Nov. 1985, and Sept. 1990 (hereafter cited as Fletcher Interviews).

25. Ibid.; Jackson *Clarion-Ledger*, Nov. 4, 1972.

26. Interview 15; Jackson *Clarion-Ledger*, Dec. 9, 1972.

27. Fletcher Interviews; Jackson *Clarion-Ledger*, Oct. 20, 1973.

28. Interview 15; L. C. Dorsey, *Cold Steel* (Jackson, 1982), p. 3.

29. Fletcher Interviews.

30. Ibid.; interviews by W. B. Taylor with Supt. Jack Reed, Parchman, Miss., July 1975, and Jackson, Miss., Feb. 1976 (hereafter cited as Reed Interviews).

31. Ibid.

32. *Inside World*, Jan. 1975.

33. Reed Interviews.

34. Ibid.; Fletcher Interviews.

35. Reed Interviews; Fletcher Interviews; Interview 15; Jackson *Clarion-Ledger*, May 2, 1974.

36. *Gates v. Collier*, 501 F. 2d. 1291 (5th Cir. 1974).

37. Lipman, p. 685.

38. State of Mississippi, Office of Building, Grounds & Real Property Management, "Incarceration Facilities Cost Comparison, 1974–1989" (comp. Jan. 15, 1990), p. 1 (hereafter cited as IFCC 1974–89).

39. J. Upchurch, "Federal Court Intervention and Substantive Living Conditions in Mississippi Corrections" (MDOC, Jan. 12, 1976), pp. 2–3.

40. Fletcher Interviews; Jackson *Clarion-Ledger*, Feb. 1, 1975.

41. 407 F. Supp. 1117 *et. seq.* (N.D. Miss. 1975).

42. MDOC, "Department of Treatment . . . 1976."
43. Fletcher Interviews.
44. Ibid.
45. Ibid.
46. *Miss. Laws,* 1976, p. 650 *et. seq.*
47. MDOC, *Annual Report, FY 1982* (Jackson, 1982), pp. 5–7.

Epilogue

1. The *Annual Reports* of the MDOC contain summaries of all the major substantive orders. For general assessment, see C. A. Brown, "Redefining the Terms of Legal Incarceration: The Case of Mississippi, 1970–1980," Honors Thesis, Univ. of Southern Miss., 1989. For the related holdings of the United States Fifth Circuit Court of Appeals, see F. E. Devine, *Holdings on Prisoners' Rights by the U.S. Court of Appeals for the Fifth Circuit* (Parchman, 1986).
2. Each *Annual Report* of the MDOC contains information on the various protections and services provided inmates.
3. Telephonic interview by W. B. Taylor with a former state politician who requested anonymity, June 1991.
4. Jackson *Clarion-Ledger,* June 15, 1986.
5. Fletcher Interviews.
6. Telephonic interview by W. B. Taylor with a state legislator who requested anonymity, June 1990 (hereafter cited as Interview 16).
7. Telephonic interviews by W. B. Taylor with an employee of the MDOC who requested anonymity, June, Oct. 1990 (hereafter cited as Interview 17).
8. Interview by W. B. Taylor with an employee of the MDOC who requested anonymity, Hattiesburg, Miss., Aug. 1990 (hereafter cited as Interview 18).
9. Telephonic interview by W. B. Taylor with a former state legislator who requested anonymity, June 1990 (hereafter cited as Interview 19).
10. Interview by W. B. Taylor with an employee of the MDOC who requested anonymity, Forest, Miss., Sept. 1986.
11. For two notable examples, see *Rudolph v. Locke,* 504 F. 2d 1076 (1979), and *Vodicka and Tyler v. C. Paul Phelps,* 624 F. 2d 569 (1980).
12. Interview by W. B. Taylor with an employee of the MDOC who requested anonymity, Forest, Miss., Sept. 1986 (hereafter cited as Interview 20).
13. *Annual Report, 1989–1990* (MDOC, 1990), pp. 36 and 38 (hereafter cited as *AR, 1989–1990*).
14. Interview by W. B. Taylor with a former employee of the MDOC who requested anonymity, Jackson, Miss., May 1991.

15. Telephonic interviews by W. B. Taylor with J. D. Cooke, Assistant to the Mississippi Commissioner of Corrections, Sept. and Oct. 1990, and Feb. and Aug. 1991 (hereafter cited as Cooke Interviews).

16. *PR*, 1955–57, p. 14; *AR, 1989–1990*, p. 19.

17. The shattering of inmate society was noted as early as 1960 by G. M. Sykes and S. L. Messinger in "The Inmate Social System," in *Theoretical Studies in Social Organization of the Prison*, ed. R. A. Cloward, et al. (New York, 1960), pp. 5–19. Since that time an immense body of literature addressing the role of ethnic and racial gangs in modern American prisons and the changed nature of prison administration has emerged. For recent assessment, see *Are Prisons Any Better? Twenty Years of Correctional Reform*, ed. J. W. Murphy and J. E. Dison (Newbury Park, Calif., 1990).

18. Interview by W. B. Taylor with a former black inmate who requested anonymity, Jackson, Miss., June 1990. The letters cited were written during 1975 and 1976 by two of Parchman's white inmates. The author was allowed to read and quote from a total of thirty-nine letters on condition that the names of the correspondents would remain anonymous.

19. Interview 20. Almost identical assessments were obtained in Interviews 17 and 18.

20. *AR, 1989–1990*, p. 38.

21. Ibid., pp. 29–32.

22. *PR*, 1955–57, pp. 34–38, constituting the report of the director of education.

23. *PR*, 1955–57, pp. 26–30; *AR, 1989–1990*, p. 38.

24. Interview 12.

25. *PR*, 1955–57, p. 6; Cooke Interviews.

26. *AR, 1989–1990*, p. 71; Interview 16; Interview 17.

27. Fletcher Interviews.

28. Letter to W. B. Taylor from an MDOC administrator who requested anonymity, June 1990. See *Hattiesburg American*, Oct. 15, 1990, reporting the continuing effort of the Mississippi Prosecutors' Association to secure legislation lengthening custodial sentences for drug offenders.

29. *Miss. Laws*, 1978, pp. 406–9; "Penitentiary Lands," pp. 42–45, 62–66, and 79–120.

30. *Miss. Laws*, 1989, pp. 200 and 271–73; interview by W. B. Taylor with D. A. Cabana, former warden of the Mississippi State Penitentiary at Parchman, April 1986; Cooke Interviews.

31. In May 1990 the penitentiary opened a new 10,000-square-foot, fully air-conditioned adult education facility equipped with modern media services (Jackson *Clarion-Ledger*, Sept. 28, 1990). Meanwhile, marketable professors and educational administrators who had not received salary increases in three years were abandoning Mississippi's institutions of higher learning, commu-

nity colleges were facing unprecedented fiscal crises, and the state's systems of elementary and secondary education were attempting to function with underpaid teachers and many decaying, overcrowded schools.

32. Interviews by W. B. Taylor with two high-ranking law enforcement officials who requested anonymity. The interviews were conducted in September 1990. The location of the interviews is withheld by the author to protect confidentiality.

33. "Inmate Population Projections 1979"; *Miss. Laws*, 1979, pp. 656–59; MDOC *Annual Report FY 1982*, pp. 20–21.

34. *Miss. Laws*, 1989, pp. 275–82; MDOC, "Monthly Fact Sheet, June 30, 1991" (hereafter cited as "Fact Sheet").

35. Jackson *Clarion-Ledger*, Sept. 12, 1978; *Miss. Laws*, 1978, pp. 739–41, and 1989, p. 206; Cooke Interviews.

36. Jackson *Clarion-Ledger*, July 18, 1978.

37. *Miss. Laws*, 1989, pp. 206 and 261–63; "Fact Sheet."

38. Ibid.; Cooke Interviews. See the indignant editorial in the *Hattiesburg American*, June 17, 1991.

39. Ibid., Oct. 8, 1990.

40. Fletcher Interviews; Interviews 16, 17, 18, 19, and 20.

41. IFCC 1974–89; *Hattiesburg American*, Oct. 8, 1990.

42. MDOC, "Inmate Population Projections 1979." See *Miss. Code*, 1989, p. 205, for the provisions of the "county option" system pertaining to the construction and renovation of satellite units.

43. MDOC, *The Multi-Million Dollar Satellite Idea: Community Correctional Treatment Centers* (Jackson, 1979), pp. 3–6.

44. Page 15.

45. IFCC 1974–89; *Miss. Laws*, 1989, p. 206.

46. "Fact Sheet"; Cooke Interviews; *Miss. Laws*, 1989, p. 206.

47. Cooke Interviews.

48. *Gates v. Mabus*, GC 71–6–LS–D.

49. Interview 17.

Bibliographical Essay

The student of American penal history must begin with an assessment of the intellectual currents of the late eighteenth and early nineteenth centuries that merged to form what later generations labeled legal "Classicism." Labeling is always risky business, and in this case it has led to an appalling degree of oversimplification. Classicism was a hopeless mesh of retributivism, libertarianism, utilitarianism, religiosity, philanthropy, infant criminological determinism, and practical politics. The divergent focuses were hammered into a weak body of theory by the iron hand of necessity. The demands of politics assured further intellectual error in the transformation of theory to public policy. And the resulting philosophical confusion largely explains two hundred years of Western penal jurisprudence.

The works of several late eighteenth and early nineteenth century thinkers reveal the extent of the intellectual conflict. The retributivist agenda was laid out by Immanuel Kant, the libertarian by Cesare Beccaria, the utilitarian by Jeremy Bentham. For insight into the retributivist and utilitarian schools, see *Philosophy of Law*, ed. J. Feinberg and H. Gross (Encino, Calif.: Dickenson Publishing Co., 1975); for the libertarian, including analysis of the crucial distinctions between Beccaria and the later British Utilitarians, see F. E. Devine, "Beccaria and the Liberal Tradition in Anglo-American Criminal Jurisprudence," *The Midwest Quarterly*, 18 (1977). For the place of religiosity and philanthropy in the equation, see the several published works of the English sheriff, John Howard; for that of early determinism, and its insurmountable conflicts with all the rest, see W. B. Taylor, "Alexander Maconochie and the Revolt Against the Penitentiary," *Southern Journal of Criminal Justice*, 3 (1978).

The principal offspring of legal Classicism was the penitentiary, and that institution's theoretical foundations reflected, and continue to reflect, the intellectual ferment of the late eighteenth century. Perhaps the most lucid analysis of the early British penitentiary is Michel Foucault's *Discipline and Punish: The Birth of the Prison* (1975; rpt. London: Peregrine Books, 1979). No publication of equal quality addresses the origins of the American penitentiary, but much valuable insight can be gleaned from the works of Thomas Eddy, the spiritual father of New York's Auburn system. Also relevant are the several publications on the Pennsylvania system sponsored by the Pennsylvania Historical Commission, and N. K. Teeters and J. D. Shearer, *The Prison at Philadelphia's Cherry Hill: The Separate System of Penal Discipline, 1829–1913* (New York: University of Columbia Press, 1957). For an analysis of the Anglo-American penitentiary movement of the late eighteenth and nineteenth centuries, see "The Foundations of Modern Penal Practice," comp. W. B. Taylor (*New England Journal On Prison Law*, 7 (Winter 1981).

Blake McKelvey's *American Prisons: A History of Good Intentions* (Montclair, N.J.: Patterson Smith, 1977) provides an able historical survey of the American penitentiary. Among a large number of works assessing the recent history of American prisons, a collection of essays edited by J. W. Murphy and J. E. Dison, *Are Prisons Any Better? Twenty Years of Correctional Reform* (Newbury Park, Calif.: Sage, 1990), is an excellent point of departure.

There are several regional histories of the American penitentiary. Perhaps one interested in the South should begin with H. J. Zimmerman's unpublished doctoral dissertation, "Penal Systems and Penal Reform in the South Since the Civil War" (Univ. of North Carolina, 1947). Every word Zimmerman wrote about Mississippi is true, but like McKelvey, she necessarily wrote too little; the subject is simply too complex for national or regional treatment.

One must tackle the study of penal law and administration with a firm grasp of the characteristics of the pertinent political entity. And one had best beware in tackling Mississippi. For things there are not always as they appear and certainly not as they are often represented by modern writers.

Mississippi scholars have contributed a number of useful general histories. The best overview is an article by P. B. Foreman and J. R. Tatum entitled "A Short History of Mississippi's State Penal Systems," *Mississippi Law Journal*, 10 (April 1938). Two graduate students at the University of Mississippi have written pertinent M.A. theses. L. G. Shivers's "A History of the Mississippi Penitentiary" (1930) is a responsible factual account, as is M. L. Hutson's "Mississippi's State Penal Systems" (1939). Also of general interest is an unpublished typescript in Parchman's library, S. Sullivan's "Prison Without Walls: A History of Mississippi's Penal System."

Narrower accounts are more abundant. Valuable for the Spanish era (pre-1798) are R. V. Haynes, "Law Enforcement in Frontier Mississippi," *JMH*, 22 (Jan.–Oct. 1960), and J. D. L. Holmes, "Law and Order in Spanish Natchez, 1781–1798," *JMH*, 25 (July 1963). Another work shedding light on crime and criminal policy during the Spanish era is Holmes's *Gayoso: The Life of a Spanish Governor in the Mississippi Valley, 1789–1799* (Baton Rouge: Louisiana State University Press, 1965).

M. C. Dunn's unpublished University of Southern Mississippi thesis,

"Criminals Along the Natchez Trace" (1970), is a good general account of criminality and criminal policy during the territorial era (1798–1817). The molding of territorial criminal policy is covered in some detail by J. Wunder, "American Law and Order Comes to the Mississippi Territory: The Making of Sargent's Code," *JMH*, 38 (May 1976); by J. T. Hatfield, "Governor William Charles Cole Claiborne, Indians, and Outlaws in Frontier Mississippi, 1801–1803," *JMH*, 27 (Nov. 1965); and by W. B. Hamilton, *Anglo-American Law on the Frontier: Thomas Rodney and His Territorial Cases* (Durham, N.C.: Duke University Press, 1953).

The only work surveying the forces that gave birth to Mississippi's antebellum penitentiary and the early years of its existence is E. B. Thompson's "Reforms in the Penal Systems of Mississippi, 1820–1850," *JMH*, 7 (April 1945). However, useful information on the design and construction of "The Walls" is available in D. N. Young's "History of the Construction of State Buildings in Jackson, Mississippi, 1822–1860" (Thesis, Miss. College, 1964). W. D. McCain's *The Story of Jackson* (2 vols.; Jackson, Miss.: J. F. Hyer, 1953) contains interesting comment on the prison as well.

After 1865 a powerful, very unhappy dialectic is discernible in state history. For insight one should consult W. C. Harris, *The Day of the Carpetbagger: Republican Reconstruction in Mississippi* (Baton Rouge and London: Louisiana State University Press, 1979); A. D. Kirwan, *Revolt of the Rednecks: Mississippi Politics, 1876–1925* (Gloucester, Mass.: Peter Smith, 1964); and V. L. Wharton, *The Negro in Mississippi, 1865–1890* (1947; rpt. New York, Evanston and London: Harper Torchbooks, 1965).

Next the student should take on two books written by C. V. Woodward: the enlarged edition of *The Burden of Southern History* (Baton Rouge: Louisiana State University Press, 1968), and the third, revised edition of *The Strange Career of Jim Crow* (New York: Oxford University Press, 1974). Then, in sequence, one should read W. F. Holmes, *The White Chief: James Kimble Vardaman* (Baton Rouge: Louisiana State University Press, 1970), C. M. Morgan, *Theodore G. Bilbo: Redneck Liberal* (Baton Rouge: Louisiana State University Press, 1986), and N. R. McMillen, *Dark Journey* (Chicago and Urbana: University of Illinois Press, 1989). Also of general interest are the articles relating to the late nineteenth and twentieth centuries in *A History of Mississippi*, edited by R. A. McLemore (2 vols.; Hattiesburg, Miss.: University and College Press of Mississippi, 1973).

For further information on twentieth century Mississippi one should see the several volumes at the William David McCain Graduate Library that have been produced by the University of Southern Mississippi's Oral History Program. Also significant, of course, are the many articles and books dealing with state history since the advent of the civil rights movement. Among them, J. Silver's *Mississippi: The Closed Society* (Harcourt, Brace and World, 1964) is required reading.

After digesting these background materials, one might be equipped to focus more narrowly on the formulation and implementation of criminal policy in postbellum Mississippi. Harris's *The Day of the Carpetbagger* provides a general account of the role of the penitentiary in state politics during the decade following the War Between the States. Kirwan's *Revolt of the Rednecks* follows Harris's book up expertly, blending penitentiary affairs into the broader realm of state politics. Professor McKelvey relates what Harris and Kirwan say about convict leasing to the entire South in his "Penal Slavery and Southern Reconstruction," *The Journal of Negro History*, 20 (1935).

R. E. Cooley presents a solid summary of trends in Mississippi between Appomattox and the advent of penal farming in the introductory chapter of her master's thesis, "A History of the Mississippi Penal Farm System, 1890–1935: Punishment, Politics and Profit in Penal Affairs" (Univ. of Southern Miss., 1981). S. Curtis addresses the political warfare that accompanied the state's long transition from convict leasing to penal farming in his M.A. thesis, "Penitentiary Reform in Mississippi, 1875–1906: A Study of Politics in Penal Affairs" (Miss. College, 1974). For an account of the transition from leasing to penal farming penned by an involved state politician, one should examine J. H. Jones, "Penitentiary Reform in Mississippi," *Publications of the Mississippi Historical Society*, 6 (1902). Vardaman's triumph over the McLaurins is covered very ably in the sixth chapter of Holmes's biography.

The previously cited works by Foreman and Tatum and by Hutson provide good general assessments carrying the story through the 1930s. Cooley's thesis also offers a good factual account of the first thirty-odd years of the twentieth century. R. F. Saucier began her M.A. thesis, "A History of the Mississippi Penal Farm System, 1935–1970" (Univ. of Southern Miss., 1982), where Cooley left off and provided a summary of events up to the eve of federal intervention.

Other useful secondary works shedding much light on twentieth century criminal policy and prison administration are N. B. Bond, *The Treatment of the Dependent, Defective and Delinquent Classes in Mississippi* (n.p., n.d.), and the several contributions of C. B. Hopper, especially his celebrated *Sex in Prison: The Mississippi Experiment With Conjugal Visiting* (Baton Rouge: Louisiana State University Press, 1969).

D. Lipman's "Mississippi's Prison Experience," *Mississippi Law Journal*, 45 (1974) covers the early years of federal intervention, and the undergraduate honors thesis of C. A. Brown, "Redefining the Terms of Legal Incarceration: The Case of Mississippi, 1970–1980" (Univ. of Southern Miss., 1989), examines relevant case law. The impeccable scholarship of F. E. Devine is also vital. His "Absolute Democracy or Indefeasible Right: Hobbes Versus Locke," *The Journal of Politics*, 37 (Aug. 1975) sheds much light on the central conflict inherent in federal intervention; his *Holdings on Prisoners' Rights by the U.S. Court of Appeals for the Fifth Circuit* (Parchman, Miss., 1986) deserves much wider exposure.

Pertinent unpublished secondary sources include two papers on file at the MDOC in Jackson: J. Upchurch, "Federal Court Intervention and Substantive Living Conditions in Mississippi Corrections" (1976), and L. C. Vincent, "The Future of Corrections: The Times They are a Changing" (1980). "Lands of the Mississippi State Penitentiary," compiled by P. J. Townsend and E. McBride (1980), is a history of purchases, sales, leases, and surveys of penitentiary lands.

Relevant unpublished manuscripts are rare indeed; there are many skeletons in the closet, and evidently the principal actors were sensible enough to cover their tracks. Excepting several letters of nineteenth century vintage, the papers of the state's governors at the Mississippi Department of Archives and History in Jackson are disappointing. Elsewhere at the MDAH are a meager number of scattered letters, ledgers, contracts, reports by legislative committees, and other documents relating to the penal system. The most important of them are the sketchy minute books of the penitentiary's boards of inspectors, trustees, and commissioners. Other manuscript collections offer little or nothing.

Several published primary works are available, but virtually all of them relate to the early nineteenth century. Useful for the territorial era are *The Mississippi Territorial Archives*, edited by D. Rowland (Nashville: Press of Brandon Publishing Co., 1905), and *Official Letter Books of W. C. C. Claiborne, 1801–1816*, also edited by Rowland (Jackson, Miss.: MDAH, 1917).

The published lives and letters of several politicians offer insight into the 1817–1861 era. The most valuable of them are *Life and Correspondence of John A. Quitman*, edited by J. F. H. Claiborne (2 vols.; New York: Harper and Bros., 1860), and H. S. Foote, *Casket of Reminiscences* (Washington, D.C.: Chronicle Publishing Co., 1874). See also J. H. Ingraham, *The South-West. By a Yankee* (2 vols.; New York: Harper and Bros., 1835).

But there, no doubt owing to the debasement of postwar politics under both Republican and Redeemer rule, published primary works all but disappear. Some of the published proceedings of the American Prison Association (later the American Correctional Association) contain sections on Mississippi, but the value of such staged performances is dubious at best. More reliable, perhaps, is the section on the state in *Handbook of American Prisons and Reformatories 1929*, edited by P. W. Garrett and A. H. MacCormick (New York: National Society of Penal Information, Inc., 1929).

The public record is useful if one understands the context of state politics. The statutory law of the state of Mississippi is an essential skeleton. The journals of the senate and house, especially the reports of penitentiary committees and the messages of governors, provide superficial insight into the forces that molded policy. Nothing, however, is more important than the annual, and later biennial, penitentiary reports. Running without interruption from 1841 through 1963, and generally confirmed by newspapers and other contemporary sources, they furnish a huge amount of information relating to the formulation and implementation of penal policy, including assessments of operations by key administrators.

Where the printed penitentiary reports leave off, less believable "progress reports," issued every four years, begin; here one discerns an attempt by state actors to hype the triumphs of the penal system and to hide anything that might be interpreted as a civil liability. The progress reports are replaced by the statistic-laden annual reports of the MDOC during the 1970s. A number of unpublished materials are in Parchman's library; others are available at the Jackson offices of the MDOC.

By necessity one must rely heavily on the state's journalists. The most useful newspapers for the territorial period are the *Washington Republican*, the Natchez *Mississippi Messenger*, the Natchez *Mississippi Republican*, the Natchez *The Weekly Chronicle*, and the Natchez *Mississippi Herald and Natchez Gazette*. Especially valuable for the early years of statehood are the Natchez *Ariel*, the Natchez *Southern Galaxy*, the Natchez *Mississippi State Gazette*, the Natchez *Mississippi Free Trader*, the Vicksburg *Herald*, and the *Woodville Republican*. After about 1840 the newspapers of the Jackson area eclipsed those of southwestern Mississippi in coverage of penal policy and administration. Thereafter, until the Civil War, the Jackson *Mississippian* and the Jackson *Mississippian and State Gazette* are the best sources.

While politicians wrote and said less about criminal matters after Appomattox, a number of newspapers in the Jackson area, each devoted to a particular political point of view, said more. The most important among them are the Clinton *Sword and Shield*, the Jackson *The New Mississippian*, and Ethelbert Barksdale's Jackson *Clarion*. Barksdale continued to devote considerable space to penitentiary affairs until the early years of the twentieth century. After his death, the Jackson *Clarion-Ledger* provided the most systematic coverage of penitentiary affairs for the twentieth century. The contributing authors have followed a general rule of citing the *Clarion-Ledger* and its predecessors in all cases unless other newspapers provide more detailed or conflicting information or an opposing point of view.

Prominent among other newspapers consulted are the Greenville *Delta Democrat-Times*, the Memphis *Commercial Appeal*, and the New Orleans *Times Picayune*. Parchman's inmate-produced newspaper, *Inside World*, is also important. What the convicts write is suspicious due to censorship; but the manner in which they write, and often what they do not write, says a great deal. There is an incomplete run of the *Inside World* at the Mississippi Law Library in Jackson; most of the gaps can be plugged via a little snooping in Sunflower County.

In covering the twentieth century, a dearth of traditional sources renders oral history essential, and the authors, after weeding out what they perceived to be obvious fabrications and otherwise shaky information, resolved to exploit testimony emanating from thirty-four persons: two law enforcement officials, fifteen former or current employees of the penal system, eight former or current state politicians, six former inmates, and three other informed parties. Of the thirty-four, only seven have been identified by name. Most of them prudently requested anonymity; the names of others have been excluded on the advice of legal counsel.

Index